I0200129

A BRIEF HISTORY OF THE HEAVYWEIGHTS 1881-2010

BY

TRACY CALLIS

WIN BY KO

Win By KO Publications
Iowa City

A Brief History of the Heavyweights
1881-2010

Tracy Callis

Front Cover: Mike Tyson (right) versus James "Quick" Tillis; Photo Courtesy of Steve Lott, Boxing Hall of Fame – Luxor Hotel Las Vegas
Back Cover: Mike Tyson (left) versus Mitchell Green; Photo Courtesy of Steve Lott, Boxing Hall of Fame – Luxor Hotel Las Vegas

(ISBN-13): 978-0-9799822-6-2
(hardcover: 50# acid-free alkaline paper)
Includes appendix, bibliography, and index.
© 2013 by Tracy Callis. All Rights Reserved.
No part of this book may be reproduced, or transmitted in any form or by any means, graphic, electronic or mechanical, including photocopying, recording, taping, or by any information storage retrieval system without the written permission of Tracy Callis.
Manufactured in the United States of America.
Win By KO Publications
Iowa City, Iowa
winbykopublications.com

Table of Contents

Acknowledgements

The author offers a "thank you" to all those who contributed to the development of this book, for assistance in various ways --

First, let me thank **Steve Lott** of the **Boxing Hall of Fame – Luxor Hotel Las Vegas**. Steve went out of his way to help make this book a reality by providing and licensing numerous photos utilized in this book.

Of great importance too was **Donna Abbatello.** Her willingness to help was remarkable. Plain and simply stated, she enabled this project to be accomplished. **Adam Pollack** also played a key role in getting this book published. When frustration set in and no satisfactory publisher could be decided upon, **Adam** and his publishing company, **Win By KO Publications (winbykopublications.com)**, came to the rescue.

Another very special thank you goes to **Barry Hugman**, the outstanding historian and compiler/editor of the **British Boxing Board of Control Yearbooks** for his advice and direction in compiling much of the data that went into this book. His research on the heavyweights was a primary reference and his suggestions were essential in the completion of this task. Barry's work can be seen at the following internet address **boxrec.com/hugman/index.php/Category:Heavyweight_Division**.

Much appreciation goes to **Ron Brammer**, a lifelong friend and knowledgeable student of boxing history, who offered valuable critique and suggestions during the writing of this book. My appreciation also goes to **Dan Cuoco** and **Kelly Nicholson**, good friends and boxing historians, who contributed a number of useful observations and suggestions. **Tony and Kathleen Triem**, valued friends, also graciously provided advice and help on a number of associated tasks.

In addition, my thank you is extended to many others who provided photographs - **Tony Triem**, from his collection, **William Schutte**, from his collection, **Dan Cuoco, Bruce Jarvis, Anthony Barton, Ed King, Jerome Shochet, Tom Hogan/HoganPhotos** (Vitali Klitschko images, page 133) and **Harry** and **Raven Shaffer (Antiquities of the Prize Ring)**. **Harry** was a wonderful man and good friend who provided valuable comments. Regretfully, he passed away while this work was in progress.

A big thank you also goes out to **Daaave Summers** (yes, **Daaave** is correct) for his outstanding skills in touching up and improving many of the old and faded photographs and to all the newspapers who so graciously gave permission for articles from their papers to be included in this work.

Further, a sincere thank you is extended to all of my other boxing friends and fellow historians whose comments and observations over the years provided deep insight into the skills and capabilities of the fighters, managers, trainers and promoters. These men include **Arly Allen, Jim Carney Jr., Doug Cavanaugh, Bob Carson, Ralph Citro, Don Cogswell, Monte Cox, Luckett Davis, Mike DeLisa, Mark Dunn, Laurence Fielding, Stephen Gordon (Gordoom), Chuck Hasson, Chuck Johnston, Eric Jorgensen, Christopher LaForce, Tim Leone, Peter Lerner, Greg Lewis, Frank Lotierzo, Dave Martinez, Bill Matthews, Clay Moyle, Joe Page, Christopher Shelton, John Sheppard, Jan Skotnicki, Kevin Smith, Bob Soderman, Jake Wegner, Paul Zabala** - and many others not named.

Last, but not least, the author also offers a huge thank you to all the members of my family for their unending assistance, patience and understanding during the writing of this book - to **Barbara Callis**, my wife, and **Tracy Jr., Jonas** and **Seth**, sons. Numerous discussions and exchanges of views and opinions transpired. Many, many hours were spent in the reading of chapters and passages by **Barbara**. Thank you, dear.

While working on the book, my oldest son, **Tracy Jr.**, passed away. He was a kind, gentle and soft-spoken young man who is deeply missed. We all love him very much. **'Til we meet again, dear son.**

Introduction

The Years 1860-1880

O n January 1, 1881, there was no true heavyweight champion of the world. No world-wide boxing commissions or official global governing bodies existed. Boxing was considered by many as an activity of ruffians, hoodlums and thugs. Yet, it held an interest for people of all social levels.

Most fights up to this time had been carried out under the old London Prize Ring Rules, the offspring of Jack Broughton's Rules of 1743 – an attempt to bring a degree of civility and safety to fistic encounters. The men used bare-knuckles. But a new set of rules, the Marquis of Queensberry, were being used more and more. Under these rules, the men fought using gloves. Some sources report that John Chambers was the primary designer of these rules.

John Sholto Douglas, the 9th Marquis of Queensberry, was a fan of the sport. He felt that the number of boxing injuries could be reduced and more fights could take place with this new set of rules - so he lent his name to them (circa 1867). The rules were adopted little by little into organized boxing contests and gradually replaced the London Prize Ring Rules that had previously governed contests.

John Sholto Douglas

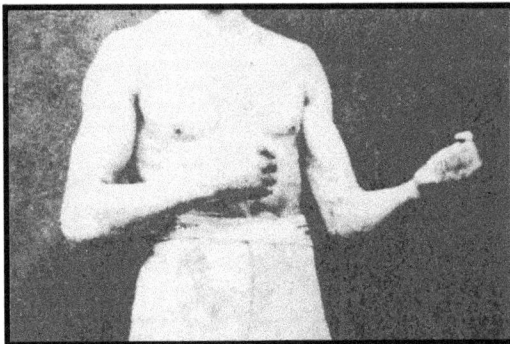

Bare-Knuckle Fighter

Until now, the man who reigned under the London Prize Ring Rules and fought with bare-knuckles was usually called champion. Many times, a man simply claimed a title if his challenge was refused or unanswered by the champion. Sometimes, when a current champion left the country for one reason or another, a challenger claimed the title. Further, many well-known men operated schools of boxing and conducted tournaments. Winners of these tournaments often claimed to be the champion of the country.

Even though there was no world-wide champion, many countries had their own pugilistic kingpin. There was much confusion. In England, several men who had been champions at one time or another had migrated to America. One of them, Joe Goss, had been considered to be the American champion. In Australia, home-grown Larry Foley had been proclaimed as the best. Championship claims were heard everywhere.

A number of the men who were prominent during the early 1880s had been active during the preceding decade. A brief look at the pugilistic history in England, America, Australia and New Zealand in the few years prior to 1881 helps to explain the confusing situation when there were no official boxing governing bodies.

In 1860, "The Brighton Boy" as Tom Sayers was called, was seen as the champion of England. He had been fighting in the prize ring ever since the 1840s and had lost only one battle. He had defeated such men as Aaron Jones, William Perry ("The Tipton Slasher"), Bob Brettle, Bill Benjamin and Tom Paddock.

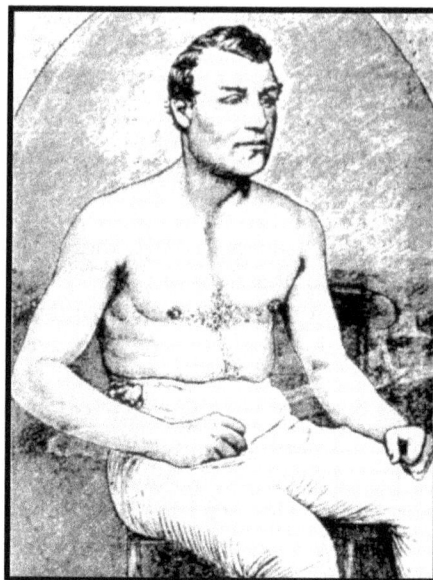

Tom Sayers

John C. Heenan had been a top contender for the championship in America for a number of years. He was famous for his battle against John Morrissey in 1858. Morrissey retired and refused to fight Heenan again. So, John challenged the world and decided to go to England, fight Sayers and establish himself as the top heavyweight.

John C. Heenan

The two men fought on April 17, 1860 in Farnborough, England for 42 rounds. Heenan seemed to have the advantage when the crowd broke into the ring.

Sayers retired and did not fight again. It was nearly four years before Heenan would fight once more.

**John C. Heenan-Tom Sayers
April 17 1860**

"Both men then left what had been the ring, Sayers, though much blown and distressed, walking firmly and coolly away, with both his eyes open and clear. His right arm, however, was helpless, his mouth and nose were dreadfully beaten, and the side of his head and forehead much punished. Heenan was almost unrecognizable as a human being, so dreadful had been his punishment about the face and neck."

**The Nonconformist (London)
April 18 1860**

Then, the fighting game experienced a decline. Interest in bare-knuckle fighting waned. To a large degree, the sport was taken over by thugs and crooks. Underhanded dealings took place. Fans who attended contests were often bullied and beaten up. Upper class society lost the interest it once held and avoided the fights.

In November of 1860, Sam Hurst beat Tom Paddock in five rounds near Hungerford, England, thus entitling him to receive the Champion's Belt from Tom Sayers. Hurst was then considered to be the champion of England.

Sam Hurst

THE CHAMPIONSHIP.—The Champion's belt was on Tuesday fought for, by one Tom Paddock, a veteran of the prize-ring, and a Lancashire man named Hurst, alias the Staleybridge Infant. The following report of the affair is from the *Morning Post:*—"The fight, after being stopped near Basingstoke, at last came off near Hungerford. Paddock, whose age is thirty-six, and height some 5 ft. 11 in., is a burley, florid, good-humoured looking fellow. He has, however, lost his former science, and years have told upon him. Hurst is a young man of twenty-three, whose height is 6 ft. 2 in.; his ordinary weight is nineteen stone, but his training had brought him down to a little under fifteen stone. He is larger and heavier than Heenan, and a clumsy fellow to look at. The "battle" was hardly worthy of the name—only five rounds were fought. Hurst drew "first blood;" but in the first four rounds both men fought very poorly. Instead of the swift, lightning-like blows and ready agility of such athletes as Sayers or Mace, there was only an exhibition of clumsy sparring, in which the men's fists described slow movements, more like those of heavenly bodies in Adams's orrery than those of boxers seeking the belt. In the fifth round Paddock delivered the only fine blow given in the course of the fight, full and straight upon the left eye and cheek of Hurst. The "Infant" fairly staggered under it, and was in the act of retiring to his corner when Paddock made an absurd rush at him unworthy of any novice. Hurst, recovering himself, turned suddenly round, and struck, with the whole force of his prodigious weight, a wild sort of blow, which happened, as luck would have it, to light on the left side of Tom, somewhere about the heart, and felled him as if a cannon-ball had struck him. He sank senseless, breathless, and prostrate. He was, of course, "knocked out of time," and the sponge thrown up. Poor Paddock was a long while in coming to himself, and was apparently in great pain. Hurst is now Champion of England, and it remains to be seen whether he will be allowed long to retain the belt he has won. From the unscientific mode in which he fought, it is expected that, notwithstanding his great weight and strength, other boxers will not be slow in challenging him."—Paddock's ribs are fractured, it seems, and he is suffering greatly from internal injuries. A short time ago he was under treatment in Middlesex Hospital for paralysis of the lower extremities.

The Illustrated Times (London)
November 10 1860

Jem Mace, a very slick boxer when fighting under the prize ring rules, had been hailed by many as the best in the land.

He was an advocate of the manly art of self-defense. As a boxer, he was clever and had perfected a number of boxing skills such as how to position the body, hold the arms, strike blows and avoid punches.

Lightly Mace moved in and out, feinting and smiling, as, with a noiseless bound, like a cat, he sprang just out of distance of the ponderous arms that seemed only required to move to crush him. Gradually they drew nearer and nearer, the giant waiting for his chance, which the other now and then appeared to give him, though, in reality, he ventured nothing. At last Mace carefully ventured in and struck his opponent slightly three or four times in the face. They were only little blows, but enough to show him that he could reach the slow, unwieldy boxer when he chose, and get out of all danger of return with perfect certainty. Apparently satisfied with this knowledge, Mace began the fight with a terrific blow, which completely closed Hurst's eye, and seemed to make his bulky frame tremble to his very feet. Before the first round, which lasted nearly twelve minutes, was over, Hurst was half smothered in his own blood, and his face so gashed that, as far as appearances went, Mace might have been assaulting him with a razor.

The Illustrated Times (London)
June 22 1861

Jem Mace

During the 1860s at one time or another, Mace was the owner of the English middleweight and heavyweight boxing titles. Some sources say the welterweight title too. Jem had a big influence on boxing during his lifetime. He traveled the world and taught boxing skills, gave lectures and conducted tournaments. Many talented pugilists were developed by him.

Mace defeated Sam Hurst on June 18, 1861. He pitted his outstanding skills and quickness against the much larger size of Hurst and came out victorious. He then claimed the heavyweight championship of England. Hurst retired shortly afterwards.

Jem followed this up with a victory over Tom King on January 28, 1862, also for the heavyweight championship.

FIGHT FOR THE CHAMPIONSHIP BETWEEN MACE AND KING.--The above fight took place yesterday morning, at Godstone, in Surrey, and about thirty miles from London. The fight began at seven minutes past nine, and after fighting one hour and eight minutes, during which time forty-two rounds were fought, King was unable to come up to the call of time, and Mace was declared the victor. King obtained first blood and the first knock-down blow. The betting at the commencement was 3 to 1 on Mace, but in the course of the encounter the odds varied to similar offers upon King. The punishment delivered up to a certain time was tolerably equal, King having slightly the best of it until the last round, when they closed and fell, King's head coming in contact with the ground, which rendered him insensible, and the sponge was thrown up in token of his defeat. The fight took place amid a steady fall of rain, but the attendance was very large, the aristocracy being very powerfully represented.

The Evening Star and Dial (London)
January 29 1862

Jem Mace-Tom King
January 28 1862

In a rematch between Mace and King on November 26, 1862, a new champion took the throne when King won in 21 rounds. Afterwards, Jem challenged King to a rematch but Tom refused.

The combatants entered the ring a few minutes past 9, when after fighting for 38 minutes, during which time 21 rounds were fought, mostly in favor of Mace, King countered him very heavily on the nose and knocked him down insensible. Previous to the last round 6 to 1 was offered on Mace. The winner was seconded by Jack Macdonald and Bos Tyler, and Mace by Bob Travers and Bob Brettle.

The British Miner and General Newsman (London)
November 29 1862

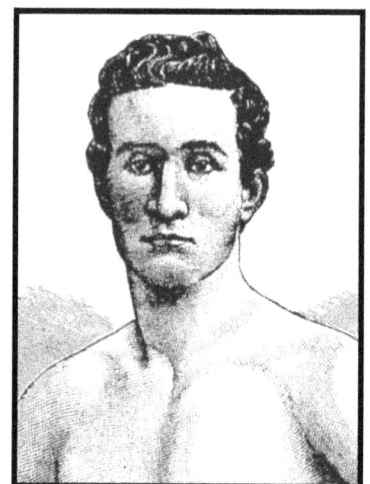

Tom King

Joe Coburn

During 1862, Joe Coburn, a quick moving American pugilist with fast hands, hurled challenges at the top men. When none responded, Coburn claimed the title.

Also on the scene was Joe Goss, a tough and tricky scrapper who had won the English middleweight title in November of 1862. During 1860-1862, Goss was unbeaten in six contests and had defeated some good men. He wanted to fight Mace.

Joe Goss

Coburn strengthened his claim for the American heavyweight title in 1863 when he defeated Mike McCoole near Charlestown, Maryland after 67 rounds. Later that year, he challenged Tom King and Jem Mace to championship fights but both refused.

Joe Coburn-Mike McCoole
May 5 1863

Mace was looking for a title after losing his heavyweight crown to Tom King. He heard the noise coming from Joe Goss and decided to tangle with him. On September 1, 1863, in a contest that was held in three rings due to the authorities trying to prevent it from taking place, Mace defeated Joe Goss in nineteen rounds to reclaim the middleweight championship of England. Mace defended himself well, pounded Goss and then finished him with a strong right hand punch.

Jem Mace-Joe Goss
September 1 1863

Andrew Marsden defeated Ned O'Baldwin in October of 1863 to become a candidate for the championship of England. Then, Tom King defended his championship against the American John C. Heenan in December of 1863 and won in 24 rounds. Heenan was dominate early in the fight but by round seventeen had tired greatly. From that round until the end, King was the better man and came out the victor. It appears that King did not fight again and the heavyweight championship was held by no one.

Jem Mace and Coburn, the American champ, tried to engage in a contest during 1864 but negotiations broke down. The two could never come to an agreement on fight conditions. Joe Wormald defeated Andrew Marsden in January of 1865 and claimed the championship of England. Mace and Wormald then arranged a title fight for September 1865 but it was cancelled when Joe suffered an injury during training. Mace claimed the English crown once again.

When the fight with Jem Mace failed to materialize, Coburn retired and a fellow named Bill Davis claimed the American title. When he lost to Jim Dunn in May of 1865, his claim was discarded.

Bill Davis

However, when Dunn turned to politics instead of fighting, Davis renewed his claim to the title.

During 1865, Jimmy Elliott challenged Joe Coburn to a fight for the championship but Coburn refused. Elliott then claimed the title. Soon afterwards, Bill Davis challenged Jimmy.

Jim Dunn

Jem Mace and Joe Goss met in May of 1866 to decide the heavyweight championship of England but it seems they did not truly want to fight. Few blows were struck. They met again in August of the same year in a more earnest mood. Mace won. Also in England, Ned O'Baldwin gained revenge for his 1863 loss by defeating Andrew Marsden in September 1866.

Jimmy Elliott

> The great prize fight for the Championship of England, between Jem Mace and Joe Goss, took place to-day, August 7th. Twenty-one rounds were fought, when Mace was declared the winner.

The Brooklyn (NY) Daily Eagle, August 9 1866
(Brooklyn Public Library-Brooklyn Collection)

In America, Mike McCoole put in his claim for the title during September of 1866 when he defeated Bill Davis in 34 rounds. In March of 1867, Joe Goss met Tom Allen, the reigning middleweight champion of England. This fight ended in a draw. Their paths would cross again in the future. On May 10, 1867, Jimmy Elliott defeated Bill Davis and maintained his claim to the title. McCoole came back with a victory over Aaron Jones in August of 1867 and was shouting his claim to the big prize loud and clear.

Mike McCoole

Jem Mace was scheduled to defend the heavyweight title in London on October 15, 1867 against big Ned O'Baldwin, who stood 6'5" and had made claims of being the champion. However, the bout was prevented by the authorities.

At this time, there was much opposition to bare-fist fighting in the country and matches were difficult to hold. So, in 1867 Goss packed his bags and left England for America. Allen came along. Jem Mace went to America a couple of years afterwards.

Tom Allen

O'Baldwin and Joe Wormald, two men who had laid claims to the English heavyweight title, went to America too. Fighting in England was at a standstill until years later.

Ned O'Baldwin

Each of these men had an undisputed claim to the title so they arranged a fight to determine who was champion. It was to be held on October 29, 1868 but as happened so often in those days, the police showed up and arrested them shortly after they began.

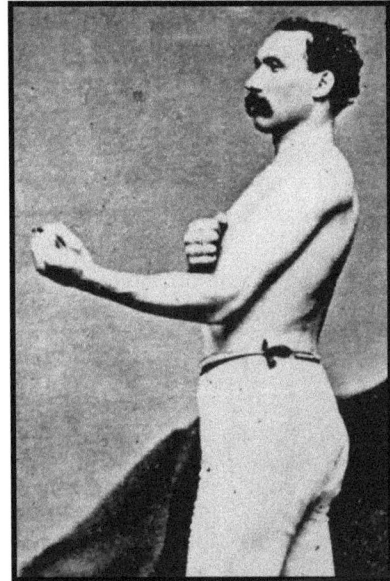

Joe Wormald

There were rumors that O'Baldwin defeated Wormald in a fight held on Election Day in November. Another story said O'Baldwin was awarded the stakes when Wormald failed to show. Yet, another report stated that they settled matters on November 11, 1868 and O'Baldwin won when Wormald failed to come out for the second round.

About daylight a ring was pitched just above Weehawken ferry, O'Baldwin being seconded by Joe Coburn and Charles Dimond, and Wormald by George Rooke and Tom Butts. As soon as the men entered the ring they set at work at one another and a more severe contest was never witnessed. Both men forced the fight, and Wormald got in two or three very good body blows, when O'Baldwin sent in his right which sent Wormald flying into his corner, he again rallied, and on coming up O'Baldwin got in another heavy blow on Wormald's jaw, which could have been heard a great distance off, and which sent him flying across the ring, where he lay for some time apparently insensible. When time was called for the second round he failed to put in an appearance, and the referee, Dan Noble, decided the fight in favor of the Giant O'Baldwin. On examination it was found that Wormald's jaw was broken.

The Brooklyn (NY) Daily Eagle, November 12 1868
(Brooklyn Public Library-Brooklyn Collection)

In January of 1869, Tom Allen defeated Bill Davis near St. Louis and claimed the American heavyweight championship. Shortly afterwards, he lost that claim in a fight against Charley Gallagher. In June, Allen lost to Mike McCoole on a foul in nine rounds. It was no surprise when McCoole put forth another claim for the American championship.

Near St. Louis in August, Allen met Gallagher again and defeated him in nine rounds to renew his claim for the American championship. Some historians report that they fought eleven rounds and the battle was declared a draw.

In 1870, Jem Mace defeated Allen for the American heavyweight title. The Mace-Allen bout was also billed as the heavyweight championship of the world. Mace's claim was not challenged since he had held the English championship and now held the American championship too.

THE ALLEN AND GALLA-GHER PRIZE FIGHT.

Desperate Encounter.

ALLEN THE VICTOR IN THE NINTH ROUND.

BOTH MEN BADLY PUNISHED

The Dubuque (IA) Herald
August 18 1869

**Jem Mace-Tom Allen
May 10 1870**

The following year, Mace twice met Joe Coburn, the former claimant for the American heavyweight championship. Each contest was ruled a draw. In the first match, few punches were thrown. The second involved a few more punches. Soon afterwards, Mace began traveling, teaching boxing fundamentals and running contests. He sparred often but engaged in few real fights.

In Australia, Laurence "Larry" Foley was the most famous pugilist at this time. He had won a championship of sorts in 1871 by "out-quicking" the larger, more powerful Sandy Ross. As a fighter, Foley combined agility and science with punching power and was a pioneer in boxing styles and techniques. He was in the lightweight to middleweight range in physical body structure but fought all comers irrespective of size.

Born in New South Wales, it was said that Foley's early years were spent as a member of a Catholic gang that roamed the inner-city of Sydney and got into street fights with the Protestant gang. Reportedly, a negro ex-convict called John Perry ("Black Perry") first taught Foley to box.

Foley rose from gang-fighting to organized prize-fighting when he gained the support of the well-to-do who enjoyed watching fist fights. He went on to become the greatest bare-knuckle fighter of his time and the founder of scientific boxing in Australia.

Larry Foley

Jem Mace made an exhibition tour in 1872 and then became inactive. Upon Mace's exit from official contests, Tom Allen again won the American championship by beating Mike McCoole near St. Louis in 1873. Allen also met Ben Hogan in a title defense and retained his crown.

McCOOLE-ALLEN FIGHT.

Allen Wins the Toss and Whips McCoole in 20 Minutes.

Only Nine Rounds Fought.

The Dubuque (IA) Herald
September 24 1873

Originally, it had been scheduled for October 28, 1873 at Chouteau [Chateau] Island, Illinois but intervention by authorities delayed the battle. According to boxing historian Arly Allen, Hogan and Allen fought their battle on November 18, 1873 in a field near Pacific City, Iowa.

It was declared a draw. However, Hogan claimed the title and Allen pursued him to Pennsylvania trying to arrange a second bout.

William Miller

William Miller was a well-known boxer, wrestler and all-around athlete during the years 1874-1876. He appeared in many locations but performed primarily in the New York area.

BOSTON MUSIC HALL.

MONDAY EVENING, JUNE 12, 1876.
The Greatest Contest of the Season.
The Grand Græco-Roman
WRESTLING MATCH
Between
PROF. WILLIAM MILLER
Of Boston (late of San Francisco), whose challenge to any man in the world has been accepted by Mr.
JOHN DWYER

The Boston (MA) Daily Globe
June 12 1876

He was often matched against Joe Goss or a talented young man named John J. Dwyer. Both Miller and Dwyer were very popular crowd favorites. In June 1876, Miller reportedly defeated Dwyer for the wrestling championship of America.

It was 1876 before Tom Allen risked the title again. Joe Goss defeated him in Kentucky and was recognized as the American heavyweight champion. The fight was held in two rings. Goss was not a big man but he was talented and capable under the London Prize Ring Rules. He knew some tricks. Following his victory, Joe made personal appearances, boxed a few exhibitions and retained the American title until 1880. Allen returned to England.

THE MAULING MATCH.

Allen and Goss Fight Twenty-One Rounds on the Bourbon-Bedewed Soil of Kentucky.

They Are Interrupted by the Authorities, Only to Resume That Allen May Lose by a "Foul."

The Vanquished Gladiator Arrested and Imprisoned.

The Dubuque (IA) Herald
September 8 1876

The boxing genius Jem Mace boxed some exhibitions with Joe Goss in London in 1875, beat Bill Davis a couple of times - 1876 and 1877 - and then went to Australia in the late 1870s. He toured with Larry Foley, giving exhibition bouts in Australia and New Zealand. While traveling with Mace, Foley further refined his skills.

Charles Smith

A number of boxing historians consider Charles Smith to be the colored heavyweight champion of the world during the mid to late 1870s. Reportedly, he began fighting at age 19 and had more than 200 bouts during his career. His manager, Bill Muldoon, called him a great fighter, terrific hitter and clever boxer.

During his career, Smith defeated such men as Mervine Thompson, Thomas "Soap" McAlpine, Harry Woodson ("The Black Diamond"), "Professor" Charles Hadley, John Donaldson, Steve Taylor, Jack Fallon, Bill Gabig and Mike Brennan.

John J. Dwyer, the young man who boxed and wrestled with William Miller, improved rapidly as he engaged in boxing contests with men like Steve Taylor, Joe Coburn and Joe Goss - and held his own. Dwyer continued to sharpen his skills with a number of contests in 1877.

In London on March 2, 1877, a man named Milsom won a heavyweight competition by defeating a fellow named Hope. The eyes of the public tuned in more and more to activities of the ring.

On May 19, also in London, John Knifton [Knifeton], big and crude but also tough and rugged, won a heavyweight competition under the Queensberry Rules with the gloves when he knocked out Jem Madden, stopped Walter Watson and then outpointed Tom Tully. Later in the same year, using the Queensberry Rules, he fought Tom Scrutton in a fight billed as the English heavyweight championship. No decision was rendered. Knifton was considered to be champion by some.

John Knifton

After the first round, which, according to the Marquis of Queensberry's rules and articles of agreement, lasted only three minutes, it was manifest that Allen was the more powerful man of the two. On the call of time for the second round, Allen, after striking his opponent three heavy blows with his left, drew the first blood, and finished by knocking his antagonist down—a double feat which elicited much applause. Gilbert was then taken to his corner, where he was carefully wiped down and restoratives administered to him, as he appeared unconscious. During the following rounds, up to the seventh and last, he received two more knock-downs. During this time the blood continued to flow freely from his mouth and nose, whilst Allen showed no marks of the unequal combat. In the last round the champion struck Gilbert two severe upper-cuts, which caused him to stagger, Allen the while standing in the middle of the ring. Upon recovering, Gilbert rushed at his opponent, seized him round the loins and attempted to throw him. On this, Allen picked him up, raised him on a level with his head, and dashed him with great force on the wooden stage, the thud resounding throughout the building.

The Week's News (London)
November 3 1877

Tom Allen rejected Knifton's title claim. Big John was willing to meet him but could not obtain the financial backing needed for the fight. In October of 1877, Allen fought and defeated a man named Tompkin [Thompkin] Gilbert in London. Some historians contend Gilbert won due to a foul. Allen then claimed the heavyweight championship under the Marquis of Queensberry Rules. It was difficult to argue with his claim because of his past record and reputation.

10

On April 4, 1878, Tom Allen beat Charles Davis in a championship fight in London. Davis was a man in bad health and should never have been fighting. During April and May, Paddy Ryan, a popular boxer-wrestler in the New York area, challenged John J. Dwyer to a fight. The match was set but cancelled when the promoter could not come up with the prize money.

There was on-going talk about Ryan fighting Dwyer for the championship of America but making it happen was the problem.

According to some sources, Morris Grant claimed the colored heavyweight championship in 1878 (or 1879). Little is known about Grant but he was said to be a strong, scrappy competitor.

Morris Grant

THE PRIZE-RING.

John Dwyer and Patrick Ryan to Fight for $2000 and the Championship of America.

(Special Despatch to The Boston Globe.)

NEW YORK, June 7.—Sporting men are getting ready for the next prize-fight according to the latest London rules, which is to take place within a few weeks between John Dwyer of Brooklyn and Patrick Ryan of Troy. The match is said to be for $2000 and, of course, the so-called championship of America.

The Boston (MA) Daily Globe
June 7 1878

On December 2, 1878, Larry Foley fought Peter Newton in Melbourne, Australia in a Queensberry Rules contest using gloves. Reportedly, the authorities intervened and the fight was called a draw. Foley dominated the action and voiced a claim for the Australian championship. Each man weighed much less than a true heavyweight.

Foley renewed his claim as the Australian champion by defeating Abe Hicken in sixteen rounds on March 20, 1879 in what has been called the last of the great bare-knuckle battles. Hicken had made several claims for the Australian title during the 1870s. The contest was first scheduled to be held in Melbourne but to avoid the police, the battle site was moved northward to a place near Echuca in nearby New South Wales Territory. Although the men were talented fighters, they weighed much less than true heavyweights would have weighed.

Abe Hicken

TWELFTH AND LAST ROUND.—This round was a terrible one. Elliott, although he was severely beaten, evidently was not quite licked. He warded off one or two blows, but Dwyer went for him with such force and celerity that he used him up inside of twenty seconds. He finally threw and fell upon him. Dwyer arose, but Elliott lay on his back just where he had fallen. Then he partially turned over, opened his eyes and fell on his back again. Without waiting to pick up their man, his seconds threw up the sponge. Elliott was knocked clean out of time. When he was dragged to his corner he fell off his chair and lay on the ground.

The referee, of course, decided that Dwyer won the fight.

The Brooklyn (NY) Daily Eagle, May 9 1879
(Brooklyn Public Library-Brooklyn Collection)

Another man of fistic fame south of the equator was Jack Hagpole in New Zealand. He was a man full of scrap and plenty capable with his fists. Jack reportedly held the title of that land for a number of years during the 1870s.

Tom Allen drew with Jem Stewart in a 24-round title contest in London on April 22, 1879 and retained the English crown. He later retired from actively fighting in the ring and relinquished his claim to the championship. Afterwards, he fought a few exhibition contests.

John J. Dwyer had developed into a very good boxer as well as a talented wrestler. He had profited from his days of scuffling with William Miller. In May of 1879, he defeated Jimmy Elliott and launched his claim for the American title.

In June, Paddy Ryan was still after Dwyer. Reportedly, John accepted Paddy's challenge and preparations were underway for a title fight between the two but it never happened.

Patrick Ryan, of Troy, New York has challenged Dwyer, of Brooklyn, to fight for $1,000 aside and the championship. Dwyer has accepted, and the articles will be signed June 5.

The Belleville (KS) Telescope
June 12 1879

Alfred "Alf" Greenfield

Following the draw with Tom Allen, Jem Stewart defeated Tompkin [Thompkin] Gilbert on September 6, 1879 in Glasgow and shortly afterwards claimed the English championship.

Alfred "Alf" Greenfield racked up some impressive victories in England during the 1877-1879 years, including wins over Sam Breeze and Jimmy Highland. He was a top candidate for champion of England. In November of 1879, Greenfield actually bested the popular and talented Denny Harrington but was declared the loser on a foul.

Charlie Mitchell, a scrappy man who fought from around 130 pounds up to 178 pounds during his career, surfaced in "Mother" England. An extremely talented man under London Prize Ring Rules, Mitchell won a number of contests at the lighter weights. Along the way, he had beaten many larger men.

During 1879-1880, a young slugger from Boston gained public attention in America with his heavy punching and great ego. His name was John L. Sullivan. He had a loud mouth, a lot of nerve and a very strong punch.

When young John L. fought, he seemed to be in an urgent rush to finish off his man. He had the "goods" and his performances caught the eye of the people. Despite his drinking and bragging, he had a magnetic personality and on his powerful young shoulders rode the resurgence of the fight game.

As the years passed into the 1880s, there was still no official fight organization to declare a champion. Each country had its combatants who claimed the championship of its territory and of the world but there truly was no heavyweight champion of the world.

On February 26, 1880, "Alf" Greenfield defeated Jem Stewart in London and laid claim to the English championship. Meanwhile, in New Zealand, a man named Herbert Slade was viewed as the best big man there in the early years of the 1880s. A man named Pettengell also made a title claim during those years.

John L. Sullivan as a young man

12

At this time, Joe Goss was still generally recognized as the American champion. However, in the state of New York, there was the Irishman, Paddy Ryan. He was a powerful man who was an accomplished wrestler and tough as nails but quite crude as a pugilist. Nevertheless, tremendous support grew for him to fight Joe Goss.

Paddy Ryan

Paddy Ryan-Joe Goss
May 30 1880

The Fight of the Heavyweights Yesterday

PADDY RYAN THE WINNER

~

Goss Badly Punished – Eighty-Six Rounds Fought

The Titusville (PA) Herald
June 2 1880

The contest was held on May 30, 1880 at Collier's Station, West Virginia. (Some sources said June 1.) Goss was much smaller than Ryan but was rather clever and quick. He was a fighter to be reckoned with under London Prize Ring Rules.

Ryan, about 6 feet tall and 210 pounds, had a definite size advantage over Goss, who stood 5'8" and weighed 160 pounds. He was stronger too. His strength served him well and he was able to overcome the skills of the crafty Goss, who was not able to come out for round 87.

John J. Dwyer

Reportedly, in June of 1880, young John L. Sullivan knocked out the famous George Rooke. In July 1880, John J. Dwyer assumed the position of Clerk of the Third District Court in Brooklyn under Justice John Courtney. He traded his muscles and fists for pencil and paper and retired from the ring. Perhaps he did not want to fight the tough, bull-strong Paddy Ryan. In contrast, young John L. Sullivan was more than willing - bring on Paddy.

PRIZE FIGHT

~

**Between Sullivan
And Donaldson**

~

**The latter badly
Beaten in ten
Rounds in
Cincinnati**

The Cleveland (OH) Herald
December 25 1880

Sullivan continued knocking people around. He was young and brash and sounding off about what he would do to Ryan and the other big boys. In December of 1880, John L. beat John Donaldson.

Cincinnati, December 24

John Sullivan, of Boston, and Prof. John Donaldson, of Cleveland, succeeded in having a fight with small hard gloves, in a hall, before a very small and select house. Ten rounds were fought. From the beginning it was apparent Donaldson was no match for Sullivan, as at the end of every round he was either knocked down or went down to avoid punishment. At the end of the tenth round Donaldson indicated that he had seen enough of his antagonist and Sullivan was declared the winner.

The Titusville (PA) Morning Herald
December 25 1880

In Australia, champion Larry Foley faced many challengers - Bill Farnan being the most prominent of these. Several attempts were made to get Foley and Farnan in the ring together but none succeeded.

To the left, Larry Foley's White Horse Hotel
Sydney, New South Wales, Australia

Larry operated a boxing school in Sydney and trained young men who aspired to be fighters. During his time, he mentored a number of young fighters who went on to world-wide fame.

There were a number of fight venues in Sydney at the time but Foley's White Horse Hotel was the most popular.

The Iron Pot, a simple wooden building covered with sheets of corrugated iron, was a favorite site of fistic action provided by Foley.

In most places, boxing (fighting) at this time was looked upon with disdain and little interest. It was an activity for the illiterate, the lower socio-economic groups, the have-nots and the criminal element or less than ethical members of society in England, Ireland, America, Australia, New Zealand and other countries of the world. Nevertheless, there were some members of the upper echelon who followed pugilism with great interest - including doctors, lawyers, judges, engineers, ministers, etc.

Chapter One

The Years 1881-1900

I n 1881, Charlie Mitchell defeated Caradoff ("The Belgium Giant"), a much larger man than he. Clever and shifty with a solid punch, Charlie also held his own against Tom Tully, another larger man. Some sources report a draw, some report a Mitchell victory in the Tully contest.

The English influence had caught on in America. Good young American pugilists were springing up all over. Patriotism abounded. Name calling was commonplace between the Americans and the English. Most of the top English boxers and other European fighters decided to venture to America and teach the young upstarts a lesson.

Charlie Mitchell

EXTRA!

FLOOD-SULLIVAN

PRIZE FIGHT.
—
SULLIVAN WINS AFTER 8
ROUNDS.

The prize fight between Jack Sullivan, of Boston, and John Flood, of this city, which has been contemplated for a long time, took place Monday night on a barge 10 miles up the Hudson River.

The Police Gazette Extra
May 17 1881

All the while, Australia had its good men. Talented young fighters came along one after the other during the early to mid-1880s - men such as Peter Jackson, Frank "Paddy" Slavin, Tom Lees and Nicholas "Mick" Dooley. They learned the trade under Larry Foley and were making noise on the world stage. Like the English, the Australians soon migrated to America to show the new world their skills.

During 1881, the cocky young warrior from Boston, John L. Sullivan, continued to make a name for himself as a knockout puncher. He would take on anybody.

Sullivan battered his opponents easily and knocked out some big fellows - Steve Taylor, John Flood, Fred Crossley, Dan McCarty, James Dalton and Jack Burns. In addition, he had plenty to say about how he would manhandle Paddy Ryan, the American champion. This irritated Paddy.

In England on May 19, 1881, Jack Burke was victorious in a splendid, skillful duel against William "Coddy" Middings. As a result, some viewed Burke as the champion of England, including Burke himself.

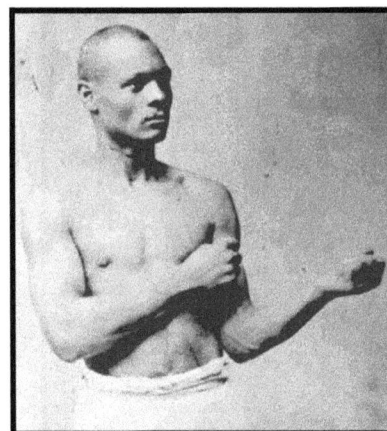

Charles Hadley

John L. Sullivan-Paddy Ryan
February 7 1882

Some historians contend that in 1881 (or 1882), Charles Hadley defeated Morris Grant and was generally considered to be the colored champion.

Paddy Ryan finally accepted Sullivan's challenge and the two men met in Mississippi City, Mississippi on February 7, 1882 for the American championship. The fight was held under London Prize Ring Rules in a 24-foot ring in front of the Barnes Hotel.

It turned out to be a one-sided affair with Sullivan scoring most of the knockdowns and falls. Ryan was bleeding badly from the nose and mouth early in the fight. After eight rounds, Ryan could not continue and John L. became the heavyweight champion of America.

As Sullivan continued his career, his fighting prowess prompted hero worship. Even the members of the upper echelon of society followed his ring encounters closely. The great warrior, along with the usage of gloves instead of bare-fists, transformed the unruly sport of boxing (pugilism) into an acceptable form of social entertainment. John L. Sullivan became a legend in his own time.

During 1882, Charlie Mitchell enhanced his reputation when he won an English welterweight (or middleweight) championship. In December of 1882, William "Coddy" Middings defeated John Knifton in a heavyweight competition. Also in December, Mitchell did the impossible when he won Billy Madden's heavyweight competition, beating several men - Bill England, Bill Springhall and Dick Roberts - in the process. In 1883, he beat the North England champion Jack Clarke by a stoppage in one round.

THE FIGHT.

The Troy Giant Whipped by Sullivan,

And the Boston Boy Now Wears the Belt.

Paddy Ryan Knocked Out of Time on the Eighth Round

The Marion (OH) Daily Star
February 8 1882

McHenry Johnson

Gilbert Odd, the famous British boxing historian, contended that in the early 1880s, Charlie Mitchell defeated John Knifton in three rounds in a heavyweight competition to capture the heavyweight championship of England. This is disputed by some historians.

Boxing lore has it that during the early 1880s, Morris Grant, Charles Hadley, George Godfrey ("Old Chocolate"), McHenry Johnson, Harry Woodson ("The Black Diamond") and Billy Wilson all declared for the colored heavyweight championship. These men fought each other frequently and numerous claims were made for the title since there was no sanctioning body.

According to boxing historian Kevin Smith, in 1882 Grant and Hadley engaged in a couple of fights and Hadley remained champion. In 1883, Hadley won over Harry Woodson in January but then lost to George Godfrey in February. Godfrey claimed the title and was a popular choice as the colored champion.

Name calling and insults had been hurled across the Atlantic from England to America and back for years. Mouthy Charlie Mitchell, claimant to the English championship, came to America in 1883, beat Mike Cleary on April 9 in New York and got into the ring with John L. Sullivan on May 14.

George Godfrey

Mitchell put big Sullivan down in the first round. John L. pushed him out of the ring in round two, pinned him to the ropes in round three and was blasting away when the police intervened. Mitchell always felt if he could get John L. onto the turf under London Prize Ring Rules, he stood a chance. However, he would have to wait.

On May 28, William Miller, now in Australia, fought Larry Foley in Sydney for the championship of Australia. The fight ended after forty rounds. Spectators rushed into the ring to save the ageing Foley from defeat and a brawl broke out among the rowdies. The police then appeared upon the scene and the contest was declared a draw. The next day, Foley conceded defeat and the winner's purse was awarded to Miller.

John L. Sullivan-Charlie Mitchell
May 14 1883

Apparently, Miller never took the title too seriously because he engaged in wrestling matches, boxing and wrestling exhibitions and traveled abroad often.

In England on June 29, "Alf" Greenfield defeated Jack Burke in the final bout of a Jem Mace English all-weight competition and solidified his claim to the championship of England.

William Sheriff, another English invader, got into the ring with the sharp-hitting American Mike Cleary on April 18, 1884 in New York. Cleary, a man with quick feet and fast hands, took care of business and finished off Sheriff in the first round.

Mike Cleary-William Sheriff
April 18 1884

In 1884, George Godfrey met McHenry Johnson in a fight for the colored heavyweight championship. This bout was called a draw and Godfrey retained the title. He would not defend for several years. Johnson still made claims to the title and fought a draw with Billy Wilson a month later, supposedly in a colored title bout.

Bill Farnan

In Melbourne on July 26, 1884, Bill Farnan, who had claimed the heavyweight title since defeating Charlie "Darkie" Richardson in 1881, strengthened his claim to the heavyweight championship of Australia. He stopped the up-and-coming Peter Jackson. Some sources report a second encounter between these men in September of that year. Farnan held the title for nearly a year before losing in twelve rounds to Tom Lees on May 20, 1885 in Melbourne.

John Knifton won a couple of victories and claimed the English championship in 1884. A July win over Jack Massey and an October victory over Wolf Bendoff sparked his claim.

"Alf" Greenfield decided to come to America in November of 1884 and try conclusions with John L. Sullivan in New York. He did well in the first round but things got hot in round two. In this round, John L. eventually got Greenfield pinned on the ropes and was pummeling him when the police interrupted the bout. Both men suffered cuts in the contest. The bout was called an exhibition and the men escaped jail time.

Back in England in December, Jem Smith made Wolf Bendoff retire after twelve rounds in a heavyweight competition. Smith won a trophy and claimed the English championship. Shortly afterwards, on January 12, 1885, John L. Sullivan beat "Alf" Greenfield in four rounds in Boston.

Jem Smith won another heavyweight competition on February 26 with a victory over Tom Longer. Meanwhile, down under, Dick Matthews was the champion of New Zealand as of 1885.

SULLIVAN AND GREENFIELD IN COURT

John L. Sullivan and Alfred Greenfield, the pugilists, who were arrested in Madison Square Garden, New York, last night, were put under bonds to appear at Jefferson Market Court this afternoon to answer the charge of having engaged in a prize fight "to the great danger of the public peace."

The Brooklyn (NY) Daily Eagle, November 19 1884
(Brooklyn Public Library-Brooklyn Collection)

Dominick McCaffrey

It was three-and-a-half years after the fight with Ryan when Sullivan defended his American title again. His opponent was a "cute" boxer named Dominick McCaffrey, who was quick and skillful - a dodger deluxe. The fight was held in Cincinnati on August 29 of 1885 under the Queensberry Rules. Some reports called it a world championship contest.

McCaffrey chose to hit-and-run. John L. decided to deliberately stalk his smaller foe, not charging ferociously as he often did but steadily pursuing his man. When he caught McCaffrey on the ropes, a strong one-two sent Dominick to the ground. McCaffrey was knocked down several times during the seven rounds and the fight went to the champion. Stubborn McCaffrey fans thought their man had won.

18

Jack Wannop drew attention when he beat Wolf Bendoff in an English heavyweight competition in November of 1885.

Many Englishmen felt that Charlie Mitchell had abandoned the English title chase when he traveled to America in 1883. So, on December 16, 1885 in Surrey, England, when Jem Smith knocked out Jack Davis [Davies] in six rounds, he asserted his claim to the heavyweight championship of England.

Jem Smith

SULLIVAN CHAMPION YET.

McCaffrey Defeated After Seven Closely Contested Rounds.

The Young Pittsburger Stands up Bravely and is Declared the Loser Because of an Alleged Foul—Details of the Contest.

CHESTER PARK, Cincinnati, August 28.

At precisely 5:17 o'clock, after several minor fights had been furnished for the entertainment of the crowd, Sullivan made his way forward to the ring and was greeted by lusty yells from ten thousand throats.

The Brooklyn (NY) Daily Eagle, August 30 1885
(Brooklyn Public Library-Brooklyn Collection)

In midwestern America, the reputation of a crunching hitter named Pat Killen was growing. Just a tap from this bruiser and his opponent fell. It was simply a matter of time. When Killen landed his punch, it was over.

His followers were convinced he would whip any man he faced. He would take out John L. for that matter. Just ask 'em! Just ask Killen! What's more, through early April of 1886, he was unbeaten and had scored knockouts in all of his bouts except for one contest where his man kept falling to avoid his punches. Killen was one of the most dangerous knockout artists of the period.

Pat Killen

Jem Smith-"Alf" Greenfield
February 16 1886

On February 16, 1886, two of the top men of the English ring, Jem Smith and "Alf" Greenfield, tangled in a fight that lasted thirteen rounds. The contest was held near Paris and after some tough fighting, Smith seemed to be the better man. However, some rowdy observers broke into the ring and the bout was declared a draw.

Patsy Cardiff, a pretty good heavyweight, tangled with George Rooke on March 5 and won a solid six-round victory. This man Cardiff would go on to be an obstacle to some top men before he would wrap up his ring career.

Tom Lees was a muscular, sturdy man with tremendous strength. He was especially well-built about the chest, shoulders and arms. After winning the Australian crown from Bill Farnan in 1885, he fought a couple more title fights with him. The last of these was a four-round stoppage near Essendon on April 20, 1886 in which he kept the title. After this, he fought a number of non-title bouts, including a win over scrappy "Mick" Dooley and a "no decision" contest against Bob Fitzsimmons.

Patsy Cardiff-George Rooke
March 5 1886

Tom Lees

On June 11, Patsy Cardiff further enhanced his reputation by fighting a five-round draw with Charlie Mitchell in Minneapolis.

At this time, there was a man in Pennsylvania building a reputation for himself as quite a hitter. Frank Herald was his name. On June 21 in New York, he tangled with Mike Conley, another man with a powerful punch. On this day, Herald was quicker and got in his blow. He knocked Conley out in a single round. Herald was not so fortunate on September 18 when he was stopped by John L. Sullivan.

Frank Herald-Mike Conley
June 21 1886

In August of 1886, Harry Laing claimed the New Zealand heavyweight title with a win over Mick Dillon. Over in Australia, Peter Jackson was back in the picture. On September 25, he defeated Tom Lees in Sydney in thirty grueling rounds to win the heavyweight championship of Australia. Big and tall, he was a serious threat to any man who entered the ring with him.

On December 2, 1886, McHenry Johnson battled Billy Wilson for ten rounds in St. Paul, Minnesota for the colored championship.

Jem Smith and John Knifton were set to fight for the English championship, also in December of 1886, but authorities intervened and prevented the bout.

Peter Jackson

If John L. Sullivan could do anything with as much zeal as fighting, it was drinking and carousing. His managers, trainers and friends had worried about his behavior ever since he had entered the game of fisticuffs.

The first real indication that his lifestyle was affecting his fighting came on January 18, 1887 in Minneapolis when he went against Patsy Cardiff. Sullivan injured his left arm that once was "made of iron." He could not finish off Cardiff. The fight was called a draw after six rounds.

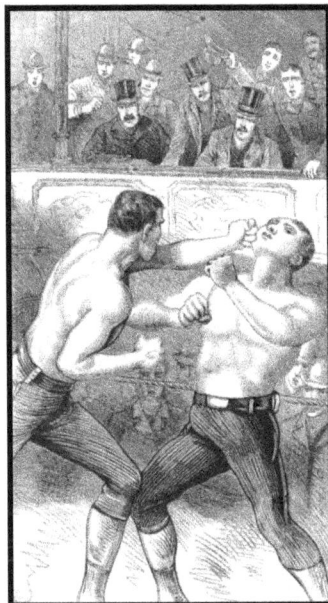

Yes, John L. should have won. But, in truth, Cardiff was a good man. He would prove to be a menace to a number of other men as well as the champion. Powerful Pat Killen would find this out later in the year.

BROKE HIS WRIST.

Slugger Sullivan Meets With a Bad Accident.

THE CONTEST WITH CARDIFF.

The Latter Has the Best of the Fight, Badly Punishing the Champion of Brutes.

Slugger Sullivan's Accident.

The Salt Lake (UT) Daily Herald
January 19 1887

A surprise occurred on March 7 when the quick and tricky Dominick McCaffrey, who had lasted seven rounds with "The Great John L. Sullivan," met Patsy Farrell. McCaffrey floored Farrell in round one but, as slick as he was, he got caught by the quick-handed Farrell and downed twice in round two. Police intervened.

Patsy Farrell-Dominick McCaffrey
March 7 1887

Richard K. Fox, of the Police Gazette, was a great antagonist of John L. Sullivan, disliking him from the first time they met. Fox had backed Paddy Ryan against Sullivan in Mississippi.

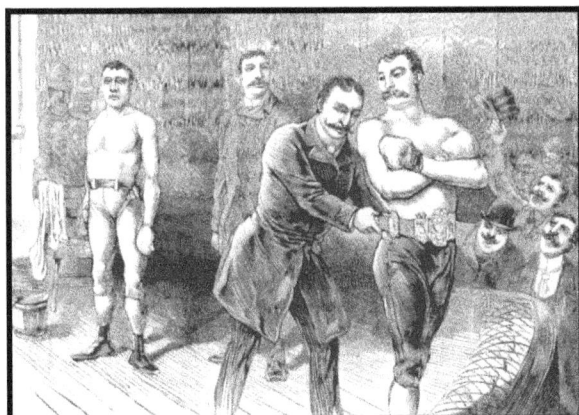

Richard K. Fox

Jake Kilrain receiving the
Fox Heavyweight Championship Belt

In May of 1887, Fox declared Jake Kilrain champion and presented him with a beautiful belt.

By August 5, Pat Killen had added more victims to his list of knockouts. Patsy Cardiff was then fed to him in Minneapolis. In another surprise, Killen - like Sullivan - could not finish this man. Cardiff lasted ten rounds and proved that a human could absorb Killen's blows. Yet, this result did not stop Killen from challenging John L. and calling him names. Sullivan responded by calling Killen a coward and a cur.

Jake Kilrain

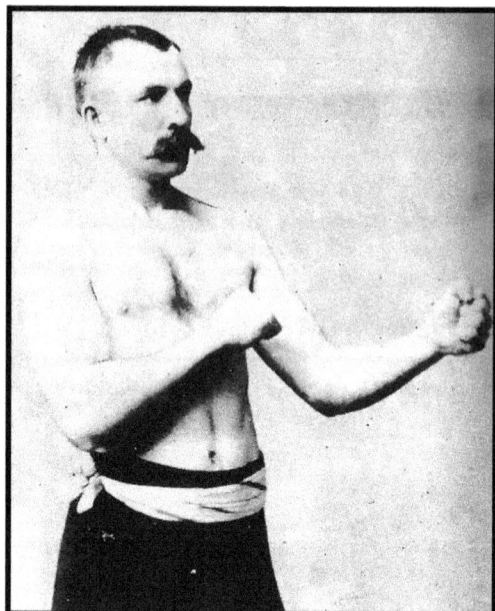

Patsy Cardiff

Over the last few years, Fox had backed Jake Kilrain and promoted him as the actual heavyweight champion. He arranged a championship contest between Kilrain and Jem Smith, the champion of England, for the Police Gazette Diamond Belt and big money. It took place on December 19 on the island of St. Pierre in the river Seine, near Rouen, France.

Kilrain was better than Smith, scoring first blood, first knockdown and fall. He clearly would have won had darkness not set in after 106 rounds. The fight lasted two hours and 31 minutes. Jake was still promoted as champion by Fox in his newspaper resources. The publicity he received needled Sullivan.

Jake Kilrain-Jem Smith
December 19 1887

John L. Sullivan-Charlie Mitchell
March 10 1888

On March 10, 1888, John L. and Charlie Mitchell got into the ring once more. This time it was near Chantilly, France and fought under London Prize Ring Rules. Some said it was for the championship of the world. A cold sleet and rain fell off and on during the fight that lasted three hours and eleven minutes. The turf was muddy and slippery and made to order for Mitchell's skills. Sullivan scored all the knockdowns but slick Charlie got in many sharp blows and a little spiking besides. Whenever Sullivan got him cornered, Mitchell went down to avoid punishment. The decision was a draw after thirty-nine rounds.

In early 1888, the magnificent Peter Jackson journeyed from Australia to America to get a fight with Sullivan but John L. refused. Jackson realized he would have to wait. So, he set about to make a reputation in America, hoping to change the champion's mind.

When Jackson left Australia, Frank "Paddy" Slavin became the top heavyweight remaining on the island continent. He was a fast-moving, hard-hitting, two-handed fighter with a vicious attitude toward other men. He came to fight.

Harry Laing reigned supreme in New Zealand from 1886 to 1888 with Dick Matthews making a couple of claims during that time. Slavin won the heavyweight crown from Laing on April 25, 1888. Then, on December 8, 1888, he defeated "Mick" Dooley and claimed the Australian heavyweight championship.

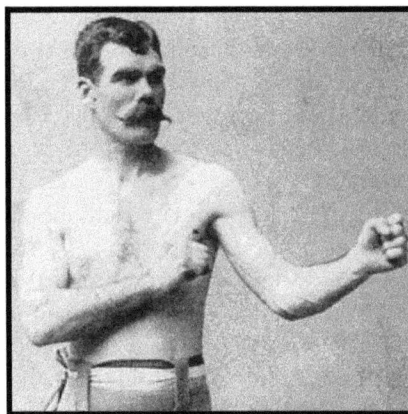

Frank "Paddy" Slavin

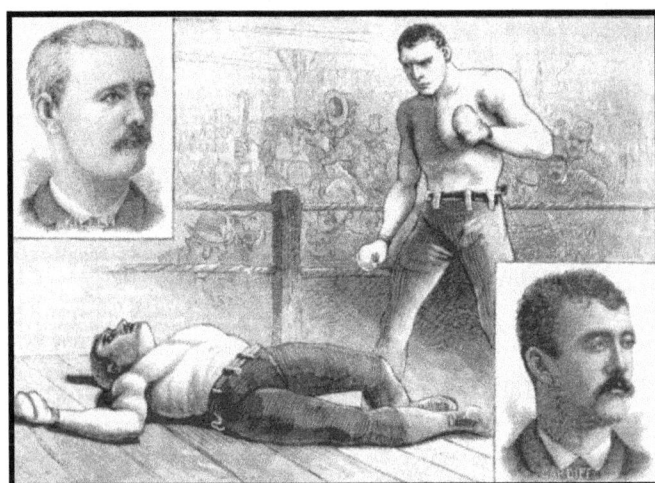

**Pat Killen-Patsy Cardiff
June 26 1888**

Pat Killen racked up several victories after his disappointing showing against Patsy Cardiff. Then, on June 26, 1888 in Minneapolis, he got into the ring with Patsy again. This time his bombs exploded and Pat flattened his man in four rounds.

**George Godfrey challenging
John L. Sullivan in 1888**

GODFREY GIVES UP.

Jackson Batters Him for Nineteen Rounds.

Game and Exciting Fight to the Close.

The Bostonian Is Badly Injured by the Australian's Heavy Blows.

**The San Francisco (CA) Chronicle
August 25 1888**

George Godfrey had a controversial bout versus Mr. McHenry Johnson in Boulder County, Colorado in January 1888. Reports say that he knocked Johnson out but was declared the loser due to a foul. Nevertheless, his claim for the colored championship was strengthened. Many still considered him to be the champion.

George was not a big heavyweight but he was quick and full of fight. He eagerly challenged John L. to a bout but it never took place. On August 24, 1888, Peter Jackson defeated the smaller Godfrey in San Francisco. Many then recognized Jackson as the colored champion. On December of the same year, Peter again proved his merit by knocking out big Joe McAuliffe in twenty-four rounds, also in San Francisco.

On April 24, 1889, with Frank "Paddy" Slavin elsewhere, Harry Laing fought a draw with "Australian" Billy Smith in New Zealand for the top prize in that country. Two days later in San Francisco, Peter Jackson stopped the nemesis of big-name fighters, Patsy Cardiff, in ten rounds. Then Jackson toured America, taking on all comers and hoping all the while to meet Sullivan. Of note was a three-round stoppage of George Peters in Detroit. Peters was known as the champion of Michigan at the time.

Richard K. Fox continued to be an irritant to the mighty John L. He promoted Jake Kilrain as champion of America and the world. The annoying challenges made by Kilrain, along with the non-ending disparaging remarks made by Fox in his publications, prompted John L. to meet Kilrain in the ring and settle matters once and for all.

Under London Prize Ring Rules, they fought on July 8 near Richburg, Mississippi, within 100 miles of New Orleans. Kilrain fought well for the first six rounds. But after that, John L. battered him, threw him about and roughed him up until Mike Donovan, Jake's second, threw in the sponge after 75 rounds.

John L. Sullivan-Jake Kilrain
July 8 1889

Joe Choynski

During the early part of 1889, an impressive young fighter in California, Jim Corbett, engaged another good young pugilist, "Chrysanthemum Joe" Choynski, three times. All encounters were very close but Corbett was better.

Joe was clever, moved well, had a natural feel for boxing and hit exceptionally hard for his weight, which was usually between 160-170 pounds. He often tangled with larger men and won. He was a pound-for-pound phenom.

Yes, Choynski was a very good fighter but Corbett - well, he was exceptional. Jim was brainy, jack-rabbit quick, could stand directly before an opponent yet avoid blows and alter fight plans in a split second to bring about victory. Hitting him with a solid blow was almost impossible, especially about the head. His star was rising.

Following Sullivan's struggle with Kilrain, Pat Killen decided to fight Joe McAuliffe, polish him off and then go after the big mouth champion. However, sometimes the best laid plans go awry.

Jim Corbett

Joe McAuliffe

On September 11 in San Francisco, McAuliffe surprised the world when he knocked out Killen in seven rounds. Reportedly, Pat injured his right shoulder in round two and fought the rest of the bout using only his left arm. He would never again be a threat to Sullivan.

Jem Smith won yet another heavyweight competition in England on September 30. This time he defeated Jack Wannop in ten rounds and once more claimed the English heavyweight championship.

In the fall of 1889, agile Peter Jackson went to England and toured, taking on all comers. He easily defeated two popular men at this time – tough Jem Smith in London on November 11 and a sharp hitting young Irishman named Peter Maher in Dublin on December 24.

Hitting? Talk about hitting! This Mr. Maher was a terrific hitter and would be heard from in the future.

Frank "Paddy" Slavin decided to show off his skills abroad and in August of 1889 traveled from Australia to England. He knocked out a couple of men in London and on December 23 fought Jem Smith near Bruges, Belgium for the heavyweight championship of England. Slavin was much better and would have won but the crowd broke into the ring. The fight was called a draw after fourteen rounds and Slavin was declared heavyweight champion.

Peter Maher

Peter Jackson was back in America in January of 1890, touring and still trying for a title shot with Sullivan. It did no good. Sullivan boxed only exhibitions following his win over Kilrain. Ring rust piled up on "The Great John L."

In a battle of puffed-up egos, Charlie Mitchell met Jem Mace on February 7, 1890 in Glasgow, Scotland. It was scheduled as an exhibition and not for the championship of England. Reportedly, Mace had been abusive in his language towards Mitchell. The younger Mitchell talked the judges into calling him the winner (see Gordon 2007 pp 388 496).

**Frank "Paddy" Slavin-Jem Smith
December 23 1889**

The young Californian Jim Corbett added another prestigious name to his list of fistic conquests on February 18. He met Jake Kilrain in New Orleans and completely outclassed the former title contender. During March in New York, he sparred with Mike Donovan, former middleweight champion, and on April 14 in Brooklyn, he easily dominated Dominick McCaffrey in a contest. He was gaining a name for himself.

In March 1890, "Alf" Idhe defeated Herb Goddard and Morry Abrahams to win a heavyweight competition and laid a claim to the Australian heavyweight title. In June of 1890, Herb's brother, Joe, defeated "Mick" Dooley and established the more generally recognized claim to the heavyweight championship of Australia. Owen Sullivan launched his own claim to this title in August of 1890 when he defeated Jim Hall.

CORBETT WHIPS KILRAIN.

The Baltimore Slugger Defeated in a Six-round Mill at New Orleans.

NEW ORLEANS, La., Feb. 18.—The fight here last night between J. J. Corbett, of California, and Jake Kilrain, who was defeated by Sullivan, is the sensation of the hour. It was the best contest ever fought in this city, and was not less exciting than the big mill between Jake and the world's champion last July.

The battle took place at the Southern Athletic club, a tony organization of New Orleans, and was stated to be for six rounds for scientific points. Corbett has licked several prominent men out in California, besting Joe McAuliffe for scientific points, and is a handsome young fellow 24 years old, and somewhat taller than Kilrain. He weighed last night 183 pounds, while Kilrain tipped the beam at 201.

The fight was a savage set-to from beginning to end, and Corbett was the only one in it in the six rounds that were fought. He won the fight, proved himself a cool, magnificent, and wonderfully scientific fighter, and blackened both eyes of Kilrain.

The Logansport (IN) Journal
February 19 1890

Joe Goddard

Joe Goddard was rough and tough, a rushing type of fighter who took punches in order to dish them out. He excelled at infighting and if he could get an opponent onto the ropes, he was a very difficult man to deal with.

While in England, Frank "Paddy" Slavin had taken the measure of the English and was ready for the Americans. On September 27 at the London Ormonde Club using gloves, he won the Police Gazette heavyweight championship when he made Joe McAuliffe retire in two rounds. He wanted more. Bring on the Americans!

Goddard fought a draw with Peter Jackson in October of 1890 and beat "Mick" Dooley twelve days later. In February 1891, he stopped Joe Choynski in four rounds, a feat he repeated five months later. Sandwiched in between the Choynski fights was a win over Tom Lees. All were Aussie title bouts.

March 13, 1891 saw Jake Kilrain and George Godfrey meet in a lengthy confrontation that lasted 44 rounds. Kilrain was slow and heavy of foot. He hit Godfrey often but lacked the power to put him out. Godfrey fought back and was game but tired as the bout wore on. He lost the fight more from exhaustion than from Kilrain's blows.

In April of 1891, Slavin came to America and challenged John L. to fight for the heavyweight championship. The match never happened. Instead, Slavin boxed some contests in New York with Charlie Mitchell and Jim Daly.

On May 21, Peter Jackson stepped into the ring in San Francisco with the young comer Jim Corbett. These two men represented the latest in boxing techniques - jabs, footwork, movement, hit-and-run tactics and the one-two punch combination.

Jackson was the more powerful of the two but was at a disadvantage because he did not know the caliber of fighter that Corbett was. On the other hand, Jim knew all about Peter Jackson. Peter, at the time of this bout, was recovering from a sprained ankle plus he had a cold. The bout lasted sixty-one rounds and resulted in a "no contest" – however, some sources report a draw. This was a moral victory for Corbett and a setback for Jackson in his attempt to get Sullivan into the ring.

Jim Corbett-Peter Jackson
May 21 1891

The talented Australian Frank "Paddy" Slavin never stopped trying to "get it on" with John L. Sullivan - to no avail. But he did manage to get Jake Kilrain into the ring.

Frank "Paddy" Slavin-Jake Kilrain
June 16 1891

SLAVIN STOPPED HIM.

The Australian Knocked Mr. Kilrain Out in the Ninth.

After the Second Round the Baltimorean Had No Chance.

Knocked Down Many Times, the Beaten Man Pluckily Fights On.

The St. Paul (MN) Daily Globe
June 17 1891

On June 16, Slavin met Kilrain in Hoboken. "Paddy" stopped him in nine rounds. There was confusion due to an electric time clock that was used. Accordingly, referee Jere Dunn would not render a decision. Actually, Slavin handled Kilrain quite easily. Some historians consider this a defense of Slavin's Police Gazette heavyweight championship. Again, Slavin challenged Sullivan. Again, there was no match. Reportedly, Sullivan had retired.

The former champion of England Jem Smith was outmaneuvered and outhit by Ted Pritchard on July 27, 1891 in London. Smith knocked Pritchard down twice in round one but ran out of gas and was stopped in round three. Pritchard laid claim to the English heavyweight title but four years later, on May 10, 1895, was knocked out by Smith who then lost to Dan Creedon in 1896.

In September 1891, the Australian Joe Goddard fought a draw with Tom Lees and afterwards beat Jack Ashton and Ned Ryan in impressive style.

Pritchard Licks Smith in Three Rounds
London, July 27. – The fight between Jem Smith and Pritchard for $10,000 took place this evening and Pritchard beat Smith in three rounds. Smith showed a strong disinclination to take punishment and was easily defeated by Pritchard. The fight lasted only ten minutes.

The Salt Lake (UT) Daily Herald
July 28 1891

Bob Fitzsimmons-Peter Maher
March 2 1892

Peter Maher came to America from Ireland in October of 1891. Shortly afterwards, he racked up his first victory in this country with a win over Jack Davis. Maher, possibly the deadliest knockout hitter of the pre-1900 years, proceeded to win nine contests, seven by knockout.

On March 2, 1892 in New Orleans, Peter confronted the outstanding middleweight fighter Bob Fitzsimmons. In a battle of sharp blows, Fitzsimmons handed Maher his second career loss when the contest was stopped in the twelfth round.

In 1892, Frank "Paddy" Slavin and Peter Jackson, two men who had bad blood between them ever since their days in Australia, went to England to fight for the English heavyweight championship that Slavin claimed. On May 30, they met at the National Sporting Club in London.

Slavin, who had never lost an official fight, fought aggressively but never came close to finishing Jackson. Peter landed accurate and telling blows throughout and his punches began to take their toll early on. After a few rounds, Slavin weakened. Jackson stopped Frank in the tenth round to win the English title. Historians say several titles were claimed as a result of this bout.

Peter Jackson-Frank "Paddy" Slavin
May 30 1892

Joe Goddard-Joe McAuliffe
June 30 1892

Joe Goddard, the tough Australian, tangled with big Joe McAuliffe on June 30 in San Francisco. The rugged man from down under knocked out the American in fifteen rounds. One more antagonist's name had been added to the list of men chasing after the heavyweight crown of John L. Sullivan.

Sullivan continued to be challenged by Jackson, Slavin, Mitchell and Corbett. He was tired of hearing from them. He was also tired of being told he was rusty and not the fighter he once was. He decided to fight again and squelch the talk.

John L. discounted Jackson because he was black. He discounted Slavin because Jackson had just beaten him. He discounted Mitchell because he felt he had already bested the Englishman twice. That left Corbett. Besides, he wanted to teach the "fancy dan" upstart from California a lesson.

CORBETT WINS

Sullivan Knocked Clean Out In Twenty-first Round.

THE BOSTONIAN SHOWS SIGNS OF SEVERE PUNISHMENT.

The Californian Finishes Without Any Signs of the Fight.

The Sun (Lowell, MA), September 8 1892
All rights reserved. Reproduced with the permission of MediaNews Group Inc.

Jim Corbett-John L. Sullivan
September 7 1892

On September 7 in New Orleans, Sullivan met Corbett for the heavyweight championship. It was no contest. Corbett was too quick, too scientific and too well-conditioned. Sullivan, fat and slow, could not touch him. Corbett knocked out Sullivan in 21 rounds. No sooner had Corbett won the crown than he was challenged by the men who had been after Sullivan. Jim ignored the verbiage and went on tour, acting in plays and sparring to keep in shape. Time passed.

Clever Steve O'Donnell fought a draw with Ned Ryan on February 14, 1893 and claimed the Australian crown. He left the country soon afterwards. In early January 1894, Harry Laing defeated Joe Goddard to win the heavyweight championship of Australia. However, Laing died in April of 1894 and "Mick" Dooley beat James "Tut" Ryan in June to claim the "big island" title.

Jim Corbett-Charlie Mitchell
January 25 1894

Sixteen months after winning the heavyweight crown, Jim Corbett decided to meet Charlie Mitchell in a title defense. This fight was held on January 25, 1894 in Jacksonville, Florida. Corbett won easily in three rounds.

Corbett then continued his touring, sparring and acting. Not really wanting to fight any more, he had some minor bouts during the next three years. Included in his appearances was a sparring session with John L. Sullivan. He also had a four-round contest with Tom Sharkey in San Francisco. Sharkey was to become a great fighter and a near-champion.

Jim had picked up a talented new challenger in Bob Fitzsimmons, the current middleweight champion. Fitzsimmons had come over from Australia and cleaned up the men of his weight class in America. Way back on January 14, 1891, he had defeated the reigning middleweight champion Jack Dempsey, "The Nonpareil," in New Orleans.

Fitzsimmons was a marvelous fighter. He was cunning and crafty. He was a two-handed fighter who hit hard with both hands. He hit from all angles. When hurt, he recuperated from unbelievable circumstances. He wanted Corbett.

Over the next three years, Corbett and Fitzsimmons became extremely antagonistic towards one another. They agreed to fight near Dallas, Texas in October of 1895 but the fight was cancelled by authorities. Corbett still lacked interest in getting into the ring for a serious battle.

Gentleman Jack - Cast of Players
1894

On November 11, 1895, Peter Maher knocked out slick Steve O'Donnell in one round in Maspeth, New York. In attendance was champion Jim Corbett. So impressive was Maher's performance that Corbett jumped into the ring, announced his retirement and awarded Maher the heavyweight championship.

Corbett later admitted he acted too quickly under the emotions of the moment. Of course, his gift of the title was withdrawn.

On November 26, Jem Smith won over Dick Burge on a disqualification to assert his claim to the English championship.

Steve O'Donnell

FITZ WINS WITH ONE MIGHTY BLOW.

Maher Falls, and as He Lies Inert the Fateful 10 Seconds Pass.

The Boston (MA) Daily Globe
February 22 1896

In Coahuila, Mexico, near Langtry, Texas on February 21, 1896, Bob Fitzsimmons met Peter Maher again. The Irishman Maher had scored numerous victories since his loss to Bob in their first fight, back in 1892. He was eager to avenge that setback. But it was not to be. Fitzsimmons knocked Peter out in the first round.

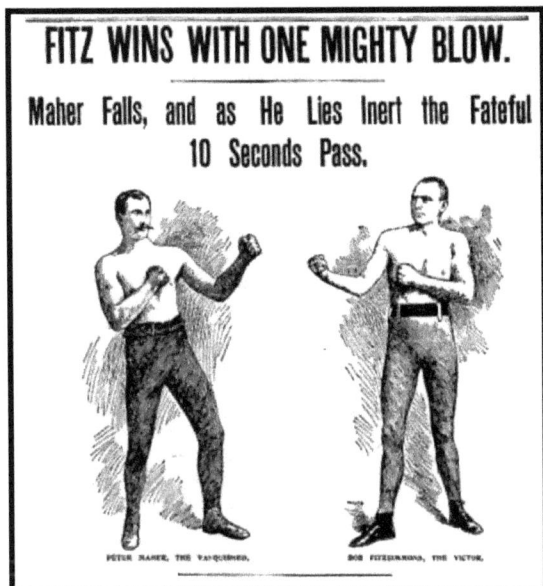

Many argued that since Corbett had given the title to Maher and Fitz defeated Maher, then Fitz was the heavyweight champion.

On June 18, 1896 in New York, two of the very best fighters of the pre-1900 years met. Peter Maher, the devastating hitter, tangled with Frank "Paddy" Slavin, once an excellent boxer-puncher. Everyone expected a war of the first degree. But what they did not realize was that Slavin's best days were behind him. The brooding over his 1892 loss to Peter Jackson, drinking, inadequate training and poor conditioning had reduced him to an ordinary man. Maher controlled the battle from start to finish and the contest was his in the fourth round when he stopped Slavin.

Joe Goddard defeated "Denver" Ed Smith in South Africa on November 7 and not only claimed the South African title but claimed the world championship as well. Joe just wouldn't quit trying.

MAHER BEATS SLAVIN.

The Irish Fighter Whips the Australian at Madison Square Garden in Four Rounds.

A SMALL CROWD SEES GOOD BATTLES

Dublin's Champion Was Too Clever for the Antipodean, and Won with Comparative Ease.

Peter Maher is a great boxer. He was the star at Madison Square Garden last night. There was but a small crowd present. If the sport-loving residents of Greater New York had realized what an excellent series of exhibitions had been arranged for them, it is very probable that the crowd would have been much larger.

Maher was pitted against Slavin, the Australian. Great things were said about Slavin. He came 3,000 miles to box the Irishman. It was an unequal match. From start to finish the Irish champion had the better of it. As a matter of fact, it looked for two rounds as if he was attempting to give the Australian a boxing lesson.

The New York (NY) World
June 19 1896

31

SHARKEY KNOCKED OUT,

BUT HE RECEIVED THE DECISION
ON AN ALLEGED FOUL.

Fitzsimmons Had All the Better of the
Big Fight at San Francisco and Fin-
ished His Man in the Eighth Round.
"Robbery." Said Fitz.

San Francisco, Cal., December 3—The feeling that exists to-day as a result of Referee
Earp's decision is great. Sharkey is in the
position of a man who has been knocked out
but ostensibly has a championship title. Fitzsimmons is credited with the victory by everybody, but the stigma of the decision remains
He says: "I have been robbed. I have always fought fairly and I did not foul Sharkey
If he was hurt it was done without my knowledge and was an unavoidable accident."

The Brooklyn (NY) Daily Eagle
December 3 1896
(Brooklyn Public Library-Brooklyn Collection)

Bob Fitzsimmons was in San Francisco on December 2 and involved in a peculiar contest. His opponent was the young, bull-like, power-hitter Tom Sharkey. Both men were chasing after the heavyweight title.

In a battle that saw terrific blows exchanged, Fitzsimmons was having the better of it. During a trade of punches in round eight, Sharkey went down. Referee Wyatt Earp ruled that Fitzsimmons had struck a low blow and awarded the bout to Sharkey on a foul. Despite losing the match, Fitzsimmons came away with the respect of observers for his outstanding fighting skills.

Historians still question this controversial call and debate whether Earp was in on a fix to have Sharkey win.

Some contended that Fitz had become champion by beating Maher and Sharkey was now the champion by winning over Fitz.

In February of 1897, Jem Smith had a ring session with George Chrisp, who avoided the bigger man until Smith lost his temper and fouled. Mr. Chrisp claimed the English heavyweight title as a result.

Bob Armstrong

Bob Armstrong was a tall black fighter who moved well and owned a good jab. He had beaten Frank "Paddy" Slavin two times. On December 21, 1896 in New York, Bob beat Charley Strong to claim the colored heavyweight title. On March 6, 1897, he stopped Joe Butler in six rounds and on April 23 made Sam Pruitt retire during the first round - in colored title defenses. In September, he stopped Jack Douglass in two rounds.

Wyatt Earp

On March 17, 1897, Jim Corbett and Bob Fitzsimmons finally fought in Carson City, Nevada for the heavyweight title. Corbett dazzled Fitzsimmons in the early rounds. Bob was going for the champion's head but could not find it. In round six, Corbett floored Fitzsimmons and had it not been for a slow count by referee George Siler, the fight would have ended then and there.

Fitzsimmons recovered and changed his attack from the head to the body - feints to the head and shots to the body. Gradually, Corbett slowed. In round thirteen, some very hard blows found the midsection of Corbett and in round fourteen, Fitzsimmons drove home the devastating "solar plexus punch" that took Corbett's wind and floored him for the count. Fitzsimmons was now the king of the heavyweight fighters.

True to the form of Sullivan and Corbett, after Fitzsimmons won the title, he turned to activities other than fighting. He toured, acted and boxed exhibitions.

Bob Fitzsimmons-Jim Corbett
March 17 1897

Bob Armstrong Knocked out.

Chicago. Jan. 29.—Bob Armstrong a colored heavy weight, who has been heralded by Parson Davies as a world beater, was completely smothered and knocked out in the second round to-night by Frank Childs another colored pugilist of this city. The affair was a special bout in the regular bi-weekly boxing contests in the gymnasium of the Chicago Athletic club. Both of the men were over the heavy weight limit. Armstrong was so badly punished that he was unable to leave the ring for several minutes after the fight was over.

The Davenport (IA) Sunday Leader
January 30 1898

Frank Childs, a talented black fighter, had surfaced on the West Coast during the early 1890s. He was short and weighed much less than many of the big boys but he could hit. He had beaten the likes of Bob Armstrong, John "Klondike" Haines, George LaBlanche and "Australian" Billy Smith and caught the attention of boxing people. January 29, 1898 saw Childs defeat Bob Armstrong again, this time in Chicago, to claim the colored heavyweight championship. During February, he beat George Grant and John "Klondike" Haines in possible colored title bouts.

On March 22, 1898 in San Francisco, Peter Jackson met Jim Jeffries, a promising young fighter from California, and was stopped in three rounds. Jackson was past his peak at this point in his career and finished as a top-notch fighter. He was also suffering from a weak, physical condition. In just a little over three years, he would be dead.

Tom Sharkey, the rough, aggressive fighter who had won over Bob Fitzsimmons on the foul call by Wyatt Earp in 1896, continued to make a name for himself. Tom was a sturdy, squat battler with dynamite in each fist. He had engaged in 34 fights, scored 24 knockouts and was claiming the heavyweight crown following the Fitzsimmons bout. He was unbeaten in subsequent bouts with Peter Maher, Joe Goddard and Joe Choynski that some called title bouts.

Jim Jeffries

33

The two promising young heavyweights, Jeffries and Sharkey, tangled on May 6, 1898 in San Francisco. In a rough and bruising twenty-round battle, Sharkey met defeat at the hands of Jeffries who then had a claim for the title.

Charles "Kid" McCoy got into the title act when he beat Gus Ruhlin in twenty rounds on May 20. The "Kid" then made his claim for the crown.

Frank Childs fought a draw with Charley Strong in June in Chicago. In doing so, he kept his colored title claim alive.

Tom Sharkey

CROWD CHEERED JEFFRIES.

Wild Enthusiasm Prevailed When the Referee Declared Him Winner.

SHARKEY FOUGHT STUBBORNLY.

The Eagerly Anticipated Meeting of the Two Heavyweights Lasted Twenty Rounds and Both Men Were on Their Feet When the Gong Sounded—Falling Tiers of Seats Nearly Created a Panic. No Serious Injuries.

The Brooklyn (NY) Daily Eagle, May 7 1898 (Brooklyn Public Library-Brooklyn Collection)

During this time, there was Hank Griffin, a well-known black who was quite capable with his fists. He is most famous for his sparring sessions with cagey Bob Fitzsimmons and his bout with Jim Jeffries in the mid-1890s.

Griffin owned a win over Harris Martin ("The Black Pearl") in 1892 and had fought a twenty-round draw with Frank Childs in 1893. In 1900, he would earn a win over Jack Munroe and would go on to defeat the famous Jack Johnson in 1901.

Hank Griffin

Another talented black fighter about this time was George Byers, who defeated Frank Childs on September 14, 1898 in New York to capture the colored heavyweight championship. But Byers did not actively campaign as the black champion. Many historians contend he disclaimed the title so Childs sought to claim it again. Frank defeated feisty Charley Strong on November 8, 1898 in Chicago and proclaimed himself to be the colored heavyweight champion.

On November 22, 1898, Tom Sharkey won on a disqualification against Jim Corbett. Then, on January 10, 1899, he ended "Kid" McCoy's aspirations for the heavyweight title. "Mick" Dooley had held the Australian heavyweight championship since 1894 although Peter Felix (1897) and James "Tut" Ryan (1898) had made claims. In February 1899, "Mick" lost his crown to Bill Doherty.

George Byers

Frank Childs was busy in early 1899 and beat Joe Butler. He then defeated Bob Armstrong in a colored title bout. However, trouble was brewing. In May, John "Klondike" Haines beat Jack Johnson, George Grant and "Scaldy" Bill Quinn in Chicago bouts that launched his claim for the colored heavyweight crown.

Nicholas "Mick" Dooley

Bob Fitzsimmons was a fighter at heart and after a while became hungry for another championship bout. He and his manager looked around and settled upon the young Jim Jeffries. The new contender had a good record and had gained public attention. He was also rather inexperienced. He was viewed as someone Fitzsimmons could take apart. It was a miscalculation because Jeffries was extremely tough, the quintessential "Iron Man."

On June 9, 1899 at Coney Island, Fitzsimmons defended the title. During most of the action-packed fight, Fitzsimmons smashed away at Jeff with hard blows. The durable Jeffries took the punishment, crouched and moved in for more. Jeffries floored the champion in round two. In the eleventh round, Jeffries finally caught up to Fitzsimmons and knocked him out to win the championship in an upset.

Bob Fitzsimmons-Jim Jeffries Ticket
June 9 1899

George Byers renewed his claim for the colored championship on July 24 with a ninth-round stoppage of Charley Strong.

The Racine (WI) Daily Journal
June 10 1899

In August of 1899, Frank Childs defeated John "Klondike" Haines and was seen by most to be the colored champion. Frank followed up this win with another victory over Haines in October of 1899 to assert his superiority.

On October 28 in Chicago, Bob Fitzsimmons was back in action. He knocked out Geoff Thorne in a little over a minute.

On November 3 at Coney Island, five months after winning the championship from Fitzsimmons, Jim Jeffries made his first defense of the title. He chose Tom Sharkey, a man he felt was deserving of a chance because of the tough fight between the two in 1898.

Sharkey came to fight. However, in Jeffries, he faced one of the most rugged men who ever entered the ring. The two men pounded each other for twenty-five rounds in a head-on confrontation. Jeffries knocked Sharkey down, broke a couple of his ribs and won by decision. Many fans at ringside thought Sharkey won the fight. After taking the brutal pounding by Jeffries' big fists, Sharkey was never again the great fighter he once was.

Jim Jeffries-Tom Sharkey
November 3 1899

In Australia, Bill Doherty followed up his February 1899 victory over "Mick" Dooley for the Australian heavyweight crown with three title defense wins. He then lost the title to Peter Felix in December of that year.

February 9, 1900 witnessed Dick Burge knock out the bigger Jack Scales in one round and claim the English championship. However, the fight did not appear to be on the level and Scales continued a claim for the title. Soon afterwards on March 16, Frank Childs fought a draw with George Byers in Chicago and remained the more popular choice as colored heavyweight champion.

The effort by Fitzsimmons to regain the title intensified in 1900 when he stopped Jim Daly in one round in Philadelphia on March 27. Then, on April 30 he disposed of big Ed Dunkhorst in two rounds in Brooklyn.

Five months after the first defense of his title, Jeffries took on Jack Finnegan in Detroit on April 6, 1900. It took fifty-five seconds and three knockdowns for Jim to make Finnegan quit.

On May 11 at Coney Island, Jeffries came within a breath of losing his title to the man who conquered John L. Sullivan. Former champion Jim Corbett boxed, jabbed, slipped punches and pounded Jeffries for twenty-two rounds. He was well ahead in the contest but in round twenty-three, he got careless and Jeffries caught him with a hook. Corbett went down and out. Years later, Corbett would laugh and say he was pitching a shutout when it happened. Actually, it was a closer fight than that.

Bill Doherty won the Australian heavyweight crown back from Peter Felix in July of 1900 and once again ruled supreme on the south side of the equator. He had two more successful title defenses before the end of the year and retained his crown.

"Ruby Robert" Fitzsimmons was determined to reach the top of the mountain once again and took on two good men within two weeks of each other during August of 1900. On August 10, he flattened Gus Ruhlin in six rounds in New York and on August 24 in Brooklyn, he easily handled tough Tom Sharkey, the brawler. Fitzsimmons put his man out in two rounds.

Frank Childs scored a knockout win over Joe Butler in a possible colored title defense in Chicago on December 15.

George Chrisp finished up the title fights for the year on December 17 with a fourteen-round knockout of Harry Smith to claim the English belt.

Bob Fitzsimmons-Gus Ruhlin
August 10 1900

Up to this point in time, the heavyweight champions of a number of countries have been discussed. Now, the championship of the world was rather well-established. Jim Jeffries was the man generally considered to be the heavyweight top dog. Since the black fighters were not allowed to fight for the championship, they maintained their own championship. In the following pages, discussion will follow the world championship lineage and the colored champions with occasional mention of bouts between top contenders. Later, the numerous modern "alphabet" titles appear on the scene.

Top Heavyweight Boxers of 1881-1900
1. Jim Jeffries
2. Jim Corbett
3. John L. Sullivan
4. Peter Jackson
5. Bob Fitzsimmons

Top Heavyweight Bouts of 1881-1900
1. Jim Jeffries-Tom Sharkey #2, November 3 1899, Coney Island, New York
2. John L. Sullivan-Jake Kilrain, July 8 1889, Richburg, Mississippi
3. Jim Corbett-John L. Sullivan, September 7 1892, New Orleans, Louisiana
4. Peter Jackson-Frank "Paddy" Slavin, May 30 1892, London, England
5. Jim Corbett-Peter Jackson, May 21 1891, San Francisco, California

John L. Sullivan-Jake Kilrain
July 8 1889

Bob Fitzsimmons-Jim Corbett
March 17 1897

Chapter Two

The Years 1901-1920

On March 16, 1901 in Hot Springs, Arkansas, Frank Childs knocked out George Byers in seventeen rounds to retain his colored heavyweight championship.

Jim Jeffries had engaged in three world title defenses since winning the crown in 1899 so he took some time off. Meanwhile, he once again heard from Gus Ruhlin, the fighter with whom he had fought a twenty-round draw early in his career.

Ruhlin always felt he was better than Jim and was sounding off. Annoyed, Jeffries decided he wanted him next. The champion had a couple of warm up fights in September of 1901, besting Hank Griffin and knocking out Joe Kennedy.

Jim Jeffries

On November 15 in San Francisco, Jeffries defended his crown against the erratic Ruhlin. Gus encountered a far different man this time. Jeffries' skills were better than before. He defended well, he punched with hard blows and he could box now. No matter how Ruhlin hit at Jeffries, he could not strike him effectively.

Jim Jeffries-Gus Ruhlin
November 15 1901

Jeffries stalked Ruhlin and near the end of round five, Jim drove his powerful left hook into Ruhlin's ribs. Down went Gus. He got up but could not fight. In pain, he back-peddled for the rest of the round. At the start of round six, Ruhlin could not come out and Jeffries retained his title. Afterwards, Gus called the punch an accidental low blow and extolled Jeffries' fearful prowess.

JEFFRIES IS THE VICTOR

Ruhlin Gives Up in the Fifth Round and Retires.

The Dubuque (IA) Telegraph Herald
November 16 1901

Jim Jeffries-Bob Fitzsimmons
July 25 1902

Frank Childs defeated Walter Johnson in a possible colored title bout in January of 1902. A month later, "Denver" Ed Martin defeated Childs to win some recognition as the colored heavyweight champion.

About eight months after defeating Ruhlin, Jeffries defended against the former champion Bob Fitzsimmons. This fight was held July 25, 1902 in San Francisco. Fitz was eager for this match against the man who dethroned him. He used every trick he knew.

Fitz pounded Jeffries unmercifully. Each punch seemed to change the shape of Jeffries' face. The rugged champion took it and bore in. At last, in round eight, Jeffries knocked out the former champ.

Some writers claimed that Fitzsimmons "loaded up" the wraps on his hands with plaster of paris for this bout but Jeffries inspected Fitz's hands in the ring before the battle began and did not object.

During the year, "Denver" Ed Martin further enhanced his image in four title defenses. He had a win against Bob Armstrong and two wins against Frank Craig. In another bout with Armstrong, there was no decision.

JEFFRIES DOES UP BOB FITZSIMMONS.

A Thorough Knockout Given in the Eighth Round, Though Jeffries Was Badly Punished Too.

The Xenia (OH) Daily Gazette
July 26 1902

"DENVER ED" MARTIN BEAT ARMSTRONG IN LONDON.

Outboxed Him and Won Easily on Points in a 15-Round Bout.

LONDON, July 25. The contest between "Bob" Armstrong and "Denver Ed" Martin, the American pugilists, for the colored championship of the world, which took place at Crystal Palace tonight, attracted a great crowd.

Armstrong started in a favorite, but his performance did not justify this, as Martin proved to be the cleverer from the outset, and never gave his opponent a chance, being declared an easy winner on points at the close of fifteen rounds.

Martin, it is announced, will challenge the winner of the Jeffries-Fitzsimmons fight in San Francisco to-night.

The New York (NY) World
July 26 1902

In October, Frank Childs fought Joe Walcott. The bout was stopped due to a Walcott injury. Many still saw Childs as the colored champion in spite of his February loss to Martin. But just a few days later, Jack Johnson defeated Childs and declared himself to be the colored champion.

Jeffries and Fitzsimmons developed a sincere respect for each other and went on an exhibition tour together. On December 20, 1902 in Butte, Montana, Jeffries ran into a well-muscled miner named Jack Munroe in a bout that caused a stir. Some said Munroe earned a victory in the contest.

Munroe was not a great fighter but he was strong and could hit. During the exhibition, he mostly ran from Jeffries. Jim slipped to the floor once as he was throwing a punch while in hot pursuit of Munroe. Some reports said Munroe knocked the champion down.

"Denver" Ed Martin lost to Jack Johnson in February 1903. Johnson would claim the colored title until he captured the world heavyweight championship a few years later, in 1908. He did lose a contest to Joe Jeannette in 1905, however.

On August 14, 1903 in San Francisco, Jeffries again met Jim Corbett. The mighty champ was a better fighter now than in his first bout with the clever Corbett who boxed the big fellow and tried new tactics.

Early in the fight, Jeffries nearly bashed in the ex-champion's right side with a powerful hook. During the contest, he floored Corbett in the fourth and sixth rounds. Then, he downed "Gentleman Jim" twice in the tenth round to stop him.

Jack Munroe

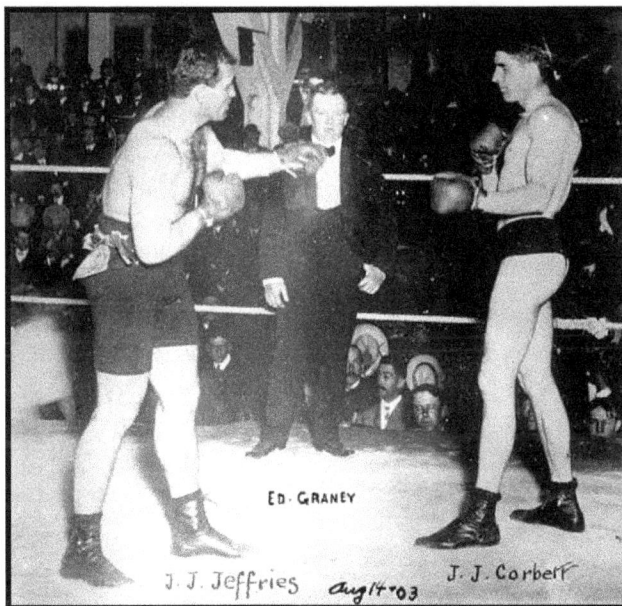

Jim Jeffries-Jim Corbett
August 14 1903

JEFF SUPREME AS PREMIER PUGILIST

Crushing Defeat of Corbett Last Night at San Francisco Stamps Victor as Pugilistic Marvel of Age.

The Lincoln (NE) Evening News
August 15 1903
Reprinted with permission of the
Lincoln (NE) Journal Star

One year later, on August 26, 1904, Jeffries met Jack Munroe in San Francisco and squelched the rumors that Munroe had beaten Jim in their exhibition fight in 1902. Jeff stopped Munroe in two rounds.

Billy Delaney

Jeffries had beaten all bonafide contenders for his title. His trainer Billy Delaney was urging him to retire since the men who looked to be good in the future were somewhat younger than he was. By the time they were ready, Jeff would be older and would get rusty if not well-challenged. In addition, he had married four months prior to the Munroe fight so it was time for him to leave the ring.

On May 13, 1905, Jeff retired. At the encouragement of financial backers, he looked over the field, suggested the names of two good men to fight for the vacated championship and agreed to referee the contest.

The two-fisted battler Marvin Hart was one of the men selected. Hart had scored many knockouts, had lost only three fights and just recently on March 28, 1905 in San Francisco, had gained a decision over Jack Johnson in twenty rounds. Jack Root was the other man chosen. Root was a former light-heavyweight champion and a very good boxer who had lost only a couple of fights.

On July 3 in Reno, Nevada with Jeffries as referee, Hart knocked out Root in twelve rounds to win the bout. Some considered the contest to be for the heavyweight championship, some did not. Making his own claim for the heavyweight title, "Philadelphia" Jack O'Brien knocked out Al Kaufman on October 27, a little over three months after Hart's victory, but this was not generally recognized.

Marvin Hart-Jack Root
July 3 1905

O'Brien followed this bout with a victory over Bob Fitzsimmons on December 20 for Bob's light-heavyweight title. His claim for the heavyweight title continued.

Marvin Hart's days as champion were numbered. On February 23, 1906 in Los Angeles, Tommy Burns defeated Hart in twenty rounds. Burns was a small man for a heavyweight, standing 5'7" and weighing around 175 pounds, but he was a little guy with a big punch. "Little Tommy" was living proof that "it's not the size of the dog in the fight, it's the size of the fight in the dog." Actually, Burns was a light-heavy.

Tommy Burns

Tommy was an active champion, winning a number of championship fights over the next two years and seven months, most of them by knockout.

By 1905-1906, there was a set of talented black fighters that had surfaced in America. These fellows made it a habit of fighting one another often along what historian Tim Leone called the "Chitlin Trail." They were evenly matched and the fights were exciting. On April 26, 1906, Jack Johnson decisively defeated Sam Langford in Chelsea, Massachusetts to clearly establish himself as the best of the blacks.

Two of Burns' important title bouts came in 1906. On October 2 in Los Angeles, he knocked out "Fireman" Jim Flynn, a tough nut, in fifteen rounds.

FLYNN KNOCKED OUT IN THE FIFTEENTH

Pueblo Champion Slow and
Awkward—Easy
to Hit

BURNS FIGHTS AGGRESSIVELY

The Washington (DC) Times
October 3 1906

On November 28 in Los Angeles, Tommy fought "Philadelphia" Jack O'Brien in what referee Jim Jeffries called a draw. In truth, Burns bested O'Brien in the bout. O'Brien boxed his usual hit-and-run style while Burns did all the hard punching. Another claimant for the title stepped forth in early 1907 when Mike Schreck won battles against John Wille and Tony Ross.

Tommy Burns-"Philadelphia" Jack O'Brien
November 28 1906

BURNS GETS DECISION

-

O'Brien Looks More Like a Sprinter Than a Fighter

-

BOUT WAS UNSATISFACTORY

-

Referee Declares Bets Off Before Fight Because Of Injury O'Brien Is Said to Have Received While Training – Big Crowd Was Present and Hissed and Hooted Principals

-

The Washington (DC) Post
May 9 1907

Burns gained three more championship wins in 1907. He earned a twenty-round win against "Philadelphia" Jack on May 8 in Los Angeles. This was the third time the two men had met in the ring and their series now stood at one win apiece and a draw.

On May 30, Mike Schreck defeated Marvin Hart. Due to his recent performances and past successes against Burns, Mike was seen as a viable candidate for the title.

Next, Tommy Burns knocked out Bill Squires of Australia in one round in Colma, California (San Francisco) on July 4. This was a surprise because a hard give-and-take battle was expected.

Afterwards, Burns traveled the world defending his title. On December 2 in London, he knocked out the two-hundred pound James "Gunner" Moir in ten rounds. By now, most followers of boxing saw Burns as the true champion.

During the years 1903-1906, Jack Johnson reportedly defended his colored championship several times against the likes of "Denver" Ed Martin, Sam McVea [McVey], Joe Butler, Black Bill (Claude Brooks), Frank Childs, Joe Jeannette, Walter Johnson, Morris Harris, "Young" Peter Jackson and Sam Langford.

Tommy Burns-Bill Squires
July 4 1907

Jack Johnson

In 1907, Johnson, the reigning colored heavyweight champion of the world, scored five knockouts in six bouts. One of these victories was on July 17 in Philadelphia over Bob Fitzsimmons in two rounds. Another was in a colored title defense against Peter Felix. Thus far in his career, Johnson had suffered one loss in 1899, two losses in 1901 and two losses in 1905. But he had not lost a bout in two years and was putting all of his skills together. He was nearing his peak.

"Little Tommy" Burns scored six knockouts in title defenses during 1908. He scored quick knockouts over Jack Palmer in four rounds in London on February 10, Jem Roche in one round on March 17 in Dublin, Ireland and Joseph "Jewey" Smith in five rounds on April 18 in Paris.

The other three finishes took a little longer. He put Bill Squires out in eight rounds in Paris on June 13 and Squires, a second time, in Sydney on August 24 in thirteen rounds. On September 2 in Melbourne, he knocked out Bill Lang in six rounds.

Tommy Burns-Joseph "Jewey" Smith
April 18 1908

"Fireman" Jim Flynn (Andrew Chiariglione) was short and stocky, hard-charging and tough. He carried a stiff punch too. Jim had begun his career back at the turn of the century and gotten better over the years.

"Fireman" Jim Flynn

KAUFMANN KNOCKS OUT FLYNN AFTER EIGHT FIERCE ROUNDS

GONG SAVES PUEBLO BOY IN EIGHTH, BUT HE IS STOPPED QUICKLY IN NINTH

The Los Angeles (CA) Herald
August 26 1908

He lost a couple of fights at the beginning of his career around 1899-1900 but afterwards lost only to Jack Root, former light-heavyweight champion (1903), heavyweight champion Tommy Burns (1906) and future heavyweight champion Jack Johnson (1907). During 1907, Flynn gained victories over such men as George Gardner, Tony Ross and Bill Squires. On August 25, 1908, the "Fireman" suffered a setback when he lost to Al Kaufman in Los Angeles.

Al Kaufman

Al Kaufman was a promising young heavyweight who had lost only one bout since starting his career. He had knocked out a number of men by the time he fought "Fireman" Jim Flynn. "Young Al" knocked out the rough, gritty and often foul Flynn in nine rounds and was the center of much attention.

By 1908, Jack Johnson had matured into a master of defense. He was smooth with quick reflexes and very difficult to hit squarely. In his offensive arsenal, he possessed a sharp jab and a vicious uppercut. Boxing historian and writer Adam Pollack (2012) called Johnson a "stylistic nightmare" for any opponent, able to confuse his man, wreck his coordination and raze his style of fighting.

Sam Langford

In addition to Johnson, there was Sam Langford who was perhaps the second best black pugilist fighting at the time. Langford began his career in the lighter weight classes and worked his way up to the heavyweight division. He was a terrific ringman, an all-time great.

Sam could box or punch and he could fight in close or at a distance. He was quick on his feet and fast with his punches. In addition, he had plenty of stamina.

Joe Jeannette

Also, there was Joe Jeannette, who was an exceptionally good pugilist. He was quick and slippery. He hooked well and was loaded with boxing savvy. Like Langford, he could fight on the outside or inside.

Up to this point in his career, Jeannette had wins over Jack Johnson, Sam Langford, Black Bill (Claude Brooks), Jim Jeffords and Morris Harris.

Sam McVea

Sam McVea was another talented battler. Sam was big and powerful. He was not a polished fighter but he was tough, immensely strong and fast on his feet for a man of his size. McVea was comparable in size to Jeffries and had a powerful structure similar to the champion. Jeffries, on the other hand, possessed a more solid chin and greater stamina than Sam.

By this time in his career, the big warrior McVea had gained victories over "Denver" Ed Martin, Fred Russell, Kid Carter, Ben Taylor and Jack Scales.

Jack Johnson followed Tommy Burns the world over seeking a title shot. At first, Burns ignored his challenges. Finally, Tommy consented and why not? He was the champion, he was quick and he had a stinging knockout punch. Besides, Johnson had been knocked out twice. Further, he had beaten Marvin Hart and Hart had beaten Johnson. Bring on the black!

Jack Johnson-Tommy Burns
December 26 1908

On December 26, 1908 in Sydney, Australia, Burns fought Johnson. The large black toyed with him. He jabbed, jeered, and tied Tommy up round after round. When he became bored with the goings-on, he belted the champion with lefts and rights until police intervened and stopped the contest in round fourteen. Jack Johnson became the first heavyweight champion of the world who was black.

From the moment Johnson beat Burns to claim the title until he eventually lost the crown, the cry rang out for a "White Hope" - a Caucasian man who would reclaim the championship.

The writer Jack London felt that Johnson was better than any of the white fighters in the ring at the time. His infamous words in **The New York Herald (December 27, 1908)** best represent the prevailing attitude -

[I] was with Burns all the way. He was a white man and so am I. Naturally I wanted to see the white man win. Put the case to Johnson and ask him if he were the spectator at a fight between a white man and a black man which he would like to see win. Johnson's black skin will dictate a desire parallel to the one dictated by white skin … But one thing remains. Jeffries must emerge from his alfalfa farm and remove the smile from Johnson's face. "Jeff, it's up to you …" (also see Fleischer 1939 pp 72 73).

The Oakland (CA) Tribune
December 27 1908

Any white man who could swing his fists or put up his guard seemed to be a viable candidate to challenge Johnson for the crown. Some of these men were good fighters, some were fair and some were not good at all. Among those who loomed as possible serious challengers for the black man at the time were Jim Barry, John "Sandy" Ferguson, Mike Schreck, Jim Stewart, Al Kubiak, "Fireman" Jim Flynn, Al Kaufman, "Philadelphia" Jack O'Brien, Tony Ross and Stanley Ketchel. Five of these men actually tangled with Johnson with the heavyweight championship at stake.

As world heavyweight champion, Johnson drew the "color line" on the good black fighters just as the previous white champions had done. He never fought an outstanding black man for the title. While Johnson was avoiding the other black scrappers, they were teeing off on each other.

Sam McVea and Joe Jeannette tangled in Paris for the colored championship in February of 1909. McVea won. Next, he defeated Billy Warren in a title defense and then fought Jeannette again, in Paris on April 17. After a slugfest in which each man was sent to the canvas several times, Jeannette won by a stoppage after round forty-nine. Later in 1909, Sam Langford bested John "Klondike" Haines and challenged Johnson for the world heavyweight title. When Jack refused to fight him, Sam claimed the colored championship.

Joe Jeannette-Sam McVea
April 17 1909

O'BRIEN IN THE LEAD

-

Philadelphian Shows Well
Against Champion

-

LACKS PHYSICAL STRENGTH

-

White Man Lands Majority of Blows
And Surprises Big Negro by His
Clever Work - Handicapped
On Weights - Blows Are Much
the Cleaner - Brady Talks Fight.

The Washington (DC) Herald
May 20 1909

Five months after defeating Burns, Johnson boxed "Philadelphia" Jack O'Brien on May 19, 1909 in Philadelphia, reportedly for the title. Two better boxers did not exist. O'Brien was impressive but Johnson retained the championship in six rounds.

Six weeks afterwards, on June 30, Johnson boxed Tony Ross in Pittsburgh, in a bout that some say was for the title. Johnson was better from start to finish. Following this bout, on the ninth of September, Johnson met talented Al Kaufman in a possible title fight in California. Johnson was easily better - this time in ten rounds.

Stanley Ketchel

Sam Langford continued to press his claim as the colored heavyweight champion and on September 28 in Boston stopped Aaron Brown ("The Dixie Kid") in five rounds.

Johnson was a hated heavyweight champion. He taunted and jeered his opponents in the ring. He was a black man who lived life in a reckless fashion. He violated social customs and laws. The white society was clamoring for someone to beat him.

Numerous boxing tournaments were held in search of a white man that could be put up against him. Pressure was put upon Jim Jeffries to come out of retirement to fight Johnson. Jeffries scoffed at this idea but Stanley Ketchel, middleweight champion of the world, did not. He stepped forward to fight the black champion.

Jack Johnson-Stanley Ketchel
October 16 1909

The Johnson-Ketchel fight took place in October of 1909 in Colma, California (San Francisco). Johnson outweighed Ketchel by thirty-five pounds. He played with the middleweight throughout the fight. In round twelve, Ketchel knocked Johnson down with a sneaky, quick right. Johnson got up and immediately knocked out Stanley.

Once again, white groups were calling upon Jim Jeffries to get back into the ring and dethrone this undesirable champion. Finally, Jeffries agreed to fight Johnson.

In November 1909, Langford knocked out John "Klondike" Haines in two rounds to keep his title of colored heavyweight champion. In December, Joe Jeannette fought Sam McVea to a draw in Paris for his version of the colored title.

Sam Langford stayed busy defending his colored crown in January of 1910 with another knockout win over Aaron Brown ("The Dixie Kid") and a newspaper win against "Battling" Jim Johnson in May. Joe Jeannette met Morris Harris on July 1 in a defense of his colored title claim. It was a "no decision" bout.

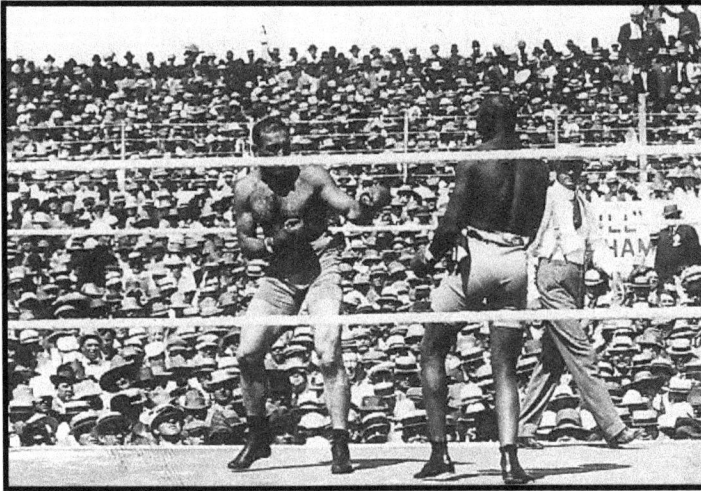

Jack Johnson-Jim Jeffries
July 4 1910

Reportedly, Jim Jeffries had weighed over 300 pounds. He trimmed down to about 230 pounds in nine months. Jim had not fought in six years and had not engaged in any real fights to prepare for the contest. Johnson had engaged in numerous fights since Jeffries had retired.

On July 4, 1910 in Reno, Nevada, Johnson met Jeffries in the ring. The temperature was over 100 degrees that day. Sounds bad for Jeffries - it was! The bout was a mismatch. Johnson was sharp. Jeffries was rusty and "over the hill." Yet it took Johnson fifteen rounds to stop Jeffries.

This victory over the once great Jeffries gave Johnson the image of invincibility that lasted for many years. It also tarnished the reputation of Jeffries. As the news of the fight spread across the country, blacks danced in the streets, store windows were smashed, riots broke out and racial fights took place. During the remaining months of 1910, Sam Langford racked up three more wins for his colored title, including a win over Joe Jeannette. He kept his title in five more bouts through September of 1911.

After a couple of years of up-and-down fighting, "Fireman" Jim Flynn got back on the winning track. On May 5, 1911, Flynn avenged his 1908 loss to Al Kaufman by scoring a tenth-round knockout in Kansas City.

JIM FLYNN DROPS KAUFMAN IN TENTH AFTER TERRIFIC BATTLE

The Colorado Springs (CO) Gazette
May 6 1911

Jack Johnson-"Fireman" Jim Flynn
July 4 1912

November 29, 1911 saw Tom Kennedy get the best of Al Palzer in a Brooklyn contest billed by some newspapers as the white heavyweight championship. Sam Langford lost his colored title to Sam McVea on December 26 but won it back on April 8, 1912.

On July 4, 1912, "Fireman" Jim Flynn fought Jack Johnson in Las Vegas, New Mexico, reportedly for the heavyweight championship. Flynn was known to fight dirty and on this day, he was determined to get Johnson. However, each time he tried to get close enough to hit Johnson, he was tied up and held. In the clinches, Flynn attempted to head-butt the champion time and time again. He was warned several times and finally the bout was stopped. Johnson remained champion.

Since claiming the colored heavyweight championship, Sam Langford had engaged in a number of contests against other talented blacks. He continued to reign as the colored champion during 1912-1913. Meanwhile, Johnson continued to avoid fighting the top black fighters for the big prize.

Luther "Luck" McCarty

There had been a number of bouts conducted to find a white heavyweight who could beat Johnson. After a while, some good men had surfaced - Luther "Luck" McCarty, Al Palzer, Arthur Pelkey, Ed "Gunboat" Smith, Carl Morris, Frank Moran, Fred Fulton and Jess Willard.

McCarty was probably the best of the bunch and might have stood a chance with Johnson. He was big, quick for his size, could hit and could box fairly well.

On May 3, 1912, McCarty knocked out Carl Morris in six rounds in Springfield, Missouri. He followed this impressive triumph with several other victories, including wins over Al Kaufman, "Fireman" Jim Flynn and Al Palzer.

Some sources called the Palzer contest a white heavyweight championship bout. He also met Frank Moran in what some papers called a white hope title defense.

At this time, Arthur Pelkey, a strong battler and a solid hitter, boasted a fine record and owned wins over Alfred "Soldier" Kearns, Jim Barry, Andy Morris and Charles "Sailor" White.

Arthur Pelkey

Arthur Pelkey-Luther "Luck" McCarty
May 24 1913

In a fight between Pelkey and McCarty on May 24, 1913 in Calgary, Canada, what appeared to be a light punch to McCarty's head in the first round put Luther down and out. He died at ringside. Some sources called this a bout for the white heavyweight championship. Following the tragic incident, Pelkey won only a handful of bouts in 26 contests. Then he quit the ring.

In Jack Johnson's private life, he was involved with woman after woman. Many times, they were white. He was asking for trouble. There existed a White Slave Traffic Act, otherwise known as the Mann Act, which forbade anyone from transporting a woman across a state line for sexual purposes. Jack was arrested in 1912 and charged with violating this act and also with smuggling jewelry into the country but the case fell apart.

In early 1913, Johnson was arrested again and on May 13 was found guilty of a technical violation of the Mann Act. In late June, with imprisonment pending, he skipped the country to avoid going to jail. He wandered from place to place and ended up in France near the end of the year.

Johnson spent money freely and carelessly. Soon, he was nearly broke. Some sources report that to survive financially, he agreed to enter the ring with Andre Sproul, a wrestler. Jack knocked him out in two rounds in Paris.

Jack Johnson and wife

"Battling" Jim Johnson

Ed "Gunboat" Smith was a sharp hitter, pretty good boxer and full of scrap. He beat Jess Willard in twenty rounds on May 20 in Colma (San Francisco) and won against Carl Morris in five rounds in New York on October 9.

On December 19 in Paris, Jack Johnson boxed "Battling" Jim Johnson, a fairly good black fighter. During the fight, Jack injured an arm. Various sources say he broke it. The fight was called a draw. Some say it was for the title. However, the French Boxing Federation (FBF) declared the talented Sam Langford heavyweight champion when he beat Joe Jeannette on December 20, also in Paris.

Ed "Gunboat" Smith defeated Arthur Pelkey on January 1, 1914 to capture the white heavyweight title.

Yet Jess Willard, the huge fighter from Kansas, loomed as the possible "White Hope" fighter who could possibly conquer Johnson.

Jess was big, strong and old school tough. However, he had lost a contest to Ed "Gunboat" Smith in 1913 and was bested by Tom "Bearcat" McMahon on March 27, 1914.

Jess Willard

Harry Wills

During 1914, Harry Wills, a big "cat-quick" 220-pounder, surfaced as one of the better black fighters. In 14 fights during the year, Wills lost just twice. He and Sam Langford met two times in colored championship battles. Harry bested, or at least drew, Sam in the first war but lost the second. He also lost to Sam McVea. Wills was very good and was on the verge of handling the top heavyweights. Langford retained the colored title throughout the year 1914 although Wills launched a claim.

Frank Moran could hit but he was not a good boxer. Jack Johnson figured he was an easy touch. Frank got his chance at the black man on June 27 in Paris. Johnson beat Moran handily in twenty rounds in a questionable title fight. On July 16 in London, Georges Carpentier defeated Ed "Gunboat" Smith on a foul to capture the white heavyweight championship.

Jack Johnson-Frank Moran
June 27 1914

On October 20, 1914, Ed "Gunboat" Smith was flattened by Sam Langford in three clangs of the bell. This loss eliminated him as a contender for Jack Johnson's crown.

On April 5, 1915 in Havana, Cuba, Johnson took on the big Kansan Jess Willard. It was a cautious fight at first with Johnson showing spurts of offense at times. As the afternoon wore on, Johnson slowed and Jess landed solid blows. In round twenty-six, he caught Johnson with a stiff punch and Jack went down and out.

LANGFORD KNOCKS
OUT GUNBOAT SMITH

Negro Heavyweight Puts Over Sleep Punch in Third Round.

The Naugatuck (CT) Daily News
October 21 1914

Jess Willard-Jack Johnson
April 5 1915

Afterwards, Johnson claimed he threw the fight. But now, Willard was the heavyweight champion and an immediate hero. He was "the man who beat Jack Johnson." People cheered him at railroad stops as he made his way to New York from the South. Unfortunately, Jess was not colorful and his popularity waned quickly during his first year as champ. With this win over Johnson, the white heavyweight championship died.

CARL MORRIS ROCKS PELKY TO SLEEP

TULSA, Okla., Feb. 12. — Carl Morris of Sapulpa, Okla., knocked out Arthur Pelky of Canada in the fifth round last night of their scheduled 15-round bout here. Pelky was floored twice in the fifth before he was knocked out. The men are heavyweights.

WILLS KNOCKED OUT BY LANGFORD

NEW ORLEANS, Feb. 12. — Sam Langford knocked out Harry Wills in the nineteenth round of a scheduled 20-round bout at a local arena last night. Until the knockout blow, neither fighter seemed to have the advantage.

The Oakland (CA) Tribune
February 12 1916

Carl Morris was a pretty good fighter who was probably at his best during the 1912-1916 years. He was big and carried a heavy punch but moved too slowly to stand a chance against Johnson. His losses to Luther "Luck" McCarty, Ed "Gunboat" Smith and Al Kubiak hurt his chances and he never got a title shot.

Carl Morris

The years 1915 and 1916 saw Harry Wills continue to get better. So much did he improve that the only men who would fight him were black. His lone official loss during these years was to Sam Langford, though he bettered Sam on several occasions. Harry, Sam, Joe Jeannette and the other Sam [McVea] - all four - claimed the colored title at times during 1915. Wills and Langford fought several times for that title in competitive battles in 1916 although Sam held the title for most of the year. Jeannette also had a 1916 claim.

On March 25, 1916, Willard boxed Frank Moran ten rounds in a dull "no decision" fight in New York City. Jess kept his crown.

Following this fight, Willard toured with a Wild West show and circus. He would engage in just two official bouts until May 12, 1923.

Jess Willard-Frank Moran
March 25 1916

While Willard was taking it easy, a young aggressive fighter named Jack Dempsey was maturing out West. During 1914-1916, Dempsey fought in saloons, mining camps and on street corners, scoring knockout after knockout. He was small for a heavyweight but he was fast, had good timing and hit extremely hard. He could take it too.

Jack stepped up in competition in 1917 and struggled. He lost to "Fireman" Jim Flynn in what some historians claim was a fixed fight and he lost a decision to Willie Meehan. Little by little he learned, modified his techniques and improved his style and skills.

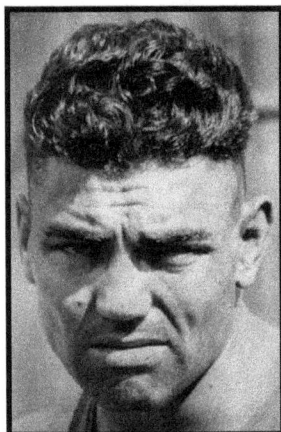

Jack Dempsey

Challenger Fred Fulton was tall and possessed a lethal jab along with a smashing cross. He had beaten many good men, including Sam Langford, but he was eliminated as a title threat by Al Palzer, Carl Morris and Harry "Texas" Tate. He never received a shot at the championship.

Sam Langford and "Big" Bill Tate battled a couple of times for the colored heavyweight title during 1917, each man winning once. Langford also fought Harry Wills two or three times for the colored crown. In addition, he fought "Battling" Jim Johnson, Joe Jeannette, Kid Norfolk and Andrew Johnson in colored title bouts.

Fred Fulton

FULTON STOPS SAM LANGFORD IN SIXTH

-

MINNESOTA PLASTERER SCORES TECHNICAL KNOCKOUT OVER THE NEGRO HEAVYWEIGHT IN BOSTON BATTLE

-

The Racine (WI) Journal-News
June 20 1917

In 1918, Jack Dempsey scored seventeen knockouts, twelve of them in the first round, against quality fighters. Among them was a revenge one-round knockout of "Fireman" Jim Flynn on February 14 in Fort Sheridan, Illinois, a one-round knockout of Fred Fulton on July 27 in Harrison, New Jersey and a one-round knockout of Carl Morris in New Orleans on December 16.

Harry Wills' star shone brightly in 1918 when he was unbeaten in seven bouts and scored four knockouts. Among his victories were a knockout and a win against Sam McVea, a knockout and a stoppage of Sam Langford and a stoppage of Jeff Clark. He reigned as the colored king for most of the year, ready for anyone.

Yes, Harry had arrived. He was unbeaten in eight bouts during 1919 and defended his colored belt several times. He was the colored champ when the year began and was still the champ at year's end, although Langford made a claim.

Dempsey blazed into 1919 with five straight one-round knockouts in official bouts. At this point in Jack's career, he was one of the greatest attacking fighters who ever entered the ring. He bobbed and weaved, he moved left and right, and he hit hard with each fist.

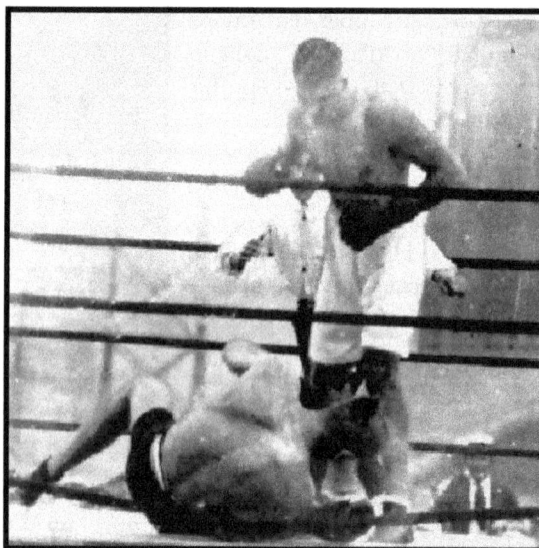

Jack Dempsey-Fred Fulton
July 27 1918

On July 4 in Toledo, Ohio, promoter "Tex" Rickard brought together this attacking challenger and the heavyweight king Jess Willard. "The Tiger in the White Trunks" mauled the champion, scoring seven knockdowns in the first round. In rounds two and three, Dempsey proceeded to pulverize Willard. The towel was thrown in at the beginning of round four. Dempsey was champion.

54

Jack Dempsey-Jess Willard
July 4 1919

At first, Dempsey was not liked by many Americans. The first world war was going on and he failed to enlist and serve in the American Armed Forces in Europe. Many called him a slacker for not serving his country. Some champion, huh? When he entered the ring for his next two fights, there were many boos and hisses among the cheers.

Harry Wills had eight bouts in 1920, reportedly involving seven colored heavyweight championship bouts in which he retained the crown. Impressively, in Newark, New Jersey on July 26, he knocked out Fred Fulton in three rounds. Wills had not lost a fight since February of 1917 when he had injured an arm against "Battling" Jim Johnson and was forced to stop. He was at his peak. A fight with Jack Dempsey was on his mind.

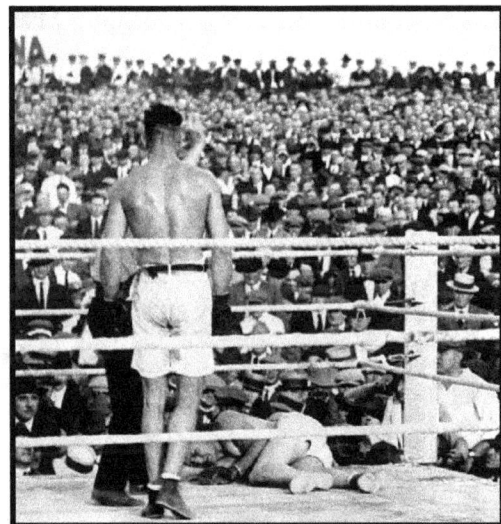

Jack Dempsey-Billy Miske
September 6 1920

On September 6, 1920 in Benton Harbor, Michigan, a little over a year after capturing the heavyweight championship, Dempsey knocked out Billy Miske in three rounds. Miske was an able boxer but was not in the best of health. He was no match for Jack.

Jack Dempsey-"K.O." Bill Brennan
December 14 1920

Dempsey battled the bruiser "K.O." Bill Brennan on December 14 in New York. After a very rough contest, Jack scored a twelfth-round knockout. Throughout the fight, Brennan belted Dempsey with rights and lefts that had Jack bleeding from his lips and one ear. "K.O." Bill seemed unafraid of Jack's punches that appeared to lack their usual steam. However, Jack was most dangerous when hurt. During round twelve action, Dempsey suddenly ripped in a heart punch and a sharp left to Brennan's midsection. These blows led to the finish and another Dempsey win. This was the last title fight of 1920.

Having fled the states for seven years, Jack Johnson returned in 1920 and surrendered to authorities. He served a year in Leavenworth prison and was released in July of the following year.

Top Heavyweight Boxers of 1901-1920
1. Jim Jeffries
2. Jack Johnson
3. Jack Dempsey
4. Harry Wills
5. Sam Langford

Top Heavyweight Bouts of 1901-1920
1. Jack Johnson-Jim Jeffries, July 4 1910, Reno, Nevada
2. Jack Johnson-Tommy Burns, December 26 1908, Sydney, NSW, Australia
3. Jack Dempsey-Jess Willard, July 4 1919, Toledo, Ohio
4. Jess Willard-Jack Johnson, April 5 1915, Havana, Cuba
5. Joe Jeannette-Sam McVea #3, April 17 1909, Paris, France

Sam Langford-Joe Jeannette
December 20 1913

Chapter Three

The Years 1921-1940

On July 2, 1921 in Jersey City, New Jersey, more than 80,000 fans saw Dempsey take on Georges Carpentier, a French war hero. The fight was promoted as an American versus a Frenchman. As a result, Dempsey received many cheers.

Carpentier, "The Orchid Man," was a former light-heavyweight champion who could hit. In round two, he rocked the heavyweight champion with a right-hand smash but Dempsey then took charge and finished him in round four.

A young light-heavyweight and ex-Marine named Gene Tunney was keeping his eye on the outcome of this bout. He was watching Dempsey's every move.

In 1921, Harry Wills supposedly had ten colored heavyweight title bouts and retained his crown in all of them. Upon release from prison, Jack Johnson toured the United States fighting exhibitions and a few official bouts.

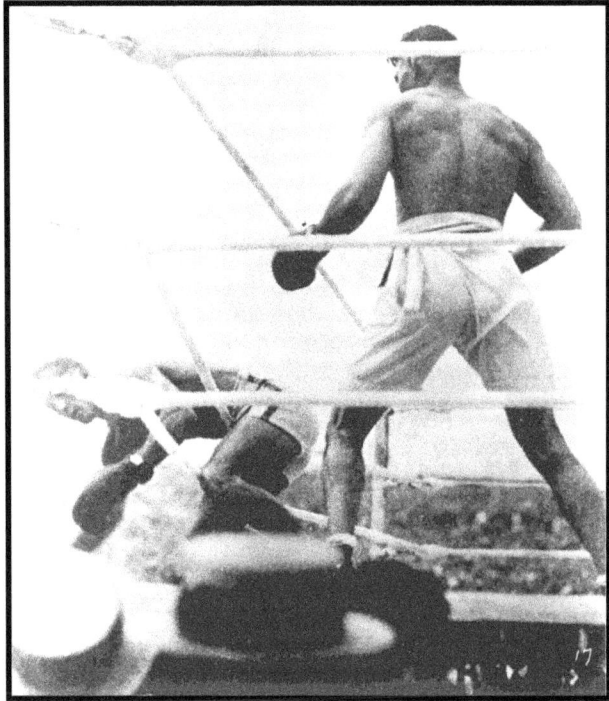

Jack Dempsey-Georges Carpentier
July 2 1921

James "Tut" Jackson and Jack Johnson
1922

During 1922 in a New York State Athletic Commission (NYSAC) title fight, Dempsey defeated Jimmy Darcy in four rounds in Buffalo. But mostly he took life easy, made public appearances and boxed some exhibitions.

From 1921 to mid-1923, James "Tut" Jackson drew much attention. During this time, he engaged in more than 50 fights, lost only five and scored 36 knockouts. Victims of Jackson included Sam Langford, "Rough House" Ware, "Denver" Jack Geyer, Eddie Civil and Clem Johnson.

"Big" Bill Tate had an interesting and lengthy career, beginning in 1912 and lasting until the late twenties. His true skills first surfaced in 1916 when he had nine fights and lost but two official bouts. That year he battled Sam Langford and Harry Wills in "no decision" contests and knocked out Rufus Cameron.

In 1917, Bill defeated Sam Langford and claimed the colored heavyweight championship but lost that title back to Langford in the same year. In December of 1921, he bested Sam Langford and from that bout until late 1925, did some of his best fighting.

In 1922, Tate who served as a sparring partner for a number of top heavyweights during his career, won from Harry Wills on a foul in an Oregon bout and claimed the colored title. A rematch ended in a draw and both men claimed the crown. Tate's claim was not generally recognized although he defended "his" title several times from February to June 1922. He lost his last title bout to Jack Thompson

"Big" Bill Tate

who received little support for his title claim. Wills was seen by most to be the colored champion. Harry went on to defend his crown several times the rest of the year. During the year, Tate bested Langford in Memphis but lost to Sam in Tulsa, Oklahoma.

Luis Angel Firpo-"K.O." Bill Brennan
March 12 1923

Langford, who fought Harry Wills seventeen times in his career, was asked how Wills would do against Dempsey. Sam replied, in *The Atlanta Constitution (June 5, 1922)*, that if they ever fought, his money would be on Dempsey. "He is the greatest fighter I have ever seen. He hits twice as hard as Jeffries and he is as fast in the ring as James J. Corbett."

Luis Angel Firpo was the reigning heavyweight champion of South America when he traveled to the United States in 1922. He scored three wins and then returned home.

In 1923, Firpo ventured to America once again and on March 12 in New York defeated "K.O." Bill Brennan in the first of eight straight wins.

A big heavyweight elimination tournament was held on May 12, 1923 in New York to find a future challenger for the champion Jack Dempsey. Included was Jess Willard, who had gotten into a bad situation and needed money. Also included was Luis Angel Firpo. Jess trained rigorously, lost some weight and tried to regain his old strength. Willard fought Floyd Johnson and stopped his man in eleven rounds. In the other bouts, Firpo knocked out Jack McAuliffe II, Jack Renault won from Fred Fulton on a foul, "Tiny" Jim Herman scored a knockout win over Al Reich and Harry Drake outpointed Joe McCann. The big names on the fight card were Willard and Firpo. Their wins on this program set up a bout between the two, the winner to meet Dempsey.

On July 4, Dempsey defended his championship in Shelby, Montana against Tommy Gibbons, a crack light-heavyweight. Gibbons was a clever, seasoned fighter and lasted fifteen rounds with Jack. Dempsey was rusty but still the better man in the fight. Financial matters for this fight were handled poorly. Dempsey received his purse but Gibbons got nothing.

BIG WILLARD
A COMEBACK
-
KANSAS MAN-MOUNTAIN AGAIN A PUGILISTIC FIGURE
-
Batters Floyd Johnson at Pleasure, Winning in the Eleventh Round Firpo an Easy Victor Over McAuliffe.

The Sunday State Journal, May 13 1923
Reprinted with permission of The Lincoln (NE) Journal Star

Jack Dempsey-Tommy Gibbons
July 4 1923

On July 12 in Jersey City, Willard was fighting again. This time he was in with Luis Angel Firpo, the big puncher from Argentina. Firpo had many victories to his credit, mostly by knockout. He was crude but he could hit.

Luis Angel Firpo

FIRPO WINNER OVER WILLARD IN THE EIGHTH
-
Leads All the Way and Finishes With a Clean Knockout

The Traverse City (MI) Record-Eagle
July 13 1923

The bout, described by some as a clumsy young man fighting a clumsy old man, consisted mostly of Willard's left jab and Firpo's clubbing right hand. There was much holding. In the fourth, seventh and eighth rounds, Firpo got Willard on the ropes and pounded away. The assault in the eighth put Jess down and Firpo was declared the winner with the former champ left sitting on the floor.

South of the border on July 27, 1923, Clem Johnson defeated Sam Langford to win the championship of Mexico and launch a colored heavyweight title claim that never amounted to much. A muscular heavyweight from Oklahoma, Brad Simmons, began getting some attention during 1923. Thus far in his career, he had earned a draw with Sam Langford and scored wins over "Big" Bill Hartwell, Jack Thompson, Clem Johnson and "Battling" Gahee.

Brad Simmons

After only a fair start to his career, Ed "Bearcat" Wright made some noise on the heavyweight scene when he defeated Sam Langford in Mexico City during August of 1923. Wright was a big, strong fellow with a mighty wallop but he sometimes tended to get quite careless during a contest.

Over the course of his career, the "Bearcat" gained victories over such men as Jack Johnson, Fred Fulton, "Long" Tom Hawkins, James "Tut" Jackson, Brad Simmons, Roy "Ace" Clark, "Big" Bill Hartwell, Cecil "Seal" Harris, Neil Clisby, "Tiger" Jack Fox, Bob Lawson and Dan "Porky" Flynn.

Ed "Bearcat" Wright

Nearly two and a half months after his fight with Gibbons, on September 14 in New York City, Jack Dempsey took on Luis Angel Firpo. It was an explosive fight. The men went at it right away and fireworks prevailed. Dempsey knocked Firpo down seven times in the first round. The champ was knocked down too. He also was knocked out of the ring.

Ringsiders grabbed the champ and pushed him up into the ring. Otherwise, he might not have made it back in ten seconds. Dempsey knocked Firpo down twice more in round two while finishing him off.

Over the next three years, Dempsey fought mostly exhibitions. He changed managers, had his nose straightened, traveled to Europe, went on stage, married and got rusty.

Jack Dempsey-Luis Angel Firpo
September 14 1923

Harry Wills made headlines by defeating the white fighter Homer Smith and beating Jack Thompson in a colored heavyweight title defense in 1923. He ranked high among heavyweight title contenders during 1924-1925 when he beat Bartley Madden, Charley Weinert and Floyd Johnson and bested Luis Angel Firpo.

Jack Johnson Flop in Simmons Fight; Monte in Victory

ENID, Okla., Sept. 7.—(AP)—Brad Simmons, Drumright negro heavyweight, was given a decision over Jack Johnson, former world's heavyweight champion, in a 10-round fight staged last night before 4000 spectators in the 101 Ranch arena.

The bout was mostly a tame affair. Simmons seemed willing enough but Johnson, who must have weighed nearly 250 pounds, stalled and contented himself with frequent clowning.

**The San Antonio (TX) Light
September 7 1926**

Wills had openly challenged Dempsey from the late teens to 1926. Jack said he would meet him but his manager, Jack "Doc" Kearns, made the final decision - they never fought each other. Several efforts were made during the early 1920s to get them together but time and again promoters backed out, not wanting another episode of the Jeffries-Johnson fight with riots and racial confrontations breaking out. So, plans for the Wills bout faded.

In August of 1926, Brad Simmons beat Sam Langford and "Big" Bill Hartwell. On September 6 in Ponca City, Oklahoma, he won a ten-round decision from the former champion Jack Johnson. Jack was older and in the midst of a six-bout losing streak.

Meanwhile, Mr. Gene Tunney was building an outstanding record. He started fighting in 1915 and by the time he fought Dempsey in 1926, had boxed more than 65 contests, scored 47 knockouts and lost only one fight - to Harry Greb. He later defeated Greb twice and bested him once in a "no decision" bout.

Gene Tunney

During this time, Tunney knocked out Georges Carpentier. He also knocked out Tommy Gibbons, something Dempsey had not accomplished. Gene was the American light-heavyweight champion before moving into the heavyweight ranks.

Tunney was a beautiful fighter with a good left jab and a sharp hitting right hand. He was the greatest ring general among the heavyweights since the days of Jim Corbett.

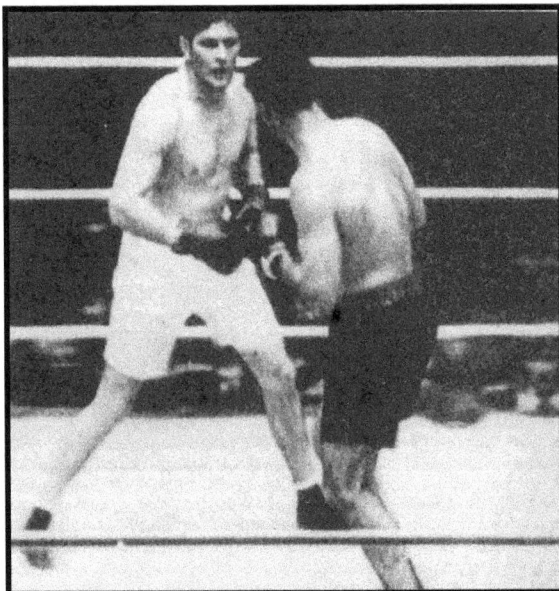

**Gene Tunney-Jack Dempsey
September 23 1926**

On September 23, 1926 in Philadelphia before more than 120,000 fans, Dempsey met Tunney for the title. Tunney was a master. He was at his best. Dempsey was rusty. Tunney won the championship in ten rounds.

Gene Tunney, the Fighting Marine, Slugs Heavyweight Crown Off Dempsey's Head

The Charleston (WV) Gazette
September 24 1926

Jack Sharkey-Harry Wills
October 12 1926

An up-and-coming puncher Jack Sharkey fought Harry Wills on October 12 in Brooklyn and defeated the black man on a foul in round thirteen. This loss gave "Tex" Rickard another excuse for not matching Harry with Dempsey and ended Wills' chances of getting a title fight.

Sharkey became a leading contender for a world championship fight while Wills joined Peter Jackson and Sam Langford as great black fighters who never got a shot at the title. However, the colored championship was still alive at this time. George Godfrey defeated Larry Gains in Buffalo on November 8 to claim it and beat Ed "Bearcat" Wright in a title defense shortly afterwards. He also beat "Cowboy" Billy Owens in a possible colored title bout in December.

Everyone wanted to see a rematch between Tunney and Dempsey but what about Sharkey? He was at the top of the list, had beaten Wills and added three wins to his record since. A contest was arranged between Dempsey and Sharkey with the winner to meet Tunney for the title.

On July 21, 1927 in New York City, Sharkey had the best of Dempsey for most of the fight. But in round seven, Dempsey sent a low punch to Sharkey's midsection. Sharkey grabbed his middle and looked towards the referee, claiming foul. Quick as a cat, Dempsey hooked his man and down he went - down and out.

Jack Dempsey-Jack Sharkey
July 21 1927

On September 22 in Chicago, Tunney met Dempsey a second time for the heavyweight crown. It was all Gene until round seven. Then Dempsey caught him on the ropes and with a flurry of punches, sent the ex-Marine to the canvas for the first and only time in his career.

In the heat of battle, Dempsey tried to get close to his man. Referee Dave Barry kept directing him to a neutral corner. Finally, Dempsey obeyed and went to the corner. Tunney was down all this time - from twelve to fourteen seconds by most counts. Tunney got up and survived the round.

In the eighth round, Gene scored a knockdown and clearly outboxed Jack the rest of the way to win in ten rounds. Reports vary on the attendance but it seems that the famous "long count" contest passed into history with at least 80,000 observers present.

**Gene Tunney-Jack Dempsey
September 22 1927**

Gene Tunney Remains World's Champion; Gets Decision in 10th Round

**The Palatine (IL) Enterprise, September 23 1927
Reprinted by permission of the Daily Herald, Arlington Heights, Illinois**

Jack Sharkey's career was stymied by his loss to Dempsey. Two fights in New York in early 1928 did not help. He drew with Tom Heeney and lost to Johnny Risko but then got back on track. He knocked out Jack Delaney and Leo Gates and defeated Arthur DeKuh to finish out the year.

On May 15, 1928 in Kansas City, "Big" Bill Hartwell added his name to the braggers' list of fighters who defeated Jack Johnson when he stopped the former champion in six rounds. Bill was a large man and plenty strong. He punched with stiff blows but he lacked good boxing skills.

His overall career was an up-and-down affair but during his ring tenure, in addition to Johnson, he gained wins over such men as James "Tut" Jackson, Cecil "Seal" Harris, Brad Simmons, Neil Clisby, Lee Anderson, Larry Gains, Bob Lawson and Roy "Ace" Clark.

"Big" Bill Hartwell

Neil Clisby

Neil Clisby was a popular fighter around this time. His career had been mediocre. However, he sported a 13-1 mark with a "no contest" and a "no decision" bout over his last 15 contests of 1927-1928. He had posted wins over "Long" Tom Hawkins, Bob Lawson, Mack House and John Lester Johnson.

Tunney fought one more time following his two victories over Dempsey - on July 26, 1928 in New York against Tom Heeney, a tough Australian. Tunney boxed his man, wore him down and stopped him in round eleven. Following this fight, Tunney retired.

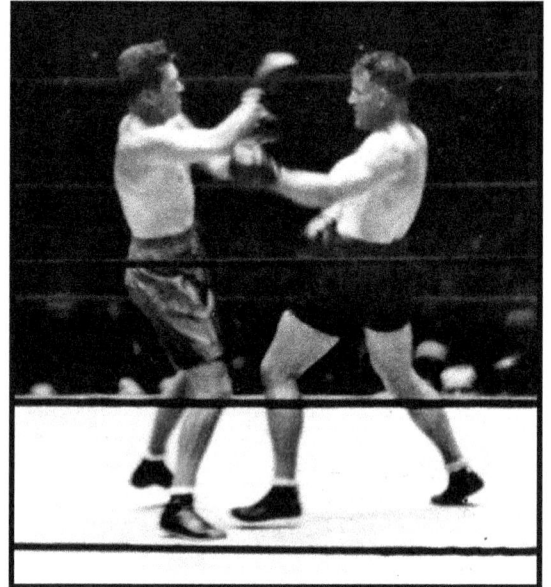

Gene Tunney-Tom Heeney
July 26 1928

The heavyweight division was without a world champion. There was no dominant fighter in the weight class at this time and none in sight. The period from 1928 until the mid-thirties when Joe Louis came on the scene has been called the "dark ages" of the division.

Cecil "Seal" Harris

At this time in 1928, powerful George Godfrey was the colored champion and considered by many to be the best heavyweight around. He had beaten Leon "Bombo" Chevalier, "Long" Tom Hawkins, Jake Kilrain and Neil Clisby in colored title defenses in 1927. He also won two other possible colored title bouts that year.

But in June of 1928, he lost to Johnny Risko, the white boxer. Then, in August he lost the colored crown to Larry Gains. In December, Gains met Cecil "Seal" Harris in a "no decision" contest. Afterwards, Gains pursued other fight interests in Europe and Harris claimed the colored title.

While there was no outstanding fighter among the heavies at this time, there were some good men. The best were Jack Sharkey, W.L. "Young" Stribling, Johnny Risko, Paulino Uzcudun of Spain and Max Schmeling of Germany.

W.L. "Young" Stribling

Paulino Uzcudun

64

Max Schmeling

On April 4, 1928 in Berlin, Max Schmeling won the heavyweight championship of Germany when he defeated Franz Diener in fifteen rounds. He carried a record of 37-4-3 with 27 knockouts at this point in his career.

Max had won the German light-heavyweight championship in 1926 and the European light-heavyweight championship in 1927. He came to America and on November 23, 1928 in New York City, knocked out Joe Monte in eight rounds.

The famous promoter George Lewis "Tex" Rickard passed away on January 6, 1929 in Miami Beach following surgery for appendicitis. Famous for being where the action was, Rickard had "wheeled and dealed" in the Klondike, in Nevada, New York, Boston and other places during his career.

"Tex" promoted some of the biggest fights in boxing history - in particular, the Jack Johnson-Jim Jeffries bout of 1910 and the second Jack Dempsey-Gene Tunney bout that attracted over 100,000 fans and garnered net receipts of more than two million dollars.

Schmeling continued his winning streak in early 1929. He beat Joe Sekyra, knocked out Pietro Corri, stopped Johnny Risko and defeated the Spaniard Paulino Uzcudun in fifteen rounds in New York City.

A Square Sport

GEORGE LEWIS RICKARD, better known as "Tex" Rickard, died Sunday morning in a hospital at Miami Beach, Fla., following an operation for acute appendicitis. He began his notable career as a promoter of the boxing game in Nevada nearly a quarter of a century ago and when death claimed him, he was manager of the new Madison Square Garden in New York, where he promoted sporting contests of every form.

The Salt Lake (UT) Tribune
January 7 1929

In April and June of 1929, Bob Lawson won against Al Walker and launched claims for the colored heavyweight championship but was not generally recognized. Lawson had made such claims since 1927. Cecil "Seal" Harris retained his colored title claim in a couple of bouts in May 1929 and then lost to "Long" Tom Hawkins in June. Tom defended three times before losing to Ed "Bearcat" Wright in October. Wright beat "Cowboy" Billy Owens a month later and won a rematch with Hawkins in January 1930. Ed lost to Al Walker in June and was out as the colored champion. Walker then fought Leonard Dixon and Carl Carter in possible colored title bouts but his claim did not amount to much as most people felt that George Godfrey was the best of the black fighters.

Jack Sharkey

Jack Sharkey kept his string of victories alive in 1929. He beat Meyer "K.O." Christner, W.L. "Young" Stribling and Tommy Loughran.

Jack could box and punch but was an up-and-down fighter. When he was "up," he could fight with most heavyweights. When he was down, he was a rather poor scrapper.

A huge heavyweight from Italy named Primo Carnera made a fine record for himself in Europe during 1928 and 1929. He came to the United States in 1930 and began to hammer the top heavies. By October, he had won twenty-three fights in twenty-four outings, including twenty-two knockouts.

During these contests, the big man had beaten the likes of Sully Montgomery, Chuck Wiggins, Jack McAuliffe II, Neil Clisby, Leon "Bombo" Chevalier, George Cook, Meyer "K.O." Christner, Jack Gross, Ed "Bearcat" Wright, Riccardo Bertazzolo and Pat McCarthy.

Primo Carnera

WIGGINS ADDED TO CARNERA VICTIMS

Italian Man Mountain Knocks Out Hoosier in Second Round at St Louis

ST. LOUIS, Mar. 18 (A. P.)—Chuck Wiggins, Indianapolis battler of policemen, found the going too tough against Primo Carnera, the Man Mountain from Venice, here last night and the Italian won his tenth straight American knockout victory, Wiggins succumbing in the second round of a scheduled ten-round bout.

The Monitor-Index and Democrat (Moberly, MO), March 18 1930

Some rated his skills very good. Historian Joseph Page (2011 Introduction) wrote, "I'll not argue that he was a great fighter, but he was adequate and at times very good."

Big George Godfrey beat Leonard Dixon in December of 1929, then further impressed boxing fans with his power and fighting skills when he knocked out Roy "Ace" Clark on March 24, 1930 and stopped Jack Rozier on May 16. All three wins were for his colored championship claim.

On February 27, 1930, Jack Sharkey stopped Phil Scott in three rounds in Miami and set the stage for a title bout with Max Schmeling. On June 12 in New York, he met Schmeling for the heavyweight title. He was "up" and punched the German around the ring. Jack was ahead on points when it happened.

During the fourth round while he was attacking, he sent a left into Schmeling's midsection. It may have been low. Schmeling acted like it was - he doubled up, grabbed himself and sank to the floor. Referee Jim Crowley, not seeing a low blow, started the count. The bell rang.

Schmeling's corner was calling for a foul. Crowley consulted with judges at ringside but they saw nothing. Some reporters began screaming for a foul. Crowley gave in, the decision was made. Schmeling was declared champion by foul.

**Max Schmeling-Jack Sharkey
June 12 1930**

George Godfrey

One contest in which the giant Italian Carnera did not finish his man was with big George Godfrey on June 23, 1930 in Philadelphia. Godfrey, a powerful man and stiff puncher, fouled Carnera in round five. After this fight, Godfrey notched three knockout wins in colored title defenses and in December of 1930 fought a draw with Ed "Bearcat" Wright for the black heavyweight title.

Big George was a force - an awesome hitter and a top heavyweight contender during the 1925-1930 years. He won 56 bouts during this time and scored 46 knockouts. At his peak, many fans thought he was the best heavyweight fighting at that time. Yet he never received a world title shot.

On August 25, 1930 in San Francisco, two very talented young battlers squared off. Frankie Campbell, whose real name was Francisco Camelli, had a record of 33-3-2 with 26 knockouts. He met Max Baer who carried a record of 23-3-0 with 19 knockouts. In the fifth round, Baer took control of the fight and landed haymakers, one of which left Campbell hanging on the ropes. Baer followed up with blow after blow. Campbell slumped to the floor unconscious. He failed to gain consciousness in the ring and was taken to a local hospital. Thirteen hours later, he died.

In the fifth round Baer backed his opponent into a corner and sent a smashing right to the jaw. Campbell undoubtedly knocked out, collapsed in a sitting posture on the ropes. He was defenseless under the blows the Livermore boxer continued to direct at him. Finally Campbell, unconscious, slipped to the floor and referee Irwin raised Baer's hand in victory without the formality of a count.

The Greeley (CO) Daily Tribune
August 27 1930

Primo Carnera's only loss during 1930 was to Jim Maloney on October 7 in Boston in ten rounds. Primo avenged his loss to Maloney on March 5, 1931 in Miami when he beat the American in ten rounds. The well-muscled Italian followed this win with six straight knockouts.

Jim Maloney

On July 3, 1931, Max Schmeling defended the championship in Cleveland against W.L. "Young" Stribling and won by a technical knockout in fifteen rounds. It was the only fight the German had engaged in since he won from Jack Sharkey in 1930. He would not fight again until 1932.

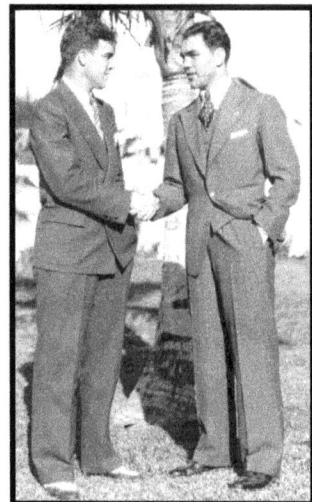

W.L. "Young" Stribling
shaking hands with
Max Schmeling

In Brooklyn on July 22, 1931, Jack Sharkey boxed a fifteen-round draw with tough Mickey Walker. Mick was the middleweight champion who had relinquished his title to move up and fight larger men. George Godfrey fought Cecil "Seal" Harris on August 24 in Toronto and won back the colored heavyweight championship. On October 12 in Brooklyn, Primo Carnera tangled with the unpredictable Sharkey for the first time. Sharkey was "up" and defeated the giant Italian in fifteen rounds.

Following this setback, Primo got busy and rang up nine wins in a row, seven of them in Europe. He suffered another loss on May 30, 1932 in London to the talented black heavyweight Larry Gains.

Larry Gains

Still determined to get a shot at the title, Carnera set out yet again and entered the ring eighteen more times in 1932. He won seventeen fights, scoring fourteen knockouts.

Sharkey got his rematch with Schmeling for the championship on June 21 in Long Island City, New York and made his dream come true. He beat Max in fifteen rounds to become champion.

Sharkey now boasted a record of 35-8-2 and had finally won the crown despite his erratic performances from time to time. What's more, he was ready to defend his title of champion.

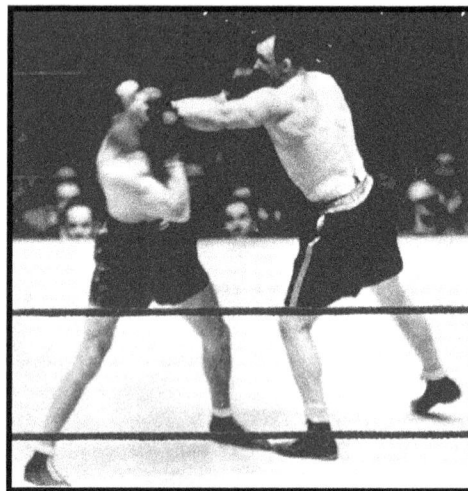
Jack Sharkey-Max Schmeling
June 21 1932

MAX BATTERS WALKER FOR RIGHT TO MEET SHARKEY AGAIN

New York Bout Has Pitiful Ending As Schmeling Pounds "Toy Bulldog" From Post to Post in Eighth—Jack Kearns Leaps to Ring to Save Mickey

The Sun (Lowell, MA), September 27 1932
All rights reserved. Reproduced with the permission of MediaNews Group Inc.

September 26, 1932 was a busy night in boxing. In New York, Max Schmeling battered Mickey Walker and stopped the gallant "Toy Bulldog" in eight rounds.

In Chicago, that tough heavyweight Max Baer beat Gerald "Tuffy" Griffiths. This was Baer's twelfth straight victory against top competition since a loss to Paulino Uzcudun in 1931. He was a man to watch.

BAER TRIUMPHS OVER GRIFFITHS

Scores Technical K. O. in Seventh, Giving Foe a Sound Beating

The Monitor-Index (Moberly, MO)
September 27 1932

Primo Carnera-Ernie Schaaf
February 10 1933

Carnera met Jack Sharkey in Long Island City on June 29 for the title and the big man knocked Sharkey out in six rounds. Carnera was now champion. According to Page (2011 p 199) "… Carnera was an adequate fighter - no Joe Louis, but an adequate fighter - who used his size, strength, conditioning and toughness to reach the pinnacle of the boxing world."

In 1933 on February 10 in New York City, Carnera knocked out Ernie Schaaf in thirteen rounds. He had earned his shot at the title. Schaaf subsequently died, likely from injuries received in this fight.

On June 8, hard-hitting Max Baer stopped the former champion Schmeling in ten rounds in New York City. The California slugger was working his way towards a shot at the heavyweight crown.

Max Baer-Max Schmeling
June 8 1933

Primo Carnera-Jack Sharkey
June 29 1933

George Godfrey retained his colored heavyweight title in defenses during late 1932 and early 1933 but on October 9, 1933 against Obie Walker, he lost. Walker, who boasted a splendid record of just two losses in 36 contests, including 21 knockouts, was now the champion.

Carnera defended his world title (also the International Boxing Union, IBU version) against Paulino Uzcudun on October 22, 1933 in Rome and won in fifteen rounds. He defended again on March 1, 1934 against Tommy Loughran in Miami and won in fifteen rounds. He was on a collision course with the hard-hitting Max Baer.

Talented Steve Hamas had a short career, 1930-1935, but an impressive one. His record during his ring tenure was 35-4-2 with 27 knockouts. Steve had earned a 29-0-0 record when he suffered his first loss to Lee Ramage in Los Angeles. During his career, he split four fights with Tommy Loughran and defeated such men as Max Schmeling, Art Lasky, Armand Emanuel, Lee Ramage and George LaRocco.

Steve Hamas

Max Baer-Primo Carnera
June 14 1934

On June 14, 1934 in Long Island City, Carnera fought Max Baer for the championship. Baer knocked Carnera down eleven times. The fight was stopped in the eleventh round and the new champion was pleasure loving Max Baer.

A hard-hitting puncher drawing attention at this time was big Art Lasky, a Minnesota product. Lasky began fighting in 1930 and was unbeaten in 14 bouts before he was bested by Dick Daniels in 1932.

Art Lasky and his wife, Ima

During 1933-1934, Art ran off another streak of 14 bouts without a loss. Word was out that his punches had some "kick" and merited concern when facing him in the ring. Before wrapping up his career in 1939, Art beat such men as "Tiger" Jack Fox, Lee Ramage, King Levinsky, Fred Lenhart, Paul Pantaleo, Joe Sekyra, Joe Doktor, George "Sonny Boy" Walker, Jack Roper, Johnny Paychek, Bennett "Buck" Everett, Harold "Millionaire" Murphy, Andy Mitchell and Tony Cancela.

Max Baer

The new champion Baer was a man with talent. He was a powerful puncher and he could take it too, but he had a major weakness. He did not like to train and it proved to be his downfall. Following his ascension to the heavyweight throne, "Good Time" Max piddled around and fought mostly exhibitions.

Another up-and-coming fighter on the scene was Lee Ramage. He had started boxing in 1930 and had gotten better over the years. A slick competitor, surprisingly the longest win streak he ever had was ten.

Not a heavy hitter, clever boxing was Lee's forte. Using it well, he was 2-1-1 against Maxie Rosenbloom in four contests and defeated such other men as Steve Hamas, Gerald "Tuffy" Griffiths, Pete Cerkan, Asa "Ace" Hudkins, Yale Okun, Sandy Garrison Casanova, Donald "Red" Barry, Ed "Unknown" Winston, Hans Birkie, Alvin "Babe" Hunt, Meyer "K.O." Christner, King Levinsky, Frank Rowsey, Leo Lomski and Jimmy Hanna during his career.

Lee Ramage

Another explosive hitter was making his way through opponents at this time. Charley Retzlaff, a blistering puncher throughout his career, began fighting in 1929 and was unbeaten in 21 bouts when he lost for the first time - by disqualification in 1930. He avenged that loss in the very next bout and ran off ten more wins until he lost to Joe Sekyra in 1931.

Before he hung up the gloves, Charley had beaten such men as Jim Braddock, Art Lasky, Al Ettore, Stanley Poreda, Johnny Risko, Tom Heeney, Les Marriner, Paul Pantaleo, Les Kennedy, Ralph Ficucello, Hans Birkie, Frank Rowsey, Dick Daniels and Emmett Rocco. He scored 52 knockouts in 75 bouts and lost just 8 times.

Charley Retzlaff

The erratic Jim Braddock was selected as Max Baer's opponent in his first defense. In his last twenty-four fights, Braddock had nine wins. He was a plodder, not flashy but fairly tough and could take it. He was the type to absorb whatever Baer dished out and keep coming. This was one style that might beat an out of shape Max Baer. The International Boxing Union (IBU) withdrew its recognition of Baer as champion for fighting Braddock.

Jim Braddock

The two men met on June 13, 1935 in Long Island City. Baer obviously took Jim lightly. He even clowned around during the bout - funny, maybe, but he lost the title in fifteen rounds. Mr. Braddock was now the heavyweight champion. Fans had questions about the result but the National Boxing Association (NBA), Great Britain and the New York State Athletic Commission (NYSAC) accepted it.

In New York on June 25, a little over a year after his loss to Baer, Primo Carnera met the young, outstanding prospect Joe Louis and was stopped in six rounds.

Jim Braddock-Max Baer
June 13 1935

On July 20, 1935 in England, Larry Gains became the colored champion when he defeated Obie Walker in fifteen rounds. Gains never defended and let the title slip into oblivion.

Things continued to go badly for Max Baer. In his next outing on September 24, just three months after losing the title to Braddock, Baer was knocked out in four rounds by Louis. Baer could hit but Louis could hit too - and Joe was quicker with his punches.

Joe Louis-Primo Carnera
June 25 1935

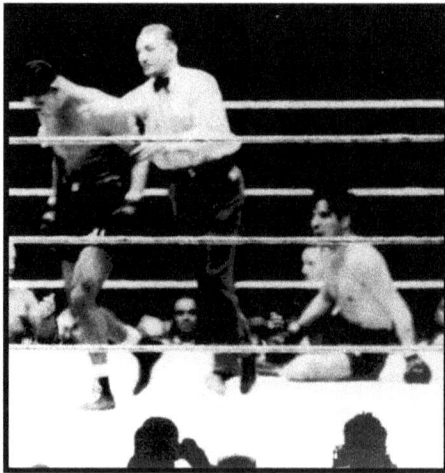

**Joe Louis-Max Baer
September 24 1935**

On October 2, 1935 in Brussels, Belgium, big George Godfrey won the International Boxing Union (IBU) heavyweight title with a victory over Pierre Charles.

Regarding the young Joe Louis, he looked like a fantastic prospect - and he was. No one realized the greatness this young man possessed but Joe's outstanding ability would reveal itself in time.

Louis was undefeated and on his way up. He could hit! Already, he had beaten many talented fighters besides Primo Carnera and Max Baer - Donald "Red" Barry, Lee Ramage, Natie Brown and King Levinsky to name four.

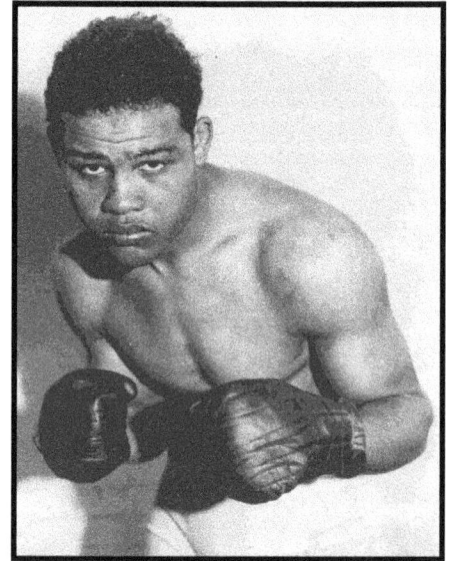

Joe Louis

On December 13 in New York City, Louis stopped Paulino Uzcudun in four rounds. Following a knockout win over Charley Retzlaff on January 17, 1936 in Chicago, Louis suffered a major setback in his sojourn to the title.

**Max Schmeling-Joe Louis
June 19 1936**

Joe fought former champion Max Schmeling in New York City on June 19 and lost by knockout in round twelve. The German's awkward style baffled Joe, who appeared to be off in his timing. He did not look like the Louis of previous fights.

The Evansville (Illinois) Intelligencer ran an article on June 20 reporting that Adolf Hitler congratulated Max Schmeling for his victory over Joe Louis. In it, "The Führer" was said to have ordered flowers sent to Mrs. Schmeling in Berlin.

Joe came right back in his next fight two months later against another former champion. This time it was Jack Sharkey in New York City on August 18. Louis knocked out Sharkey in three rounds. He was on track and won three more fights in 1936. It would be 1950 before Joe lost again.

Joe Louis was almost the perfect fighter. He was patient and he had a quick, stiff jab. He punched with fast combinations and always kept his balance. He did not say much. Instead, he let his fists do the talking and the echoes can still be heard. However, he could be boxed. It was best to keep away from him and not encourage him to mix it up. His greatest weakness probably was his chin. He could be hurt.

On June 22, 1937 in Chicago, Jim Braddock fought Louis for the heavyweight championship. Joe won by a knockout in eight rounds. The division again had a dominate fighter and champion. He would become perhaps the most dominate fighter in heavyweight history.

Louis defended his title two months later on August 30 in New York against Tommy Farr from Wales. The Welshman had beaten Tommy Loughran and Bob Olin in 1936 and Max Baer in early 1937.

Joe Louis-Jim Braddock
June 22 1937

Joe Louis-Tommy Farr
August 30 1937

Farr was an excellent boxer whose style confused Joe. Tommy was aggressive and tenacious throughout the fight and made it competitive. Louis cracked Farr's nose in the first round on his way to a fifteen-round decision win. Many fans thought Farr won but most agreed with the official verdict.

Louis defended three times in 1938. On February 23 in New York City, he knocked out Nathan Mann in three rounds.

On April 1 in Chicago, Joe knocked out Harry Thomas in five rounds.

Joe Louis-Nathan Mann
February 23 1938

Thomas Goes Out In Fifth

Brown Bomber Now Looks Toward Schmeling

Chicago (AP)—Brown Bomber Joe Louis, with another notch in his blazing fistic guns, trained his sights today on the only man ever to bring him down—Max Schmeling.

A slashing, fifth round knock-out last night of Harry Thomas, Louis' third successful heavyweight title defense since he won the crown last June, was "just another fight" to the youthful Detroit Negro. Ahead of him, and constantly in his mind, was the long-awaited chance of settling an old score.

"I'll go at Schmeling from the start and I know I can beat him," he said after the Thomas victory, the Bomber's 38th in 39 professional battles. "I been thinking of Schmeling ever since he knocked me out two years ago and I'll even things up."

The Hutchinson (KS) News
April 2 1938

The champion gained a revenge knockout win over Max Schmeling on June 22 in New York. The contest turned out to be a grudge fight. Instead of coming out in his usual steady shuffle, Louis moved quickly towards the German and shot out quick hard jabs. He brought over a straight, stiff right hand - flush on Schmeling's jaw. He moved in and pounded home lefts and rights. Schmeling was floored three times before his corner threw in the towel. Joe won in the first round.

Joe Louis-Max Schmeling
June 22 1938

Joe defended four times in 1939. On January 25 in New York City, he finished John Henry Lewis in a single round. On April 17 in Los Angeles, he polished off Jack Roper in one round.

On June 28, Louis met the rowdy "Two-Ton" Tony Galento in New York. Galento was a sturdy, squat brawler who claimed he had never been downed. He fought from a low-slung crouch, striking out and leaping forward with hard shots.

Joe was going through his usual motions of shuffling, jabbing, stalking, tossing a hook here, a cross there when it suddenly happened. In round three, Galento caught the champion with a shot and down went Joe. "The Brown Bomber" got up somewhat dazed but lasted the round and ended matters in the next round.

A little over two months later, Galento got into the ring again. On September 15 with his "I'll moida da bum" attitude, he met Lou Nova in Philadelphia in what turned out to be one of the roughest, dirtiest brawls ever. Referee George Blake should have disqualified

Joe Louis-Tony Galento
June 28 1939

Galento early on but he let him continue. Tony thumbed Nova in his eyes frequently - among other foul tactics - and eventually won the bout that was stopped in round fourteen.

On September 20, 1939 in Detroit, Louis fought Bob Pastor, a superb, clever boxer who had gone ten rounds with Joe in 1937. At this point in time, Bob had wins over some good men - Al McCoy, Lee Ramage, Steve Dudas, Al Ettore, Chuck Crowell, Freddie Fiducia and Tony Shucco to name a few. Pastor was floored several times early in this bout but then kept his distance and boxed cautiously. Joe caught up with him in round eleven and ended it.

In 1940, Louis defended four more times. On February 9 in New York City, he had the toughest challenge of the year. His opponent was Arturo Godoy from Chile.

Bob Pastor

Joe Louis-Arturo Godoy
June 20 1940

Godoy was rough, durable and strong. He fought in an unorthodox low, crouching style which bothered Joe. Louis seemed to be "off" throughout the fight but won in a fifteen-round split decision.

Following the win over Godoy, Louis stopped Johnny Paychek on March 29 in two rounds. In a return match with Godoy on June 20, Joe finished his troublesome foe in eight rounds.

The last title fight in 1940 was on December 16 when Louis met Al McCoy. Joe had not fought in nearly six months and was a little rusty. McCoy was an experienced fighter with 90 contests under his belt but was on the decline and had lost five of his last eight bouts. Louis stopped McCoy in six rounds.

Louis Looks Forward to Conn Fight After Battering McCoy

The Sun (Lowell, MA), December 17 1940
All rights reserved. Reproduced with the permission of MediaNews Group Inc.

Top Heavyweight Boxers of 1921-1940

1. Jack Dempsey
2. Joe Louis
3. Gene Tunney
4. Max Schmeling
5. George Godfrey

Top Heavyweight Bouts of 1921-1940

1. Jack Dempsey-Luis Angel Firpo, September 14 1923, New York, New York
2. Joe Louis-Max Schmeling #2, June 22 1938, New York, New York
3. Gene Tunney-Jack Dempsey #2, September 22 1927, Chicago, Illinois
4. Billy Miske-"K.O." Bill Brennan #4, November 7 1923, Omaha, Nebraska
5. Max Baer-Primo Carnera, June 14 1934, Long Island City, New York

Jack Dempsey-Georges Carpentier
July 2 1921

Chapter Four

The Years 1941-1960

Joe Louis vowed to be a fighting champion. In 1941, he fought one title bout a month for the first six months. Writers called his opponents "The Bum of the Month Club." Actually, some of these fighters were pretty good.

On January 31 in New York City, Louis knocked out "Red" Burman in five rounds. Two weeks later, on February 17, he knocked out Gus Dorazio in two rounds in Philadelphia.

Gus Dorazio

On March 21 in Detroit, Joe fought huge Abe Simon, a 254-pounder who was ponderous but tough and durable. It took Joe thirteen rounds to dispose of him.

In St. Louis on April 8, Louis stopped cagey Tony Musto in nine rounds. Then, on May 23 in Washington, DC, Joe ran into big and tough Jacob "Buddy" Baer, the brother of former champion Max Baer.

**Joe Louis-Abe Simon
March 21 1941**

Louis Stops Buddy Baer In Rousing Title Fight

**The Salt Lake (UT) Tribune
May 24 1941**

In round one, Baer smashed the champ with a powerful hook that toppled him over the ropes onto the ring apron. Joe climbed back into the ring and proceeded to hammer away at Baer. At the end of round six, Louis fired some punches which Baer claimed were deliberately tossed after the bell. He refused to answer the bell for round seven. Louis won by disqualification.

Conn Stops Knox In Eighth Round

Pittsburgh Bill Pounds Dayton Boy Into Helplessness in Smoky City

The Salt Lake (UT) Tribune
May 27 1941

Billy Conn, the cracker jack boxer and talented light-heavyweight champ of the world, readied himself for his title bout against Joe Louis by finishing off Charles "Buddy" Knox in eight rounds in Pittsburgh. Conn was such a clever boxer that fighting men much larger than he was posed no problem.

On June 18 in New York City, before more than 54,000 fans, Joe had a close call against the quick Conn. Billy was cocky and confident. He boxed superbly against the champion and was ahead on two judges' cards after twelve rounds. Advised to box and stay away from Joe for the remaining rounds, Conn chose to move in and try for a knockout. Louis ended the fight in round thirteen.

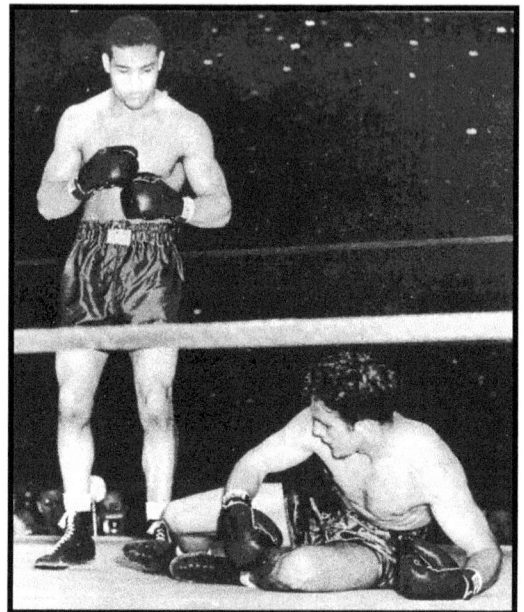

Joe Louis-Billy Conn
June 18 1941

The champion next fought Lou Nova on September 29 in New York City. It was a rather quiet fight until round six when Nova became aggressive. He hit Louis with a hard right to the ear. Louis responded with a hook to the head. Nova again fired a punch at the champion which grazed the chin. Once more, Louis came back - with a shot that missed.

Then, in a flash, Louis cracked Nova flush on the button and down went the challenger. He struggled to his feet and wobbled around the ring with Louis in pursuit. Joe finally knocked him to the floor again. The fight ended in this round.

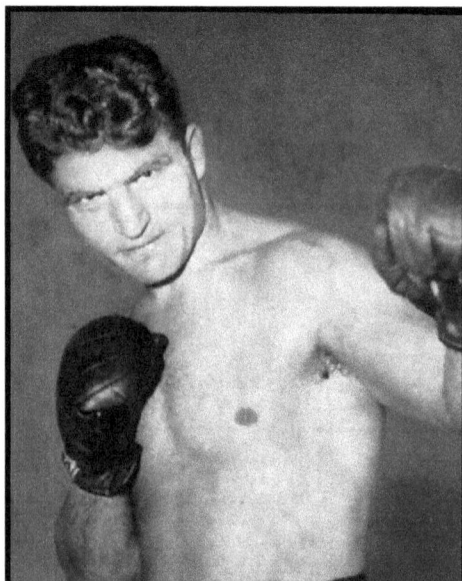

Lou Nova

On January 9, 1942, Louis fought "Buddy" Baer in a rematch in New York City. Louis was ready for this one. He exploded quickly and knocked Baer out in round one. The champion donated his purse to the Navy Relief Fund.

On March 27, Louis again fought a rematch. This time it was with big Abe Simon in New York City. It took Louis six rounds to stop Simon. Joe donated this purse to the Army Relief Fund.

Louis entered the United States Army in 1942 and boxed exhibitions during 1944 and 1945. The New York State Athletic Commission (NYSAC) recognized a win over Johnny Davis in 1944 as a title fight. Upon leaving the Army, he got down to business once again.

Joe Louis-Jacob "Buddy" Baer
January 9 1942

Lee Savold began fighting in 1933 and fought through 1952. He was perhaps at his best during the early 1940s. Always a rugged and durable warrior, Savold went through periods of winning and losing but kept hammering away at the profession he loved. He is probably best known for his fights against Joe Louis in 1951 and Rocky Marciano in 1952, both six-round losses. Lee was just plain tough.

Lee Savold

Some of the top men Lee defeated during his career were Gus Dorazio, Joe Baksi, Lou Nova, Lem Franklin, Tony Musto, Bruce Woodcock, Nate Bolden, Charles "Buddy" Knox, Maurice Strickland, Solly Krieger, Erv Sarlin, Ted Wint, Bill Poland and Al Hoosman.

On June 19, 1946 in New York, Joe Louis fought a rematch with Billy Conn who had also served in the United States Army and boxed exhibitions. By now both men were older with slower footspeed. This hurt Conn more than Louis. During the fight, Conn did little or no leading. He just ran. Fans booed. Louis caught up with him in round eight and finished him off.

Louis defended the championship once again in 1946. It was on September 18, also in New York, against Tami Mauriello. In the first round, Tami struck a blow that sent Louis across the ring and came close to downing the champ. As soon as Joe recovered and put in the punches, it was over.

Joe Louis-Tami Mauriello
September 18 1946

Jimmy Bivins

Jimmy Bivins was a talented boxer of the 1940s who began as a middleweight, moved up to light-heavyweight and then on to heavyweight. He ran off 19 straight wins at the start of his career. Then, following a tough 7-5 stretch, Bivins went on a 26-0-1 tear. Jimmy could box and smack too.

Elmer "Violent" Ray was a big banger during the 1940s. Elmer had a so-so career when he first began but from March 1940 until March of 1947 when he fought "Jersey" Joe Walcott in Miami, he had earned sixty-six wins in sixty-nine bouts. Included was a victory over crafty Walcott in November of 1946.

Elmer "Violent" Ray

Walcott won a ten-round decision in their 1947 contest. Ray then ran off seven wins and claimed a win over Ezzard Charles in doing so. Charles gained revenge on May 7, 1948 in Chicago when he stopped Ray in nine rounds.

Joe Louis boxed a number of exhibitions after his win over Mauriello and then, on December 5, 1947 in New York City, he fought "Jersey" Joe Walcott for the crown. This bout was the closest Joe had come to losing his title since he had won it in 1937.

Joe Louis-"Jersey" Joe Walcott
December 5 1947

Louis defended poorly and had slow reflexes. He threw some good punches but not like the Louis of old. Walcott knocked him down in round one and again in round four. He hit the champion with good, solid punches time and time again. Walcott cost himself a decision win by retreating too much and not counter-punching. Louis won a split decision in fifteen rounds.

80

Six months later, on June 25, 1948 in New York, Louis met Walcott a second time for the championship. Walcott was his usual cagey self and slipped Louis' punches repeatedly. This time, however, Louis was the clear winner, knocking out Walcott in the eleventh round.

During the remainder of 1948 and early 1949, Louis boxed exhibitions. On March 1, 1949, Louis retired as an unbeaten champion. He continued to box exhibitions the rest of 1949 and through April of 1950.

Upon Louis' retirement, Walcott was a natural selection to fight for the title due to his two good efforts against Joe. The other man chosen to fight for the crown was Ezzard Charles, the highly skilled light-heavyweight who beat up on heavyweights.

Charles had lost only one fight since 1943. Louis backed these two men as contenders for the relinquished crown. The NBA recognized the contest between the two as a world title match. However, the New York State Athletic Commission (NYSAC) and the European Federations did not.

Ezzard Charles

On June 22, 1949 in Chicago, Charles defeated Walcott in fifteen rounds to win the NBA heavyweight championship.

Great Britain and the European Boxing Union (EBU) recognized Lee Savold as world heavyweight champion in June of 1950 when he defeated Bruce Woodcock.

Ezzard Charles-"Jersey" Joe Walcott
June 22 1949

Charles followed the Walcott victory with three straight wins in NBA title defenses. On August 10, 1949, he stopped Gus Lesnevich in seven rounds in New York, on October 14 in San Francisco, he knocked out Pat Valentino in eight rounds and on August 15, 1950, Ezzard finished Freddie Beshore in fourteen rounds in Buffalo.

Pat Valentino

Rocky Decisions La Starza in N.Y.

The Oakland (CA) Tribune
March 25 1950

Earlier in 1950, on March 24 in New York City, two outstanding battlers - Rocky Marciano, 25-0-0, and Roland LaStarza, 37-0-0, fought each other. In a very close fight, Marciano won a disputed decision. Rocky was a brawling power puncher who caught the eye of boxing people with this win.

Meanwhile, Joe Louis was in financial trouble with the United States Government over a matter concerning taxes. Many folks were encouraging him to fight once again for the title. Joe heard their voices and thought about the money he owed Uncle Sam. Finally, he challenged Charles to a fight and Ezzard accepted.

On September 27, Charles met Louis in New York and the very good, very sharp champion easily outpointed the old former champ in fifteen rounds. Charles was now recognized as the heavyweight champ by the NBA and the New York State Athletic Commission (NYSAC). Europe continued to recognize Lee Savold.

Rex Layne, a talented young fighter from Utah who had 25 victories and 18 knockouts against 1 loss and 2 draws, met "Jersey" Joe Walcott on November 24 in New York. Rex pulled off a big surprise by winning a ten-round decision over the crafty old warrior.

Ezzard Charles-Joe Louis
September 27 1950

The future looked bright for Layne who was moving up the heavyweight ladder very fast. After his win over Walcott, he would run off eight straight wins before meeting the greatest challenge of his career - Rocky Marciano in 1951.

Charles fought once more in 1950, on December 5, and knocked out Nick Barone in eleven rounds in Cincinnati in defense of his NBA heavyweight title.

Rex Layne-"Jersey" Joe Walcott
November 24 1950

During 1951, Ezzard made three successful NBA title defenses. He stopped Lee Oma in ten rounds on January 12 in New York City. Oma was a man with a long career that began in 1939. After some up-and-down fighting with streaks of talented boxing, he ran off a 15-1 record with one "no contest" bout that earned him the shot at the title. Following the loss to Charles, Oma retired.

Lee Oma

Charles Injured In Title Clash; To Be Sidelined For Two Months

Champ Retains Crown, Scores Booed Decision

Next, Ezzard won a fifteen-round decision over "Jersey" Joe Walcott on March 7 in Detroit but sustained an injury to his left ear in the process. Then, he won a fifteen-round decision over Joey Maxim, light-heavyweight champion, in Chicago on May 30.

The Kingsport (TN) Times
March 8 1951

Eddie Eagan weighs Rocky Marciano
as Rex Layne watches, July 12 1951

After Joe Louis defeated Lee Savold in June of 1951, the British Boxing Board of Control (BBBC) acknowledged Louis as heavyweight champion. The young slugger Rocky Marciano hit stride in mid-1951 by defeating another major contender on July 12 in New York City. He knocked out tough Rex Layne in six rounds.

It was a sweet victory for Rocky. Layne was a formidable opponent who sported a 34-1-2 record at the time with 24 knockouts. He had beaten such men as "Jersey" Joe Walcott, Bob Satterfield, Cesar Brion, Henry Hall, Albert "Turkey" Thompson, Joe Kahut, Bob Dunlap and Dave Whitlock.

A week later, on July 18 in Pittsburgh, Charles once again defended his title against "Jersey" Joe Walcott. This was the third time Charles and Walcott had fought for the heavyweight crown. Charles was a six to one favorite. In round seven, Walcott surprised Charles and the world by polishing off Ezzard to become the new champion.

"Jersey" Joe Walcott-Ezzard Charles
July 18 1951

83

"Jersey" Joe Walcott

At this point in time, Walcott was 37 years of age and one of the oldest fighters to win a world championship. "Jersey" Joe seemed to get better with age and had captured the most treasured prize in sports - the heavyweight championship of the world. Following this bout, all major organizations recognized Walcott as heavyweight champion.

One month after the Walcott-Charles fight, on August 27 in Boston, Marciano knocked out Freddie Beshore in four rounds. On October 26 in New York City, Rocky gained his greatest victory yet when he fought old Joe Louis.

Rocky Marciano-Joe Louis
October 26 1951

The former champion hit the young "Rock" with many good shots but his "steel-headed" opponent shook them off and continued his pursuit. He knocked Louis onto the ring apron in the process and won by a technical knockout in round eight.

A big man who had a splendid career during the 1940s and 1950s was Nino Valdes. Nino was good but never sensational in his ring contests.

Nino Valdes

From December of 1945 through June of 1952, he fought sparingly and lost only one contest. Following a downturn, he picked it up and was unbeaten from July of 1953 to his May of 1955 bout against Archie Moore. One last outstanding streak ran from October of 1956 to March of 1959 when he worked up a 12-1 mark.

From the beginning of his career, Bob Baker was a sterling prospect. He ran off 25 wins and a single draw prior to fighting Clarence Henry on November 23, 1951 in New York. His record at the time included wins over Marty Marshall, Jimmy Bivins, Omelio Agramonte, Rusty Payne, Sid Peaks, Abel Cestac and Elkins Brothers.

Bob Baker

Clarence Henry

Baker lost to Henry and struggled through his next few fights. Then, starting in May of 1954, he ran off a streak of 13 wins before losing to Tommy "Hurricane" Jackson on February 3, 1956 in New York. After this loss, Baker settled into mediocrity the remainder of his career.

Henry Upsets Baker in Explosive Eighth-Round Kayo
Hard-Hitting Californian Wants to Meet Rocky Marciano—First Defeat for Bob

The Sun (Lowell, MA), November 24 1951
All rights reserved. Reproduced with the
permission of MediaNews Group Inc.

Clarence Henry was light for a heavyweight but he threw sizzling punches. He weighed in the 180-190 pound range for his entire career and never worried much about the weight of his foes. The man could hit - no doubt about it.

Henry had been fighting since July 6, 1948 and had a record of 28-2-1. He finally got the attention he deserved when he knocked out the unbeaten Bob Baker. However, his career declined starting the very next year. Clarence had chalked up a 31-2-1 record heading into the last few of years of his career. His punch fading at this point, he lost four of his last seven contests and retired.

Roland LaStarza

On December 21, 1951 in New York City, Roland LaStarza fought the hard-hitting Dan Bucceroni. Roland had won ten fights without a loss since his 1950 fight against Marciano. He was a clever boxer and a solid hitter who owned a 47-1-0 mark.

Bucceroni was lean and lanky and a very explosive hitter. He boasted a record of 36-2-0. In a big surprise, Dan upset LaStarza in a ten-round decision. It now looked like a Bucceroni-Marciano head-on collision was forthcoming - but it never took place. LaStarza, however, had the title fight looming in his future.

Dan Bucceroni

Rocky Marciano roared into 1952 with three impressive wins - against Lee Savold, Gino Buonvino and Bernie Reynolds. He was now in a strong position to challenge for the title. Walcott had seen him and called him a "bow-and-arrow" puncher, not too hard to read.

Jersey Joe Decisions Charles To Keep Heavyweight Title

The Salt Lake (UT) Tribune
June 6 1952

On June 5, 1952, "Jersey" Joe Walcott met Ezzard Charles for the fourth time in a title bout. This time it was held in Philadelphia. Walcott was up to the task and defeated Charles in fifteen rounds to retain his crown.

On July 28 in New York City, Rocky Marciano met the experienced Harry "Kid" Matthews, a clever boxer who was expected to give the brawler from Brockton plenty of trouble. Rocky knocked him out in two rounds. The stage was set for the undefeated knockout puncher to rumble with the crafty old champion "Jersey" Joe Walcott.

At this time there was a lighter man - Bob Satterfield - who could punch with the best hitters ever. This fellow was at his best when weighing in the 180-185 pounds range. When speaking of sizzling hitters, one must talk about Bob.

Harry "Kid" Matthews

Bob Satterfield-Harold Johnson
August 6 1952

To the left, Satterfield floors Harold Johnson in 1952. When Bob fought, the seats were filled early because there was going to be red-hot action. Someone was going out - either Bob or his man.

Rocky Marciano was a throwback to the old days of fighting. He was a determined, relentless puncher - one of the hardest hitters ever. He was also one of the strongest. Marciano was not clever and his style was crude - but he had never been beaten! Bring on "Jersey" Joe!

On September 23 in Philadelphia, Walcott met Marciano for the crown. Right off the bat, in round one, "Jersey" Joe caught the challenger with a shot that put him down for the first time in his career. Rocky got up quickly and pursued Walcott. The aged slickster was no pushover.

Rocky Marciano

Rocky Marciano-"Jersey" Joe Walcott
September 23 1952

The fight was a good one with Walcott boxing cleverly and pasting Marciano with good hard shots off and on. Both men were punished by round six. Walcott was clearly ahead after twelve rounds. Marciano had to score a knockout to win.

In round thirteen, just as the men were entering an exchange of punches, Rocky's right-hand punch - "Suzy Q" - clipped Walcott on the chin. "Jersey" Joe tilted forward and collapsed onto the floor, knocked out. Marciano was the new heavyweight champion.

Eight months later, on May 15, 1953, the two men were matched in a return go in Chicago. In the first round, Marciano nailed Walcott with a good punch but not a great one. Walcott went down. It was over. Marciano retained his title.

Rocky Kayoes Joe in 2:25 of 1st

The Racine (WI) Journal-Times
May 16 1953

The disputed win over Roland LaStarza in 1950 had always bothered Marciano. He aimed to make it right. On September 24, 1953 in New York City, they met again - this time for the championship. LaStarza held his own against Rocky for six rounds but the heavy blows of the champion finally took their toll. In round eleven, Rocky stopped LaStarza to keep the crown.

Marciano defended against former champion Ezzard Charles in New York on June 17, 1954. Charles was slick. Rocky had his hands full. It was a contest that went the full fifteen rounds. Rocky won a close decision in a great fight!

Rocky Marciano-Roland LaStarza
September 24 1953

Exactly three months to the day in New York, the two men fought again for the title. Charles split the Rock's nose and it got bad.

Referee Al Berl considered stopping the fight after seven rounds. Warned of the referee's intentions, Marciano set out to end it and end it he did, in round eight.

Rocky retained the crown after a scare - still champion, still unbeaten.

Rocky Marciano-Ezzard Charles
June 17 1954

Don Cockell

On May 16, 1955 in San Francisco, Marciano took on Don Cockell, the British heavyweight champion. Rocky was easily better but struggled to finish off the European. He tossed one blockbuster punch after another but Cockell weathered the storm. Finally, Marciano stopped his man in round nine. Afterwards, he considered retirement.

Rocky defended one more time, against Archie Moore on September 21, 1955 in New York. Clever Archie dropped the champion in round two. Rocky got up and went after his man. He pounded his challenger throughout the contest, decked Moore five times and ended the battle in round nine. On April 27, 1956, Marciano retired unbeaten with a mark of 49-0-0.

Floyd Patterson, a former Olympic Gold Medal Champion, had accumulated a 29-1-0 record since turning professional in 1952.

He defeated Tommy "Hurricane" Jackson in twelve rounds on June 8, 1956 in New York City. The victory earned him a bout with Archie Moore to determine Marciano's successor as heavyweight champion.

Floyd Patterson

**Floyd Patterson-Archie Moore
November 30 1956**

On November 30, the young Patterson fought the aged but cagey Archie Moore in Chicago. He knocked out "The Old Mongoose" in five rounds to become the youngest heavyweight champion in boxing history.

Eight months passed and on July 29, 1957, Floyd and his extremely fast hands defended against Tommy "Hurricane" Jackson in New York City. Patterson won by a technical knockout in ten rounds. Jackson was bleeding from the mouth, nose and both brows. He was taken to the hospital the next day for his excessive bleeding.

Patterson then pulled a weird stunt by fighting the amateur heavyweight champion Pete Rademacher for the professional crown on August 22 in Seattle. It was a mismatch but not without excitement. Pete floored the champion in round two, exposing his weak chin. Floyd rose from the canvas and knocked out Rademacher in six rounds.

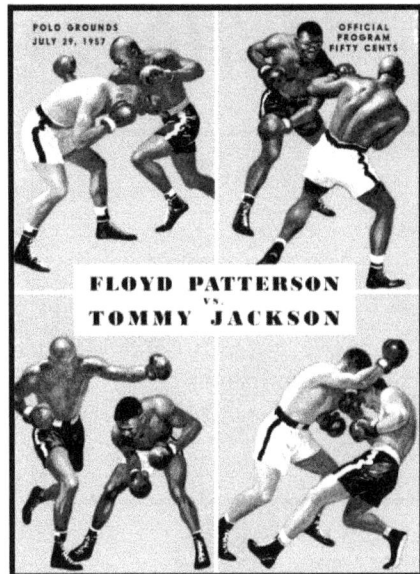
**Floyd Patterson-Tommy Jackson
Program, July 29 1957**

Eddie Machen

One year later on August 18, 1958 in Los Angeles, Patterson defended against the unbeaten Texan, Roy Harris, the "Pride of Cut and Shoot." The champion polished off the courageous Harris after twelve rounds of fighting.

Patterson was indeed a talented fighter with very fast hands but he had a fragile chin. However, he was a gallant warrior who persisted in getting up when downed.

There were some good heavies around at this time who were not getting their chance at the title - Eddie Machen, Nino Valdes, Cleveland "Big Cat" Williams, Zora Folley, Ingemar Johansson and Charles "Sonny" Liston - to name six.

Machen was 24-0-1 and a very good boxer who possessed a fine left jab and fast hands. Pressure was put upon the champion by writers to meet him next but Floyd ignored them. In Europe, Johansson was 20-0-0 and talked a lot about the good fighters he had knocked out - Hein Ten Hoff, Franco Cavicchi, Henry Cooper, Joe Erskine and Heinz Neuhaus. Johansson was not a clever boxer and he did not like to train - but he could hit!

Ingemar Johansson

Swede KOs Machen In 2:16 of 1st Round

The Tokyo (Japan) Pacific Stars and Stripes
September 15 1958

Machen went after the Swede. A win against a man with an unbeaten record just might get him a title shot. He should have been more careful.

On September 14, 1958 in Goteborg [Gothenburg], Sweden in the first round, Eddie walked into a right hand punch that Ingemar often referred to as the "Hammer of Thor." The bout ended then and there. Machen was now 24-1-1 and Patterson forgot about him. In Europe, Johansson was talking about a title shot.

Meanwhile, awesome "Sonny" Liston cleaned up some other contenders, defeating top men like Julio Mederos, Wayne Bethea, Frankie Daniels and Bert Whitehurst in 1958 and Mike DeJohn in 1959.

Cleveland Williams

An explosive puncher, Cleveland Williams was sporting a 43-2-0 record with 35 knockouts when he met Liston on April 15, 1959 in Miami Beach. Williams, "The Big Cat," pumped plenty of leather to "Sonny" but the man with the tough chin took it all, pounded Cleveland down and won in three rounds.

It was May 1, 1959 in Indianapolis when Patterson put his title on the line against Brian London. Floyd stopped the durable Britisher in eleven rounds.

Charles "Sonny" Liston

Patterson Retains Title By Knocking Out London in 11th

Republished with permission of The Galveston County (TX) Daily News
May 2 1959

At this point, Liston was 24-1-0 but Patterson did not want to meet this awesome creature in the ring. Instead, Floyd chose the Swede Johansson. Much ado had been made about Johansson's knockout win over Machen. Patterson trained diligently for the fight. Johansson, on the other hand, came to America, said he already had trained and did very little. He worked out lightly, sparred some, lounged around, walked in New York's Central Park

Casual Challenger
Ingo to Quit Training Five Days Before Bout

The Sun (Lowell, MA), June 18 1959
All rights reserved. Reproduced with the permission of MediaNews Group Inc.

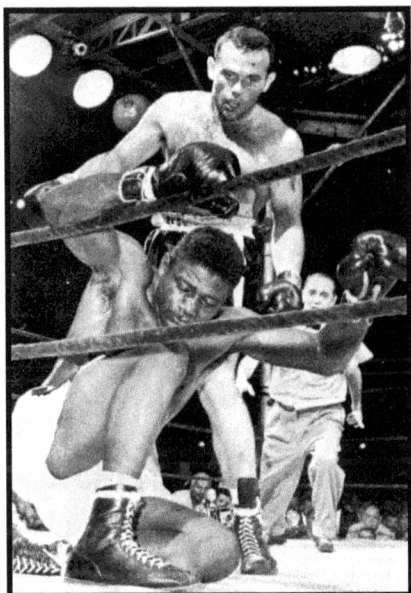

with his girl friend and said he was "letting the strength flow back into his bones." He referred to his left and right fists as "toonder and lighting." Writers scoffed at his remarks - but he was not kidding.

On June 26 in New York, Patterson met Johansson for the heavyweight championship. Patterson was bobbing and weaving in his usual style. Johansson was flicking out his left jab lightly. Suddenly in round three, it happened! "Ingo's Bingo," the booming right hand, crashed upon Patterson's chin. He went down. Up, down, up, down, up, down - seven times. Referee Ruby Goldstein stopped it and Johansson was the new heavyweight champion.

When asked by writers if he was surprised when he hit the heavyweight champion of the world and he went went down. Johansson responded, "No, I was surprised when he kept getting up."

Ingemar Johansson-Floyd Patterson
June 26 1959

The world was shocked and impressed. However, when former champion Rocky Marciano was asked if he could beat Johansson, Rocky replied, "If I said I could, I'd be bragging. If I said I couldn't, I'd be lying."

Liston went on to knockout Nino Valdes in August and stop Willi Besmanoff in December, both in 1959. Then, in early 1960 he stopped Howard King, Cleveland Williams (a second time) and Roy Harris. "Sonny" was now sporting a 29-1-0 record and waiting his turn for a title shot. It looked like that chance would never come.

Charles "Sonny" Liston-Cleveland Williams
March 21 1960

On June 20, 1960 in New York City, Johansson met Patterson in a return bout and he should have trained harder for this one. Floyd had. Patterson won by a knockout in five rounds to become the first heavyweight ever to regain the title. This was the last title fight of 1960.

Meanwhile, "Sonny" Liston continued to hammer the top heavyweights, knocking out Zora Folley in July and beating Eddie Machen in September.

Top Heavyweight Boxers of 1941-1960
1. Joe Louis
2. Charles "Sonny" Liston
3. Rocky Marciano
4. Ezzard Charles
5. Cleveland Williams

Top Heavyweight Bouts of 1941-1960
1. Rocky Marciano-"Jersey" Joe Walcott #1, September 23 1952, Philadelphia, Pennsylvania
2. Joe Louis-Billy Conn #1, June 18 1941, New York, New York
3. Rocky Marciano-Ezzard Charles #1, June 17 1954, New York, New York
4. Charles "Sonny" Liston-Cleveland Williams #1, April 15 1959, Miami Beach, Florida
5. Ingemar Johansson-Floyd Patterson #1, June 26 1959, New York, New York

Joe Louis, Ingemar Johansson and Jack Dempsey
1960

Chapter Five

The Years 1961-1980

On March 8, 1961 in Miami Beach, Charles "Sonny" Liston stopped Howard King in three rounds. This was the second time he had polished off King. He was now 32-1-0 and still waiting his turn at the title.

Floyd Patterson met Ingemar Johansson in the rubber match of their series on March 13 in Miami. Floyd emerged as the winner by a sixth-round knockout. It was a thrilling fight in which each man got in his punches.

Patterson had one more fight in 1961, beating Tom McNeeley in four rounds on December 4 in Toronto, Canada. Liston also fought on that date in Philadelphia and annihilated Albert Westphal in one round. When asked about fighting Liston, Patterson said he had denied him a title match due to his criminal record. He felt that if "Sonny" won, he would be an undesirable champion. But after years of declining to meet "Sonny," Floyd gave in to public pressure and scheduled "The Black Bear" for a title bout.

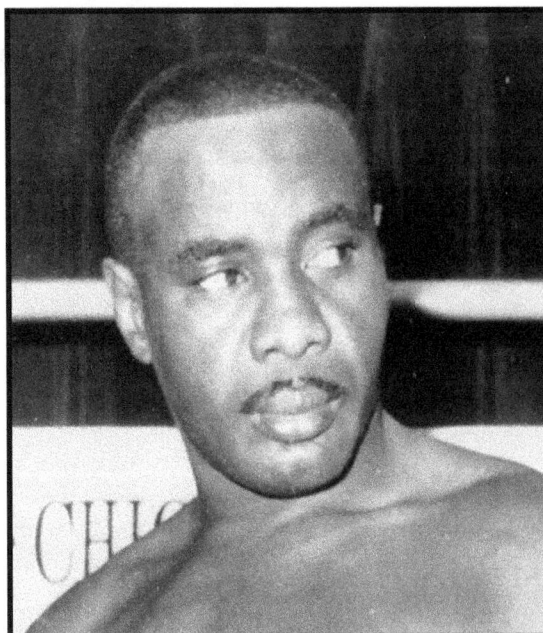

Charles "Sonny" Liston

Charles "Sonny" Liston-Floyd Patterson
September 25 1962

From 1958 until the day of the fight, "Sonny" Liston probably was the best heavyweight in the division. "Sonny" was a big man, very strong and a solid boxer with a thudding jab. He could deliver powerful smashes and take awesome punches. In addition, he had the resolute temperament to be a fighter. Until now, he had been unable to get a title fight.

Patterson often fought a lower-ranked man in defense of the title. Liston, on the other hand, made it his business to destroy the highest ranked man he could get into the ring.

On September 25, 1962 in Chicago, Liston got his chance with Patterson. The result was the same as most of Liston's fights, a knockout. He finished Floyd in round one. "Sonny" Liston was now heavyweight champion of the world, something he likely should have been for several years.

Ever since 1960, a young Olympic champion from Louisville named Cassius Clay had gained lots of attention by running his mouth and winning bout after bout. He was young and had much to learn but he was fast and he was talented. On March 13, 1963, he defeated the more experienced Doug Jones in a close ten rounder to raise his record to 18-0-0.

Clay Forced to Rally to Whip Doug Jones

The Racine (WI) Journal-Times
March 14 1963

Liston gave Patterson a rematch on July 22 in Las Vegas. Floyd felt he had learned something from the first fight and was ready to face his conqueror again. The result was the same, a one-round knockout. It lasted four seconds longer than the first bout.

Many felt that Liston would reign a long time. His punching power, his ability to take hard shots and his surly appearance were all convincing arguments. But that was not the case. He would lose the next time out.

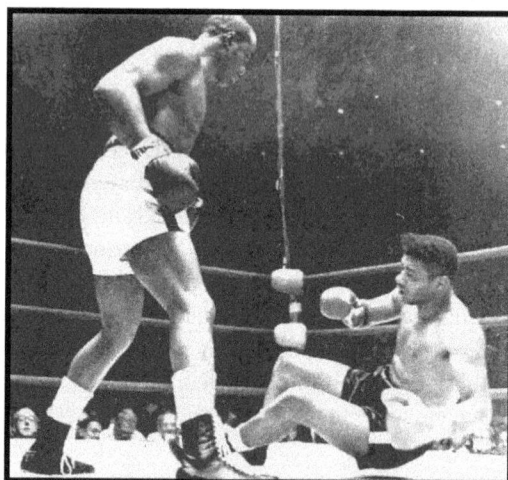

Charles "Sonny" Liston-Floyd Patterson
July 22 1963

After his win over Doug Jones, the brash young fighter from Louisville was talking even more, telling people just how pretty and how great he was. Often, he predicted the round in which he would win his bouts. He even called himself "The Greatest."

Hank Kaplan and Cassius Clay
1964

Yes, young Cassius Clay was sounding off again. After a knockdown scare in London on June 18, he stopped the dangerous hitter Henry Cooper in five rounds and boasted a record of 19-0-0 with 15 knockouts. He made insulting remarks about Liston's ability. He rattled off abusive comments in public about the personality of "Sonny." He belittled the champion in just about every way possible. "Sonny" wanted to shut this kid up in a bad way.

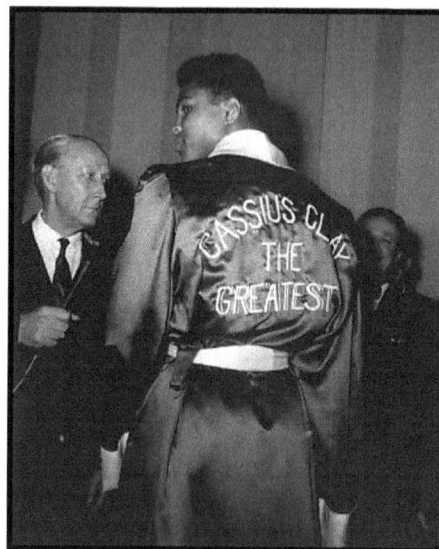

Cassius Clay, "The Greatest"

On February 25, 1964 in Miami Beach, Cassius Clay defeated Liston and won the heavyweight title when "Sonny" retired after six rounds. The unbelievable had happened. The invincible one had been destroyed by a saucy kid. The new young champion could indeed "float like a butterfly and sting like a bee."

What most fight fans failed to realize was that young Cassius was no ordinary fighter. He was destined to become one of the greatest fighters in heavyweight history. It took a fighter of this caliber to beat Liston.

Clay was quick and he could box, make no mistake - fast hands, fast feet, fast head movements and fast with words. He was fluid. He moved gracefully and knew

Cassius Clay-Charles "Sonny" Liston
February 25 1964

where he was at all times. He measured distance to the inch and moved out of harm's way by a fraction. He boxed well, hit in combinations and possessed one of the fastest jabs ever. His "punches in bunches" were beautiful to behold.

When Clay defeated Liston, the World Boxing Association (WBA) was rid of bad "Sonny." But now Clay wanted to meet Liston in a return contest. If "Sonny" happened to win and most people felt he would, the WBA would have Liston and his image problem back again.

Ernie Terrell

Dramatic changes soon took place in Clay's life. After winning the title, he changed his name to Muhammad Ali and professed to becoming a Muslim. He became more outspoken and actively involved in many black causes. In September of 1964, the WBA withdrew its recognition of Cassius Clay as heavyweight champion due to his political activism. He was still considered to be the world heavyweight champion by most but did not have the WBA backing.

On March 5, 1965 in Chicago, Ernie Terrell defeated Eddie Machen in fifteen rounds to win the vacant WBA heavyweight crown.

Ernie Terrell Awarded Decision over Machen

The Racine (WI) Journal-Times
March 6 1965

95

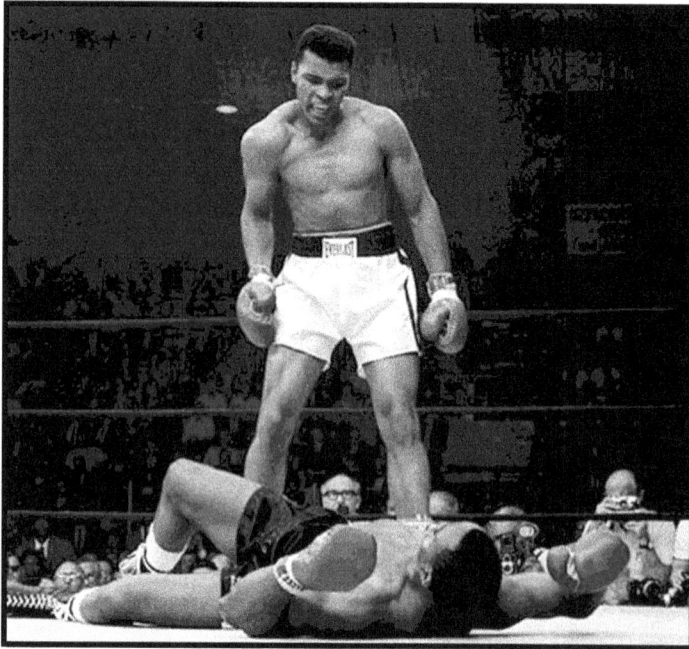

Muhammad Ali-Charles "Sonny" Liston
May 25 1965

In the rematch with Liston on May 25 in Lewiston, Maine, mouthy Muhammad Ali [Cassius Clay] won on a suspicious one-round knockout. "Sonny" Liston, one of the toughest of heavyweights, was flattened by Ali, who was not known as a crunching knockout puncher.

Many ringside observers claimed they did not see the punch that downed Liston. Most of those who did see it said it wasn't hard enough to drop most heavyweights, much less Liston.

There were rumors of a fix - not that Ali was involved. It was a questionable event.

On November 1, 1965 in Toronto, Terrell defended his WBA title against George Chuvalo, a powerful but somewhat ponderous fighter who possessed the ruggedness of the old-time heavyweights. Terrell won a fifteen-round decision.

Three weeks later on November 22 in Las Vegas, Muhammad Ali [Cassius Clay] met Floyd Patterson and won by a technical knockout in twelve rounds.

George Chuvalo

Ali decided to try the tough Chuvalo in a championship fight in Toronto on March 29, 1966. Terrell could not take out Chuvalo and neither could Ali. Muhammad won a decision in fifteen rounds.

Two months after this fight, on May 21 in London, Ali defended against Henry Cooper, the man who flattened him in 1963 and almost knocked him out. This time, Ali bloodied up Cooper and scored a technical knockout in six rounds.

Muhammad Ali-Henry Cooper
May 21 1966

On June 28, 1966, Terrell defended his WBA crown in Houston, Texas against Doug Jones, a very good boxer. The talented Jones had come close to defeating Ali in 1963 when the young Cassius Clay was working his way up the heavyweight ladder. Terrell won this bout in fifteen rounds.

Terrell Retains Title Amid 'Low Blow' Yells

The Logansport (IN) Pharos-Tribune
June 29 1966

In England on August 6, Ali knocked out the Britisher Brian London in three rounds and on September 10 in Frankfurt, Germany, he scored a technical knockout over left-handed Karl Mildenberger in twelve troublesome rounds.

Two months later on November 14, back in the United States in Houston, Ali met "Big Cat" Cleveland Williams in a title fight. Williams, once a brutal puncher, was "over the hill" but still dangerous.

Ali boxed his man, tantalized him and lured him on. When Williams was in strong pursuit, the champion stopped, braced himself and shot out straight punches which made the challenger quiver from head to toe. Ali won a technical knockout in three rounds.

Cleveland Williams

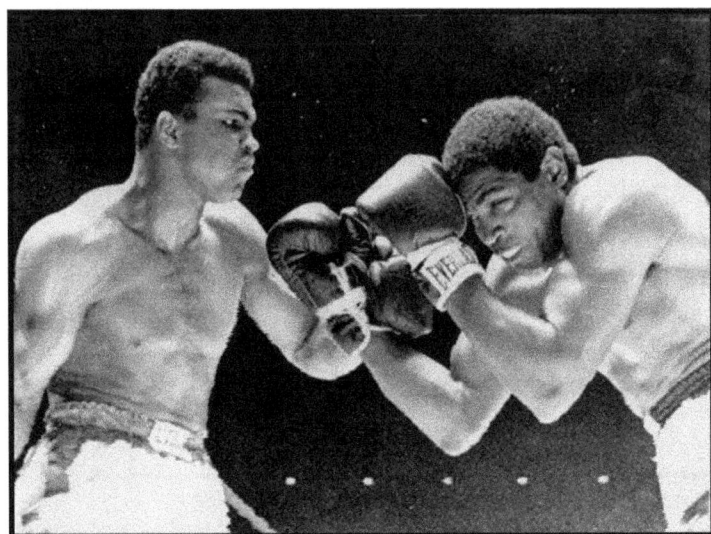

Muhammad Ali-Ernie Terrell
February 6 1967

Ali and Terrell developed ill feelings towards each other over time. Ali made insulting comments about Ernie's skills and praised his own Muslim religion, which annoyed Terrell and many followers of boxing. A war of words was raging between the two when they met on February 6, 1967 in Houston to unify the title. Ali won in fifteen rounds.

On March 22 in New York City, Ali fought and scored his last world championship win for the next four years. He knocked out clever Zora Folley in seven rounds.

97

On April 28, the WBA once again removed its recognition of Ali as heavyweight champion. This time the action was taken due to Ali refusing to serve in the United States Army when called in the draft. For the same reason, the New York State Athletic Commission (NYSAC) also withdrew its recognition of Ali as champion.

Out in California, a bright young prospect named Jerry Quarry had surfaced. He sported a record of 23-1-4 with his only loss coming against highly regarded Eddie Machen. In addition, on June 9 he had fought a draw with former heavyweight champion Floyd Patterson. Quarry was good-looking and popular. He would be heard from over the next few years.

Jerry Quarry

Joe Frazier

Two major boxing organizations held different views on how to find a successor to the title. An elimination tournament involving its top-rated fighters was set up by the WBA. The New York State Athletic Commission (NYSAC) decided to have a championship fight. Joe Frazier was selected as one of its choices. As a result, Frazier refused to compete in the WBA tournament.

In New York City on March 4, 1968, Frazier, a hard-punching young heavyweight, stopped the huge Buster Mathis in eleven rounds to capture the New York (NYSAC) version of the title. Seven weeks later, on April 27 in Oakland, Jimmy Ellis captured the vacant WBA heavyweight crown by defeating Quarry ("The Bellflower Belter") in fifteen rounds.

Joe Frazier racked up two more NYSAC title wins in 1968. On June 24 in New York City, he stopped Manuel Ramos in two rounds and on December 10 in Philadelphia, he won a fifteen-round decision over Oscar "Ringo" Bonavena even though Oscar floored Joe twice in this contest.

Jimmy Ellis defended his WBA title against the former champion Floyd Patterson on September 14 in Stockholm, Sweden. Ellis won in fifteen rounds. After this, Jimmy did not fight an official battle for the next seventeen months.

Jimmy Ellis

Jimmy Ellis Retains WBA Heavyweight Title

The Logansport (IN) Pharos-Tribune and Press
September 15 1968

Frazier engaged in two NYSAC championship bouts in 1969 and won both short of the scheduled distance. He put the lights out on Dave Zyglewicz in one round in Houston on April 22 and retired Jerry Quarry after the seventh round in New York City on June 23.

Olympic king Foreman making noise as a pro

The Jefferson City (MO) Daily Capital News
August 20 1969

Big George Foreman had made progress in the heavyweight division since making America proud with his triumph in the 1968 Olympic Games. On August 18, 1969, George stopped Chuck Wepner in three rounds for his fourth victory in four bouts. Yes sir, big George was making a good start to his professional career.

Frazier and Ellis settled matters and unified the heavyweight championship on February 16, 1970 in New York City. Jimmy was a talented boxer who moved well, boxed well and had plenty of savvy. Joe, on the other hand, was very strong, possessed a solid chin and threw paralyzing punches from both sides. Frazier won when Ellis could not come out for round six. He now owned the WBA and World Boxing Council (WBC) titles along with the New York (NYSAC) version.

Joe Frazier Is The Undisputed King Of Heavyweights After Victory Over Jimmy Ellis, But Now Has No One Left To Fight

The Gettysburg (PA) Times
February 17 1970

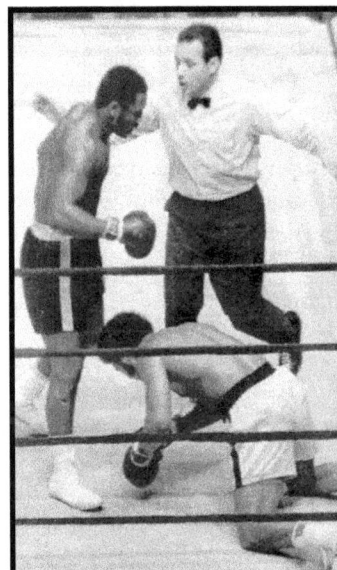

Joe Frazier-Jimmy Ellis
February 16 1970

George Foreman continued taking big steps towards the top of the heavyweight heap on April 17, 1970 in New York when he stopped James J. Woody in three rounds. Fighting often, George now boasted an 18-0-0 record with 15 knockouts or stoppages.

On October 26 in Atlanta, Muhammad Ali fought his first official ring battle since his departure from the square circle back in 1967. He was heavier now and hit harder than before. Ali met Jerry Quarry, cut up his man and won by a technical knockout in three rounds. He was after "his" title - but it was held by Joe Frazier.

George Foreman-James J. Woody
April 17 1970

Frazier defended his WBC and WBA titles by meeting the sharp-hitting light-heavyweight Bob Foster on November 18 in Detroit. Foster could hit but could not withstand the powerful blows of a genuine heavyweight and went out after two rounds.

Oscar "Ringo" Bonavena

On December 7 in New York City, Ali was back in the ring, this time against the ponderous, tough Argentinian Oscar "Ringo" Bonavena. Ali pounded Bonavena, wore him down and finally stopped him in round fifteen. He wanted "his" title back and he was after Joe Frazier!

The newspapers had a heyday publicizing and promoting the inevitable showdown between Ali and the current champion Frazier for the WBC and WBA titles. Fans clamored for the confrontation between the two great fighters. Frazier wanted it and Ali was eager for it – too eager.

Frazier was at his peak. Muhammad was getting back into fighting condition. On March 8, 1971 in New York, Frazier won the most important victory of his career. He decisioned Ali in fifteen rounds, knocking down the great fighter in the process. A sturdy roadblock stood between Ali and "his" title(s).

Frazier won a couple of WBC and WBA title defenses in 1972. On January 15 in New Orleans, he stopped Terry Daniels in four rounds. On May 25 in Omaha, he stopped Ron Stander.

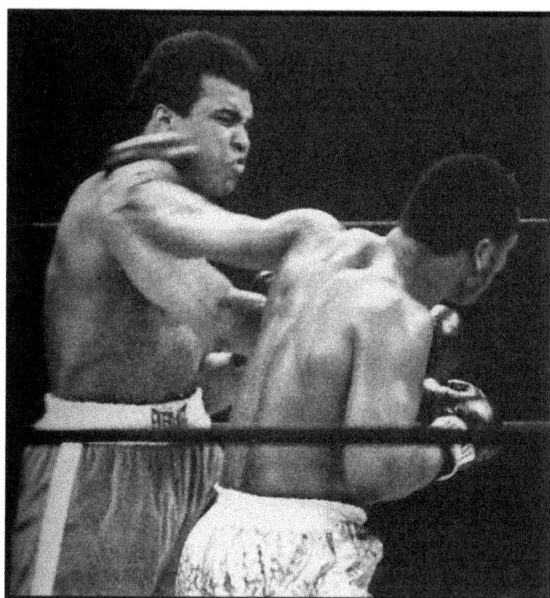

**Joe Frazier-Muhammad Ali
March 8 1971**

**Ken Norton-Jack O'Halloran
March 17 1972**

In San Diego on March 17, a couple of months before the Frazier-Stander bout, a tremendous prospect named Ken Norton overcame a huge height and weight disadvantage and pounded out a victory over big Jack O'Halloran.

100

O'Halloran stood 6'6" and weighed over 240 lbs. He was tough and durable and came in with a fairly good record that included ten knockouts. After the win, Norton's record stood at 25-1-0 and he was looking for some big fish to fry. O'Halloran, after his ring years, began a career in the motion pictures.

On January 22, 1973 in Kingston, Jamaica, young George Foreman, who had built himself a fine 37-0-0 record, scored a technical knockout over Frazier to dethrone Joe. The immensely powerful former Olympic champion knocked Frazier down six times in two rounds to take the WBC and WBA heavyweight titles away from Smokin' Joe.

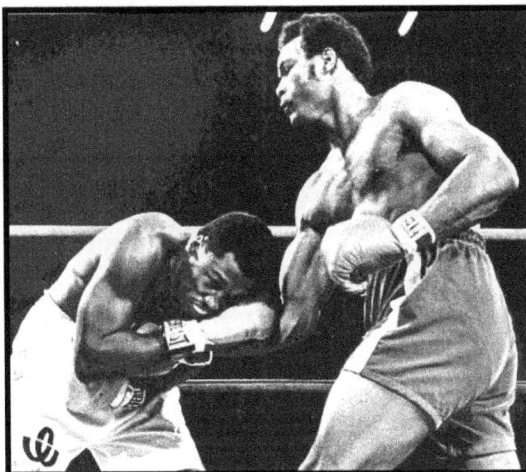

George Foreman-Joe Frazier
January 22 1973

Ken Norton-Muhammad Ali
March 31 1973

Sure enough, Ken Norton found a big fish. On March 31, 1973 in San Diego, Muhammad Ali suffered another setback in his attempt to regain the title. He met the powerful, hard-hitting Norton who respected Ali but did not fear him. Ken had a style that matched up well against Ali and he came out the winner, breaking Ali's jaw in the process. But like a true great champion, Ali did not abandon his quest to regain the title and restore his image.

Meanwhile, on July 2 in London, Joe Frazier was back in the ring for the first time since being dethroned by Foreman. He won a twelve-round decision against Joe Bugner. He was too good to let the only loss of his career slow him down.

On September 1 in Tokyo, Foreman defended his WBC and WBA titles for the first time and pummeled Jose "King" Roman in a single round to remain champion.

Frazier Decisions Britain's Bugner

The Naugatuck (CT) Daily News
July 3 1973

In defense of world heavyweight title
Foreman dethrones 'King' Roman in two minutes

The Great Bend (KS) Tribune
September 2 1973

Nine days later, on September 10 in Inglewood, California, Norton and Ali fought a second time. This time Ali worked his magic and won a twelve-round decision. His loss to Norton was avenged although most sportswriters at ringside scored the contest as a win for Norton.

Muhammad Ali-Joe Frazier
January 28 1974

Ali still had some unfinished business on his agenda - to get even with Joe Frazier, the first man to beat him. In New York City on January 28, 1974, he met Frazier in a rematch.

Frazier applied constant pressure with his ever-aggressive attacking style. He threw many hard punches and landed a number of stiff blows.

Ali moved, boxed well and when cornered on the ropes by Frazier's relentless aggression, smothered Joe's attack. After twelve competitive rounds, Ali won by a decision. Revenge was sweet.

Ken Norton's nice fighting style worked well against Ali, the clever boxer, but it did not fare so well against a super slugger like George Foreman. Big George met Norton for the WBC and WBA championships on March 26 in Caracas, Venezuela and simply overpowered Ken. It was over in two rounds. Foreman was still king of the heavies.

George Foreman-Ken Norton
March 26 1974

Once again the stage was set for a showdown with the WBC and WBA heavyweight championships at stake. This time the fighters were George Foreman as champion and Muhammad Ali as challenger. The massive champion met his "Waterloo" in Kinshasa, Zaire (Democratic Republic of the Congo) on October 30, 1974.

Ali regained the title with a stunning eighth-round knockout, becoming the second man ever to do that. It was a battle of styles and as happens many times, the boxer won over the slugger.

Muhammad Ali-George Foreman
October 30 1974

It was this fight and the victories he recorded over the next three years that inspired the public to believe that Ali was perhaps what he had claimed to be all along - "The Greatest."

In 1975, Ali won four WBC and WBA title defenses. On March 24 in Richfield, Ohio (Cleveland), he scored a technical knockout over the battler Chuck Wepner in fifteen rounds. On May 16 in Las Vegas, he scored an eleven-round technical knockout over hard-hitting Ron Lyle. On July 1 in Kuala Lumpur, Malaysia, he won a fifteen-round decision over troublesome Joe Bugner. This set the stage for a "rubber" match with Joe Frazier, one of the two men who had beaten him.

On October 1 in the Philippines, the two great fighters tangled in "The Thrilla in Manila." It was one of the best fights in heavyweight championship history. Each man wanted to win badly. Each man gave it everything he had. Each man was pressed to the limit. Each man wanted to quit at some time during the fight. Finally, just before round fifteen, Frazier's corner called it quits - against Joe's will. Ali won by a technical knockout.

Trying to get back into his former awesome fighting shape, George Foreman tangled with power-hitting Ron Lyle on January 24, 1976.

Muhammad Ali-Joe Frazier
October 1 1975

Ron Lyle

In a "rock-em-sock-em" affair, each bruiser pummeled the other. Each man hit the deck twice. Finally, Foreman, almost totally drained, finished off the worn-out Lyle in the fifth round to take home victory. Afterwards, George ran off three more wins during the year, including another conquest of Joe Frazier.

During 1976, "The Greatest" was a busy fighter. Ali defended his WBC and WBA titles four times and also competed in an exhibition with the great Japanese wrestler Antonio Inoki.

In Ali's title defenses, two were easy wins - a five-round knockout over Jean-Pierre Coopman on February 20 in Puerto Rico and a five-round technical knockout over Richard Dunn on May 25 in Munich, Germany.

The other two championship battles were close calls. On April 30 in Landover, Maryland, Ali fought Jimmy Young, a good but erratic boxer. When inspired, Young was an excellent fighter and on this night he was electric. Jimmy more than held his own with the champion. He boxed, hit in combinations and defended well. But on occasions when Ali was attacking, Young ducked under the ropes to avoid punishment instead of back-peddling or running. This action probably cost him the fight. Ali was awarded a fifteen-round decision but many observers thought Young won the fight.

Jimmy Young

Muhammad Ali-Ken Norton
September 28 1976

The other close call was a "rubber" match with Ken Norton on September 28 in New York. Norton pressed the fighting, landed hard and often with overhand rights and straight lefts and rights. Ali used his old trick of fighting the first thirty seconds and last thirty seconds of each round to impress the judges. Ali was awarded a fifteen-round decision.

A panel of sportswriters reviewed this fight on a special television program a few months later and scored the bout. The result was a draw in rounds with Norton well ahead on points.

The contest with the wrestler Antonio Inoki took place on June 26 in Tokyo. The curiosity of everyone was aroused but the event was a major disappointment. Inoki lay on the floor for most of the fifteen rounds, kicking at Ali when he got close. As a result, Ali kept his distance for fear of being injured. It was called a draw.

On May 16, 1977 in Landover, Maryland, Ali met Alfredo Evangelista, the European heavyweight who boasted a record of 14-1-1. The WBC and WBA titles were at stake. Muhammad won an easy fifteen-round decision. Evangelista was an awkward but durable fighter who could not match Ali's speed nor hit the champion effectively.

Earnie Shavers

Muhammad had a brain-rattling experience on September 29 against Earnie Shavers in New York. Earnie was an awesome hitter. When he won, it was usually by a knockout. Ali outboxed Shavers to win a decision in fifteen rounds and keep his WBC and WBA titles but was forced to hang on desperately throughout the battle when struck by Shaver's powerful stunning blows.

Most great fighters become overweight with the passage of time. Some become overconfident. Ali was no exception. Consequently, on February 15, 1978 in Las Vegas, he lost the WBC and WBA championships in a surprise upset to a young fighter named Leon Spinks.

Leon Spinks-Muhammad Ali
February 15 1978

There was talk of a Spinks-Ali rematch but the WBC ruled that Spinks must fight Ken Norton as his next opponent. The young Spinks defied the WBC and scheduled a return engagement with Muhammad Ali.

In retaliation, the WBC proceeded to strip Spinks of its version of the championship. That organization rated both Ken Norton and Jimmy Young highly. Since Norton had defeated Young in a non-title fight on November 5, 1977 in Las Vegas, he was subsequently declared the WBC heavyweight champion of the world.

Norton then fought Larry Holmes and lost the WBC title to the unbeaten warrior on June 9, 1978 in Las Vegas. It was an exciting, close fight. Both men were exhausted at the final bell. No one realized that a future great fighter had won the title.

Ali defeated Spinks in their rematch on September 15 in New Orleans to win back the WBA championship. This was the third time as a heavyweight king for Ali.

Larry Holmes made the first defense of his WBC title on November 10 in Las Vegas. He fought Alfredo Evangelista, the durable Spaniard who had lasted fifteen rounds with Ali. The aggressive Holmes finished his man in seven rounds.

Larry Holmes-Ken Norton
June 9 1978

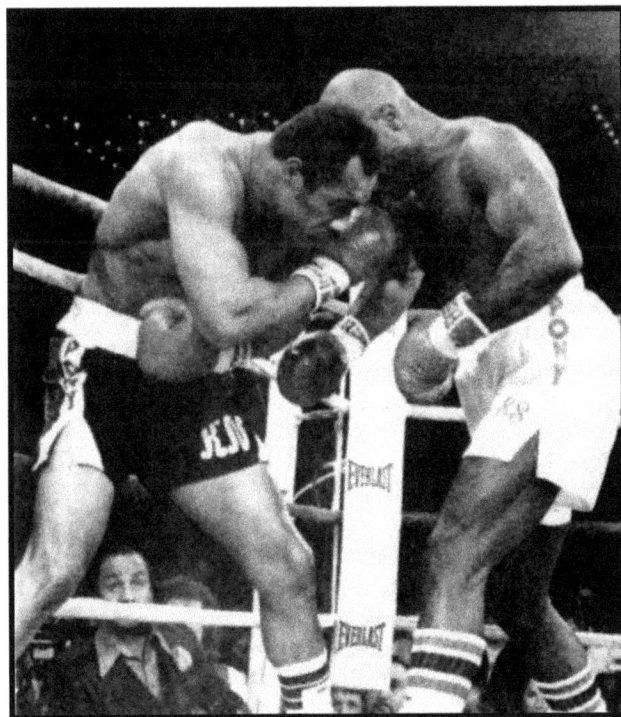

A little over four months afterwards, on March 23, 1979, Holmes defended again. He met Osvaldo "Ossie" Ocasio in Las Vegas. This contest lasted only seven rounds. Holmes retained his WBC title. On the same card, Ken Norton met the stiff punching Earnie Shavers and was knocked out in the first round. Ken's fine career was winding down.

Two very interesting WBC championship bouts followed for Larry. He was hard pressed and forced to call upon the grit that great champions possess in order to win. These bouts were the "heat that tempered the steel."

Earnie Shavers-Ken Norton
March 23 1979

On June 22, 1979, Larry met Mike Weaver in New York. While clearly outboxing Weaver throughout most of the fight, Larry was belted and floored. Upon getting up, he was forced to hang on and fight his way back against the aggressive challenger. Holmes won by a technical knockout in round twelve.

After reigning for a year without fighting, Ali announced his retirement as WBA champion on September 6. Once again, the WBA had no champion.

On September 28, Holmes met Earnie Shavers, the heavy-handed slugger, in Las Vegas. Again, Holmes was outboxing his man when suddenly he was rocked and floored. He got up, fought back and won by a stoppage in round eleven.

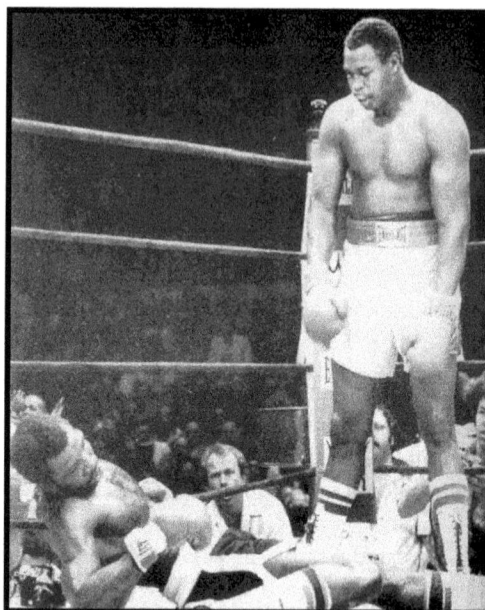

Larry Holmes-Mike Weaver
June 22 1979

John Tate

Pretoria, Transvaal [Gauteng], South Africa was the scene on October 20 where John Tate, a huge American fighter, defeated Gerrie Coetzee, the South African heavyweight, to capture the vacant WBA championship.

Meanwhile, over in the WBC, Larry Holmes was "King of the Jungle." Holmes, who possessed one of the best jabs in heavyweight history, also had a sneaky, powerful overhand right accompanied by a stiff right uppercut. Larry knew how to fight. He would prove to be one of the best champions ever. The WBC championship was in good hands.

On February 3, 1980, Holmes disposed of Lorenzo Zanon in six rounds in Las Vegas. It was his fifth defense of the WBC title. The WBA, on the other hand, went through a quick change in champions.

On March 31 in Knoxville, just five months after winning the WBA crown, John Tate lost to Mike Weaver by a knockout in round fifteen. On the same date in Las Vegas, Larry Holmes defended his WBC heavyweight crown against huge Leroy Jones. Larry had his wonderful array of punches in fine working order. He punished Jones and stopped him in round eight.

Irish Gerry Cooney was a sensational heavyweight from New England. He continued to draw raves upon himself when he stopped Jimmy Young in four rounds in Atlantic City on May 25. Cooney then owned a 23-0-0 record with 19 knockouts. Meanwhile, Larry Holmes defended his WBC crown again and on July 7 in Bloomington, Minnesota, he stopped Scott LeDoux.

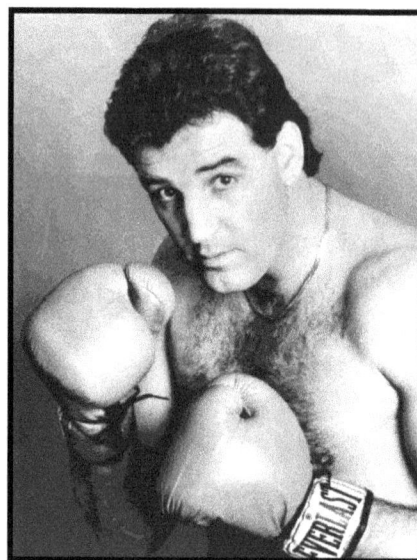

Gerry Cooney

In a WBC championship defense on October 2, 1980 in Las Vegas, Holmes defeated the once-great Muhammad Ali who had come out of retirement. Holmes had the highest respect for the aging Ali and was reluctant to deliver hard finishing punches when the former champion was on the ropes and ready to go. Finally, the contest was stopped.

"He shouldn't ever fight again, and I'm sure he won't . . . His time has come." **Larry Holmes**

The Logansport (IN) Pharos-Tribune
October 3 1980

Larry Holmes-Muhammad Ali
October 2 1980

Big Gerry Cooney kept in step with the champion by knocking out Ron Lyle in one round in Uniondale, New York on October 24. Holmes and Cooney, two hard-hitting heavyweights, were on a collision course.

Cooney boasted a 24-0-0 record. Boxing fans everywhere were eagerly awaiting the match between Gerry and Holmes, who had compiled a 36-0-0 mark at this point in his career.

Gerry Cooney-Ron Lyle
October 24 1980

On October 25 in Sun City, Bophuthatswana [North West], South Africa, Mike Weaver defended his WBA championship against Gerrie Coetzee in his first fight as champion. The challenger Coetzee was big, a good boxer and a strong hitter. But Weaver wore him down and stopped him in thirteen rounds. This was the last title fight of 1980.

On December 17 in White Plains, New York, a promising heavyweight Renaldo Snipes knocked out Dwain Bonds in eight rounds for his eighth win of the year, six by knockout. Snipes' record was 18-0-0. He was headed for the top.

Top Heavyweight Boxers of 1961-1980

1. Muhammad Ali (Cassius Clay)
2. Charles "Sonny" Liston
3. Larry Holmes
4. George Foreman
5. Joe Frazier

Top Heavyweight Bouts of 1961-1980

1. Muhammad Ali-Joe Frazier #3, October 1 1975, Quezon City, Philippines
2. Joe Frazier-Muhammad Ali #1, March 8 1971, New York, New York
3. George Foreman-Ron Lyle, January 24 1976, Las Vegas, Nevada
4. Larry Holmes-Ken Norton, June 9 1978, Las Vegas, Nevada
5. Floyd Patterson-Ingemar Johansson #3, March 13 1961, Miami Beach, Florida

Doug Jones and Joe Frazier
1967

Chapter Six

The Years 1981-2000

Larry Holmes had three WBC heavyweight championship fights during 1981. On April 11 in Las Vegas, he decisioned Trevor Berbick in fifteen rounds, on June 12 in Detroit, he stopped Leon Spinks in three rounds and on November 6 in Pittsburgh, he got off the canvas to stop Renaldo Snipes in the eleventh round. "Mister" Snipes came close - but no cigar!

Another big fight of 1981 was held on May 11 in New York City. Gerry Cooney met Ken Norton in what turned out to be a startling victory for the Irishman. Cooney stopped Norton in the first round to boost his record to 25-0-0 with 21 knockouts. A showdown with Larry Holmes was imminent.

Nearly a year after his last defense, Mike Weaver defended his WBA championship. On October 3, 1981 in Rosemont, Illinois (Chicago), he met James "Quick" Tillis for the crown and won a fifteen-round decision.

Renaldo Snipes

Larry Holmes-Gerry Cooney
June 11 1982

Larry Holmes met Gerry Cooney in Las Vegas on June 11, 1982 for the WBC heavyweight championship. This was expected to be a crucial test for the champion and it was. In a very competitive fight, Holmes outlasted Cooney. When big Gerry ran out of gas, the champion gained a TKO in round thirteen.

Holmes was in action again on November 26 in Houston against tough Randall "Tex" Cobb. Larry won a fifteen-round decision against the stubborn Cobb for the WBC crown.

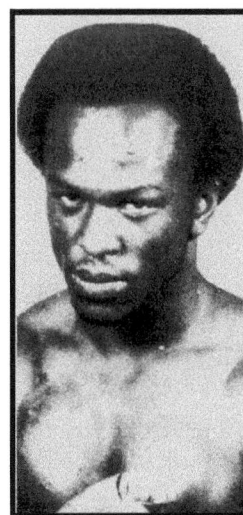
Michael Dokes

In Mike Weaver's third defense of the title, he experienced a catastrophe. He fought Michael Dokes in Las Vegas on December 10 and lost a one-round technical knockout in 63 seconds on a controversial call by referee Joey Curtis. Dokes was now the WBA heavyweight champion.

Larry Holmes had four bouts in 1983 and defended his WBC championship three times. He won on all four occasions. In title contests, he defeated Lucien Rodriguez in twelve rounds in Scranton, Pennsylvania on March 27, won a difficult and close twelve-round battle against Tim Witherspoon on May 20 in Las Vegas and stopped Scott Frank in five rounds on September 10 in Atlantic City. Then, he finished off Marvis Frazier in the opening frame in Las Vegas on November 25 in what some sources called a title event.

Holmes survives bout with Witherspoon

The Cedar Rapids (IA) Gazette
May 21 1983

Also on May 20, 1983 in Las Vegas, Michael Dokes met Mike Weaver in a rematch for the WBA crown. This time it went the distance and was declared a draw. Dokes retained the title.

On September 23, Dokes defended his WBA title against the big South African Gerrie Coetzee who sported a record of 28-3-1 with 17 knockouts.

**Gerrie Coetzee-Michael Dokes
September 23 1983**

Coetzee had earned victories over such men as Leon Spinks, Ron Stander, Mike Schutte, Kallie Knoetze, Pierre Fourie, Ibar Arrington, Stan Ward, Scott LeDoux and Mike Koranicki. Dokes lost by a knockout in the tenth round. This fight was held in Richfield, Ohio (Cleveland).

About the time that Coetzee beat Dokes, Larry Holmes had a falling out with the WBC and gave up that title. The young International Boxing Federation (IBF), however, recognized Larry as its king.

The game of "musical chairs" for the titles began when the division entered a period of large, ponderous, ill-conditioned and overweight fighters. Titles changed hands frequently. Different governing bodies got into the picture. Only two dominate fighters appeared - Larry Holmes and Mike Tyson.

On March 9, 1984, Tim Witherspoon beat Greg Page for the WBC championship vacated by Larry Holmes, but soon lost it to Pinklon Thomas. This bout was held in Las Vegas.

Witherspoon decisions Page to capture title

The Hutchinson (KS) News
March 10 1984

110

Thomas defeated Witherspoon on August 31 in Las Vegas in twelve rounds. He would not defend this title for nearly a year.

Pinklon Thomas-Tim Witherspoon
August 31 1984

Larry Holmes defended his prize possession, the IBF championship, on November 9 in Las Vegas against rugged James "Bonecrusher" Smith. Larry won on a twelfth-round stoppage.

James "Bonecrusher" Smith

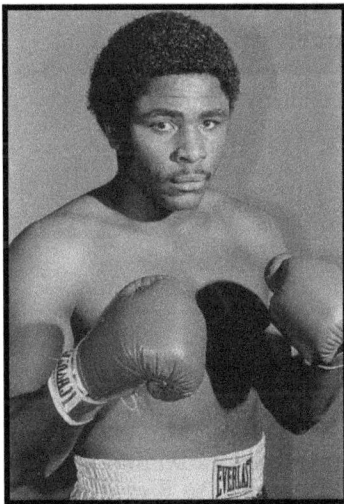
Greg Page

A little more than fourteen months after winning the WBA title, Gerrie Coetzee made the first defense of his championship on December 1 in Sun City, Bophuthatswana [North West], South Africa. He went against Greg Page and lost by knockout in the eighth round.

Page KOs Coetzee for WBA crown

The Intelligencer (Doylestown, PA)
December 2 1984

Larry Holmes, ever the busy champion, was back in action on March 15, 1985 in Las Vegas and stopped David Bey in ten rounds to retain his IBF title. No question about it, Holmes was the real heavyweight champion.

Greg Page lost in his first WBA title defense against Tony "TNT" Tubbs in fifteen rounds. This bout was held on April 29 in Buffalo.

Tony Tubbs

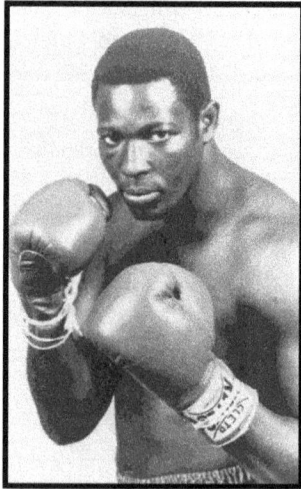

Carl Williams

On May 20 in Reno with his IBF title at stake, Larry Holmes won a close fifteen-round encounter with Carl "The Truth" Williams. Holmes appeared unbeatable at this time but a surprise was coming in the near future.

Pinklon Thomas finally defended his WBC title after nearly ten months of inactivity. On June 15 in Las Vegas, he met the former WBA champion Mike Weaver and finished him off in the eighth round.

On September 21, Larry Holmes met Michael Spinks in defense of his IBF heavyweight crown. In a surprising and questionable verdict, young Spinks was victorious over Holmes in fifteen rounds. Larry was quite vocal about a rematch and many observers supported his demand.

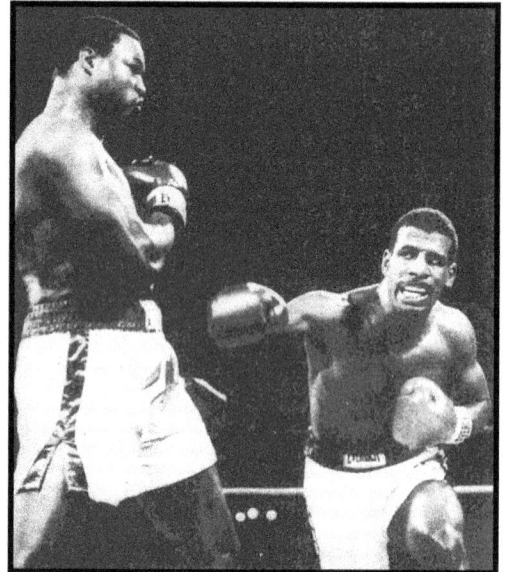

**Michael Spinks-Larry Holmes
September 21 1985**

The reigning WBA champion, Tony Tubbs, was a "Jack Johnson" type of fighter. He was a crafty, skillful boxer who possessed a good jab and quick reflexes. He was not a power hitter but he could stand before a man and slip punches. Had he been more serious about his boxing, perhaps he could have been more successful.

On January 17, 1986 in Atlanta, Tubbs lost to Tim Witherspoon in his first defense. This was the second time Witherspoon had held a world heavyweight championship.

Tim Witherspoon

Witherspoon batters Tubbs

ATLANTA — Tim Witherspoon got back a piece of the heavyweight championship Friday night, then said, "Now I want it all." Witherspoon, battering Tony Tubbs' body for most of the fight, won the World Boxing Association championship with a 15-round majority decision at the Omni.

**The Daily Herald (Chicago, IL), January 18 1986
Reprinted by permission of the Daily Herald
Arlington Heights, Illinois**

Tim was a good two-handed fighter with a fine left and a vicious overhand right. It was best to fight him from angles with accompanying good footwork, not head-on. Like Tubbs, Witherspoon was a talented fighter who could have been exceptional. However, he squandered his talents by poor conditioning and an unfortunate mental attitude.

112

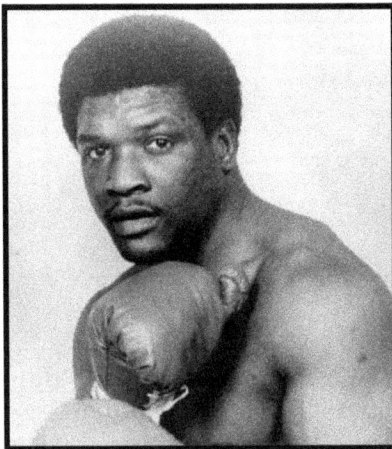
Trevor Berbick

On March 22 in Las Vegas, Pinklon Thomas lost in twelve rounds to Trevor Berbick. The WBC heavyweight championship changed hands once again.

Seven months after his shocking loss to Michael Spinks for the IBF championship, Larry Holmes tried to regain his treasured title. He was unsuccessful. Spinks defeated Larry in another close fifteen-round contest in Las Vegas on April 19.

Tim Witherspoon tangled with big Frank Bruno, a strong hitter from England, in a WBA title defense on July 19. Tim stopped Bruno in the eleventh round to retain the crown.

Frank Bruno

Michael Spinks quietly went about the business of defending his IBF title by meeting Steffen Tangstad on September 6 in Las Vegas. Spinks stopped Tangstad in four rounds to hold on to the crown. He subsequently refused to fight Tony "TNT" Tucker and was stripped of the title in February 1987.

During 1985 and 1986 while these champions were winning and losing their titles, a hungry young fighter named Mike Tyson was wading through the contenders. He racked up a 27-0-0 record with 25 knockouts. Among those he defeated were Jesse Ferguson, James "Quick" Tillis, Mitchell Green, Marvis Frazier, Jose "El Nino" Ribalta and Alfonso Ratliff. In fifteen of these fights, he required only a single round to come home the winner.

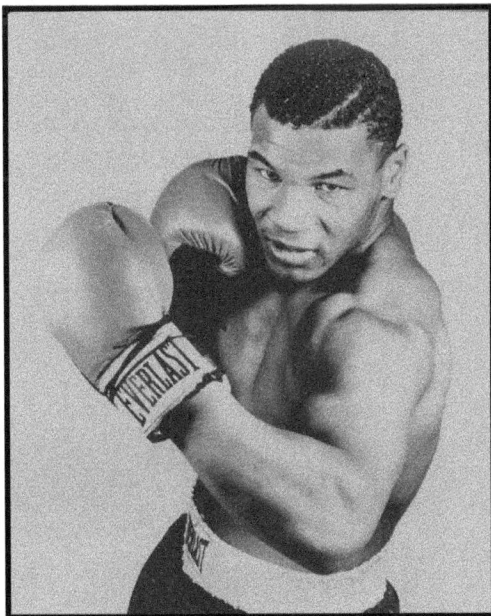
Mike Tyson

Mike got a shot at the WBC championship when he met Trevor Berbick on November 22 in Las Vegas. Berbick was a magnificent specimen of manhood - large, muscular and powerful. He delivered sledge-hammer blows. But Tyson stopped him in two rounds and then set about unifying the heavyweight championship.

Tyson was a powerful, stocky fighter like John L. Sullivan of the 1880s, Tom Sharkey of the 1890s, Rocky Marciano of the 1950s and Joe Frazier of the 1970s but was bigger than any of them. He was a devastating hitter, an aggressive gladiator who came to fight and one of the most powerful men in heavyweight history.

113

Shortly after Tyson won over Berbick, Tim Witherspoon defended the WBA championship against James "Bonecrusher" Smith on December 12, 1986 in New York City. Witherspoon had gone through several squabbles with promoter Don King over money and consequently made a poor showing. Tim lost to Smith on a first-round technical knockout. The "Bonecrusher" was the new WBA heavyweight champion.

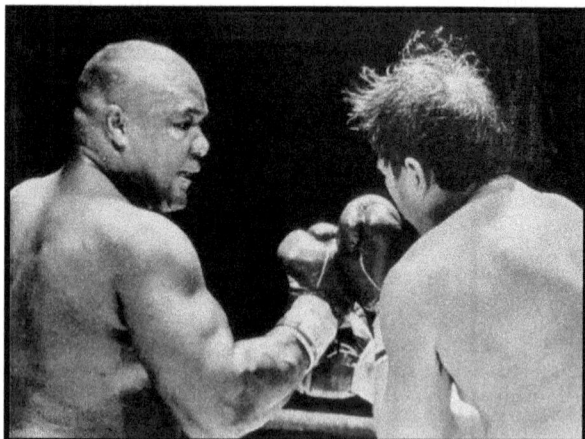

George Foreman-Steve Zouski
March 9 1987

In Las Vegas on March 7, 1987, Tyson met Smith and added the WBA title to his collection. Tyson defeated the clinching, holding "Bonecrusher" in twelve rounds. The new title went well with Mike's WBC crown.

In March of 1987, big George Foreman, the former champion, came out of retirement and started working his way up the heavyweight ladder by scoring a four-round technical knockout over Steve Zouski. Always a tremendous puncher, George had been watching the current crop of heavies and felt he could regain the title. He scored four more knockouts during 1987.

Mike Tyson next met Pinklon Thomas in Las Vegas on May 30 and stopped him in six rounds. This bout was for the WBA and WBC championships. On the same card, Tony Tucker defeated James "Buster" Douglas for the vacant IBF heavyweight championship.

Spinks decks Cooney in fifth round

The Intelligencer (Doylestown, PA)
June 16 1987

Michael Spinks was in the ring on June 15 in Atlantic City. His rusty opponent was Gerry Cooney who had come out of retirement to meet Michael. Spinks stopped the big fellow in five rounds.

Mike Tyson and Pinklon Thomas
weigh in

Tyson won two more title fights during 1987. On August 1 in Las Vegas, he decisioned Tony Tucker in twelve rounds to retain the WBC and WBA titles and capture the IBF crown. On October 16 in Atlantic City, he stopped Tyrell Biggs in seven rounds, defending all three titles.

Mike Tyson-Tony Tucker
August 1 1987

Mr. Tyson started off 1988 by meeting the former great champion Larry Holmes in Atlantic City on January 22. The ex-champion had not fought since losing twice to Michael Spinks almost two years earlier. Mike stopped Holmes in four rounds. Tyson next met the crafty former champion Tony Tubbs in Tokyo on March 21 and blasted him out in two rounds. These were scheduled WBC, WBA and IBF title fights but reportedly Japan did not recognize the Tubbs contest as an IBF title bout.

Almost on a monthly schedule, big George Foreman added nine more wins in 1988, all against minor opponents. The world was watching the former champion with a skeptical eye.

Next, Tyson met Michael Spinks with the WBC, WBA and IBF heavyweight titles at stake. The two undefeated champions got together on June 27, 1988 in Atlantic City. Mike decked Spinks in 91 seconds, one of the fastest finishes in heavyweight championship history. Now there was no question as to who was king - Mike Tyson!

Mike then scored two more knockouts in championship bouts. On February 25, 1989 in Las Vegas, he stopped Frank Bruno in five rounds. This was the last bout in which one man held all the major titles. The World Boxing Organization (WBO) came into existence and had its champion prior to the next Tyson fight. On July 21 in Atlantic City, Mike stopped Carl "The Truth" Williams in one round on a questionable call by the referee.

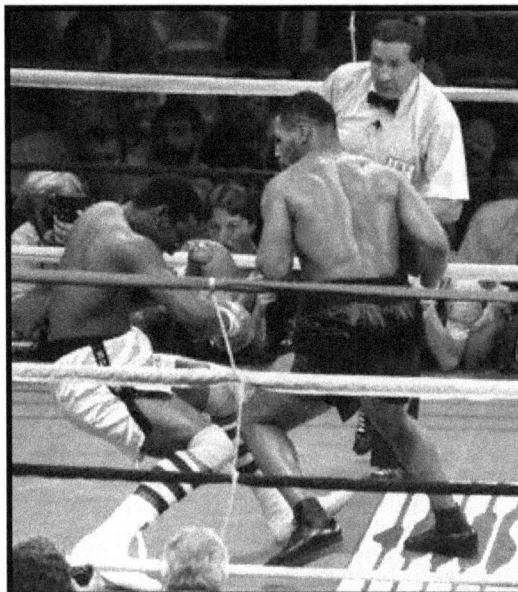

Mike Tyson-Michael Spinks
June 27 1988

Tyson's personal life became a mess. Fame and fortune had come quickly to this young man from the streets with a limited education. His championship had brought him money, power and contact with influential people and beautiful women. He was dazzled and befuddled.

Mike Tyson and Robin Givens

His mentor Cus D'Amato died before Tyson won the title. That bothered Mike. Next, Jimmy Jacobs, another of his managers, died. Bill Cayton, a third manager, could not handle him. Then, promoter Don King got into the act and things got much worse.

Mike had married actress Robin Givens in February of 1988. The odds of success were 2-1 against him (Robin and her mom Ruth Roper versus "Iron Mike"). This brought him more problems than he ever had in the ring. There were frequent domestic problems. His name was in the news for striking his wife, crashing automobiles and getting into skirmishes in public. In October 1988, eight months after the marriage, Mrs. Tyson filed for divorce.

Still there were rumors of violent episodes at shopping centers, parking lots and night clubs. Tyson also ended his relationship with Kevin Rooney, an excellent trainer who always had Tyson ready for battle. After this, Tyson trained himself.

While Tyson was having his problems, the World Boxing Organization (WBO) crept into the picture in the late 1980s and received much attention in Europe. On May 6, 1989 in Italy, Francesco Damiani knocked out the South African Johnny du Plooy in three rounds to win the newly established WBO heavyweight championship.

In spite of many critical remarks about his age and weight, George Foreman added five more wins to his record in 1989. He was gaining public support for a title shot. Many of the top contenders seemed to be dodging him.

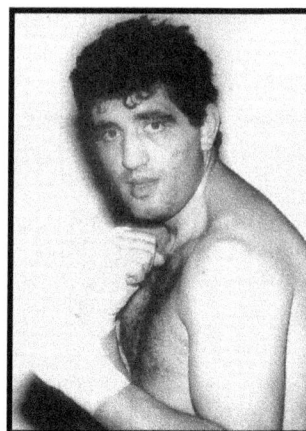

Francesco Damiani

Francesco Damiani defended his WBO crown again on December 16 in Italy. This time his challenger was Daniel Eduardo Neto. The contest lasted only two rounds as Damiani stopped his man.

Foreman eyes title after KO

By JOHN NELSON
AP Sports Writer

ATLANTIC CITY, N.J. (AP) — The ring bowed under the weight. The turnbuckles groaned. And thunder began to rumble in George Foreman's big right hand.

You could hear it in the distance. Start counting. One thousand one. One thousand two. One thousand three.

And the lightning struck.

It crashed into Gerry Cooney's jaw, crushed him to the ground and scattered what little was left of his heavyweight boxing career to the four winds.

From an Associated Press article published in The Ukiah (CA) Daily Journal, January 16 1990

On January 15, 1990 in Atlantic City, old George Foreman lured Gerry Cooney back into the ring for a rumble. Both men were huge punchers in their day. Foreman won this bout on a second-round technical knockout. Big George went on to add four more knockouts to his credit in 1990. Public sentiment ran high for George to get a title shot. The top men in the heavyweight division were watching and listening now. He could no longer be put off. Soon, he would get his chance to regain the cherished crown.

On February 11 in Tokyo, Mike Tyson took on challenger James "Buster" Douglas with three major heavyweight titles at stake. It was expected to be another knockout for Tyson but someone forgot to tell Douglas. Mike was out-boxed and knocked out by "Buster."

James "Buster" Douglas-Mike Tyson February 11 1990

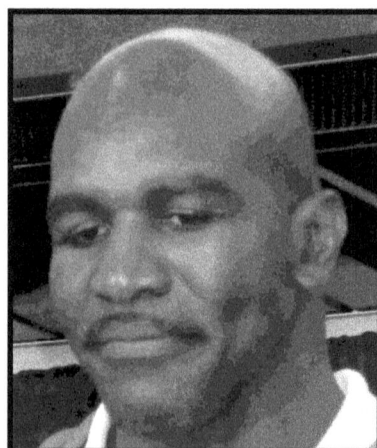

Evander Holyfield

Eight months later, on October 25 in Las Vegas, Douglas lost in three rounds to Evander Holyfield, 24-0-0, the former cruiserweight king. Holyfield now owned the WBC, WBA and IBF heavyweight titles. On December 14, Phil Jackson beat Olian Alexander to capture the new International Boxing Council (IBC) heavyweight title.

Ray Mercer, a hard-hitting heavyweight with a 16-0-0 record and a tough chin, got into the act on January 11, 1991 in Atlantic City. He knocked out Francesco Damiani, 27-0-0, in nine rounds to win the WBO title. Boxing writer Peter Lerner asked, "Who knows how his [Damiani's] career would have gone if his fight with Ray Mercer had finished differently? After being on top for most of the fight and cracking numerous big shots off the famous iron chin of the ex-marine he took a huge hybrid left hook-uppercut on the nose and was stopped."

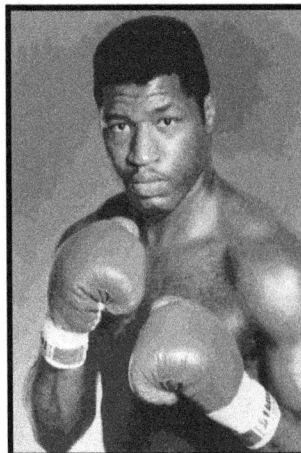

Ray Mercer

On March 18 in Las Vegas, Mike Tyson met tough Donovan "Razor" Ruddock as part of his plan to get back into the heavyweight title picture. After a battle, Tyson came away victorious by a technical knockout in round seven.

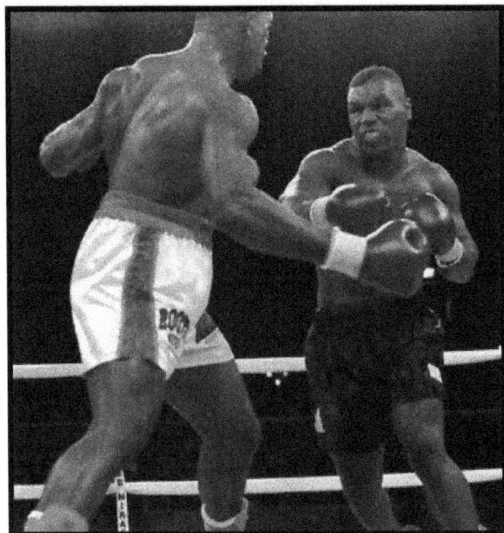

Mike Tyson-Donovan "Razor" Ruddock
March 18 1991

With Tyson no longer reigning as heavyweight king, Larry Holmes appeared on the scene once again. Larry had always maintained that aside from Tyson, he was still the best man in the division. He intended to prove it. On April 7, he stopped Tim Anderson in a single round. He picked up four more victories during the year.

George Foreman finally got his wish and fought for the heavyweight championship once again. Evander Holyfield defended his titles for the first time on April 19 in Atlantic City and defeated George in twelve rounds.

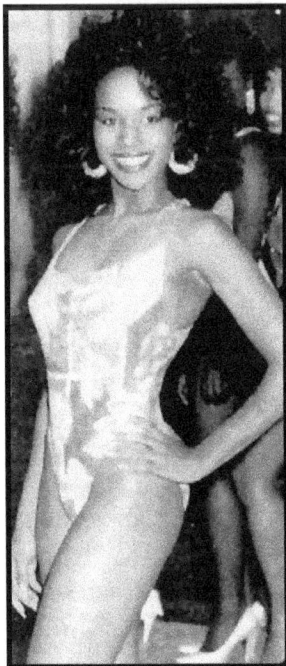

Desiree Washington

On June 28 in Las Vegas, Mike Tyson met the tough Canadian Donovan "Razor" Ruddock a second time. He won by decision in twelve rounds. Mike was working his way back to the top.

Holyfield tops Foreman in 12
Unanimous verdict for champ

Associated Press

ATLANTIC CITY, N.J. — The "Battle of the Ages" went to youth, and it was more of a battle than most thought it would be.

Evander Holyfield retained the heavyweight championship with a unanimous 12-round decision over George Foreman Friday night, but the 42-year-old challenger managed to thumb his nose at Father Time with a game and gritty performance.

"Senior citizens everywhere can be proud of themselves," Big George said.

His first loss since returning to the ring was nothing to be ashamed of, he said.

"We kept our dignity and there was no retreat," Foreman said. "I was ahead on points, but I took pity on him at the end. We proved that the age 40, 50 or 60 is not a death sentence. It will be 50 years until the world sees something like this again."

Most of the estimated crowd of 15,000 at the Convention Center rooted him on, but it was not to be. Holyfield never let Foreman get set and simply outpunched Big George.

The Daily Herald (Chicago, IL), April 20 1991
Reprinted by permission of the Daily Herald
Arlington Heights, Illinois

Tyson accused of rape

The Cedar Rapids (IA) Gazette
July 27 1991

On July 19 in Indianapolis, Mike Tyson was involved in an unfortunate incident. Tyson invited a young beauty queen Desiree Washington to his hotel room in the wee hours of the morning. According to Washington, Tyson attacked her there. Afterwards, she filed rape charges against him. Tyson denied the charges.

On September 9, a further development in the Mike Tyson rape case took place. Tyson was indicted on the rape charge and three other charges. Eventually, Mike was convicted and sentenced to time in prison. No longer was he a major player on the heavyweight scene.

BOXING

ATLANTIC CITY, N.J. — Unbeaten heavyweight **Ray Mercer** scored a fifth-round knockout over previously undefeated **Tommy Morrison** to suddenly end a scheduled 12-round bout early Saturday morning.

Referee **Tony Perez** finally stepped in to stop the bout 28 seconds into the round as Morrison lay defenseless on the ropes with Mercer raining rights and lefts to his face.

Mercer, 30, of Short Hills, N.J., was defending the World Boxing Organization title he won in January with a come-from-behind ninth-round knockout of **Francesco Damiani**. **Evander Holyfield** holds the title in boxing's three other major organizations and is considered the true champion.

**From an Associated Press article published in
The Gettysburg (PA) Times, October 19 1991**

Tommy "The Duke" Morrison, a hard-punching heavyweight, had built a record of 28 straight wins with 24 knockouts from 1988-1991. In spite of his impressive record, experts questioned his stamina and chin. He was the first challenger for Ray Mercer's WBO title.

The Mercer-Morrison contest was held on October 18 in Atlantic City. Morrison exploded on Mercer during the first four rounds with dynamite punches but the sturdy, durable chin of Mercer withstood the attacks and Morrison tired.

Suddenly in round five, Mercer opened up and caught Morrison with a series of blows that finished Tommy. The chin of Morrison let him down and Mercer retained his title. Later, Mercer was stripped of the WBO title for agreeing to fight Larry Holmes instead of Michael Moorer.

One month later, on November 23 in Atlanta, Evander Holyfield had a troublesome time of it in the second defense of his WBA and IBF belts. His opponent was Smokin' Bert Cooper who knocked the champion down and had him hanging on. But Holyfield, who had the knack of finding a way to win, came back to stop Cooper in the seventh round.

Bert Cooper

By February of 1992, three promising young heavyweights surfaced who had built fine records for themselves since 1988. They were Riddick Bowe (28-0-0), Lennox Lewis of England (18-0-0) and the former cruiserweight champion Michael Moorer (26-0-0). All three would eventually hold a heavyweight championship title.

Larry Holmes-Ray Mercer
February 7 1992

In a non-title fight on February 7, 1992 in Atlantic City, Ray Mercer met Larry Holmes. This was Larry's strongest test since returning to the ring. He won a twelve-round decision. This victory propelled him into a shot at the title.

Three days later, on February 10, Mike Tyson was found guilty of rape by an Indianapolis court. He was held in custody awaiting sentencing to take place a month later. On March 26, he was sentenced to six years in prison.

In Atlantic City on May 15, Michael Moorer stopped Bert Cooper in five rounds to become the new owner of Mercer's vacated WBO title. Each man was floored twice. Several months later, Moorer gave up the WBO title in order to become ranked by the other boxing organizations.

Evander Holyfield once again decided to give a former champion a title shot. This bout was held on June 19 in Las Vegas for three titles against Larry Holmes. Holyfield won in twelve rounds. Next, the IBC heavyweight title changed hands. On June 26 in Cleveland, Donovan "Razor" Ruddock defeated Phil Jackson.

Holyfield then chose to take on one of the young stallions who was after his crown. On November 13 in Las Vegas, he met Riddick Bowe, a talented big man with a good left jab, powerful overhand right and sneaky, lethal uppercut. Bowe defeated Evander in a terrific fight to capture the WBC, WBA and IBF world heavyweight championships.

Against Bowe, Holyfield did not fight his usual clever style but stood toe-to-toe with the bigger man and tried to match him punch for punch. Round ten was a rare example of action-packed heavyweight fighting. This was the first loss of Holyfield's career. On the undercard, Michael Moorer stopped Bill Wright in two rounds.

On November 14 in Greenville, South Carolina, Pinklon Thomas picked up the not so well-known International Boxing Organization (IBO) heavyweight title with a victory over Craig Payne. Thomas never defended this title.

Split decision
Bowe trashes WBC belt; organization names Lewis heavyweight champ

The Santa Fe (NM) New Mexican
December 15 1992

The WBC threatened to withdraw its recognition of Bowe as champion because Riddick planned to fight Michael Dokes for the title. On December 14, he relinquished the title and within a few hours the WBC declared Lennox Lewis as its champion. Bowe accepted the WBC ruling and fought Dokes.

In Columbia, South Carolina on January 29, 1993, Lawrence Carter stopped Pinklon Thomas in seven rounds to capture the World Boxing Federation (WBF) heavyweight title. Carter never defended his crown.

Riddick Bowe met Michael Dokes on February 6 in New York City and stopped the former champion in one round to retain the WBA and IBF versions of the heavyweight championship. Also on this date, Ray Mercer was involved in a controversial bout with Jesse Ferguson in New York City. Mercer allegedly offered Ferguson a bribe to take a "dive."

On February 23 in Reseda, California, Lionel Butler met Tony Willis for the IBO heavyweight title. Butler won by a stoppage in round five to take over the vacant IBO championship. Butler never defended this title.

Lennox Lewis

February 27 saw Michael Moorer defeat James "Bonecrusher" Smith in ten rounds in Atlantic City. Lennox Lewis defended the WBC heavyweight championship and defeated Tony Tucker in twelve rounds in Las Vegas on May 8. With this victory, Lewis was now the bonafide WBC heavyweight champion.

Tommy Morrison-George Foreman
June 7 1993

On May 22 in Washington, DC, Riddick Bowe stopped Jesse Ferguson in two rounds and retained the WBA and IBF heavyweight championships. However, the IBF title was withdrawn from Bowe for meeting Ferguson.

The heavyweight picture was a bit cloudy now. Riddick Bowe was the WBA champion, Lennox Lewis was the WBC champion, and the IBF and WBO commissions were without champions.

Sure is confusing with all these titles!

Tommy Morrison, now 36-1, met George Foreman for the vacant WBO heavyweight crown on June 7 in Las Vegas. Morrison fought a smart fight, hit hard and moved well against the powerful but older former champion. "The Duke" gained a twelve-round decision and the title. This was perhaps the best performance of Morrison's career. During August of 1993 in Kansas City, Tommy beat Tim Tomashek in four rounds to successfully defend his crown.

On July 23 in Townsville, Queensland, Australia, Jimmy Thunder met Melton Bowen for the vacant WBF championship. The contest ended in the fifth round when Thunder stopped Bowen to capture the crown.

Michael Bentt

Holyfield regains crown; fight delayed by chutist

Evander Holyfield defeated Riddick Bowe Saturday night to regain the heavyweight boxing title in a bizarre fight delayed for 20 minutes by a parachutist who landed in the ring at Caesars Palace in Las Vegas.

The unidentified parachutist caused pandemonium when he landed on the apron of the ring during the seventh round of the bout and fell into the crowd, reportedly breaking his neck. Bowe's pregnant wife, Judy, fainted during the incident.

Holyfield's victory came just one week short of a year from the date he lost the title on a unanimous decision to Bowe, also in Las Vegas.

On Saturday, Holyfield won by a majority decision, with one judge scoring it a tie. Holyfield became only the fourth boxer to hold the heavyweight title twice.

The Colorado Springs (CO) Gazette Telegraph
November 7 1993

Lennox Lewis stopped Frank Bruno in seven rounds to retain his WBC championship in Cardiff, Wales on October 1. On October 29 in Tulsa, just twenty-eight days after Lewis' victory over Bruno, Tommy Morrison's unstable chin let him down once more. Boxing fans expected an easy win for Tommy but in a first-round slugfest, Michael Bentt stopped Tommy to take possession of the WBO title.

On November 6 in Las Vegas, Evander Holyfield challenged Riddick Bowe in an effort to recover the WBA and IBF versions of the heavyweight championship. This time Holyfield moved, boxed and won a close twelve-round decision. He was champion once again. Rock Newman, handling Bowe, called this a bout between "the Pit Bull from Georgia and the junkyard dog from Brooklyn." Incidentally, this bout was held out of doors and was delayed during the seventh round by James Miller, known as "Fan Man," who dropped in by parachute.

November 19 saw Jimmy Thunder go into action against Johnny Nelson to defend his WBF title. The bout was held in Auckland, North Island, New Zealand. In a battle that lasted twelve rounds, Nelson took the title from Thunder.

Michael Bentt took on unbeaten Herbie Hide in London on March 19, 1994 and was outclassed by this fast, stiff-punching young fighter. Hide knocked out Bentt in round seven to become the new WBO champion.

Herbie Hide

One month after this bout, on April 22 in Las Vegas, Michael Moorer surprised the world by defeating Evander Holyfield in twelve rounds to capture the WBA and IBF heavyweight championships.

Lennox Lewis defended his WBC belt again on May 6 in Atlantic City against Phil Jackson, an impressive American fighter who carried a 30-1-0 record. Lewis stopped Jackson in the eighth round to retain the title

In Mashantucket, Connecticut on August 4, Danell Nicholson beat John Ruiz in twelve rounds to win the vacant IBO heavyweight crown. However, he never defended it.

Michael Moorer

On September 24 in London, Lewis again defended his WBC championship, this time against Oliver McCall. He was caught by a left hook and a stiff right-hand punch as he attacked the challenger in round two. Lewis went down and was too shaky to continue when he arose. McCall was the new WBC champion. McCall was not a flashy fighter but possessed a granite chin and carried a stiff punch.

Oliver McCall

George Foreman-Michael Moorer
November 5 1994

On October 29, Jimmy Thunder became the next IBO heavyweight champion when he defeated Richard Mason in twelve rounds in Atlantic City.

The impossible happened on November 5 in Las Vegas. Forty-five year old George Foreman knocked out Michael Moorer in ten rounds to win the WBA and IBF heavyweight championships. Big George became the oldest man to ever win a heavyweight title. After his victory, Foreman was stripped of the WBA crown for not fighting either of its top two contenders. He retained his IBF title, however. Also on November 5, Johnny Nelson defeated Nikolay Kulpin in Thailand to retain his WBF crown.

The "ABC" titles were clicking. December 3 saw Tim Puller stop Sherman Griffin in Harlingen, Texas to claim the IBC crown and on December 6, Jimmy Thunder won a twelve-round decision over Tony Tubbs in Auburn Hills, Michigan (Detroit) to retain his IBO crown. Riddick Bowe knocked out Herbie Hide in six rounds to win the WBO title on March 11, 1995 in Las Vegas. Bowe floored the tense Hide seven times during the bout.

On March 25, Mike Tyson was released from prison and made plans to resume his pugilistic career. The first fight in his comeback was scheduled for late summer against Peter McNeeley. This would give him five months to get into fighting condition.

Oliver McCall took on the aging but still able Larry Holmes in his first title defense on April 8 in Las Vegas. Holmes clearly outboxed McCall early in the fight but McCall stepped up the pace in the late rounds to win a twelve-round decision and retain the WBC title.

Former champion Tyson ends 3-year prison term

Former heavyweight champ Mike Tyson returned to his mansion Saturday in the rolling hills of eastern Ohio after three years in prison as the boxing world anxiously waited to see if he can mount a comeback.

Tyson's five-car caravan arrived at his Southington, Ohio,

mansion about 9 30 a m

Tyson left prison at dawn after three years behind bars for the rape of an 18-year-old beauty pageant contestant and was hustled into a waiting black stretch limousine surrounded by bodyguards and his promoter, Don King. See story in Sports.

The Daily Herald (Chicago, IL), March 26 1995
Reprinted by permission of the Daily Herald
Arlington Heights, Illinois

Bruce Seldon

The WBA also crowned its new champion on April 8 in Las Vegas when Bruce Seldon stopped Tony Tucker in seven rounds to win the vacant title. The muscular Seldon was criticized in his win and continued to receive negative press about his skills in the months that followed.

In Las Vegas on April 22, George Foreman defended his IBF heavyweight championship against the young German Axel Schulz. Also at stake was the new World Boxing Union (WBU) title. Schulz stood 6'3", weighed 221 pounds and carried a 21-1-1 record. Among his victories were wins over Ricky Parkey, Kimmuel Odum and former champion James "Bonecrusher" Smith.

To everyone's surprise, Schulz outboxed and outhit Foreman. Most observers felt he clearly won a decision over the champion. But as often happens in boxing, the judges saw it differently. Foreman retained his IBF title by decision. Following the bout, IBF officials ordered Foreman to meet Schulz in a rematch for the crown. Foreman refused and relinquished the title.

George Foreman-Axel Schulz
April 22 1995

Following a brief retirement due to chest problems, Evander Holyfield returned to the ring against a major opponent on May 20 in Atlantic City. Ray Mercer was the foe. In a close ten-round contest, Holyfield was declared the winner. The vacant IBC belt was captured on June 10 when Tommy Morrison stopped Donovan "Razor" Ruddock.

On June 17 in Las Vegas, Riddick Bowe defended his WBO title against Jorge Luis Gonzalez. Jorge stood 6'7", weighed 237 pounds and carried a 23-0-0 record with 22 knockouts. He had defeated Bowe in the amateur ranks. The talk by both men before the bout was aggressive. However, Bowe had fought much tougher men than Gonzalez since those amateur days. The experience paid off as Bowe knocked Gonzalez out in six rounds.

Jimmy Thunder stopped Ray Anis in seven rounds to retain his IBO heavyweight championship on August 8 in Coachella, California. But the main focus of boxing fans in August was on Mike Tyson who began his comeback with the intention to dominate the heavyweight division once again.

Tyson makes quick return — 1:29

Associated Press

LAS VEGAS — Mike Tyson's comeback fight was fast, furious and disappointing.

But don't blame Tyson.

Tyson knocked Peter McNeeley down twice and had a sellout crowd at the MGM Grand Garden roaring when suddenly McNeeley's manager-trainer, Vinny Vecchione, jumped into the ring and caused his fighter to be disqualified with the fight only 89 seconds old.

After three years in prison and more than four years since his last fight, Tyson had no chance to show whether he still has the skills that once made him the most feared fighter in the world.

It was over that fast, not even lasting as long as the national anthem.

The crowd changed from roaring to chanting obscenities and a dis-

gusted Tyson left the ring before the official decision was announced.

Iron Mike indicated later, however, that maybe the disqualification was the best thing for McNeeley.

"Eventually he would have gotten hurt," said Tyson. "I'm a blood man. I like to win."

"He's back. He got over the hurdle," said McNeeley, Tyson's first opponent in a little less than 50 months.

McNeeley turned out to be not even a speed bump, much less a hurdle.

"The speed (of Tyson) was the major factor in my stopping it," Vecchione said. "This young fighter is 26 years old. He's got a long ways to go."

How far he will go in boxing after Saturday night remains to be seen.

As for Tyson, he looked strong

and fast and wild, but certainly the fight gave no indication how the long layoff affected the man who was once the most feared fighter in the world.

"I'm not surprised at anything," Tyson said. "He came out punching as soon as the bell rang. I just tried to counter him."

The 29-year-old Tyson nailed the swarming McNeeley with a short left hand that dropped him about 15 seconds into the fight.

McNeeley got up immediately and as Tyson stood in a neutral corner ran around the ring until referee Mills Lane could stop him and give a standing 8-count.

The 224-pound McNeeley again swarmed to the attack and backed Tyson into the ropes, where they exchanged punches toe-to-toe exchange, missing more than they landed.

After Tyson, 220, got off the ropes, he hurt McNeeley with a right to the head, then knocked him down with a left and right uppercut to the head. McNeeley bounced up but fell against the rope and that's when Vecchione jumped into the ring, causing the disqualification at 1:29.

McNeeley then went to his corner and, with a smile on his face, hugged his mother who had come up the steps and then he gave high fives to friends in the crowd of 16,736.

"What?" was Tyson's first reaction to the surprise ending, and he obviously was not happy at the way he earned $25 million.

The victory in 89 seconds was the 12th-shortest fight in Tyson's 42-fight career, in which seven opponents have lasted less than a minute. Tyson, a 15-1 favorite, now is 42-1 with 36 knockouts.

The Daily Herald (Chicago, IL), August 20 1995
Reprinted by permission of the Daily Herald, Arlington Heights, Illinois

On August 19 in Las Vegas, Tyson knocked Peter McNeeley down two times in the first round. Vinnie Vecchione, McNeeley's trainer, jumped into the ring to save his fighter. Tyson won by disqualification. On the same card, Bruce Seldon defended his WBA championship against tough Joe Hipp and won by a stoppage in round ten.

In Sao Paulo, Brazil on August 22, Adilson Rodrigues took the WBF title from Johnny Nelson on a twelve-round decision.

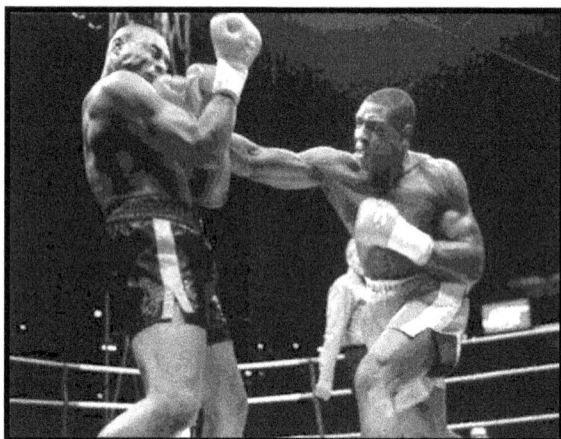
Frank Bruno-Oliver McCall
September 2 1995

September 2 saw Oliver McCall defend his WBC heavyweight championship for the second time. His opponent was hard-hitting Frank Bruno who had tried without success to win the title three times before - against Tim Witherspoon, Mike Tyson and Lennox Lewis.

Bruno won the early rounds but had to hang on as McCall stepped up the pace and battered him around the ring the last three rounds. But Bruno made it through and won the title.

On October 7, the IBC title changed hands yet another time when the large mitts of Lennox Lewis took it from Tommy Morrison in six rounds in Atlantic City.

Riddick Bowe and Evander Holyfield fought for the third time on November 4 in a non-title "rubber" match of their awesome three-bout series. This fight was held in Las Vegas. Each man could still hit with power but each had declined somewhat in his defensive skills. Some observers describe the contest as a brutal fight in which many heavy blows were thrown as the men faced off before each other. Bowe, who disliked training, perhaps was not at his best while Holyfield, on the other hand, was definitely past his peak.

After a close five rounds, Holyfield dropped Bowe in the sixth and had he been a younger man, quite possibly could have finished the contest then and there. But he was no longer that extraordinary young warrior. Bowe fought back, floored Holyfield twice in round eight and stopped the former champion.

Adilson Rodrigues pulled a repeat against Johnny Nelson on December 3 in Sao Paulo when he won a twelve-round decision to retain his WBF heavyweight crown.

In Stuttgart, Germany on December 9, Francois "Frans" Botha and Axel Schulz fought for George Foreman's abandoned IBF heavyweight title. Botha, 35-0-0, was an active fighter and won nearly all the early rounds. Schulz played a cautious waiting game and came on strong towards the end. But his rally fell short and the confident South African Botha won a twelve-round decision to become the new IBF champion. Later, he tested positive for illegal substances and the bout was ruled a "no contest."

Francois "Frans" Botha-Axel Schulz
December 9 1995

On December 15 in New York City, young Shannon Briggs, who stood 6'4" and weighed 224 pounds, scored another victory, this time over Calvin Jones. His record was then 25-0-0 with 20 knockouts. He was setting his sights on the big-time boys.

Mike Tyson continued his comeback in Philadelphia on December 16 against Buster Mathis Jr. There was little doubt about the outcome. Mathis could not hold off Tyson and his feet were too slow to run. Mike scored a third-round knockout.

Big Brian Nielsen, unbeaten and tough, stopped Tony LaRosa in two rounds on January 12, 1996 in Copenhagen, Denmark to become the new IBO heavyweight champion.

On March 15 in Atlantic City, a "Night of Heavyweights" was held with six promising young big men matched against each other. Unbeaten Darroll Wilson stopped unbeaten Shannon Briggs in 3 rounds, unbeaten Andrew Golota stopped Danell Nicholson in 8 rounds and unbeaten David Tua knocked out John Ruiz in one round. The victors were getting attention and moving up.

Frank Bruno was the first champion to meet Tyson in his comeback effort to recapture the heavyweight championship. Bruno and Tyson fought on March 16 in Las Vegas for Bruno's WBC title. In a battle between the two awesome hitters, Tyson won by a technical knockout in round three.

Shannon Briggs

In Copenhagen on March 29, Brian Nielsen stopped Phil Jackson in six rounds in defense of his IBO crown. On May 18 in Araraquara, Brazil, Adilson Rodrigues knocked out Dave Fiddler in three rounds to remain WBF heavyweight champion. In Copenhagen on May 31, Nielsen stopped Mike Hunter in five rounds, also in an IBO defense. Michael Moorer and Axel Schulz met on June 22 in Dortmund, Germany for the vacant IBF heavyweight championship. In a close fight in which Schulz made a lazy start, Moorer won a twelve-round decision. Next, on June 28, Jerry Ballard stopped Corey Sanders in six rounds in Upper Marlboro, Maryland to add his name to the list of IBC champions. Titles, titles, titles. Roll on "alphabet" titles, roll on.

Henry Akinwande, who began his career in 1989, owned a nice 29-0-1 record that included wins over Tony Tucker, Axel Schulz, Jimmy Thunder, Mario Schiesser, Johnny Nelson, J.B. Williamson, Kimmuel Odum and Eddie Taylor. Akinwande stood 6'7" and weighed 232 pounds when he tangled with Jeremy Williams for the vacant WBO heavyweight championship on June 29 in Indio, California. Williams was coming off an impressive string of eleven straight victories but Akinwande polished him off in three rounds.

Riddick Bowe looked around for a man with a respectable record who could provide a good fight. He settled on big Andrew Golota, the Polish street-fighter turned heavyweight. On July 11 in New York in a surprise, Golota pounded Bowe round after round. It was a contest in which each man fought rough and dirty. When Bowe got rough, Golota got rougher. When Bowe got dirty, Golota got dirtier. On several occasions the Pole struck low. In round seven when it appeared that Golota had the bout won, he delivered another low blow and Bowe went down. It was difficult to determine whether Bowe was hurt or simply wanted out of the grueling battle. Golota was disqualified.

A couple of months later, on September 7 in Las Vegas, Mike Tyson collected title number two in his comeback when he met Bruce Seldon for the WBA title. The beautifully-muscled but timid Seldon was hardly a match for the aggressive "Iron Mike." A hard tap from Tyson sent Seldon down for keeps in less than two minutes.

The WBC crown was not at stake for this bout. Tyson had an earlier agreement to meet Lennox Lewis for that. Shortly after the Seldon bout, Tyson relinquished the WBC title and made plans to meet Evander Holyfield for the WBA crown.

Riddick Bowe-Andrew Golota
July 11 1996

George Foreman met unbeaten Crawford Grimsley on November 3 in Japan in a less-popular version of the heavyweight title. The WBU championship was on the line and George pounded out a twelve-round win over his blond foe. The big fellow also picked up the International Boxing Association (IBA) championship.

November 9 was a big night for boxing in Las Vegas. Three world heavyweight championship fights were on the card. Henry Akinwande, at 238 pounds and sporting a record of 30-0-1, defended his WBO title against Alexander Zolkin who was 6'5" and 235 pounds with a record of 24-2-0. In what was expected to be a tough test for Akinwande, the taller champion boxed and punched his way to a knockdown in round four and a tenth-round stoppage to retain his crown.

In the battle for the IBF title, Michael Moorer, 37-1-0, battled it out with the unbeaten "Frans" Botha, 35-0-0 (with one "no contest" bout). The bout was fought in spurts by each man. Moorer's sharper punching took its toll. Botha was forced to quit in round twelve and accept his first loss.

The Colorado Springs (CO) Gazette Telegraph
November 10 1996

Mike Tyson and Evander Holyfield met in the third title contest of the evening. The two men who had dominated the scene eight years earlier got into the ring together at last. At stake was the WBA title held by Tyson. Mike started aggressively but the sharp-punching by Holyfield held him off time and again.

To the surprise of many onlookers, Evander staggered and pounded Mike on several occasions in the early going. In round five, Holyfield knocked Mike to the canvas and the tide turned. Tyson lost steam and confidence. On the other hand, Evander seemed to gain strength and stamina.

As the contest wore on, it became apparent that Tyson in his comeback effort to recapture the heavyweight championship, had reached too high, too soon. He was in the ring against a man who was just too good. Holyfield battered Tyson around and the bout was stopped very early in round eleven. Holyfield was the new WBA king. It was a shocking upset to many boxing fans. The ambition of "Iron Mike" was there in full-force but his skills had waned. Holyfield had an answer for everything Tyson tried.

On November 22 in Denver, John Kiser defeated George Stephens to become the new IBC heavyweight king. On a larger scale, Riddick Bowe and Andrew Golota fought a second time on December 14 - same men, same kind of fight, same result. Early in the bout each man was knocked down. Golota hammered away and as the bout progressed, the former champion Bowe weakened. Andrew was on the verge of scoring a knockout win. In round nine it happened! For no apparent reason, Golota tossed a low blow. Down went Bowe and Golota was disqualified.

On January 11, 1997, Akinwande was back in the ring, this time defending his WBO prize in Nashville, Tennessee against Scott Welch, 6'2" and 229 pounds.

Welch had a record of 19-2-0 and had scored 16 knockouts. He was a tough guy. Nevertheless, Henry boxed well and won a lopsided twelve-round decision. He later gave up his WBO crown to fight Lennox Lewis for the WBC title.

Henry Akinwande-Scott Welch
January 11 1997

Lionel Butler met Marcos Gonzalez on January 23 in Reseda, California for the vacant WBF heavyweight championship. In the first round, Butler scored a knockout to become the new WBF champion.

Larry Holmes was back in the ring on January 24 in Brondby, Denmark in an attempt to regain a share of the heavyweight title. His adversary was Brian Nielsen, proud owner of a 31-0-0 record and the reigning IBO heavyweight champion. Larry was unsuccessful in his effort as Nielsen won in twelve rounds.

Since his loss to McCall in 1994, Lennox Lewis had been working his way back to regaining his lost title and along the way had beaten Lionel Butler, Justin Fortune, Tommy Morrison and Ray Mercer. He was primed! On February 7 in Las Vegas, Lewis got his chance. In a startling occurrence, Oliver McCall was clearly under emotional stress and froze, unable to fight. Lewis pounded his man but McCall simply stood his ground, took the punches and eventually broke into tears in his corner. Lewis won the vacant WBC crown with a fifth-round stoppage.

The IBF championship held by Michael Moorer was the reward for the winner on March 29 in Las Vegas. The challenger was Vaughn Bean. Oddsmakers thought Moorer would finish his man quickly but Michael posted a twelve-round decision win in a dull fight.

George Foreman defended his WBU crown on April 26 in Atlantic City against Lou Savarese, a talented but lesser-known fighter who carried a 36-0-0 record with 30 knockouts. Lou hit quicker and sharper in the early part of the fight and was winning. Then Savarese, who had gone more than eight rounds only once, tired. The strength, chin and surprising stamina of big George stepped forward. The forty-eight year old youngster turned the contest around and won a split decision in twelve rounds.

Michael Grant won the IBC title with a victory over Alfred "Ice" Cole on June 20 in Atlantic City and on June 28 in England, Herbie Hide captured the vacant WBO championship when he stopped big Tony Tucker in two rounds. This was the second time Hide had won this title. For the next three years, the WBO title would reside in Europe but in the hands of different fighters.

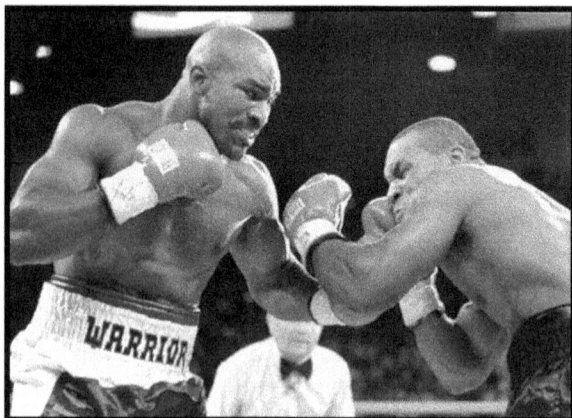

Evander Holyfield, a little more than seven months after his surprising victory over Mike Tyson, met "Iron Mike" in a WBA title rematch in Las Vegas, also on June 28.

This one was even more surprising than the first. In a "no love lost" contest, with some rough and rowdy tactics taking place, Tyson bit Holyfield's ear twice in clinches, claiming Evander was butting him. Evander won by disqualification in round three.

Evander Holyfield-Mike Tyson
June 28 1997

During 1997, following his February win over Oliver McCall, Lennox Lewis racked up WBC title bout victories over Henry Akinwande on July 12 and Andrew Golota on October 4. On July 29 in New York, Bert Cooper knocked out Richie Melito in the first round to become the new WBF heavyweight kingpin. A few months later on November 7, Michael Grant beat Jorge Luis Gonzalez for another IBC title win and on November 8 in Las Vegas, Holyfield added the IBF heavyweight championship to his collection when he stopped Michael Moorer in eight rounds. In Copenhagen on November 14, Brian Nielsen knocked out Don Steele in an IBO title defense and on November 15, Corrie Sanders took a twelve-round decision from Ross Puritty to win the WBU crown once held by George Foreman. Are all these titles confusing or what?

During 1998, Lennox Lewis defeated Shannon Briggs on March 28 and Zeljko Mavrovic on September 26 in WBC title fights. Evander Holyfield scored a win over Vaughn Bean in a contest for the WBA and IBF heavyweight championship titles. Michael Grant picked up a couple more IBC title wins and Herbie Hide won WBO title bouts against Damon Reed and Willi Fischer. In addition, Corrie Sanders stopped Bobby Czyz in two rounds in Uncasville to keep his WBU crown, Lou Savarese beat James "Buster" Douglas for the IBA title, Joe Bugner defeated James "Bonecrusher" Smith for the WBF crown when Smith injured a shoulder and Brian Neilsen retained his IBO championship against Lionel Butler. Keep on rolling, "alphabet" titles, keep on rolling!

In a heavyweight championship bout to unify the WBC, WBA and IBF titles, Holyfield and Lewis battled to a twelve-round draw on March 13, 1999 in New York.

In St. Charles, Missouri on June 25, Joe Hipp battled Everett "Big Foot" Martin for the title that men kept abandoning - the WBF heavyweight championship. Hipp won a decision.

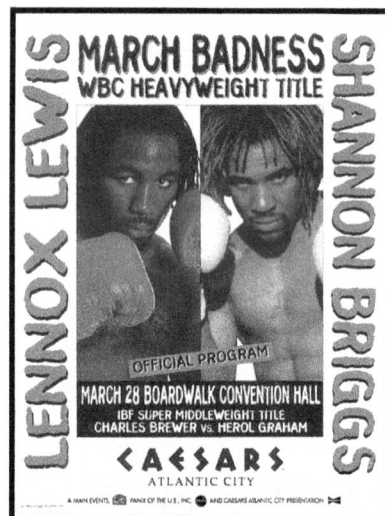

Lennox Lewis-Shannon Briggs
Program, March 28 1998

Herbie Hide next took on big Vitali Klitschko in London on June 26. Vitali knocked Herbie out in two rounds to take the WBO championship. On July 2, Corrie Sanders stopped Jorge Valdes in the first round of a WBU title defense.

Vitali "K" followed his victory over Herbie Hide with two successful defenses of the WBO title - on October 9 he stopped Ed Mahone in three rounds and on December 11 he retired Obed Sullivan in nine rounds. Both bouts were held in Germany.

In Las Vegas on November 13, in a follow-up contest to settle matters, Lennox Lewis imposed his will and won a victory over Evander Holyfield to claim three major titles – WBC, WBA and IBF - plus the vacant IBO championship. In a dispute with the WBA over his next opponent, Lennox Lewis gave up his WBA title shortly after the victory.

Early in 2000 on January 14, Brian Nielsen defeated Troy Weida in Denmark to win the vacant IBC crown and then won a second IBC victory on April 28 when he beat Jeremy Williams.

Corrie Sanders kept a firm hold on his WBU crown by stopping Alfred "Ice" Cole in the first round of a title defense in Brakpan, Gauteng, South Africa on February 19, 2000. However, during May in Atlantic City, he lost his WBU title to Hasim Rahman by a seventh-round stoppage.

Vitali Klitschko defended his WBO championship against Chris Byrd in Berlin on April 1. During the course of the bout, Klitschko injured a shoulder and was forced to retire from the contest - while leading on all the judges' score cards. Byrd was the new champion. As was a practice with the Klitschko brothers, Wladimir then challenged Byrd for the WBO title in October and won a decision over twelve rounds. He now wore the WBO crown.

Lennox Lewis-Michael Grant
April 29 2000

On May 12, 2000, Mike Bernardo captured the vacant WBF crown by stopping Daniel Jerling in Szekszard, Hungary.

Since his loss to David Tua in 1996, John Ruiz had been impressive, winning eleven bouts - ten by knockout. Ruiz met Evander Holyfield on August 12 in Las Vegas for the vacant WBA heavyweight championship. Holyfield emerged victorious.

During the year 2000, Lennox Lewis placed his WBC, IBF and IBO titles on the line on three occasions and won all three battles - against Michael Grant, "Frans" Botha and David Tua.

The big champion knocked out Grant in two rounds, stopped Botha in two rounds and won a convincing one-sided twelve-round decision against Tua.

Top Heavyweight Boxers of 1981-2000
1. Larry Holmes
2. Mike Tyson
3. Lennox Lewis
4. Riddick Bowe
5. Evander Holyfield

Top Heavyweight Bouts of 1981-2000
1. Riddick Bowe-Evander Holyfield #1, November 13 1992, Las Vegas, Nevada
2. James "Buster" Douglas-Mike Tyson, February 11 1990, Tokyo, Japan
3. Larry Holmes-Gerry Cooney, June 11 1982, Las Vegas, Nevada
4. Michael Spinks-Larry Holmes #1, September 21 1985, Las Vegas, Nevada
5. Evander Holyfield-Mike Tyson #1, November 9 1996, Las Vegas, Nevada

Larry Holmes-James "Bonecrusher" Smith
November 9 1984

Chapter Seven

The Years 2001-2010

John Ruiz led off this topsy-turvy period when he won the WBA heavyweight championship. On March 3, 2001 in Las Vegas, he defeated Evander Holyfield in twelve rounds for the title.

Ruiz knocked Holyfield down in the eleventh round. Holyfield was struggling to make it through the fight and looked like the aging fighter that he was.

John Ruiz defeats Holyfield in decision

The Logansport (IN) Pharos-Tribune
March 4 2001

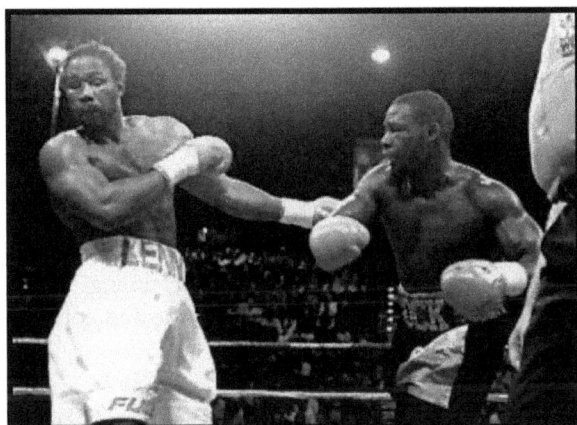

**Hasim Rahman-Lennox Lewis
April 22 2001**

On March 24 in Munich, Germany, Wladimir Klitschko, known as "Dr. Steelhammer," stopped Derrick Jefferson in two rounds to retain his WBO crown.

Hasim Rahman pulled off a big upset on April 22 in Brakpan, Gauteng, South Africa when he knocked out Lennox Lewis in five rounds. The win gave Rahman the WBC, IBF and IBO heavyweight titles.

The "alphabet" titles were rolling. Mike Bernardo stopped Peter McNeeley in round one on June 8 in a WBF title defense. Brian Nielsen defeated Orlin Norris in Denmark on June 16 to chalk up another IBC title win and on August 4, Wladimir Klitschko defeated Charles Shufford in Las Vegas to keep his WBO title.

On October 1 in Helsinki, Finland, Dirk Wallyn stopped Jukka Jarvinen in nine rounds to capture the IBU championship.

Lennox Lewis gained revenge against Rahman on November 17 in Las Vegas when he knocked out Hasim in four rounds and took back his WBC, IBF and IBO heavyweight titles.

A week later in London, Johnny Nelson defeated Alexander Vasiliev in twelve rounds to win the vacant WBU crown.

A rematch between Ruiz and Holyfield occurred on December 15 in Mashantucket, Connecticut. This was the third title fight between the two and it ended in a twelve-round draw. Ruiz kept his WBA title.

**Lennox Lewis-Hasim Rahman
November 17 2001**

Jukka Jarvinen made another attempt at the IBU crown against Adnan Serin on February 4, 2002 in Helsinki but was unsuccessful in a third-round stoppage. On March 16, Wladimir Klitschko stopped "Frans" Botha in eight rounds to remain the WBO heavyweight champion. This bout was held in Stuttgart, Germany.

The vacant WBF crown was at stake and won by Furkat Tursunov on May 11 in Munich when he defeated Ralf Packheiser. On June 8 in Memphis, Lennox Lewis gave Mike Tyson a lesson in fighting when he knocked out the man with the abusive talk in eight rounds to retain his WBC, IBF and IBO heavyweight championships. Wladimir Klitschko followed shortly afterwards on June 29 in defense of his WBO title and stopped Ray Mercer in six rounds in Atlantic City.

To retain his WBA title, John Ruiz earned a win over Kirk Johnson on July 27 in Las Vegas. Johnson was disqualified in the tenth round.

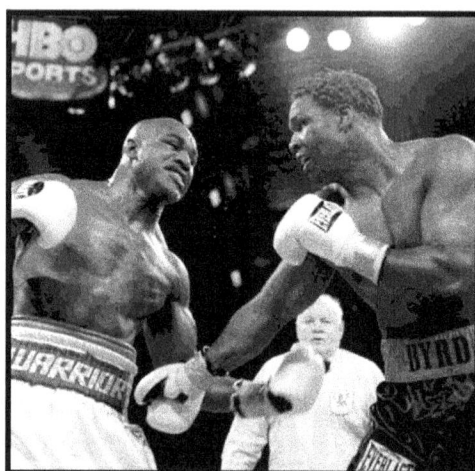

Chris Byrd-Evander Holyfield
December 14 2002

Wladimir Klitschko won again on December 7 in Las Vegas when he defeated Jameel McCline in ten rounds for the WBO championship.

In Atlantic City on December 14, Chris Byrd decisioned Evander Holyfield in twelve rounds and won the vacant IBF heavyweight championship. According to Byrd, "Now the world sees I can stay in there with the great heavyweights because I just beat one of them."

Holyfield once again showed slippage in his career as Byrd handed out a boxing lesson. Chris exhibited fine timing, hit in flurries and moved quickly. As always, Evander showed courage despite his wild swings and misses.

The vacant WBU title was up for grabs on December 21 when George Kandelaki met Alexander Vasiliev in St. Petersburg, Russia. On a twelfth-round stoppage, Kandelaki emerged as the winner.

On March 1, 2003, the talented Roy Jones Jr., who had moved up in weight over the years, was successful in his quest to capture a version of the heavyweight championship title. He won a twelve-round decision over John Ruiz in Las Vegas and became the WBA heavyweight champion.

Thus, Jones Jr. joined Bob Fitzsimmons as a former middleweight champion who won the coveted heavyweight championship. This goal achieved, Jones Jr. relinquished the crown and moved back down to fight in the light-heavyweight division. But let's not forget that Tommy Burns, once a top middleweight contender, won the heavyweight crown in 1906.

On March 8, the hard-hitting South African Corrie Sanders stopped Wladimir Klitschko in the second round to win the WBO heavyweight title. Sanders was a big hitter who coming into this contest had lost only two fights. One of them was on May 20, 2000 in Atlantic City against Hasim Rahman for the WBU heavyweight crown.

Roy Jones Jr.

Lennox Lewis-Vitali Klitschko
June 21 2003

Richel Hersisia won the vacant WBF crown when he knocked out Sandro Abel Vazquez in nine rounds in The Hague, Netherlands on May 16, 2003.

On June 21, Lennox Lewis saw the "writing on the wall" when he tangled with big Vitali Klitschko in Los Angeles with his WBC and IBO heavyweight titles at stake. In a give-and-take slugfest, Lewis won on a sixth-round stoppage when Klitschko received a bad gash. Each man knocked the other around the ring with powerful blows. At times, each man was hanging on and it seemed that just one more solid punch would finish the fight. Lewis retired from the ring soon afterwards.

Shannon Briggs won the IBU championship on July 19 in Fort Lauderdale, Florida when he stopped John Sargent in the first round. Richel Hersisia decisioned Sami Elovaara on August 9 in Salzburg, Austria to hang onto his WBF title. Chris Byrd beat Fres Oquendo in Uncasville, Connecticut to keep his IBF title on September 20 and on December 13, John Ruiz, "The Quiet Man" as he was called, captured the interim WBA heavyweight championship when he defeated Hasim Rahman in a twelve-round contest in Atlantic City.

Early in 2004, Corrie Sanders gave up his WBO crown in order to fight Vitali Klitschko in a WBC title bout. As a result, Lamon Brewster moved into the heavyweight picture. On April 10 in Las Vegas, he won a fifth-round stoppage against Wladimir Klitschko for the vacant WBO heavyweight championship. Klitshcko pounded Brewster around the ring, floored him and did everything but take him out.

Just about the time it looked like it was curtains for the courageous Brewster, Klitschko ran out of gas and was forced to surrender. Once again, stamina proved to be a big Wladimir weakness.

Klitschko Ponders Future

The Harrisonburg (VA) Daily
News-Record, April 12 2004

Vitali Klitschko-Corrie Sanders
April 24 2004

In New York on April 17, John Ruiz solidified his WBA title claim with a win over Fres Oquendo while Chris Byrd fought a draw with Andrew Golota in defense of his IBF crown.

On April 24, revenge for the Klitschko family took place in Los Angeles. Vitali stopped South African Corrie Sanders in the eighth round to win the vacant WBC heavyweight crown. This victory evened the score for the Klitschkos since Sanders had stopped Wladimir on March 8, 2003 in Germany. It gave them a major world title too.

133

In Temecula, California on September 23, 2004, James "Lights Out" Toney won a twelve-round decision against Rydell Booker for the IBA heavyweight title. Thus, Toney became the third former middleweight champion to win a heavyweight title although it was not recognized as a major one.

Lamon Brewster followed up his Wladimir Klitschko victory with a WBO title win against Kali Meehan in September in Las Vegas. In New York on November 13, John Ruiz beat Andrew Golota to keep his WBA belt. On the same card, Chris Byrd defeated Jameel McCline to retain his IBF title. In Las Vegas on December 11, Vitali Klitschko stopped Danny Williams for his WBC crown.

On February 25, 2005 in London, Matt Skelton stopped Fabio Eduardo Moli in six rounds to win the vacant WBU heavyweight championship. Lamon Brewster stopped Andrew Golota in one round to hold onto his WBO title belt on May 21 in Chicago. In Philadelphia on March 24, Robert Hawkins defeated John Poore to take the IBU title in five rounds.

One of those controversial moments in boxing took place on April 30 in New York when John Ruiz met James Toney for the WBA championship. (Some sources say the bout was for the IBA title too.) Ruiz was a busy man during the fight but Toney did the more effective hitting and won a unanimous decision.

Following the battle, Toney tested positive for a banned substance and the verdict was changed to a "no decision" by the New York State Athletic Commission (NYSAC). Ruiz kept his title and Toney kept his IBA title.

**James Toney-John Ruiz
April 30 2005**

Eddie Chambers claimed the IBU crown when he defeated Robert Hawkins in twelve sessions in Philadelphia on July 9. Hasim Rahman roared back into the heavyweight picture on August 13 in Chicago when he won a twelve-round decision over Monte Barrett. There was talk of Vitali Klitschko meeting Hasim for the WBC crown but a Klitschko injury in training ended that possibility. The WBC gave Vitali a time limit to heal and defend his crown. But Klitschko's injured knee required surgery and he could not be ready by the given date. He retired on November 9. The WBC Board of Governors then voted and on November 10 declared Rahman to be the new WBC heavyweight champion.

Wladimir Klitschko met Samuel Peter on September 24 in a North American Boxing Federation (NABF) heavyweight championship bout that was also seen as an IBF and WBO heavyweight championship elimination bout. Peter was a big power-puncher with long arms and decent quickness for a heavyweight. His record was 24-0-0 with 21 knockouts. Wlad, at this point, was sporting a 44-3-0 mark. Peter attacked, threw bombs and managed to knock Klitschko down three times during the bout. But other than the knockdowns, Klitschko outboxed Samuel and was the winner in twelve rounds.

In Hamburg, Germany on September 28, Lamon Brewster defeated Luan Krasnigi in nine rounds in a WBO title defense. On October 1 in Reno, Chris Byrd won over DaVarryl Williamson to hold onto his IBF championship and James Toney beat Dominick Guinn to keep his IBA crown.

Nikolai Valuev-John Ruiz
December 17 2005

Tomasz Bonin became the new IBC champion on November 26 with a decision victory over Fernely Feliz in Chicago.

On December 17 in Berlin, the enormous Nikolai Valuev defeated John Ruiz in twelve rounds to win the WBA heavyweight crown. Valuev was a giant, standing 7'0" and weighing 324 pounds. He now possessed an unbeaten record of 43-0-0 with one "no contest" bout and was gunning for fifty wins to surpass the Rocky Marciano mark of 49-0-0.

March 18, 2006 saw Hasim Rahman and James Toney fight to a draw for the WBC championship in Atlantic City. Rahman kept his title. On April 1 in Cleveland, Sergei [Serguey] Liakhovich won a twelve-round decision over Lamon Brewster to capture the WBO heavyweight championship.

On April 22 in Mannheim, Germany, Wladimir Klitschko stopped Chris Byrd in seven rounds to win the IBF and vacant IBO heavyweight championships. Wlad was a Russian holding world heavyweight championships at the same time that other Russians were holding major heavyweight titles.

Six months after winning the IBC crown, Tomasz Bonin knocked out Adenilson Rodrigues in three rounds to retain that title on May 20 in Poland. On the same date, Gene Pukall defeated Ingo Jaede on a third-round stoppage in Bautzen, Germany for the IBU heavyweight title and on June 3, Nikolai Valuev won a WBA title fight over Owen Beck in Hannover, Germany.

Oleg Maskaev

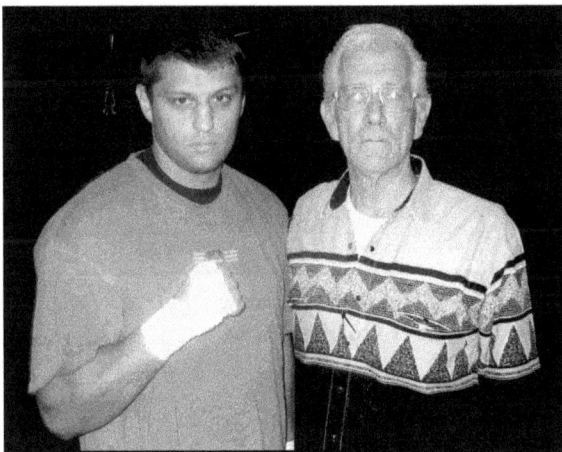

Sergei [Serguey] Liakhovich and Tony Triem,
historian, October 23 2006

In Las Vegas on August 12, yet another Russian won a world heavyweight title when Oleg Maskaev stopped Hasim Rahman in the twelfth round for the WBC crown. This seemed to be the new rule - Russians or former Russians hold the world heavyweight championships. This was the same crown that Vitali Klitschko had won in 2004.

Samuel Peter took the IBA crown away from James Toney by winning a twelve-rounder against the "Lights Out" man on September 2, 2006 in Los Angeles. On October 7, Nikolai Valuev won another WBA title fight, this time against Monte Barrett in eleven rounds. On November 4 in Phoenix, Shannon Briggs stopped Sergei [Serguey] Liakhovich in the twelfth round to win the WBO heavyweight title. November 11 saw Wladimir Klitschko defeat Calvin Brock to hold onto his IBF and IBO belts.

On December 10, 2006 in Moscow, Oleg Maskaev defeated Peter Okhello in twelve rounds to successfully defend his WBC title. In Basel, Switzerland on January 20, 2007, Nikolai Valuev defeated Jameel McCline to keep his WBA crown while Wladimir Klitschko defeated Ray Austin in a contest for the IBF and IBO titles on March 10 in Germany.

Ruslan Chagaev won the WBA heavyweight championship by defeating Nikolai Valuev in twelve rounds on April 14 in Stuttgart, Germany. This was Valuev's first defeat and eliminated his chance of surpassing Rocky Marciano's mark. At this point in his career, Chagaev had built a 23-0-1 mark.

Ibragimov beats Briggs

ATLANTIC CITY — The Cannon never fired.

Shannon Briggs' hold on the heavyweight title slipped away Saturday night at the quick hands of Sultan Ibragimov, who easily outpointed the WBO champion.

Briggs, nicknamed "The Cannon" and the only American with a share of the heavyweight crown, wasn't even a water pistol against Ibragimov. The left-handed Russian consistently landed lefty leads and often followed with more quick lefts.

The Salina (KS) Journal
June 3 2007

In Atlantic City on June 2, Sultan Ibragimov outworked Shannon Briggs over twelve rounds and defeated Briggs to take the WBO heavyweight championship. Wladimir Klitschko tasted sweet revenge over Lamon Brewster on July 7 in Cologne, Germany when he stopped his man in six rounds in defense of his IBF and IBO heavyweight titles. At this stage in his career, the big blows from his previous battles had caught up to Brewster and his tough chin. He could no longer last against this big hitter and succumbed.

The author, Tracy Callis, stands in front of a large billboard in Moscow
prior to the October 13 2007 Sultan Ibragimov-Evander Holyfield bout

Ruslan Chagaev-Matt Skelton
January 19 2008

Samuel Peter got his chance at the WBC title when Oleg Maskaev pulled out of a scheduled bout due to a back injury. Peter then fought Jameel McCline on October 6 in New York in an interim title bout and won in twelve rounds. Sultan Ibragimov had a WBO heavyweight title unification bout on October 13 against Ruslan Chagaev cancelled when Chagaev developed a medical condition. Ibragimov went ahead and successfully defended his crown against Evander Holyfield in Moscow.

Ruslan Chagaev defended his WBA heavyweight title on January 19, 2008 in Dusseldorf, Germany against Matt Skelton. Matt was a big fellow fighting out of England. He stood 6'3", weighed 254 ¾ pounds and sported a 21-1-0 record.

Skelton started strong but Chagaev defended well and made it through the tough going. Using a good left hand, Ruslan took control of the contest in the fourth round and worked his way to a twelve-round decision to retain his crown.

Nikolai Valuev picked up another win, this time against Sergei [Serguey] Liakhovich on February 16 in Nuremberg, Germany. He defeated his man in twelve rounds. This was a WBA heavyweight championship elimination bout.

Wladimir Klitschko won the WBO heavyweight championship in twelve rounds on February 23 in New York when he defeated Sultan Ibragimov. Klitschko now owned the IBF, WBO and IBO heavyweight crowns.

Samuel Peter defeated Oleg Maskaev in six rounds in Cancun, Mexico on March 8 for the WBC heavyweight championship. Peter now sported a 30-1-0 record with his only defeat coming at the hands of Wladimir Klitschko on a twelve-round decision in September of 2005 in Atlantic City.

Wladimir Klitschko-Sultan Ibragimov
February 23 2008

A WBA heavyweight championship bout set for May 31 between Ruslan Chagaev and Nikolai Valuev was cancelled when Chagaev came down with a viral infection that interrupted his training. John Ruiz, the #2 ranked heavyweight by the WBA, stepped forward to take Chagaev's place but was ignored by the WBA. The Chagaev-Valuev bout was rescheduled for July 5 in Hannover, Germany but when Chagaev suffered a complete tear in the Achilles tendon in his left ankle while training it was put off again. The WBA declared Chagaev to be a "champion in recess" and gave him time to heal before fighting for the title. Nikolai Valuev and John Ruiz were then scheduled to fight in August in Berlin.

Wlad Klitschko continued his winning ways on July 12 in Hamburg, Germany when he met Tony Thompson and put the IBF, WBO and IBO heavyweight titles on the line. It was a slow, cautious fight for the early rounds but gradually turned into a hard-hitting affair. Klitschko stopped Thompson in round eleven.

Nikolai Valuev and John Ruiz fought in Berlin on August 30 for the vacant WBA heavyweight championship. The huge man won a twelve-round decision over Ruiz. He was now champion and Ruslan Chagaev needed to fight him by June 26, 2009 for a chance to regain the WBA championship.

Vitali Klitschko-Samuel Peter
October 11 2008

Vitali Klitschko got back into the heavyweight picture on October 11, 2008 in Berlin when he ended a four-year absence from the ring to tangle with Samuel Peter for the WBC championship. Still big, still strong and still armed with a very tough chin, "Dr. Iron Fist" banged on Peter until the big fellow retired from the contest after round eight. Vitali was back. This was just the second loss of Peter's career - once again to a Klitschko.

Wladimir Klitschko was back in the ring on December 13 in Mannheim, Germany when he took on Hasim Rahman with three heavyweight titles at stake - the IBF, WBO and IBO. The careful Klitschko methodically outboxed the lethargic Rahman and in round seven, landed some blockbuster smashes that brought a stop to the contest.

James Toney was also in the ring on December 13. He was in Cabazon, California where he won a decision against Fres Oquendo in twelve rounds for the IBA crown. In Zurich, Switzerland on December 20, big Nikolai Valuev ended the championship fighting for the year when he won a dull, twelve-round decision over Evander Holyfield to hold onto his WBA title.

On February 7, 2009, Ruslan Chagaev won a technical decision in six rounds over Carl Davis Drumond in Rostock, Germany and retained his WBA "champion in recess" status. An accidental headbutt terminated the contest. Chagaev was ahead on all judges' cards. Vitali Klitschko stopped Juan Carlos Gomez, his former sparring partner, in nine rounds on March 21 in Stuttgart, Germany in a successful defense of the WBC title. Gomez frustrated Klitschko early in the fight by defending well and landing blows of his own. But the tide turned in round four and from that point on, Vitali dominated the contest except for round six when Gomez mounted a strong attack. Hector Ferreyro decisioned Cisse Salif on April 18 in Laredo, Texas to become the new IBC heavyweight champion.

In Gelsenkirchen, Germany on June 20, tall Wladimir Klitschko won a convincing ninth-round stoppage over tough Ruslan Chagaev to retain his IBF, WBO and IBO heavyweight titles. It was a one-sided match and an overwhelming victory for the big man. This bout ended the WBA recognition of Chagaev as "champion in recess."

Following the fight, Klitschko stated that he felt he was fighting at the best level ever during his ring career. He did not think any of today's heavyweights could beat him, pointing out that he had not lost in five years. Wladimir also said jokingly that he did not want to risk his chin because it was made of glass and he could not take a punch as his critics had said. Therefore, he preferred to simply dominate his fights and avoid the blows.

Klitschko stops Chagaev:
Wladimir Klitschko again proved his dominance of the heavyweight division, stopping Ruslan Chagaev in a hastily put together title fight Saturday night before 61,000 at a German soccer stadium in Gelsenkirchen. The IBF and WBO champion added the Ring Magazine belt to his haul, knocking down Chagaev in the second round and opening a cut over the Uzbekistan-born fighter's left eye in the eighth. Referee Eddie Cotton stopped the fight before the 10th round.

The Daily Herald (Chicago, IL), June 21 2009
Reprinted by permission of the Daily Herald
Arlington Heights, Illinois

In Laredo, Texas on August 21, Hector Ferreyro knocked out Matt Hicks to retain his IBC heavyweight crown. On September 26, Vitali Klitschko jabbed and landed thudding right handers throughout the contest against the somewhat inexperienced Chris Arreola who could not seem to get going. Klitschko dominated the encounter and won by a tenth-round technical knockout. The WBC title bout was held at the Staples Center in Los Angeles. "Frans" Botha met Pedro Carrion on October 24 in Dessau, Germany for the vacant WBF heavyweight championship. This was a twelve-round bout that ended in a draw.

On November 7 in Nuremberg, Germany, Nikolai Valuev lost a twelve-round decision to the outstanding former cruiserweight David Haye, who was quicker and carried a solid punch. Valuev was huge and quite strong - yet slow.

David Haye

Two judges scored the bout in favor of Haye while the third scored it a draw. Winning this bout, Haye became the generally recognized WBA heavyweight champion.

In his first ring appearance since losing his WBO title to Sultan Ibragimov in 2007, hard-hitting Shannon Briggs began a comeback and met Marcus McGee in New York on December 3. Briggs ended it in a single round but tested positive for an illegal substance and the official verdict was changed from a knockout win to a "no contest" decision.

Vitali Klitschko was back in the ring on December 12 in Bern, Switzerland. His WBC heavyweight championship was on the line and his opponent was the unbeaten Kevin Johnson. Kevin was a big fellow but Vitali was bigger. His punch was certainly bigger as he methodically jabbed and thudded Kevin throughout the contest. Johnson seemed content to stay on the ropes and counter-punch but that wasn't enough to beat the towering Klitschko. Vitali won the twelve-round decision.

Another big fight for Evander Holyfield was scheduled for January 16, 2010 against "Frans" Botha for the WBF heavyweight championship. It ran into problems and was rescheduled for February 20 in Kampala, Uganda. The bout was then postponed for the second time when the promoter did not come up with the initial money payment to the fighters. The bout was rescheduled for April in Las Vegas.

Wladimir Klitschko, 53-3-0, put his three heavyweight titles - the IBF, WBO and IBO - on the line against the American challenger Eddie Chambers, 35-1-0, on March 20 in Dusseldorf, Germany. In his usual deliberate manner, Klitschko threw his solid jab and occasional powerful overhand right that landed hard on Chambers. Eddie fought in a somewhat cautious style. Wladimir floored Chambers in round two but waited until round twelve to stop his man.

In Laredo on March 26, Hector Ferreyro won a decision against Arron Lyons to keep the IBC championship. On April 3 in Manchester, England, David Haye defended his version of the WBA title against the perpetual contender John Ruiz and won by a stoppage. Haye floored Ruiz early in the first round and again towards the end of the round. He also knocked Ruiz down in rounds five and six but the former champion refused to stop. Haye's accurate punching throughout the contest finally brought surrender when Ruiz's corner called it quits during the ninth round.

Evander Holyfield and "Frans" Botha finally got together on April 10 in Las Vegas. Both men were former top performers in the heavyweight division but for this one they displayed tarnished skills. Holyfield won an eighth-round stoppage to capture the WBF heavyweight title. Evander scored a knockdown in the last round, prior to termination of the contest. At the time of the stoppage, Botha was ahead on two scorecards but behind on the third. He was warned about his punches several times in the early rounds although he wobbled Evander in the second round with a solid right.

Tony Triem, historian, and Evander Holyfield
April 7 2010

Shannon Briggs was back in the ring in Hollywood, Florida on April 13 and ended the contest in one round when he knocked out Rafael Pedro. Briggs then met Dominique Alexander in New York on May 21 and stopped him in one round.

On May 22 in Rostock, Germany, Ruslan Chagaev met Kali Meehan in a contest viewed as a WBA heavyweight elimination bout. Chagaev won in twelve rounds. Chagev, who had been declared the WBA heavyweight "champion in recess" back in 2008, had claimed that title ever since. He fought Carl Davis Drumond in February of 2009, reportedly for the title. However, Nikolai Valuev and David Haye had been active WBA champions and were more generally recognized. On the same card, Sergei [Serguey] Liakhovich, former WBO heavyweight champion, stopped Evans Quinn in nine rounds.

The heavyweight fireworks continued on May 28 in Norfolk, Virginia when Shannon Briggs stopped Rob Calloway in the first round. On May 29 in Gelsenkirchen, Germany, the next big heavyweight bout took place between Vitali Klitschko and Poland's Albert Sosnowski. Albert gave up his European Boxing Union (EBU) heavyweight title to meet Klitschko for the WBC crown. Klitschko jabbed and punched his way to a stoppage in round ten to retain his crown. The IBC title was on the line on August 6 in Laredo when Hector Ferreyro defended against Homero Fonseca. Ferreyro won in twelve rounds.

Wladimir Klitschko was in the ring again on September 11 in Frankfurt, Germany and defended his IBF, WBO and IBO heavyweight titles against the hard-hitting Samuel Peter. Klitschko used a variety of solid punches and stopped Peter in ten rounds to retain his belts. Big brother Vitali then appeared in the ring on October 16 in Hamburg, Germany to defend his WBC crown against Shannon Briggs. In a one-sided encounter, Klitschko won the decision as he pounded Briggs, who withstood the punishment.

On November 13 in Manchester, England, David Haye, 24-1-0, put his version of the WBA heavyweight championship on the line against big Audley Harrison, former EBU heavyweight champion and owner of a 27-4-0 record with 20 knockouts. Haye stopped Harrison in the third round to keep his crown.

The former WBA champion Ruslan Chagaev defeated Travis Walker in Hamburg, Germany on November 19. Evander Holyfield was scheduled to defend his WBF title on December 9 in Detroit, Michigan against Sherman Williams but it did not take place. Likewise, Wlad Klitschko was supposed to meet Dereck Chisora in Mannheim, Germany on December 11 for his IBF, WBO and IBO titles but this bout was cancelled when Wlad tore an abdominal muscle that kept him out of the ring for nearly six weeks.

Top Heavyweight Boxers of 2001-2010
1. Lennox Lewis
2. (tie) Vitali Klitschko and Wladimir Klitschko
4. Hasim Rahman
5. (tie) Samuel Peter and Corrie Sanders

Top Heavyweight Bouts of 2001-2010
1. Lennox Lewis-Vitali Klitschko, June 21 2003, Los Angeles, California
2. Vitali Klitschko-Corrie Sanders, April 24 2004, Los Angeles, California
3. Corrie Sanders-Wladimir Klitschko, March 8 2003, Hannover, Germany
4. Hasim Rahman-Lennox Lewis #1, April 22 2001, Brakpan, South Africa
5. Roy Jones Jr.-John Ruiz, March 1 2003, Las Vegas, Nevada

The All-Time Top Fifteen Heavyweight Bouts

RANKING THE ALL-TIME GREAT BOUTS

What is it that makes a great boxing contest or an outstanding bout? Is it the action? Is it some controversial event that took place? Is it some personal characteristic of the observer? Talk to different boxing historians and fight fans and different views and reasons will surface.

The main reasons for ranking bouts as great contests involves such things as (1) the caliber of the fighters involved, (2) whether the fighters were in their prime years (or close), (3) the near-equal competitiveness of the men during the fight, (4) the amount of action taking place in the fight, (5) the type of action taking place (running, slugging, boxing, brawling, etc.), (6) the length of the fight (number of rounds), (7) the duration of the fight (how much actual time was involved), (8) the historical significance, social impact, etc., of the fight, (9) any special facts related to the fight (whether it was a controversial or remarkable event) and (10) any special conditions related to the fight (freezing weather, sweltering temperature, etc.)

John L. Sullivan-Paddy Ryan
February 7 1882

To be considered as a great action fight, a bout should be competitive. The men may be great fighters or they may be less skilled with their fists. However, if the fighting is exciting, give-and-take and loaded with action, it merits attention. Since a close, near-even match can occur at any skills level, other factors such as the caliber of the fighters, whether they are close to their peaks or not and historical impact must be analyzed along with the competition exhibited. Sometimes, these other factors compel a fight to be rated as great even if the action is limited.

When the topic of great fights is brought up, naturally bouts that involved a lot of action come to mind. Indeed, there have been a number of exciting contests where explosive action was abundant - Peter Jackson-Frank "Paddy" Slavin (1892), Joe Jeannette-Sam McVea #3 (1909), Jack Dempsey-Jess Willard (1919), Jack Dempsey-Luis Angel Firpo (1923), Max Baer-Primo Carnera (1934), Rocky Marciano-"Jersey" Joe Walcott #1 (1952), Rocky Marciano-Ezzard Charles #1 (1954), Charles "Sonny" Liston-Cleveland Williams #1 (1959), Ingemar Johansson-Floyd Patterson #3 (1961), George Foreman-Joe Frazier #1 (1973), George Foreman-Ron Lyle (1976), Larry Holmes-Ken Norton (1978), Mike Tyson-Evander Holyfield #1 (1996), Lennox Lewis-Vitali Klitschko (2003) and many others.

More examples of outstanding action-packed bouts are Jim Corbett-Joe Choynski #3 (1889), Jim Jeffries-Tom Sharkey #2 (1899), Jim Jeffries-Bob Fitzsimmons #2 (1902), Muhammad Ali-Joe Frazier #1 (1971), Muhammad Ali-Joe Frazier #3 (1975), George Foreman-Ron Lyle (1976) and Larry Holmes-Ken Norton (1978). These fights involved many power-laden punches being thrown, many boxing tactics being utilized, etc. In these contests, the men were very close to their peaks or in their primes.

Among the historical bouts that deserve consideration are the John L. Sullivan-Jake Kilrain fight (1889) and the Jim Corbett-John L. Sullivan bout (1892). The Sullivan-Kilrain match was the last major bare-knuckle fight. Kilrain was nearly at his best whereas Sullivan was somewhat past his peak. In the Corbett-Sullivan confrontation, it was a clash of styles. The new style of movement, footwork, jabs, combinations and hooks was exhibited by the young Corbett while the old man Sullivan relied upon the brute strength method of the past. Another outstanding contest of different styles was the Joe Louis-Billy Conn #1 bout in 1941.

A bout of social importance was the Jack Johnson-Tommy Burns bout (1908) in which a black man fought for the heavyweight championship for the first time - and won. It signified the end of the "color line" as a reason for preventing negroes from fighting for the biggest prize in boxing. The Joe Louis-Max Schmeling #2 contest in 1938 was another bout of historical and social importance due to the proclamation of Aryan racial superiority by Adolf Hitler.

Bouts involving controversial or remarkable events such as Billy Miske-"K.O." Bill Brennan #4 (1923), Gene Tunney-Jack Dempsey #2 (1927), Primo Carnera-Ernie Schaaf (1933) and Evander Holyfield-Mike Tyson #2 (1997) merit consideration too. Occurrences that are rare and do not happen often make such contests important. Miske fought under terrible extenuating physical circumstances, Tunney was down for the "long count," Schaaf died following surgery for a cranial hemorrhage as the result of this fight and Tyson savagely bit the ear of Holyfield in that fight.

Certainly, bouts in which the men are topflight fighters are likely important ones. Further, if these men are fighting at or near their peaks or primes, then the contest would be quite meaningful and important. If such a contest were a title bout, it would be even more significant.

It is difficult to argue that a bout between two top-notch men - at or near their peaks – with lots of action, is competitive and lasts for many rounds is not a great fight. Such was the Jim Corbett-Peter Jackson contest (1891). Of course, when bouts continue over an unbelievable number of rounds, the action slows as the men match each other and tire – also, as in the Corbett-Jackson bout.

In ranking the bouts, this writer has considered historical impact (upon society and upon boxing or its methods and techniques) to be as important as action fights with top-caliber fighters involved. There are many record compilations for boxers of the past - a number of them have conflicting results. Records from the internet boxing database at www.boxrec.com (February 2013) are used when describing the top bouts because of the popularity of the website and the many boxing historians contributing data.

There have been many outstanding bouts since 1881 that are worthy of being ranked among the greatest ever. Deserving of consideration are those bouts that were competitive and loaded with action between top caliber men that could have gone either way and did not leave much to choose from between the warriors. Doubtless, every fan has his favorite. But remember, special occurrences as well as historical and social factors are extremely important too. A few are talked about in the following paragraphs.

The Jim Corbett-Joe Choynski war of June 5, 1889 on a barge in the Carquinez Strait near Benicia, California merits strong attention. The shifty boxing strategist, "Gentleman Jim," met

---

Choynski Knocked Out by Corbett

Benecia, Cal., June 5. – The prize fight between Jim Corbett and Joe Choynski, which was interrupted on the 20th near San Anselmo, was concluded near here at daylight this morning. Twenty-seven hardly contested rounds were fought. In the last Choynski was knocked out.

The Boston (MA) Daily Globe
June 6 1889

143

the all-around fighter and terrific puncher, "Chrysanthemum Joe," in a bloody war in which each young man was battered, bruised and ready to collapse before it ended.

The Jim Corbett-Peter Jackson marathon on May 21, 1891 in San Francisco lasted 61 rounds - until the men could fight no longer. The two talented boxers tried every trick they knew on each other to no avail. Their splendid quickness turned into slow, mechanical movement before it was clear that neither man could win.

The Peter Jackson-Frank "Paddy" Slavin bout on May 30, 1892 in London and the Jim Corbett-John L. Sullivan bout on September 7, 1892 in New Orleans involved similar combatants - a man with considerable boxing skills and a fighter. The Jackson-Slavin fight was a battle that Jackson dominated. At times during the encounter, Slavin seemed on the verge of getting an attack going but Jackson responded and came out the victor after wearing Slavin down. In the case of Sullivan, he was out of fighting condition, too fat and actually too far "over the hill" to offer real opposition to the young, slick Corbett in this historic contest. Corbett, the dancing master, showed fast feet, fast hands and keen judgment in thoroughly whipping "The Great John L." The fight stands out in boxing history because, after years of reigning as the heavyweight king, Sullivan was finally bested.

Bob Fitzsimmons, one of the greatest all-around performers the ring ever produced, proved his mettle when he challenged Jim Corbett on March 17, 1897 in Carson City, Nevada. Fitz, with that rare combination of boxing craftiness and power, won the heavyweight championship that day but it wasn't easy.

On May 2, 1899, Peter Maher met Gus Ruhlin in New York at the Lenox Athletic Club. The warriors went at each other from the start, displaying little in the way of science, only exhibiting the desire to blast the each other unconscious. Both were badly punished during the bout in what was called by many the hardest heavyweight fight ever held. Others described it as vicious. It ended in a twenty-round draw.

The Jim Jeffries-Bob Fitzsimmons bloodbath on June 25, 1902 in San Francisco was a hard fought encounter in which each man was "busted up" rather badly. Fitz employed every trick he knew and battered the bigger man with blow after blow. Jeffries delivered bruising blows in return. Finally, Fitz gave out. The boxing skills of each man were at a high level but the punching power by each took its toll.

FOUGHT A DRAW

Maher and Ruhlin Put Up a Terrific Battle.

Irish Champion's Eyes Closed From the Fourth Round.

Had His Opponent Groggy Several Times After That.

Result a Huge Surprise to Old Ring Followers.

Fastest 20-Round Heavyweight Bout Ever Contested.

The Boston (MA) Daily Globe
May 3 1899

The Joe Jeannette-Sam McVea slugfest of April 17, 1909 in Paris was a combative match in which each man gave his all. Jeannette was the smaller man but overall better boxer who had a nice punch while McVea was the larger - and not much slower - power hitter. Joe got the worst end of the early fighting, going down numerous times. But his skills prevailed. He tired out the bigger man and finished him off after many rounds of fighting.

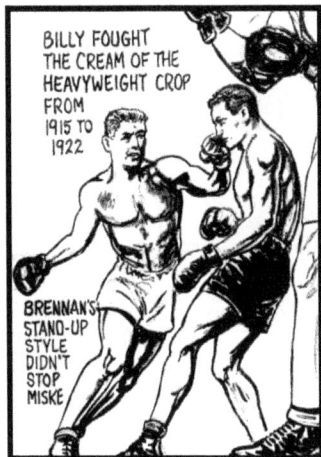

Billy Miske-"K.O." Bill
Brennan, November 7 1923

On April 5, 1915, big Jess Willard brought closure to the search for a "Great White Hope" to defeat Jack Johnson and terminated the rule of the black man as heavyweight king. The battle took place in Havana, Cuba under a burning sun and lasted for twenty-six rounds. Big Jess, who moved quickly for a large man, held his own in the early rounds against the clever Johnson. As the fight wore on, Jess reached "Black Jack" more often and in the last round, put him down and out. Later, Johnson claimed he threw the fight. In some photographs, he appeared to be shading his eyes as he lay on the canvas.

The circumstances surrounding the Billy Miske-"K.O." Bill Brennan bout of November 7 in 1923 were tense, frightening, miraculous and remarkable! It was a contest between a "dead man fighting" and a brutal puncher. Everyone who knew the circumstances held their breath. Miske was critically ill and should not have been in the ring. He could have easily died during the battle.

The Max Baer-Primo Carnera bout on June 14, 1934 in Long Island City, New York certainly ranks as one of the most action-filled contests. In this bout, the power-hitting Baer stopped the huge Italian in round eleven and captured the heavyweight crown. He scored eleven knockdowns in the process.

The Rocky Marciano-Ezzard Charles confrontation on June 17, 1954 in New York was once called "the toughest fight in my career" by Rocky. In this peak-Marciano versus the older-but-wiser Charles battle, "The Cincinnati Cobra" (Ezz) gave as good as he got. It was a close fight but Rocky eeked out a decision win.

Max Baer-Primo Carnera
June 14 1934

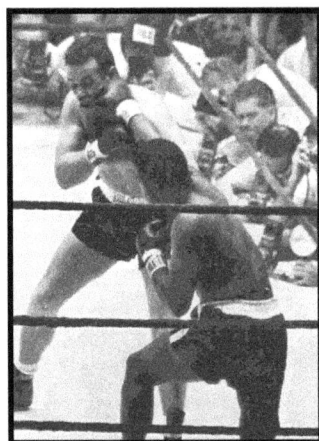

Floyd Patterson-Ingemar
Johansson, March 13 1961

Exactly three months later, on September 17, 1954, they fought again. This time, Rocky floored Ezz early in the fight and built up a good lead. But in round six he suffered a split nose. In round seven he received a cut over his left eye. Afraid that referee Al Berl might stop the bout, Marciano stepped it up and knocked Charles out.

The Charles "Sonny" Liston-Cleveland Williams brawl on April 15, 1959 in Miami Beach, Florida must not be overlooked either. Two great power-hitters teed off on each other with "Sonny" winning out.

The Floyd Patterson-Ingemar Johansson bout on March 13, 1961 in Miami Beach was the rubber match of the series between these two. Johansson had knocked out Patterson in their first encounter and taken the heavyweight title. Floyd regained the title in the rematch. It appeared that Johansson had brought his power with him from his first matchup but after three or four rounds he tired considerably and Floyd finished him off in the sixth round.

Muhammad Ali figured in two shocking contests when he scored unexpected victories - against Charles "Sonny" Liston on February 25, 1964 and George Foreman on October 30, 1974. As fans observed the magnificent Ali plying his trade to the awesome punchers, it became apparent that neither could handle the all-time great boxer's skills. Liston aged considerably in his fight and Foreman's stamina weakness was revealed in his.

Highly touted George Foreman, sporting a 37-0-0 record with 34 knockouts, challenged heavyweight king Joe Frazier, 29-0-0, on January 22, 1973. The bout took place in Kingston, Jamaica. The big man dropped Frazier three times in round one and three times in round two before referee Arthur Mercante stopped the contest. It was a great surprise to most boxing fans who had believed that big George was not yet ready for Smokin' Joe.

The rubber match between Muhammad Ali and Ken Norton that took place on September 28, 1976 in New York is another outstanding battle that merits consideration. The two great fighters tangled this third time for the WBC and WBA heavyweight titles. Ali won a close but unanimous fifteen-round decision. A panel of boxing people later reviewed the fight on national television and judged the bout as a draw with Norton winning on points. Norton had surprised the boxing world when he defeated Ali on March 31, 1973 for the NABF heavyweight championship and broke Ali's jaw in the process. Muhammad gained sweet revenge on September 10, 1973 when he won a twelve-round split decision in Inglewood, California for the NABF heavyweight championship. Most reporters at ringside saw Norton as the winner in that one.

Michael Spinks, holder of three major light-heavyweight titles, took on IBF heavyweight champion Larry Holmes on September 21, 1985 in Las Vegas in what *The Ring* magazine declared as the "1985 Upset of the Year." Michael won a close fifteen-round unanimous decision that ruined Holmes' quest to match Rocky Marciano's 49-0-0 mark. Seven months later, Spinks won a fifteen-round split decision against Larry.

The James "Buster" Douglas-Mike Tyson contest on February 11, 1990 in Tokyo, Japan was a shocking upset to most boxing fans as was the first Ingemar Johansson-Floyd Patterson bout on June 26, 1959 in New York. In each contest, the reigning champion took a shellacking.

The George Foreman-Michael Moorer bout in Las Vegas on November 5, 1994 ranks among the most memorable bouts because "old man" Foreman succeeded in his quest to regain the heavyweight title and in doing so, became the oldest boxer ever to win the coveted prize. Moorer, ahead on the cards, had boxed well throughout the bout but got careless in round ten. When Foreman's hard left hook landed, followed by a solid right, the reigning heavyweight king was flattened for keeps.

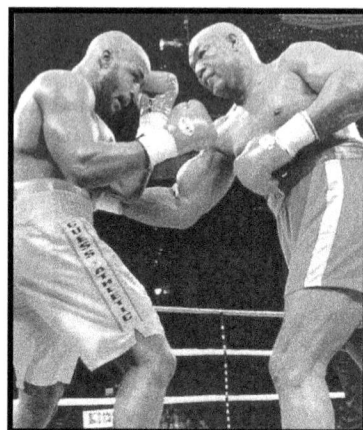

George Foreman-Michael Moorer
November 5 1994

The Evander Holyfield-Mike Tyson bout on November 9, 1996 in Las Vegas was a surprise. Tyson was on the comeback trail and serious about regaining the heavyweight title. Problem was he jumped too high too quickly. His handlers got him in against a man who was too skilled before he was truly ready. Holyfield won by knockout in round eleven.

146

On March 1, 2003, the great Roy Jones Jr. took on the WBA heavyweight champion John Ruiz in a quest for the grand prize in boxing. Jones Jr. exhibited quickness, accurate punching and solid defense in capturing the title from the larger man. In doing so, Jones Jr. joined Bob Fitzsimmons as a middleweight champion who won the heavyweight crown.

Lennox Lewis tangled with Vitali Klitschko on June 21, 2003 in Los Angeles and to the surprise of American boxing fans, but not the European fans who had seen him in action, big Klitschko held his own and gave as good as he got. He had Lewis hanging on at times. Each man was big, each man could hit and each man could take it. Unfortunately, Vitali experienced a bad gash that caused the fight to be stopped. Otherwise, they might still be fighting. It was a thrilling contest.

Some hot action --

**Luther "Luck" McCarty-Al Palzer
January 1 1913**

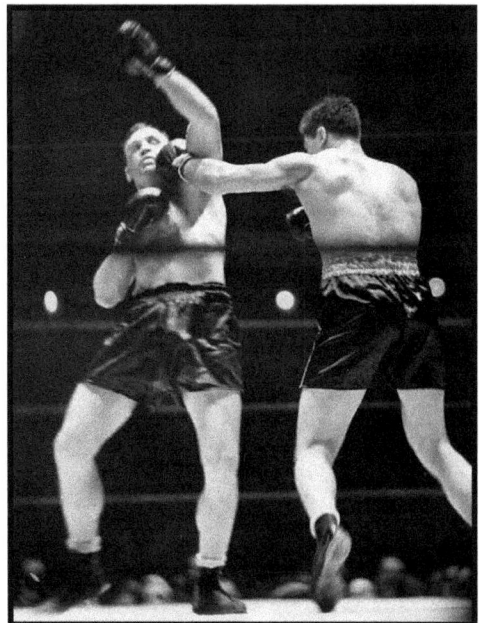

**Jimmy Adamick-Harry Thomas
February 18 1938**

"Two-Ton" Tony Galento-Lou Nova
September 15 1939

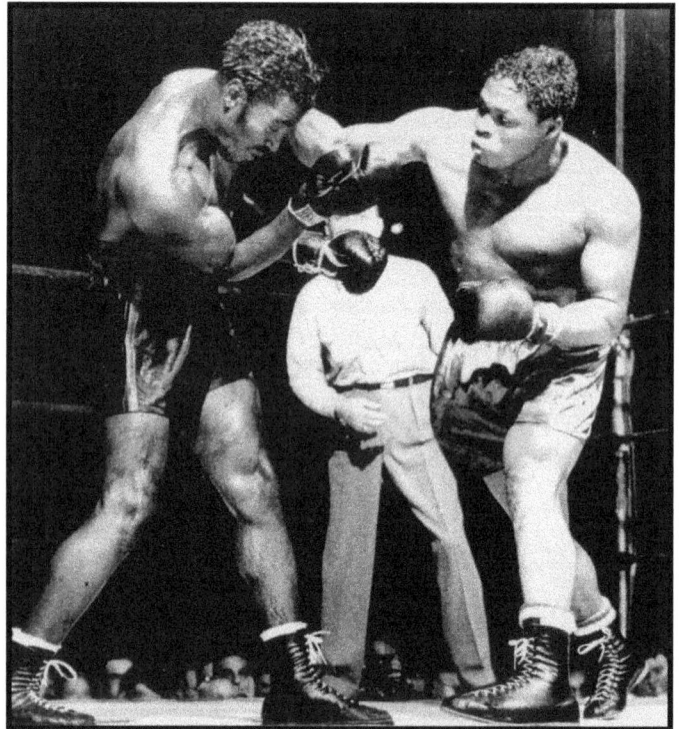

Lee Q. Murray-Albert "Turkey" Thompson
July 28 1944

Now, let's take a look at the all-time top fifteen heavyweight bouts.

15 Riddick Bowe-Evander Holyfield #1
November 13, 1992 … Las Vegas, Nevada

Evander Holyfield

Evander Holyfield was unbeaten and the holder of the WBC, WBA and IBF heavyweight championship titles. He owned a record of 28-0-0 with 22 knockouts. He was a muscular, talented fighter who could box or punch and tangling with larger men did not daunt him. He began as a light-heavyweight, moved up to cruiserweight and then heavyweight. He had won over such men as George Foreman, Larry Holmes, James "Buster" Douglas, Pinklon Thomas, Michael Dokes, Dwight Qawi (twice), Adilson Rodrigues, Alex Stewart, Bert Cooper, Carlos DeLeon and Ricky Parkey.

Riddick Bowe was a large, powerful heavyweight bruiser who possessed a good left jab, a strong overhand right and a wicked uppercut. He was unbeaten in 31 contests and had scored 27 knockouts. He had beaten such men as Tony Tubbs, Pinklon Thomas, Bruce Seldon, Bert Cooper, Tyrell Biggs, Pierre Coetzer, Philipp Brown, Art Tucker, Rodolfo Marin and Elijah Tillery (twice).

These two outstanding heavyweights battled three times before they finished their careers, the first two being for versions of the heavyweight championship. Each contest was action-packed. In the view of this writer, the first bout was the most exciting bout and ranks among the greatest fights of all-time.

Holyfield was the heavyweight champion but there was some question about his skills since he had not beaten the best of heavyweight competition. Among his victims, Foreman and Holmes were old men when he defeated them. Thomas, Dokes, Rodrigues, Stewart and Cooper were good boxers but not major champions. The other top opponents were of lighter weights. So, Evander had something to prove against the huge, powerful challenger.

Bowe was a bonafide heavyweight and the younger man but he hated to train. From his amateur days, he had the false reputation as a quitter. His victims included some good men but like Holyfield, he had not beaten many top-of-the-line heavyweight fighters.

Outweighed 235-205, Holyfield figured to move, dodge, attack and escape - but he did not. Instead, he waded into his former sparring partner, trading punches - not just punches, but haymakers. Bowe responded with blockbuster shots. The first two rounds were loaded with action. Big bombs were being tossed. Each man was taking it to the other - trying to level his foe.

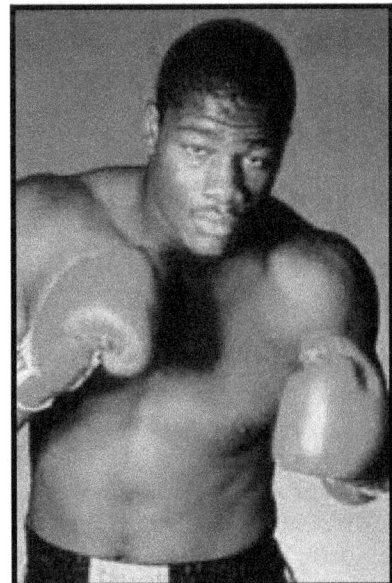

Riddick Bowe

The third round saw Holyfield slack off in his attack while Bowe kept shooting his long left jab at the champion. Bowe landed some stiff swinging blows too.

Riddick Bowe-Evander Holyfield
November 13 1992

The men battled hard throughout the fight. Each was battered and bruised. In round nine, action picked up even more. Bowe wobbled the champion with blows to the head. Holyfield worked through the attacks but was jolted again late in the round.

Round ten stood out as the most action-packed session of the encounter. Bowe had Holyfield nearly out early in the round and was knocking the champion about the ring. The smaller man was clearly hanging on - with the heart of a lion. Then suddenly, as if switching on a light, Holyfield turned the tables on his big opponent and attacked, driving him backwards.

There was no letup in round eleven as Bowe continued his jabbing and pounding on the champion. In this round, the big challenger finally scored a knockdown as Evander hit the deck. Almost exhausted, Holyfield managed to rise and finish out the fight. Bowe won a unanimous decision and captured the heavyweight championship. Each man showed the wages of battle. The right eye of each was swollen, Holyfield's almost closed. The beaten champion also had a cut over his left eye.

Even though he lost, this fight was one of Holyfield's best performances in the ring. He battled a talented, much bigger man tooth-and-nail, fought on when the going got rough (he could easily have quit) and gained the respect of everyone.

14 Larry Holmes-Ken Norton
June 9, 1978 ... Las Vegas, Nevada

Ken Norton

Ken Norton was the current WBC heavyweight champion of the world, having been declared so after his victory over Jimmy Young. (Leon Spinks was stripped of the WBC title when he met Ali in a return match instead of Norton.) Ken was a solid puncher who displayed a relentless attack that featured a powerful overhand right. He owned a record of 40-4-0 and had scored 32 knockouts. In addition to his win over Young, he had wins over Muhammad Ali, Jerry Quarry, Boone Kirkman, Ron Stander, Jose Luis Garcia, Duane Bobick, Larry Middleton, Lorenzo Zanon, Pedro Lovell, Henry Clark, Jack O'Halloran and James J. Woody (twice).

Larry Holmes was an excellent up-and-coming ringman who could box or punch. He was tall, muscular and the owner of an awesome jab. He moved well and utilized wonderful savvy. He had a record of 27-0-0 with 19 knockouts and had beaten such men as Earnie Shavers, Ibar Arrington, Rodney Bobick, Tom Prater, Roy Williams and Fred Houpe (Young Sanford).

Norton had been in the ring with Muhammad Ali (three times), George Foreman and many other top contenders. Against Ali, he had won the official verdict in the first bout. The other two contests were very close encounters and many people felt Norton had won those too. But he had lost to Foreman.

Holmes was less experienced but had won over Earnie Shavers, a formidable hitter, in his biggest victory. He had that beautiful jab, good power and knew how to box. He could deal with blockbuster hitters.

Norton thought Holmes had a big mouth. He did not like some of the things Larry had said before the bout. He stalked Holmes throughout the contest but what he received for his effort was a constant thudding with Larry's great jab.

Opinions at ringside varied as to which fighter held the advantage as the battle raged on. When it appeared that one man had taken control of the bout, dominance switched to the other. It was like this for fifteen rounds.

Larry Holmes

151

Holmes used his jab frequently in the early rounds and kept out of Norton's way. Ken kept coming on, however, as Larry speared him with sharp blows. By round five, Norton began jabbing well too, avoiding many of Holmes' shots and keeping up his attack.

Larry Holmes-Ken Norton
June 9 1978

In round eight, Norton drew blood from Holmes' mouth with a solid head shot. He was getting in good punches to the body too. Round nine saw more attacking by Norton and the pressure seemed to be slowing Larry.

Through round 11, Holmes continued his moving and evading. Norton was puffy about the eyes from Larry's steady punches. In round 12, Ken raised a swelling about Holmes' right eye and appeared to be gaining control of the fight. He was jabbing well and landing hooks and effective body punches.

During the last three rounds, Norton came on strong but not as strong as Holmes. In round 13, the tide turned. Near the end of the session, Holmes had Norton reeling from punches to the head and almost down at the bell. But Ken came back in round 14 with hard body blows and an uppercut. The bout was dead-even going into the last round. Round 15 saw toe-to-toe exchanges. Holmes' hard blows to the head had Norton on rubber legs. Again, he was in danger of going down.

At the end, the judges' scorecards read as follows: 143-142 for Holmes, 143-142 for Norton and 143-142 for Holmes. After the fight, Norton said he felt that he won but Holmes was a lot tougher than he had expected. He thought he should have put more pressure on Holmes early in the fight and not let those rounds slip away. Holmes was exhausted at the end. He commented, "I'll fight anybody except I don't want to fight Norton again."

13 John L. Sullivan-Jake Kilrain
July 8, 1889 ... Richburg, Mississippi

John L. Sullivan

John L. Sullivan was an unbeaten young heavyweight from Boston who claimed he could whip any man in the world. He owned a record of something like 38-0-2, consisting mostly of knockouts, with one "no contest" bout. (Fight reports from this time period vary greatly due to the illegal aspect of fighting and the lack of official data.) His raw strength, stamina, chin and determination made him an awesome warrior. At the sound of the bell, he attacked his man with forceful aggression and delivered relentless smashes until his foe was overpowered. He had defeated such men as Paddy Ryan (twice), Jimmy Elliott, Charlie Mitchell, Dominick McCaffrey, "Alf" Greenfield, "Professor" John Donaldson, Steve Taylor and Frank Herald.

Jake Kilrain was a sturdy bruiser who possessed great stamina, delivered solid blows and was a very good wrestler. Although he was not a classy, skilled boxer type, he was one of the best fighters among the heavyweights at that time. He had a record of 18-0-9 with 11 knockouts and two "no decision" bouts and owned victories against George Godfrey, Joe Lannon, Frank Herald, Jack Ashton, "Alf" Greenfield and John Clow and was better than Jem Smith, the English champion, in a draw in France.

Early in his career, the young Sullivan had offended Richard K. Fox, editor of the National Police Gazette organization. Fox responded by making disparaging remarks about Sullivan in his weekly publication. In addition to his statements about Sullivan's skill as a fighter, Fox established his own heavyweight championship belt and went so far as to proclaim Kilrain the Fox heavyweight champion of Ameica and the world. Sullivan, predictably, was irked by these comments, boasted that he was world heavyweight champion and vowed that he would knock Kilrain out.

The fight between Sullivan and Kilrain was for the heavyweight championship of America - and the world, according to Fox. It was a gut-wrenching battle that took place on a hot, muggy, uncomfortable Mississippi day. According to reports, the temperature was at least 100 degrees Fahrenheit. The ring was quickly put together overnight so as to avoid the authorities.

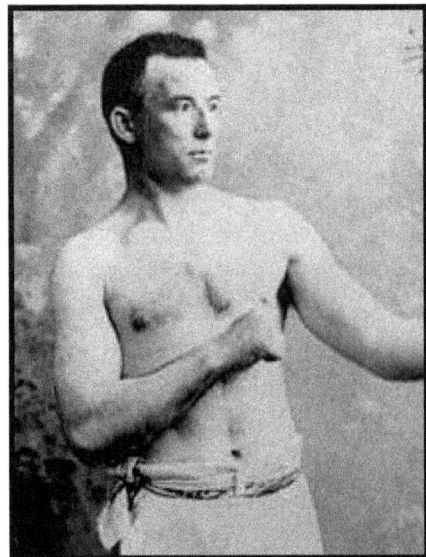

Jake Kilrain

At ringside were many of the famous fight people of the day. One was Charlie Mitchell, the Englishman who disliked Sullivan and in return, was hated by John L. Throughout the contest, Mitchell and Sullivan hurled insulting remarks toward each other. As the battle wore on, it was Sullivan who dominated the fighting and rendered a severe beating to Kilrain. The brave Jake fought on, however, in an effort to outlast his mighty foe. At last, hardly able to stand or walk, he yielded to Mike Donovan in his corner, who threw in the sponge.

Below, Sullivan on the left, faces Kilrain in one of the most brutal heavyweight fights in history - a "finish" fight with bare-knuckles under the London Prize Ring Rules. Sullivan bore into Kilrain, round after round, like a Pit Bull. Kilrain changed his tactics from round to round but mostly focused on avoiding the Sullivan rushes, clinching or trying wrestling tactics to throw John L. to the turf.

John L. Sullivan-Jake Kilrain
July 8 1889

From the start, Kilrain avoided toe-to-toe slugging and sidestepped the rushes of Sullivan. From time to time, he got in some hard blows of his own. His evasive tactics irritated John L. who yelled challenging remarks throughout the fight. Charlie Mitchell's antics at ringside further enraged John.

In round one, Sullivan pursued Kilrain but was grabbed and thrown to the ground. John L. continued to throw hard punches over the next few rounds and some landed. Much scuffling and grappling transpired. In the clinches, each man threw solid shots to the body and ribs of the other. A number of observers thought Kilrain never recovered fully from a blow to the ribs he received in round three. Kilrain scored "first blood" in round six with a bash to Sullivan's left ear. John L. scored the first knockdown in the next round. Blood flowed as the brawl continued and a scorching sun burned their backs. John drank tea and brandy between rounds and vomited during round forty-four.

Many felt Sullivan, the excessive drinker, would tire as the fight progressed but it was Kilrain who wilted. John L. was dominant throughout and scored all the knockdowns and most of the falls. Jake was game, though, and refused to quit even when some thought his neck was broken. Battered, shaky and unsteady on his feet, he came to scratch round after round. Finally, when time was called for round seventy-six, in spite of Kilrain's objections, the sponge was tossed in from his corner. This was the last major bare-knuckle fight in ring history and lasted more than two hours. The referee was John Fitzpatrick who would go on to become mayor of New Orleans. Bat Masterson of Dodge City fame was present at ringside.

Andrew English (2008 p 106) wrote, "Today the fistic field of battle is a grassy turnaround at a not yet urban crossroads. A plaque marks the spot where the determined sons of immigrants bashed themselves to glory. The locals talk about it still."

12 George Foreman-Ron Lyle
January 24, 1976 … Las Vegas, Nevada

George Foreman

George Foreman was a former world heavyweight champion and boasted a record of 40-1-0 with 37 knockouts. He was big and powerful and viewed as being close to invincible. He threw blockbuster punches and could take out anyone he could hit. George had beaten such men as Joe Frazier, Ken Norton, George Chuvalo, Gregorio "Goyo" Peralta (twice), Chuck Wepner, Boone Kirkman, Jose "King" Roman, Luis Faustino Pires, Miguel Angel Paez and Jack O'Halloran.

Ron Lyle was a top heavyweight contender who had a record of 31-3-1 with 22 knockouts. He delivered bashing blows and like George, could take out anyone he could hit squarely. He had beaten such men as Jimmy Ellis, Oscar "Ringo" Bonavena, Earnie Shavers, Gregorio "Goyo" Peralta, Buster Mathis, Jose Luis Garcia, Boone Kirkman, Jurgen Blin, Larry Middleton, Luis Faustino Pires, Vicente Rondon, Bill Drover and Jack O'Halloran.

These men were not finesse boxer-types and no one expected a classic boxing contest when they got together. Right on! It was a brawl. Each man tossed big bombs frequently during the battle. Each fighter was rocked about, knocked down and battle weary before it was all over.

If all out slugging between two super specimens of strength and power accompanied by non-stop action makes a great fight, this was surely one.

This bout was for the North American Boxing Federation (NABF) heavyweight championship but these two gladiators went to war as if it were for the undisputed heavyweight championship of the world. Pride was on the line.

Except for some exhibition bouts, Foreman had not fought since losing to Muhammad Ali on October 30, 1974. It was apparent that he was rusty. Many of his swings were ponderous and wide. He missed many punches but when he connected, he jolted Lyle.

Lyle hit with great power shots too and many rocked Foreman. Consequently, this bout could have gone either way.

Ron Lyle

The bout started slower than many expected but got hot towards the end of the first round. Foreman was staggered by a right and hurt in the ensuing action. The second round lasted only two minutes due to a malfunction of the electric timer. Foreman had Lyle hurt and in trouble when the round came to its sudden end. "Big George" controlled the third session with his stronger punching. He kept Lyle pinned in a corner and on the ropes for most of the round.

Foreman was down early in round four from a left-right combination from Lyle. But he rose quickly and mounted a wild-swinging attack that put Lyle down. Just before the bell, Lyle put George down again with a hard left. The two big heavyweights had put on quite a demonstration of power-hitting. After four rounds, two judges had Lyle ahead and the other had it even.

During the fifth and last round, both men appeared to be exhausted. Lyle staggered Foreman who recovered and charged back with a number of lefts and rights, backing Lyle up and finally putting him down and out. This was the first time Lyle had actually been counted out in a fight. Afterwards, George said that he must fight more often to avoid being so rusty and commented, "It was most definitely THE toughest fight I've ever had."

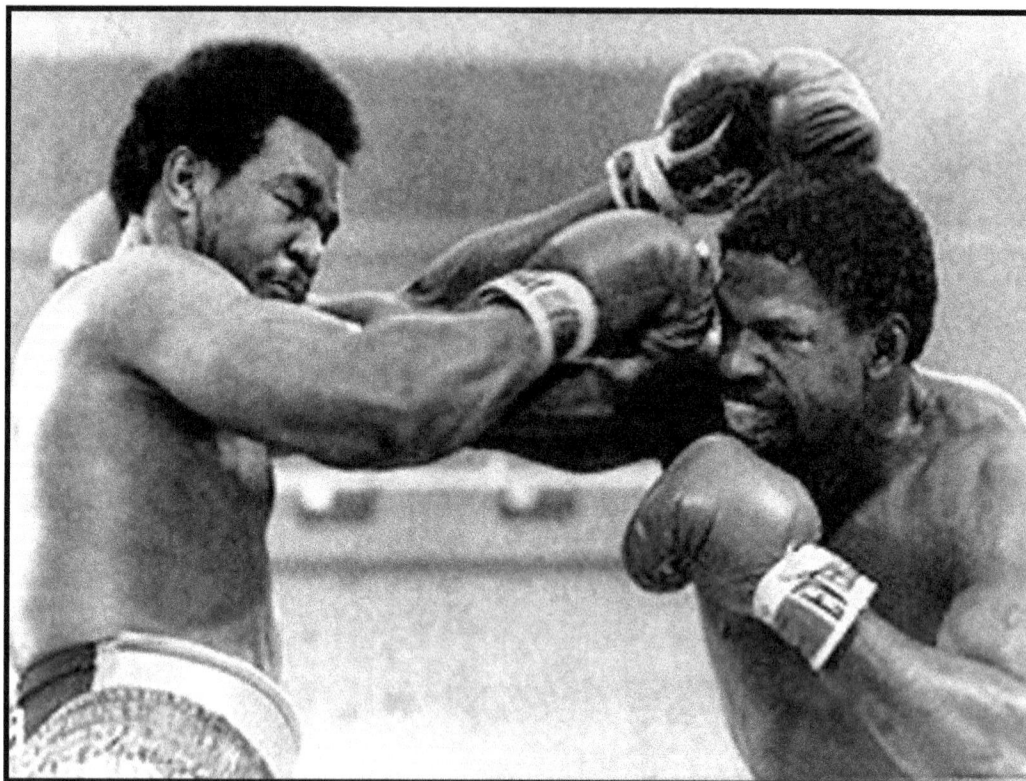

George Foreman-Ron Lyle
January 24 1976

The Foreman-Lyle donnybrook was one the most exciting slugfests in heavyweight history. George came to fight and Ron did too. Before it was over, each man had been down twice and each was staggering around almost wiped out. Finally, Foreman put across the finisher and came out of the contest with a knockout win. Many boxing people consider it one of the all-time great fights and indeed, it was a thriller.

11 Joe Louis-Billy Conn #1
June 18, 1941 ... New York, New York

Joe Louis

Joe Louis was the heavyweight champion of the world and sported a record of 49-1-0 with 41 knockouts. His timing and hitting power was at its peak. He was one of the greatest heavyweight fighters ever and arguably the best hitter among the big boys. He had beaten such men as Max Schmeling, Jim Braddock, Max Baer, Primo Carnera, Jack Sharkey, Bob Pastor (twice), Paulino Uzcudun, Charley Retzlaff, Harry Thomas, Tommy Farr, Jacob "Buddy" Baer, Abe Simon, Nathan Mann, Al Ettore, King Levinsky, Lee Ramage (twice), Tony Galento, Gus Dorazio, Donald "Red" Barry, Arturo Godoy (twice) and Roy Lazer.

Billy Conn was lean and lanky, quick and capable. He had excellent footwork, boxing savvy and feared no man - large or small. He owned a record of 59-9-1 with 13 knockouts and had beaten such men as Gus Lesnevich (twice), Bob Pastor, Al McCoy, Young Corbett III, Fritzie Zivic, Eddie "Babe" Risko, Solly Krieger (twice), Fred Apostoli (twice), Melio Bettina (twice), Teddy Yarosz (twice), Vince Dundee, Lee Savold, Gunnar Barlund, Gus Dorazio and Charles "Buddy" Knox. At this point in time, he had defeated nine men who had held world titles.

Louis had won the heavyweight title in 1937 and defended it 17 times. Joe possessed fast hands, dynamite in his punches and the remarkable ability to handle much bigger men in the clinches.

Conn had worked his way up through the weight classes, from welterweight to light-heavyweight. Now, he was going for the grand prize in boxing - the heavyweight crown. Billy had that special skill of reading his man, figuring out what it took to disrupt his foe's attack and then getting his man out of sync and off balance.

After a cautious first couple of rounds in which Conn was careful and Louis patient, Billy opened up and boxed skillfully. Joe seemed confused. Continuing his boxing lesson, Conn manipulated the fight to where he boxed as he pleased and gave the heavyweight champion a thorough fistic schooling.

However, Conn's confidence reached the point where caution was thrown to the wind. Billy decided he was going to flatten the champion instead of playing it safe and keeping his distance. As he moved in close, Louis, quick as a flash, connected with a series of solid punches to end it.

Billy Conn

Joe Louis-Billy Conn
June 18 1941

Someone once wrote that boxing fans came hoping to see a good fight and left, knowing that they had. "Cocky" Billy Conn - shame on him! He had the heavyweight championship in his pocket and blew it. As it is written in Proverbs 16:18, "Pride goeth before destruction and a haughty spirit before a fall."

Above, Conn attacks Louis. An excellent boxer, Conn began the contest by keeping out of Louis' reach and feeling out the great fighter. Louis started off in a relaxed manner, somewhat mechanical in his movement. In round three, Conn began applying his wonderful boxing magic on Louis. He hit the big man often, especially with his left hand. The more punches that were thrown, the more confident Billy became. Louis had difficulty landing solid blows.

With the passing of rounds, it was clear that Conn had matters going his way. Billy's movement was good and his defense was excellent. He dodged, slipped and blocked the champion's attempts at hitting him. His punching was masterful with jabs and combinations. "Cocky" Billy's fight was going according to plan. Boxing people were impressed. Writers were surprised. Fans in attendance sat in awe. Everyone was shocked - but not Billy. He was taking Joe to school.

In round twelve, Conn hooked Louis to the jaw and Joe wobbled. This blow likely cost Billy the fight. He sensed that he could knock the champion out and finish the fight. Ignoring instructions from his corner prior to round thirteen, Conn decided to have it out and do the impossible - win the heavyweight championship by a knockout. That was a big mistake! During the round, when Billy got close enough to trade punches, Louis' explosive rights and lefts reached Conn and the matter was settled.

10 Rocky Marciano-"Jersey" Joe Walcott #1
September 23, 1952 … Philadelphia, Pennsylvania

"Jersey" Joe Walcott

"Jersey" Joe Walcott was the heavyweight champion of the world at the time of this bout. He was the oldest heavyweight champion yet, was still muscular and could hit. "Jersey" Joe was crafty and slick - and knew every trick in the book. He could fool an opponent with his moves and he carried a dangerous punch. Walcott had a record of 51-16-2 with 32 knockouts and had beaten such men as Ezzard Charles (twice), Joey Maxim (twice), Elmer "Violent" Ray (twice), Curtis "Hatchetman" Sheppard (twice), Harold Johnson, Tommy Gomez, Lee Oma, Jimmy Bivins, Lee Q. Murray, Steve Dudas, Joe Baksi, Willie Reddish and Freddie Fiducia.

Rocky Marciano was the up-and-coming "new kid on the block." He began his career five years earlier and worked his way up through the ranks, scoring knockout after knockout. In battle, Rock was aggressive, belligerent and threw an endless barrage of punches - all blockbusters. On defense - uh, well, he had a solid chin. He owned a record of 42-0-0 with 37 knockouts and had wins over such men as an older Joe Louis, Roland LaStarza, Rex Layne, Harry "Kid" Matthews, Lee Savold, Freddie Beshore, Gino Buonvino (twice), Bernie Reynolds, Keene Simmons, Phil Muscato, Pat Richards, Bill Wilson, Carmine Vingo, Johnny Shkor and "Tiger" Ted Lowry (twice).

Walcott had been in the ring with the best - namely, Joe Louis and Ezzard Charles. Joey Maxim and Harold Johnson weren't bad either. Against Louis in December of 1947, "Jersey" Joe had floored "The Brown Bomber" twice and many observers felt like he deserved the decision. But, to his surprise and the Bomber's surprise too, the judges ruled Louis the winner. In a return match, Louis stopped Walcott in round eleven.

Joe tangled with the splendid Ezzard Charles on four occasions. Ezz won the first two contests by comfortable decisions. But once "Jersey" Joe figured him out, he was the winner. He knocked Charles out in the third battle and won a decision in the fourth fight.

The challenger Marciano carried dynamite in his punches but he tended to cut during a fight and besides, he was a "bow-and-arrow" puncher according to "Jersey" Joe. He thought that Rock tended to draw back before throwing a punch and this made him easy to anticipate.

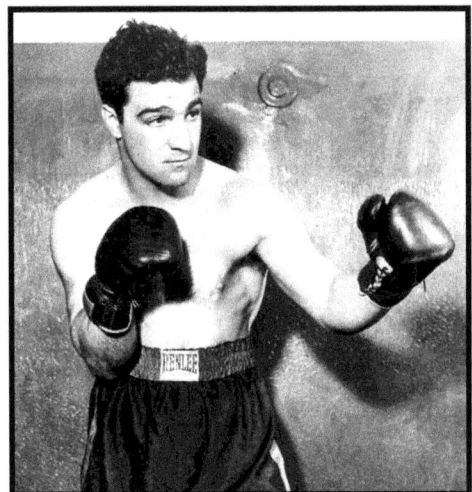

Rocky Marciano

When the bout began, Walcott took the lead with good, solid punching that tilted Rocky at times. Early in the bout, Joe dropped Marciano for one of the two knockdowns in Rocky's career. He rose quickly. As the battle raged on, Walcott took a dominant lead, consistently landing solid punches. He was comfortably ahead but Marciano's "refuse to lose" philosophy was never more apparent. There was no quit in him. Like a tenacious bulldog, he continued to try to get in close and land his haymakers.

Rocky Marciano-"Jersey" Joe Walcott
September 23 1952

As the fight entered round thirteen, it seemed that Rocky was in over his head and was going to lose his first professional fight. Suddenly a deadly, well-timed right snapped Joe's head to the side and he dropped forward onto the canvas - out cold. One knee was twisted under him and his forehead rested on the floor. Referee Charlie Daggert counted off the seconds ... eight, nine, ten. Rocky Marciano had knocked out "Jersey" Joe Walcott and captured the heavyweight championship of the world.

Eight months later, Marciano knocked Walcott out in a rematch to retain his title. Then, he defeated Roland LaStarza, Ezzard Charles (two times), Don Cockell and Archie Moore - all championship fights and all knockout wins except for the first Charles bout. Rocky retired unbeaten with a 49-0-0 mark.

Some years later, Joe Louis, Ezzard Charles and "Jersey" Joe Walcott - all three - stated that Marciano was among the easiest of all their foes to hit with solid punches. They also stated - all three - that Marciano was the hardest of all their foes to hurt or discourage.

160

9 Jack Dempsey-Jess Willard
July 4, 1919 … Toledo, Ohio

Jess Willard

Jess Willard was the heavyweight champion of the world and sported a record of 21-3-1 with 19 knockouts and six "no decision" bouts. His size, strength, stamina and chin had won the title for him against the big boys. Among those he had beaten were Jack Johnson, Dan Daily, George "Boer" Rodel (twice), George "One-Round" Davis and Alfred "Soldier" Kearns. In addition to his official wins, Willard was seen as the better man in most of his "no decision" contests.

Jack Dempsey was smaller than Jess but muscular, with a build made for quick movement and power hitting. He was one of the most devastating hitters in heavyweight history and was exciting in his attacking style, eager to get at his man. He carried a record of 53-4-9 with 44 knockouts (many coming in the first round), six "no decision" bouts and a "no contest" bout. He had beaten such men as Fred Fulton, Carl Morris (three times), Ed "Gunboat" Smith (twice), "K.O." Bill Brennan, "Battling" Levinsky, Arthur Pelkey, "Fireman" Jim Flynn, Bob Devere, Homer Smith and Willie Meehan.

Willard had been a "White Hope" chasing after Jack Johnson during the early teens. The effort to take the title from the talented black had brought forth many big, strong men who could hit with tremendous power. However, most of these men lacked top boxing skills. Big Jess fit into this category. Further, since defeating Johnson in 1915, Willard had seen little action, besting Frank Moran nearly a year after his win over Johnson and winning a decision over "Sailor" Burke in September of 1916. It had been nearly three years since he had been in a real fight.

Dempsey, on the other hand, had been extremely active. He had engaged in twelve fights in 1917, twenty-one fights in 1918 and five thus far in 1919. Coming into this fight, Jack had scored seven straight knockouts, six in the first round.

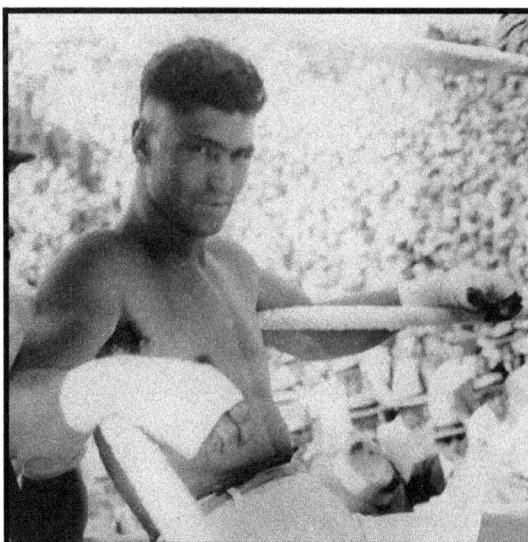

Jack Dempsey

The fight took place on a still, scorching day near Maumee Bay. Dempsey ("The Tiger in the White Trunks") was eager to "get it on." He had grabbed the ropes and was bouncing up and down when Willard entered the ring. Jess was relaxed and very confident but did not realize what a finely tuned fighting machine was waiting for him. His ring-rust proved to be a detriment in trying to keep up with and trade punches with the fast, lithe Dempsey.

Jack Dempsey-Jess Willard
July 4 1919

At the opening bell, Dempsey went into action, moving left and right, bobbing up and down, crouching and weaving. However, the actual fighting started slowly with Dempsey moving around, luring Willard to come after him as Jess cautiously sent out jabs. Gradually, the big man leaned forward more and more. Several times, he was overextended on his jabs and standing flat-footed.

In a flash, Dempsey moved in, shot out that bashing left hook and Willard went down. He got up and was quickly pounded down again. Over and over this scene was repeated. Dempsey's attack was unstoppable.

Above, Dempsey gets inside on Willard and pounds away. His two-handed attack was too fast and too vicious for Jess to withstand. Willard showed true grit, got up time and again, only to receive more punishment - heavy, powerful blows from a left hand, then a right hand. Finally, he was counted out.

Dempsey left the ring but was called back. Amidst all the crowd noise, the bell had rung and no one had heard it. For the next two rounds, Dempsey methodically pulverized Willard who gamely took the battering. Finally after round three, the towel was tossed in from Willard's corner.

A physical examination of Willard after the fight puzzled the doctors. They were amazed that Jess withstood such a beating. Many stories persist of the mauling that took place and the injuries that Willard incurred - some true but some likely exaggerated - his nose smashed, a cheek bone bashed in, his jaw broken, some front teeth broken off, a couple of ribs broken and the partial loss of hearing in one ear. Whatever the true extent of injuries, one more round of punishment and he possibly could have been beaten to death.

8 Jack Johnson-Tommy Burns
December 26, 1908 ... Sydney, NSW, Australia

Tommy Burns

Tommy Burns was the heavyweight champion of the world and had a record of 42-3-8 with 31 knockouts. He was short and stocky but possessed quickness and a dynamite punch. He had worked his way up through the ranks and had defeated such men as "Philadelphia" Jack O'Brien, Marvin Hart, "Fireman" Jim Flynn, Bill Squires (three times), Bill Lang, Jack Palmer, Joseph "Jewey" Smith and James "Gunner" Moir.

Jack Johnson was tall, muscular and "cat-quick." He possessed an excellent jab, uppercut and overall assortment of punches. On defense, he was extremely difficult to hit squarely. He carried a record of 35-5-8 with 23 knockouts, 15 "no decision" bouts and one "no contest" bout. He had beaten such men as Sam Langford, Joe Jeannette, Sam McVea (three times), Frank Childs (twice), "Denver" Ed Martin (twice), George Gardner, John "Klondike" Haines, Fred Russell, Jim Jeffords, Joe Butler, Black Bill (Claude Brooks; twice), Bill Lang, "Fireman" Jim Flynn, Peter Felix and an older Bob Fitzsimmons.

After he won the heavyweight crown from Marvin Hart in 1906, Burns then fought several title contests in California. Following these bouts and wanting to be a true world champion, he took a voyage around the world meeting the champions of a number of nations. He defeated Moir and Palmer in England, Jem Roche in Ireland, Smith and Squires in France, and Squires (again) and Lang in Australia - all in heavyweight championship bouts.

Johnson had been clamoring for a heavyweight championship bout for years. As far back as 1904-1905, he had challenged the then-reigning champion, Jim Jeffries, to no avail. Once little Tommy Burns captured the title, Johnson followed him around the world in an effort to get a chance at the crown.

Burns finally tired of the incessant verbiage and agreed to fight Jack with the title at stake. This was the first time a black man had the opportunity to win the valued title of heavyweight champion of the world. At last the barrier had been removed. The "color line" was being crossed.

Jack Johnson

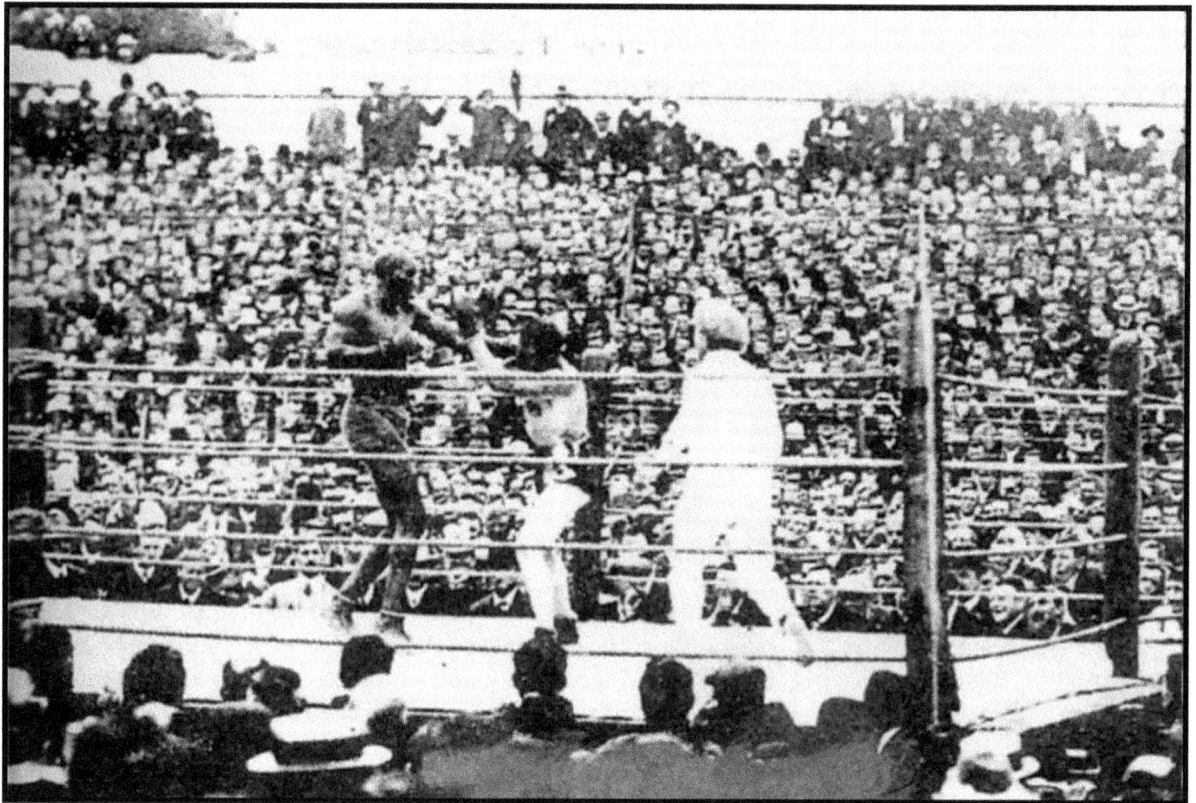

Jack Johnson-Tommy Burns
December 26 1908

It was true. A black man was fighting for the heavyweight championship of the world - and the odds could not be better for a win. Tommy was quick and bouncy on his feet but was short in height and had a limited reach. Johnson was tall, strong and fast - with a long reach. He was able to fight his usual cautious fight but with all the advantages leaning his way.

Burns was known for his quickness but it didn't matter against Johnson who was even quicker. Tommy carried an explosive right hand punch but could not land it solidly for Johnson was too evasive. It was a frustrating afternoon for Tommy and he paid the price for fighting Jack Johnson.

It was a one-sided contest from the very start. Johnson toyed with Burns throughout the fight. Jack had center-stage and he liked it. The big black relished the situation and worked it for his own pleasure. He knocked Burns down early in the bout, then talked to him and taunted him - round after round. Finally, like a cat playing with a mouse, when he tired of the goings-on, he finished off Tommy.

When all was said and done, poor Tommy was battered and humiliated and a black man was finally the heavyweight champion of the world. It was an historical event.

7 Joe Frazier-Muhammad Ali #1
March 8, 1971 … New York, New York

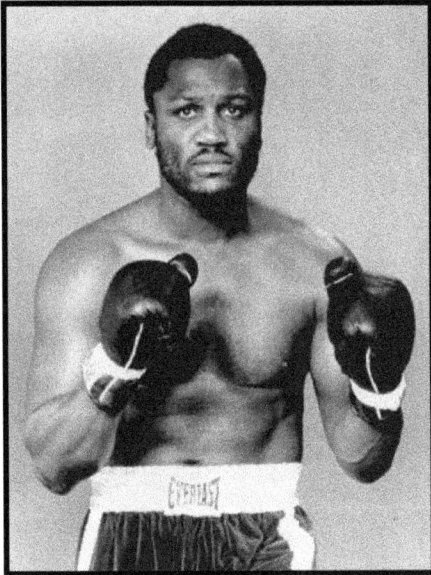

Joe Frazier

Joe Frazier was the heavyweight champion of the world with a 26-0-0 record with 23 knockouts coming into the bout. He was a solid puncher and a relentless, willing fighter. Joe had a good left hook to go along with his steady barrage of left and right punches to the body and head. Frazier had beaten such men as Jimmy Ellis, Jerry Quarry, George Chuvalo, Oscar "Ringo" Bonavena (twice), Eddie Machen, Buster Mathis, Bob Foster and Doug Jones.

Muhammad Ali was a former heavyweight champion of the world and sported a record of 31-0-0 with 25 knockouts. He was known for his speed of hand and foot and his constant movement. He had beaten such men as Charles "Sonny" Liston (twice), Floyd Patterson, George Chuvalo, Henry Cooper (twice), Ernie Terrell, Jerry Quarry, Cleveland "Big Cat" Williams, Oscar "Ringo" Bonavena and Zora Folley.

At this time, Ali was coming back from exile. He had taken a stand against the Vietnam War and refused to be drafted into the Armed Services of the United States. Consequently, he lost his license to fight in the United States and was forced into a three-year ring absence. This bout was part of his comeback effort to regain the title that had been taken from him.

Frazier was a man of great pride. Ali's constant barrage of derogatory remarks about Joe's skills and what he [Ali] was going to do to him, insulted Joe. He had difficulty dealing with it. Back when Ali changed his name, Joe refused to call him by that moniker and referred to him as Clay. He even commented that he could never be Ali's friend. Frazier's determination to win a fight was never greater.

At this stage of his career, many questioned the courage of Ali. Did he have the will to take punishment? Did he have the heart? His chin was also a topic of discussion. Could he take the solid punches of a hard hitter such as Frazier? Such questions would be answered in this contest.

The hype for this bout was sensational. Two unbeaten, outstanding fighters in their primes were squaring off against each other. Both were unbeaten. Both were dominant. Both were confident. What could be better?

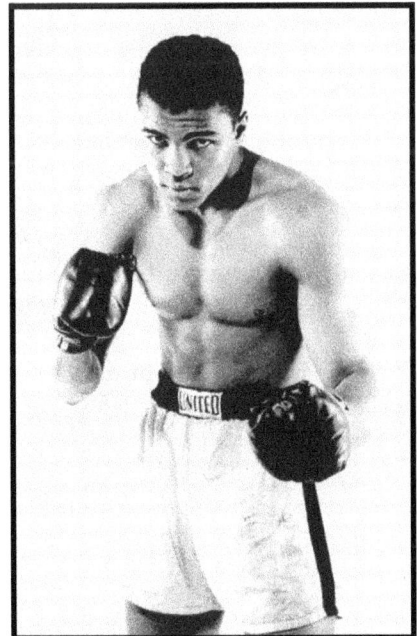

Muhammad Ali

Below, on the left, Ali boxed and moved in an effort to hold off Frazier. He resorted to clinching and holding when necessary to calm the forceful attack of Frazier. Joe moved forward applying pressure and trying to pin Ali on the ropes where he could land pulverizing blows. It was a close fight but when Frazier scored a knockdown in round 15, it settled the contest. Joe was definitely the better man in this encounter. But remember, Ali had been out of the ring for nearly three years.

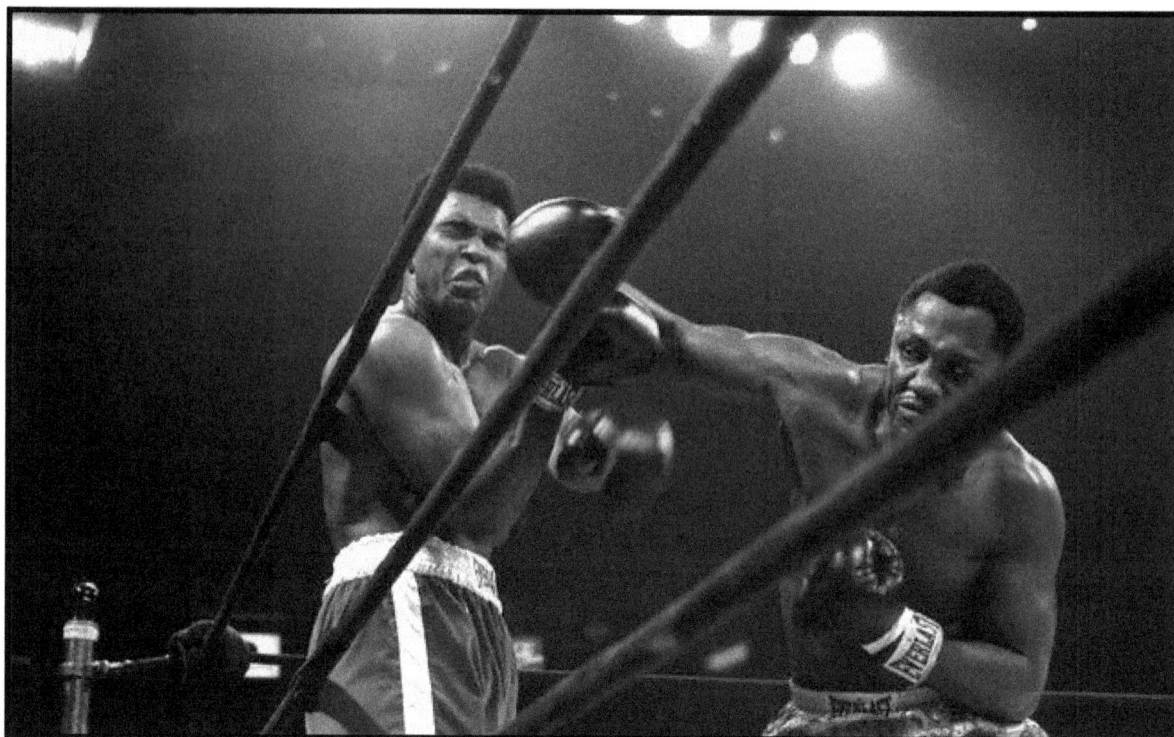

Joe Frazier-Muhammad Ali
March 8 1971

Joe kept up the attack throughout the battle in spite of a bloody nose and swollen eyes. Ali used his longer reach to strike as the relentless Frazier bore in. Up to the ninth round, the fight was close. Frazier seemed to take control of the contest in round ten. In the next stanza, he landed a hard left to Ali's head and followed up with several solid smashes that seemed to have Ali in desperate trouble.

In round fifteen, he floored Ali to insure the victory. Muhammad was up at the count of four and struggled to finish the round as Frazier landed several solid punches to the head and body. The judges scored the bout at 9-6 and 11-4 while referee Arthur Mercante had it at 8-6-1.

Following the fight, both men showed consequences of the battle. Ali suffered bruises and a swollen jaw. Joe was battered too. In defeat, Ali said that Joe was not a great boxer. Instead, he called him a great street fighter.

Following this bout, the true quality of each man was revealed. To have them in the ring against each other - both men unbeaten and as good as they were - made this one of the greatest bouts of all-time.

6 Gene Tunney-Jack Dempsey #2
September 22, 1927 ... Chicago, Illinois

Gene Tunney

Gene Tunney was the heavyweight champion of the world and sported a record of 63-1-1 with 47 knockouts, 18 "no decision" bouts and one "no contest" bout. His intelligence, quickness and effective hitting had won the title for him. He had beaten such men as Harry Greb (twice), "Battling" Levinsky, Chuck Wiggins, Charley Weinert, Erminio Spalla, Georges Carpentier, Tommy Gibbons, Joe Borrell, Fay Keiser and Bartley Madden. He had beaten Jack Dempsey too. In addition to his official wins, Tunney was seen as better in almost all of his "no decision" contests.

Jack Dempsey was the former heavyweight champion and was set on winning back his title from Tunney, the man who had taken it from him. His record was 61-5-9 with 50 knockouts, six "no decision" bouts and a "no contest" bout. `He was older at the time of this bout but was yet strong, tough and willing. Although his timing was not what it once was, his punches were paralyzing and could finish a man quickly. He had beaten such men as Jess Willard, Fred Fulton, Carl Morris (three times), Ed "Gunboat" Smith (twice), "K.O." Bill Brennan (twice), "Battling" Levinsky, Arthur Pelkey, "Fireman" Jim Flynn, Bob Devere, Homer Smith, Willie Meehan, Billy Miske, Georges Carpentier, Tommy Gibbons, Luis Angel Firpo and Jack Sharkey.

Tunney, finely tuned and well-conditioned, had won Dempsey's title from him on September 23, 1926 in Philadelphia. Moving quickly, peppering the champion with sharp jabs and crosses, Gene convincingly defeated the rusty heavyweight king.

The toll of easy living and the Hollywood lifestyle had affected Dempsey severely. The once-brutal battler was off his game. His punches lacked the former explosiveness and his fast leg speed was missing.

Determined to win back the ultimate prize in boxing, Jack had worked hard to get himself back into fighting shape. He then defeated the top contender Jack Sharkey to earn the chance to regain the crown. Gene, in the meantime, kept a close watch on Jack, continuing to study and learn everything he could about "The Mauler" - staying in excellent physical condition and awaiting the next challenge to his title.

Jack Dempsey

In this bout, Tunney went about his business in the usual manner - moving, jabbing, landing solid blows when the opportunity presented itself and tying up his man when he got too close or when the inside fighting got dangerous. Dempsey followed in pursuit - crouching, bobbing and weaving.

Gene Tunney-Jack Dempsey
September 22 1927

Round after round went by with Tunney piling up a lead. But during round seven when Dempsey closed quickly, Tunney backed away and was pinned on the ropes momentarily. Jack's lefts and rights fired like pistons. Down went Tunney. Referee Dave Barry moved in, but Dempsey, like a panther after its prey, moved around trying to get closer to Gene. Barry tried to get the excited Dempsey to go to a neutral corner. Finally, after the lapse of a few seconds, Jack obeyed and the referee started his count.

By then, Tunney's head had cleared and he was ready to get up and continue fighting. Gene boxed well the remainder of the bout and won a convincing ten-round decision to retain his heavyweight title. He even knocked Dempsey down in round eight.

Above, Tunney is down. How long was he down? Some say it was fourteen seconds. Could he have gotten to his feet in time? Opinions vary. Did Dempsey actually regain his title? These questions will never be answered. It's up to us to ponder and decide for ourselves. This bout was called the "Battle of the Long Count" and was an historic event.

5 Jack Johnson-Jim Jeffries
July 4, 1910 … Reno, Nevada

Jack Johnson

Jack Johnson was the heavyweight champion of the world and had a record of 37-5-8 with 24 knockouts, 17 "no decision" bouts and one "no contest" bout. In addition to his official wins, Johnson was seen as better in nearly all of his "no decision" contests. His overall boxing skills, quickness and amazing defensive capability had served him well and with these talents, he had won the title. He had beaten such men as Tommy Burns, Sam Langford, Joe Jeannette, Sam McVea (three times), Stanley Ketchel, Frank Childs (twice), "Denver" Ed Martin (twice), George Gardner, John "Klondike" Haines, Fred Russell, Jim Jeffords, Joe Butler, Black Bill (Claude Brooks; twice), Bill Lang, "Fireman" Jim Flynn, Peter Felix and an older Bob Fitzsimmons. For a final touch on his record, he had beaten Jack Jeffries, Jim's brother.

Jim Jeffries was the former champion heavyweight and was still recognized by many as the true champion. Jim was back in the ring to win the crown from a man many felt should not be champion because he was black. The former champion's record was 19-0-2 with 16 knockouts and one "no decision" bout. He was older now and ring-rusty, having not fought an official contest since August 26, 1904, almost six years earlier. But all this was ignored by those who yet saw him as the invincible one.

His timing was not what it once was but his punches were still powerful as was seen during his training sessions. True, he was still strong and tough but was his heart really into fighting once more? Years earlier, he had beaten Bob Fitzsimmons, Jim Corbett and Tom Sharkey two times each. He had also defeated Gus Ruhlin, Hank Griffin, Joe Goddard, Bob Armstrong, Jack Munroe, "Mexican" Pete Everett and an old Peter Jackson.

This was going to be a vengeful fight for Johnson. He was going to make the white man pay for not fighting him when Jim was champion. For years, Jack campaigned to fight Jeffries for the title but was denied. He had support from many fans and also from many writers of newspapers. However, it was not to be. Jeffries drew the "color line" as had all the heavyweight champions before him.

The older Jim Jeffries

In fairness to the unbeaten Jeffries, it should be noted that Johnson had lost fights to John "Klondike" Haines and Hank Griffin, been knocked out by Joe Choynski, been pounded in a winning effort against John "Sandy" Ferguson and had absorbed an official loss to Marvin Hart just a month before Jim retired in 1905. In addition to not wanting to fight a black man for the title, Jeffries did not see Johnson as that much of a threat.

Shortly after Johnson defeated Tommy Burns for the title, the chant began for Jeffries to come out of retirement to fight Johnson and win back the crown for the white race. Writer Jack London was a prominent leader of the crusade. Jeffries' response was that he was retired and would never fight again. After all, it was Burns' own fault for fighting Johnson in the first place. As time passed and the pressure to fight Johnson mounted - plus an offer of big money - Jeffries gave in. Jim trained hard to get himself into fighting condition and physically looked quite able. However, he was not.

Many reports state that the day of the fight was hot with a temperature over 100 degrees. Johnson was at his peak, having fought thirty contests since Jeffries had retired. Jeffries, on the other hand, was rusty, older and had fought no one in an official fight since leaving the ring. It was apparent after the first few rounds that the Jeffries of earlier years was not in the ring. Instead, it was an older man, still plenty tough and making the effort but lacking his former fighting talents. He was a "shell" of his former self.

Jack Johnson-Jim Jeffries
July 4 1910

One round after another, Johnson did his typical thing - boxed cautiously, punished Jeffries and taunted him while taking control of the fight. Then, in round fifteen, Jack sent in several punches that caused Jeffries to cave in. Down went Jim for the first time in his career. Referee "Tex" Rickard counted as Jim slowly arose. Johnson followed up with two more knockdowns and Jeffries' corner threw in the towel.

Jack admitted years later that the only time he had ever known fear in the ring was on July 4, 1910 in Reno, Nevada when the bell rang for the first round and Jim Jeffries turned and started towards him. But he overcame that fear and handed out a boxing lesson to the rugged Jeffries who took an unbelievable amount of punishment before yielding to Johnson's boxing skills.

The first great "Battle of the Century" was history, a shining example of the wonderful skills of one man, a total disaster for the other. Unfortunately, this futile image of Jeffries is what is most people remember about the man and it tarnishes his legacy as a great fighter.

Ironically, after Johnson won the heavyweight title, he drew the "color line" on his black brothers, only meeting a former sparring partner "Battling" Jim Johnson in Paris when Jack was low on funds and needed money.

4 Joe Louis-Max Schmeling #2
June 22, 1938 ... New York, New York

Joe Louis

Joe Louis was the heavyweight champion of the world and had a record of 35-1-0 with 29 knockouts. His hitting power and fighting skills were at their peak. At this time, he may well have been the greatest heavyweight who ever entered the ring. He had beaten such men as Jim Braddock, Max Baer, Primo Carnera, Jack Sharkey, Bob Pastor, Paulino Uzcudun, Charley Retzlaff, Harry Thomas, Tommy Farr, Nathan Mann, Al Ettore, King Levinsky, Lee Ramage (twice), Donald "Red" Barry and Roy Lazer.

Max Schmeling was a former heavyweight champion and a formidable challenger for the title held by Louis. He had won his last seven bouts, including a win over Joe in 1936. In style, he was a "straight-up" fighter who pawed at his man but delivered solid blows when attacking. He carried a record of 52-7-4 with 37 knockouts and had wins over such men as Jack Sharkey, Steve Dudas, W.L. "Young" Stribling, Steve Hamas, Ben Foord, Harry Thomas, Paulino Uzcudun (twice), Walter Neusel, Johnny Risko, Franz Diener, Mickey Walker, Billy "Gipsy" Daniels, Joe Sekyra and Hein Domgörgen.

The first fight between Louis and Schmeling on June 19, 1936 had been a shocker. Louis was unbeaten at 24-0-0 with 20 knockouts as he climbed the heavyweight ladder towards a title fight. Schmeling was more experienced (59 bouts) with a good eye for openings.

Max had claimed that he spotted a weakness in Joe's defense and planned to take advantage of it. As their fight progressed, he did just that. In round twelve, he broke through Louis' defense and put Joe down to win by a stoppage. Louis made no excuses.

Upon his return to Germany, Max was declared a national hero by Adolf Hitler and proclaimed to be an example of Aryan superiority. Reluctantly, Schmeling went along with this propaganda. Failure to do so might have proved disastrous for him and his family.

Following this setback in his career, Louis went to work with renewed determination and knocked off some top contenders. Always a great draw and crowd pleaser, he was in the watchful eye of champion Jim Braddock. On June 22, 1937, Joe knocked out Braddock to win the heavyweight championship. After winning the title, Joe defended it three times successfully. Then, he fought Schmeling with revenge on his mind.

Max Schmeling

Schmeling had engaged in but three bouts since defeating Louis in 1936. Joe had won eleven, including the heavyweight title. Max still felt he knew Joe's weakness and considered this to be an advantage. Joe was determined to get even.

Sportswriters were picking Joe to win. The story about writer Jimmy Cannon talking to Louis prior to the fight is worth mentioning. Cannon told Joe that he picked him to win by a knockout in six rounds. Louis responded, "It go one!"

Joe Louis-Max Schmeling
June 22 1938

At fight time when the opening bell rang, Louis came forward, methodically working those wonderful punches of his. Joe, perhaps the best hitter ever among the heavyweights, was dead-serious and Max had no chance. He used lefts, rights and combinations - all splendidly thrown – and backed Max into the ropes were he unloaded bombs.

Max tried to cover up but was hurt and soon went down. In two minutes and four seconds, it was all over. "The Brown Bomber," one of the greatest champions ever, had kept his title, gained his revenge and destroyed the Nazi myth of superiority. It ranked as an historical event.

3 Jack Dempsey-Luis Angel Firpo
September 14, 1923 ... New York, New York

Jack Dempsey

Jack Dempsey was the reigning heavyweight champion and had a record of 59-4-9 with 48 knockouts, six "no decision" bouts and a "no contest" bout. He was supposedly at his peak but had been in Hollywood too long and was beginning to slip a bit. Yet, he still had that element of quickness accompanied by phenomenal power for a man of his size. Jack had beaten such men as Jess Willard, Fred Fulton, Carl Morris (three times), Ed "Gunboat" Smith (twice), "K.O." Bill Brennan (twice), "Battling" Levinsky, Arthur Pelkey, "Fireman" Jim Flynn, Bob Devere, Homer Smith, Willie Meehan, Billy Miske, Georges Carpentier and Tommy Gibbons.

Luis Angel Firpo was a big South American heavyweight contender who had a record of 25-2-0 with 21 knockouts. He had also been in a "no contest" bout and a "no decision" contest. Luis was not particularly quick or agile but if he could hit a man squarely with his sledge-hammer blows, that man would go down or out. He had won against Jess Willard, "K.O." Bill Brennan, Charley Weinert, Homer Smith and Jack McAuliffe II.

This was not expected to be a cautious boxing contest. Power was evident. These men were loaded with it. Firpo, definitely not a polished boxer type, could furnish blockbuster punches that would render a man unconscious with one big bear-like swipe. Dempsey, on the other hand, was one of the quickest, most murderous hitters who ever stepped into the ring. But Jack had not fought in three years except for what might be called a tune-up contest against Tommy Gibbons in July of 1923, two months earlier.

At the opening bell, the fighters got right to it. The big bombs were exploding. Dempsey's timing was better than Firpo's, as expected, and Luis went down quickly in the opening round. In fact, he went down seven times - but he kept getting up. That's not all. Dempsey went down too. Twice he left his feet and once he left the ring when the bigger man finally caught him with one of those ponderous blows.

Luis Angel Firpo

By the time the bell rang to end the first session, Firpo looked tired and worn out. He had taken a battering - a terrific barrage of blows - and managed to weather the ordeal. Dempsey was tired too - partially from throwing so many hard blows in an effort to take Firpo out and partly from his long layoff from fighting.

If fans liked action, this one was it. It featured all out punching between two battlers known for their hitting. Two super punchers, power and non-stop action makes for a great fight.

Dempsey's title was on the line and did not look to be in danger until Firpo landed that blow that sent Jack out of the ring and into the laps of observers seated at ringside. Then, suddenly, it was a fight. To Firpo's dismay, Jack got back into the ring and went to work.

Jack Dempsey-Luis Angel Firpo
September 14 1923

At the sound of the bell for the second round, Dempsey went after Firpo like the Pit Bull he was. Bouncing up and down, shooting hard left hooks and right crosses, Jack dropped Firpo and Luis got up slowly. More action followed with the desperate Firpo trying to land a blow to hold off his attacker but Dempsey was outpunching him three-to-one. Finally, after a combination of hard lefts and rights, the big Argentinian went down for the full count. The war was over.

Dempsey was famous for his brutal punching and his handling of bigger men with ease. This one proved to be no exception. Although not in the best of fighting condition, Jack was a formidable warrior. The fast-paced slugfest was one of the most exciting in heavyweight history. Luis came to fight and needless to say, Jack did too - he always did.

2 Muhammad Ali-Joe Frazier #3
October 1, 1975 … Quezon City, Philippines

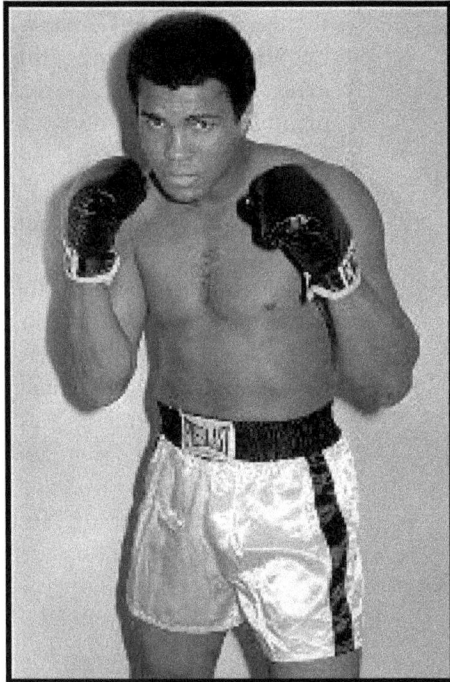

Muhammad Ali

Muhammad Ali was the heavyweight champion of the world and had a record of 48-2-0 with 34 knockouts. He was a great boxer who had beaten such men as Charles "Sonny" Liston (twice), George Foreman, Floyd Patterson (twice), George Chuvalo (twice), Ken Norton, Ron Lyle, Jimmy Ellis, Doug Jones, Henry Cooper (twice), Ernie Terrell, Jerry Quarry (twice), Cleveland "Big Cat" Williams, Oscar "Ringo" Bonavena, Zora Folley, Joe Bugner (twice) and Buster Mathis. He had beaten Joe Frazier too.

Joe Frazier, shorter than Ali, was stocky and powerful. He boasted a 32-2-0 record with 27 knockouts coming into the bout. He was considered to be one of the most powerful hitters in heavyweight history and was relentless and aggressive in his attacking style. Joe had a vicious left hook to go along with his steady barrage of hard lefts and rights to the body and head.

Frazier had beaten such men as Jimmy Ellis (twice), Jerry Quarry (twice), George Chuvalo, Joe Bugner, Oscar "Ringo" Bonavena (twice), Eddie Machen, Buster Mathis, Bob Foster and Doug Jones. Also, he had beaten Muhammad Ali.

Ali's previous two bouts with Frazier had been torturous contests in which the powerful Frazier bore in, seeking to land his bashing shots to the body and head. Ali moved, dodged, clinched and peppered Joe with jabs, crosses and combinations of lefts and rights.

In their first bout on March 8, 1971 in New York, Frazier was heavyweight champion. Ali, coming back from exile, boxed and moved in his usual style, clinching and holding when necessary to withstand the pressure attack of Frazier. It was a close fight but when Frazier scored a knockdown in round 15, it was decided.

For their second fight on January 28, 1974 in New York, neither man was champion. Frazier fought moving forward. Ali stayed on the move. Ali peppered Joe with punches throughout and from time to time, landed heavy combinations of blows. He clinched often when Joe cornered him. Joe threw the harder punches and threw them often, landing many. Opinions varied as to who won the fight but Ali gained the official decision and most fans agreed.

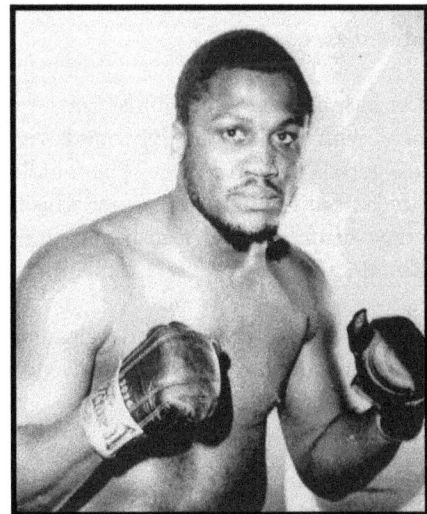

Joe Frazier

This third bout, known as "The Thrilla in Manila," had both men exhausted at the end. Throughout the fight each man landed heavy blows on the other. Ali was in pain and wanted to quit. Joe's eyes were swollen shut. Finally at the bitter end, Joe's corner threw in the towel and Ali, aching and sitting in his corner, won.

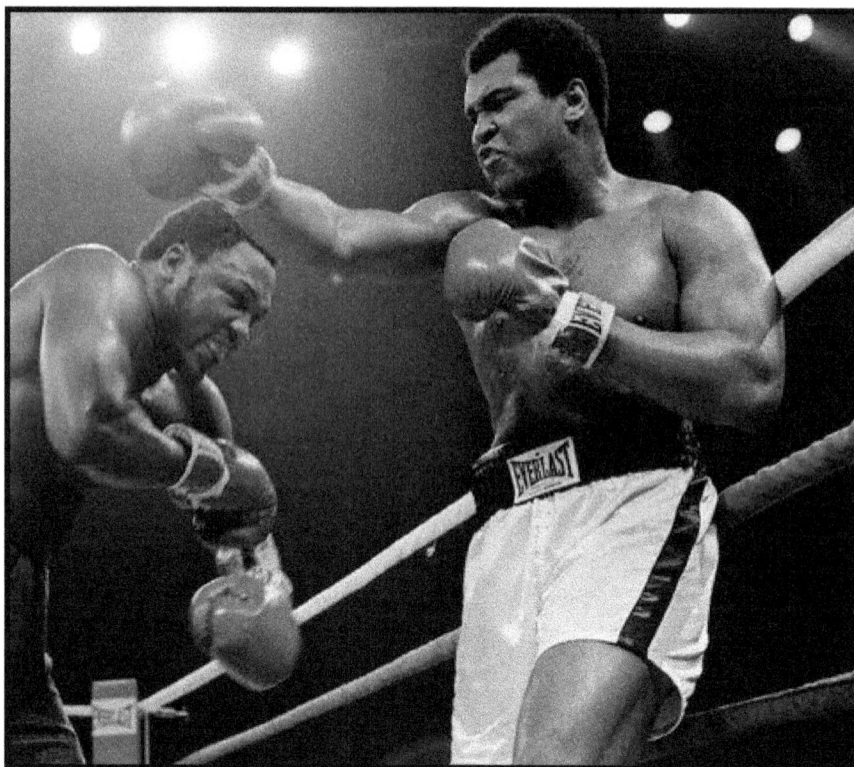

Muhammad Ali-Joe Frazier
October 1 1975

Seen here, Ali on the right, throws a punch at Frazier as he moves in during this exhausting, vengeful and painful heavyweight title fight. Ali had declared that he was going to "put a whuppin" on Joe Frazier. Instead of dancing and moving, he began the contest by throwing bombs of his own. He stood flat-footed in front of Frazier and tossed effective hard combinations of punches. Frazier seemed to be dazed. At times, he was jolted and staggered during these first few rounds as the fight was dominated by Muhammad.

Frazier kept pressing forward, however, delivering blasts to Ali's body at close range. In doing so, he took considerable punishment. Ali tired from his tactics as the battle continued. He had wanted to end it as soon as he could but Joe refused to lose. Instead, he stepped up the pace in an effort to get Ali on the ropes and pound away.

During the next few rounds, Frazier continued his belligerent offense and punished Ali about the body and head with hard hooks. By rounds six and seven, Frazier seemed to be in control of the bout. He had even staggered Ali with a blow. The middle part of the match was dominated by the sturdy Joe. Ali was unable to hold off the relentless Frazier who landed often with his hard shots. Ali appeared to wilt and be on the verge of defeat. Then, in rounds ten and eleven, Joe tired and Ali was able to move away and escape the brutal Frazier firepower. Momentum shifted.

Over the next three rounds, Frazier received considerable punishment but would not quit. Finally, after round fourteen, Frazier's trainer Eddie Futch stopped the fight. Afterwards, Ali claimed it was the closest to dying he had ever been.

1

Jim Jeffries-Tom Sharkey #2
November 3, 1899 ... Coney Island, New York

Jim Jeffries

Jim Jeffries was the heavyweight champion of the world and sported a record of 11-0-2 with nine knockouts, numerous exhibitions and perhaps many more fights that we do not know about. His strength, stamina and chin had taken him straight to the top and he got there in record time. He had beaten such men as Bob Fitzsimmons, Peter Jackson, Hank Griffin, Joe Goddard, Bob Armstrong and "Mexican" Pete Everett. He had beaten Tom Sharkey too.

Tom Sharkey was short and stocky - built like a tank. He was one of the most powerful hitters in heavyweight history and was rough and bruising in his fighting style. He carried a record of 30-2-6 with 27 knockouts and a "no decision" bout. He had beaten such men as Jim Corbett, Bob Fitzsimmons, Charles "Kid" McCoy, Joe Choynski, Joe Goddard, Gus Ruhlin and Jim Williams.

The first fight between young Jeffries and the belligerent Sharkey had been a grueling, toe-to-toe matchup in which the two powerful hitters smashed each other for twenty rounds. The green but stronger Jeffries finally came away the winner, handing "Sailor Tom" a pounding.

After winning the title from Fitzsimmons in June of 1899, Jeffries felt that a fighter as good as Sharkey deserved a chance at the top prize in fighting. So, five months later, the two squared off again.

The fight had been scheduled for October but was delayed a time or two due to an injury Jeffries experienced to his left shoulder during training. Finally, disregarding the medical doctor's advice, Jeffries decided to go ahead with the contest.

Fighting under extremely hot lights placed much too close above the ring, the scorched fighters went at each other for twenty-five rounds. Both men were pressed to the limit but each persevered and lasted the entire fight. Jeffries landed the harder blows. Sharkey landed the more frequent blows. Like a bulldog, Sharkey bore in, tossing blockbuster punches only to be driven back by Jeffries' monster knocks.

Tom Sharkey

But Tom kept attacking. He came to fight and fight he did - in a rough, "winner take all" manner. He was not in there for friendship. Jeffries took exception to some of his tactics and returned in kind.

Jim Jeffries-Tom Sharkey
November 3 1899

Above, Jeffries (facing the camera) battles Sharkey in one of the most brutal, combative heavyweight fights in history. Sharkey was the aggressor for most of the fight, attacking and throwing bombs in an effort to knock Jeffries out. Jim smashed his rushing opponent with sledge-hammer blows of his own, driving his man back and protecting his championship.

Sharkey was relentless in his attack and kept it up throughout the contest. Many observers felt that he had won the battle but referee George Siler knew that "Big Jim" had landed the harder, more telling blows and came out the better man. Jeffries knocked Sharkey down in the second round and broke a couple of ribs along the way. Only towards the end of the fight, did Sharkey become battle-weary and lose his starch for battle. Then, Jeffries took over and pounded him convincingly for the last 4-5 rounds.

The Brooklyn Daily Eagle (November 4, 1899) had these observations -- "... in no twenty-five round fight ever seen before was there such terrific punching, from start to finish, combined with an ability to take it as fast as it came and go back for more ... The sailor was running into punches as often as he landed them and Jeffries seemed to be content to let the fight go that way ... Some of the blows that Sharkey landed on Jeffries' jaw would have put an ordinary heavyweight out of the game ... The intense white lights directly over the heads of the fighters produced a temperature that must have been easily a hundred in the ring, possibly more ... Sharkey used an elbow in clinches a number of times and roughed it at all times ...

178

[Jeffries' punches] took the steam out of Sharkey and left him groggy at the finish, with a good prospect of being knocked out had the fight been prolonged ... Sharkey is probably the most wonderfully aggressive man in the ring today ... Sharkey was foul at times. He hit low at different times and hit in the clinches while holding ... Siler's decision seemed to be an eminently fair one."

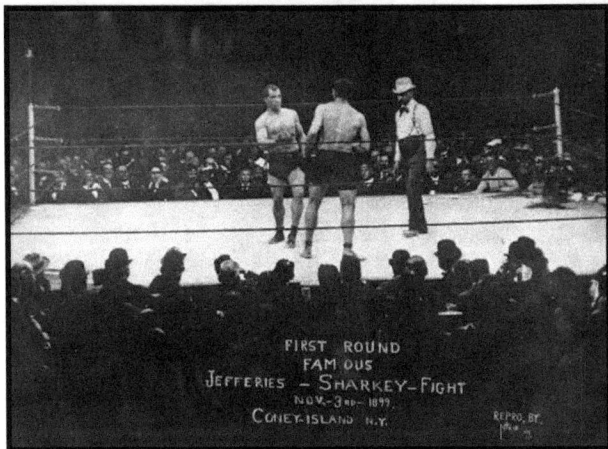

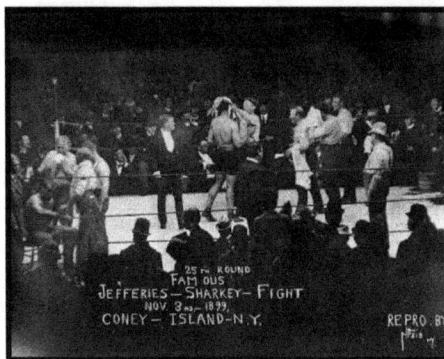

FIRST ROUND
FAMOUS
JEFFERIES – SHARKEY–FIGHT
NOV. 3RD – 1899.
CONEY-ISLAND N.Y.
REPRO. BY

THIRD-ROUND
FAMOUS
JEFFERIES – SHARKEY FIGHT
NOV. 3RD – 1899.
CONEY-ISLAND–N.Y.
REPRO BY

17TH – ROUND
FAMOUS
JEFFERIES – SHARKEY-FIGHT
NOV. 3RD – 1899
CONEY-ISLAND –N.Y.
REPRO. BY

25TH ROUND
FAMOUS
JEFFERIES – SHARKEY – FIGHT
NOV. 3RD – 1899.
CONEY – ISLAND-N.Y.
REPRO. BY

Where Are They Now?

WHEN JIM JEFFRIES (*right*) won the heavyweight crown from old Bob Fitzsimmons in 1899, he was ready for all comers, and on November 3 he was matched with Tom Sharkey, the Fighting Sailor, at Coney Island. For 25 grueling rounds they traded blows. But with the final bell, both contestants, weary and ring-marked, walked to their corners, and Jeffries was still champion.

Recently, the two battlers met on a nation-wide radio hookup and relived the drama of that fateful night. Now, half a century after the epic struggle, both live quietly in California, Jeffries tending his farm, Sharkey working in near-by Albany. The smell of resin and leather is far behind them.

Coronet, October 1949 p 14

179

JEFFRIES'S ANXIOUS EXPRESSION AS HE SEES A FACE BLOW COMING.

SHARKEY DODGING A LEFT-HAND BLOW FROM JEFFRIES.

A "KIDNEY BLOW" IN THE SECOND ROUND.

THE REFEREE'S CLOSE WATCH ON THE CONTEST.

THE SPECTATORS' QUICK INTEREST IN A CHIN BLOW.

THE MARVELOUS RESULTS ATTAINED BY THE BIOGRAPH WITH ARTIFICIAL LIGHT.

These pictures are published to show the advance made in instantaneous work by electric light. A full description of how it was done appears in to-day's main sheet. Photographs, copyright, 1899, by the American Mutoscope and Biograph Company.

American Mutoscope and Biograph Company
1899

Tom Sharkey, Gene Tunney and Jim Jeffries

180

The All-Time Top Fifteen Heavyweight Boxers

RANKING THE ALL-TIME GREAT BOXERS

Why do people rank the all-time great boxers the way they do? The reasons for doing so are quite varied - age, knowledge of boxing, preference for styles and eras, the sex and personality of the viewer, media coverage, the race of the viewer and boxer, personal favorites and the passing of time, are but a few.

The age of the individual assigning the ranks often has a bearing on the position given to different boxers and bouts. If a person is a follower of boxing, surely he is aware of the fighters of his own time. His evaluation of their abilities is rather objective. However, the younger an individual the less likely he will be familiar with fighters and bouts of 50-100 years ago.

This applies to writers of publications too. Most boxing publications do an adequate job of covering the activities taking place in the boxing world. However, the large bulk of this coverage is about contemporary pugilists with the result being that readers/fans tend to exaggerate the skills of the fighters of their own time in relation to those of other eras. With the emphasis upon more recent times, bouts of recent years rate higher. Then too, older individuals remember bouts of years past and possibly magnify the importance of bouts from those years.

The effect of age continues through the years as well. In many instances an individual continues to rate the good fighters of his generation over those to come (and those of the past). John Durant, author of *The Heavyweight Champions*, disclosed in private correspondence (1977) to this writer, "When the sportswriters of today grow old, they will rate the fighters of their youth above all that will appear in the future."

Jimmy Cannon (1978 p 157) writes: "Memory deforms the past. The old champions are cherished by nostalgic men who were young when they were. The kids will be that way about Cassius Clay (Muhammad Ali) and Joe Frazier in a couple of years. The heavyweight title fight incites recollections that are often either slanderous or reverent with the flattery of lies. It is a personal matter, and a sports reporter's descriptions of athletes are influenced as much by feeling as by truth."

The knowledge and understanding of boxing strategy and skills that an individual possesses is another factor in determining how that person will rank the fights and contestants. An experienced person in this field is aware of strengths and weaknesses in the various boxers, their styles, techniques, etc. This definitely affects the ranks assigned. A person who is not familiar with the ins-and-outs of the sport will likely assign ranks differently.

The perceived levels of skill of the various eras in history affect the appreciation. Fighters of the past were once viewed as more rugged and durable, harder hitters and better conditioned. They were considered superior. Recent opinions consider modern boxers to possess better movement, improved skills and greater power. The persuasion of the individual doing the rankings affects the choices.

Preference for style figures in - the slugger or swarmer with his power and endurance, the classic boxer with his speed and motion or the boxer-puncher with his all-around ability - is a major influence. There are strong arguments for each style. There have been outstanding fighters of each type.

The sex and personality of a person could be an influence in the choices made. Attraction to a particular kind of fighter and an affinity to one's nature and attitude could affect the ultimate selections. It should be noted that the ever-increasing coverage of fights by television, radio, newspapers, magazines and films since the twenties has caused widespread popularity of the good fighters and fights during the years since.

The race of the individual making choices as well as that of the fighters in the bout might be a factor. Black fighters dominate boxing today. For example, in the heavyweight division, from 1937-1998, only a handful of champions were white.

A resurgence of white heavyweights has occurred in recent years with the arrival of Wladimir and Vitali Klitschko, Oleg Maskaev, Sultan Ibragimov, Nikolai Valuev, Sergei [Serguey] Liakhovich and Ruslan Chagaev. However, many people still feel that blacks are superior fighters.

Sociologists do not agree. They say it is a matter of conditioning, mental as well as physical. A rougher lifestyle makes better fighters. Since blacks and Hispanics are apt to come from the lower socio-economic sphere, they are the "have-nots" of recent years.

Understand, this was not always the case. During the early years of this country, nearly everyone struggled to make it. In the period of fifty to one hundred years ago, the white society also did without and produced many exceptional fighters. Many European countries still experience tough times.

Weinberg and Arond (1952 p 460) point out that boxing has been dominated by different ethnic groups through the years and write, "The tradition of an ethnic group, as well as its temporary location at the bottom of the scale, may affect the proportion of its boys who become boxers."

One must not forget that the idea of personal favorites enters the picture too. If an observer likes a particular fighter, for whatever reason, then that fighter is likely to be rated highly.

For the most part, over the years as fans and writers age and fade away and new, younger faces appear, the more recent fighters rise to the top of any list and the older ones drop. It should be remembered that very probably, the best fighters of any period in history could fight with each other on a highly competitive and near-equal basis.

A number of men come to mind when speaking of the very best heavyweight boxers of all-time. They hail from all periods of history. A look at a few of them follows.

Bob Fitzsimmons was a true all-time great, ranking among the best in the middleweight, heavyweight and light-heavyweight divisions. For most of his career, he fought against men 15 to 35 pounds heavier and still won big. He claimed to have had around 350 bouts and he might have - he loved to fight. During his career, he lost only eight battles: "Mick" Dooley (early in Fitzsimmons' career), Jim Hall, (rumored to be a fix), Tom Sharkey (on a questionable foul call by Wyatt Earp), Jim Jeffries (twice), Jack Johnson, "Philadelphia" Jack O'Brien (late in Fitzsimmons' career) and Bill Lang (late in Fitzsimmons' career).

Tom Sharkey was a short and stocky brawler of the 1890s who fought much like Rocky Marciano of the 1950s. Built like a tank and loaded with power, Sharkey tangled with the very best of his era and usually won. Owning knockout power in each fist, "Sailor Tom" tangled with the likes of Jim Jeffries, Bob Fitzsimmons, Jim Corbett, Peter Maher, Gus Ruhlin, an older John L. Sullivan and many other top contenders. Quite possibly, he would have been heavyweight champion in any other era.

Sam Langford was such a versatile fighter and puncher that Charley Rose ranked him as the #1 heavyweight of all-time while Nat Fleischer ranked him as #7. Herb Goldman ranked Sam as the #2 all-time light-heavyweight. Sam fought his way from the lightweight division all the way up to the heavyweight division. Although he was a force as a heavyweight, he was much better carrying a little less poundage as a light-heavyweight. His career record shows 314 bouts, just 33 losses and 127 knockouts. Many boxing people call Sam the greatest fighter to never get a shot at the heavyweight title.

Harry Wills deserved a chance at the world heavyweight title but never got it. Six-foot-three-inches tall and long-armed, Wills was an outstanding boxer who had a nice punch. He pursued without success the crown held by Jack Dempsey for years. A look at Wills' record shows he fought Sam Langford 17 times and lost only twice. His career record was 68-9-2 with 19 "no decision" bouts. Harry scored 54 knockouts.

Evander Holyfield was a man who found a way to win. Put in difficult and unfamiliar circumstances, he usually worked himself into an advantageous position and came out on top. He began as a light-heavyweight, moved up to cruiserweight and ended up fighting as a heavyweight against men who were naturally much bigger. Evander is most famous for his wins over Mike Tyson and his three-fight series against big Riddick Bowe. Many knowledgeable boxing people rank Holyfield among the all-time best heavyweights.

Riddick Bowe was a huge heavyweight who stood 6'5" and weighed from 218 to 252 pounds during his prime. He had 45 fights during his career and lost just one. He owned a nice left jab and hit with blockbuster punches from either hand. Bowe defeated such men as Pinklon Thomas, Tony Tubbs, Michael Dokes, Bruce Seldon, Larry Donald, Herbie Hide, Andrew Golota and Evander Holyfield.

Lennox Lewis was a big man with big skills. He could box and punch. Tall at 6'5" and long-armed with a nice jab and a thundering right hand, Lennox could beat a foe by jabbing him all night long or by putting him to sleep quickly with a quick right-cross. Lennox had 41 bouts, won 38, lost 2 and had one draw. He scored 32 knockouts. He was a true great from the modern world.

There are many others who might be considered for all-time greatness - Max Baer, Joe Jeannette, Max Schmeling, Frank "Paddy" Slavin, Pat Killen, Peter Maher, George Godfrey, Ezzard Charles, "Jersey" Joe Walcott, Floyd Patterson, Ken Norton, Earnie Shavers, Cleveland Williams, Wladimir Klitschko and Vitali Klitschko - to name a few first class pugilists.

Now, let's take a look at the all-time top fifteen heavyweight boxers.

15 Peter Jackson ... Smoother Than Joe Louis
(Revised article - from The Cyber Boxing Zone, WAIL! - September 1999)

Peter Jackson

Peter Jackson was tall, smooth and elusive on the order of the modern boxer yet he possessed the ruggedness that typified the "old school." He had size, quickness and strength, accompanied by great ring science.

Jackson was among the first of the heavyweights to fight up on his toes. A perfectionist in his style, he developed as fine a "one-two" sequence as the ring has ever known. His punches had the kick of a mule with either hand.

Grombach (1977 p 45) stated, "While he was of the old school, he used a powerful one-two punch in various combinations which made him a tricky adversary." Fleischer (1938 p 150) said Jackson threw his punches with lightning rapidity while Lardner (1972 p 78) wrote, "Jackson's two blows landed almost simultaneously."

Always in a position to hit, Peter could feint, counter, block, or slip punches by a few inches and avoid a blow by the narrowest of margins. He was a master boxer and a stinging hitter.

He was a gentleman in every sense of the word and yet John L. Sullivan, the man generally recognized as heavyweight champion of the world at that time, would not fight him. Fleischer (1949 p 103) wrote that Sullivan drew the color line in order to evade a match with Peter Jackson and added it was well he did because Jackson probably would have won decisively, just like Corbett did a few years afterwards (see Langley 1974 p 20 and Fleischer 1942 p 34). Grombach (1977 p 44) said Sullivan ducked the fight by using the color line as an excuse.

Jim Corbett called Jackson one of the most intelligent pugilists who ever graced the ring and said it didn't matter whether it was a box or slug affair, Peter could adapt himself to it. Corbett often said Jackson could defeat any fighter he had ever seen and Jim lived until 1933 (see Corbett 1926 pp 132 145 326).

In describing Jackson, Lardner (1972 p 77) wrote, "He is considered by many experts to have been the greatest heavyweight who ever lived." He added, "Corbett ranked him with Jeffries as one of the two greatest heavyweights of all time."

Corbett related that he once saw speedy Joe Choynski spar with Jackson and not manage to touch him with a glove. He added that on another occasion, Jackson boxed with Bob Fitzsimmons in an exhibition and it was like a professor giving a pupil a lesson (see Fleischer 1938 p 123).

Corbett and Jackson fought sixty-one rounds in 1891 in one of the ring's greatest battles. Jackson entered the contest with a cold and a sprained ankle. These two conditions caused him to stop training ten days prior to the fight. Yet, Corbett was hard-pressed by Jackson at times during the contest.

Frank "Paddy" Slavin, a hard-hitting scrapper of the modern Jack Dempsey mold, who fought Jackson in another of the ring's notable fights, called Peter, "unbeatable ... the greatest of all masters" (Langley 1974 p 60).

Bob Fitzsimmons refused to meet him in an official fight, calling him the greatest fighter who ever breathed. Fitz said that Jackson was the daddy of them all and that he [Fitz] did not care for the fight (see Fleischer 1938 p 124 and Petersen 2011 p 38).

Jim Jeffries once commented on the stiffness of Peter's punches - short, crisp and hard. Lardner (1972 p 77) said, "Jeffries later used the memory of a punch Jackson had thrown at him as the basis for comparison with all the other single devastating punches he had received."

Lord Lonsdale of England, early president of London's National Sporting Club and the man for whom the Lonsdale Belt was named, said that although Jack Johnson was the best heavyweight of his time, he [Johnson] never equaled Jackson for science and skill (see Langley 1974 p 61).

Carpenter (1975 p 30) called Jackson "one of the great fighters of the time." Durant (1976 p 30) said Jackson "may have been the greatest ringman of any age." Burrill (1974 p 95) wrote, "One of his time's most feared and popular boxers."

Fleischer (1938 p 159) said Jackson was "regarded as the greatest boxer of his era." He went on to say that few fighters could be rated superior to Jackson and described him as a sharpshooter and two-fisted scientific hitter. Nat described him as having a powerful left, an excellent jabbing and hooking game, and a wicked right-hand chop.

John Chambers, the man most often credited with developing the Marquis of Queensberry Rules and perhaps the foremost boxing authority in America at the time (see Lardner 1972 p 79) said, "He's a wonder, make no mistake about his ability. He is one of the finest specimens of fighting man I've ever seen" (see Fleischer 1938 p 141).

Farnol (1928 p 177) elaborated on Jackson, "Perhaps for his size the most finished and beautiful boxer ever seen; magnificently shaped from head to foot, his every move was graceful; also he was incredibly quick and very sure."

Lardner (1972 p 78) described Jackson in battle as moving out carefully, throwing punches with a puma-like grace, stalking his man about the ring, avoiding blows with ease and hitting his adversary so hard it took a quart of whiskey to revive him. He added that Jackson was like a hurricane tearing through the ranks of the Australian heavyweights, knocking out everyone and later turning to "right-hand barred" exhibitions in which he was not allowed to hit with his right.

Eugene Corri, who was considered by many to be the greatest referee of modern times (see Grombach 1977 p 183), called Peter Jackson the best boxer he ever saw (Farnol 1928 pp 179 180). In other articles, Corri called Jackson the greatest heavyweight he had ever seen. Gilbert Odd, boxing historian, wrote (1989 p 63), "Jackson never won the world title, but some boxing experts consider him the greatest heavyweight of the late 19th century."

Jackson was a Muhammad Ali look-alike. He boxed rather than slugged and moved gracefully, quickly and easily about the ring, avoiding punches. He was almost the same physical size as Ali but never allowed himself to get as heavy as did Ali in his later career. He even looked enough like Ali in his facial features to have been his brother. His personality was likeable and almost everyone who met him developed a genuine affinity for him. He, perhaps, was not as quick as Ali (but almost) but he hit a little harder.

Jackson was like Sam Langford in that he was so good the champions of his time would not risk their titles against him. These two powerhouse fighters, Peter and Sam, were probably the greatest pugilists never to fight for the heavyweight championship of the world.

Reportedly, Jackson was more scientific than Jack Johnson, was faster and smoother than Joe Louis and hit just as hard and possessed footwork somewhat similar to Muhammad Ali. In the opinion of this writer, Jackson was one of the greatest fighters in the history of the heavyweight division and deserves to be ranked among the all-time best heavyweights. Due to the lack of fight film, he ranks as #15.

Jackson was inducted into The Ring Boxing Hall of Fame in 1956, the International Boxing Hall of Fame in 1990 and the World Boxing Hall of Fame in 1999.

Peter Jackson in a fighting pose **Older Peter Jackson**

187

14 John L. Sullivan ... I Can Lick Any Man
(Revised article - from The Cyber Boxing Zone, WAIL! - March 1999)

John L. Sullivan

John L. Sullivan was one of America's first sports idols. He was a flag-waving patriot who reflected the spirit of a vibrant, young nation. Strong, aggressive, confident and outspoken, Sullivan was a natural showman.

Shirtless, clad in knee-breeches and stockings, wearing fighting boots (shoes with spikes), "The Great John L." fought using either bare-knuckles, skin-tight gloves or padded gloves. He battled under both the London Prize Ring Rules and the Marquis of Queensberry Rules. McCallum (1974 p 3) called him "the true link between the bare-knuckle and glove eras."

At the call of "time," Sullivan with black mustache, high cheekbones and sunken cheeks charged out - glaring, scowling, snorting and swinging - trying to land the "Boston Special," his powerful right-hand punch. He was surprisingly fast for a 195-pounder. He used a straight-up stance, employed feints and threw the "one-two." In addition, he launched powerful left and right swings.

John could also take a good punch. In his prime, he quickly disposed of power hitters and because of his endurance, was able to catch and defeat his greatest problem as a fighter - the "hit-and-run" tactician. But over the years, his drinking and riotous living habits did him in. He even drank and smoked cigars during training (and probably in some bouts).

His knockout ability has been challenged in recent years but he most certainly belongs in the special class of power-punchers like "Sailor" Tom Sharkey of the 1890s, Rocky Marciano of the 1950s, Joe Frazier of the 1970s and Mike Tyson of recent years. He fought in a day when a man received credit for a knockout only if he scored a knockout. There were no technical knockouts. If a fight was stopped by a referee because of an injury such as a broken arm or by the police to prevent a brutal beating - there was no knockout. If an opponent quit fighting or ran from the ring - there was no knockout. The verdict was a "win."

There are many such bouts on Sullivan's record that could be called knockouts by today's rules but were simply recorded as wins in his day - Joe Goss, Johnny "Cocky" Woods, Dan Dwyer, Steve Taylor, John Flood, "Tug" Collins, Charlie Mitchell, John Laflin, "Alf" Greenfield, Paddy Ryan (1885) and Frank Herald.

There were many "no decision" bouts on his record and doubtless, if the details of these matches were known, he would have many more knockouts. Durant (1976 p 24) wrote that Sullivan is estimated to have knocked out some 200 men during his career while fighting all types of men - lumberjacks, blacksmiths, local strong boys and professional fighters.

For various reasons during the early years, records were often in error. Even top-notch fighters were apt to let many victories over minor opponents slip away unrecorded.

Odd (1989 p 125) wrote, "A virile, stout-hearted fighter, Sullivan was known as the 'Boston Strong Boy' and his favourite saying was that he could lick anyone in the world. Certainly he was never beaten until the end and he had some tough customers to deal with."

There is no question that John L. could hit. Langley (1973 pp 27 29) recorded, "As a knockout specialist John's record remains unbeaten. No other fighter in history has left such a trail of broken and aching jaws behind him." Old ring lore tells us that Tim Scannell, 200-pound competitor, was lifted up and out of the ring by a Sullivan punch. Charlie Mitchell and John Donaldson were also knocked out of the ring.

He knocked many men "cold" and battered numerous others into helpless submission. John Flood, Paddy Ryan, Jake Kilrain, John Laflin and Frank Herald were among those who had to be carried from the ring. He broke jaws and bashed in faces with abandon. Johnny "Cocky" Woods, Kilrain, Scannell, Laflin and Ryan were numbered among those who carried distorted features in the years following their pounding by "The Great John L."

Paddy Ryan said, "When Sullivan hit me, I thought a telegraph pole had been shoved against me endways" (see Durant and Bettman 1952 p 79; Durant 1976 p 22). "Professor" Mike Donovan commented on Sullivan's style, "It wasn't boxing. It was like being hit by a runaway horse." The "Professor" called John L. the strongest man he ever fought and added, "He used his right as a blacksmith would use a sledge hammer ..." (see Durant and Rice 1946 and McCallum 1974 p 10).

Charlie Harvey, old time manager, described Sullivan as a "rushing, tearing-in, two-fisted fighter with a power punch" and called him "... big, fast, and courageous" (see Fleischer 1972 p 207). Diamond (1954 p 10) wrote about Sullivan - "He was quick on his feet - as quick as any modern heavyweight. And what a punch he had! A knockout in each hand! He was not a scientific boxer but a slugger, depending mainly on a vicious right swing to the jaw."

Durant and Rice (1946) stated, "He was superbly fast with his hands and he moved always forward, growling as he advanced." Grombach (1977 p 43) described Sullivan in this way, "According to the writers of his time, he was a great burly, slugging fighter with bull-like tactics, mighty fists, and little science. He was good-natured, generous, conceited, blustering, and extremely popular."

Durant and Bettman (1952 p 79) stated that "... he was more than merely strong. He was amazingly fast for a big man and had a knock-em-dead punch in either hand. Ring science was not for John L. He never bothered much with defense. He brushed aside blows and kept moving forward, always punching. His was a hurricane attack."

McCallum (1974 pp 10 11) described him, "He was far from being muscle-bound. He was a 'natural' puncher. His punches were perfectly timed, seldom wild, and fast. In the ring, he was extraordinarily fast. His hands were large. His shoulders enormous, his chest was remarkably deep ..."

Lardner (1972 p 43) wrote that Sullivan was a bully, a boozer, and a braggart and later adds that he looked like a conqueror with his florid face, black brow, black hair, mustache and aggressive fighter's jaw. Burrill (1974 p 181) said he was "notorious for drinking and tavern brawls." Tom Langley (1973 p 31) said that "Sullivan implicitly believed in his invincibility and wasted no time in passing on this information to the world."

Billy Roche, famous referee, rated Sullivan as the greatest of all heavyweights and said that John L. had the best "one-two" punch that he ever saw (see McCallum 1974 p 4). Gilbert Odd, boxing historian, once wrote that John L. in most of his early years, only had to hit a man one time. If he did not knock the man out of the fight, he knocked the fight out of the man.

Jim Jeffries called Sullivan the greatest fighter in ring history (see Fullerton 1929 p VIII). Cooper (1978 p 103) called "… John L., the Champion of Champions to everybody who saw him fight …"

Grombach (1977 p 46) wrote "… if the strength, speed, hitting power, fighting instinct, and ring ferocity of Sullivan had been developed in the school of modern boxing, and were he around today, he would be a dangerous challenger to any champion."

If being the man who brought boxing to the fore indicates greatness, then John L. Sullivan must be considered among the greatest ever heavyweights, perhaps the very greatest. John L. took the sport from an outlawed, rowdy, ruffian occurrence to a main street, popular social event. His awesome presence in the ring and his escapades outside the roped square brought him fame and popularity unequaled for many years. It should be remembered that he was a pretty good puncher besides. If there were some existing film of him in action, there's a good chance he would rank among the very best at the top of the ladder. Due to no available fight film, this writer ranks him as the #14 all-time heavyweight.

Sullivan was inducted into The Ring Boxing Hall of Fame in 1954, the World Boxing Hall of Fame in 1983 and the International Boxing Hall of Fame in 1990.

John L. Sullivan-Jake Kilrain
July 8 1889

John L. Sullivan

13 Joe Frazier ... Black Marciano
(Revised article - from The Cyber Boxing Zone, WAIL! - October 1999)

Joe Frazier came out "smoking" at the opening bell and was still smoking 15 rounds later, if necessary. He was a swarming, non-stop, perpetual motion attacker who fought from a crouch. A sturdy man with a tough jaw, powerhouse left hook (his right wasn't bad either) and tremendous endurance, Joe came straight at his man, bobbing and weaving as he moved in.

Smokin' Joe wiped out most competition easily and quickly. Only the better fighters could go any distance with him. He won the title by degrees, following the action which stripped Muhammad Ali of the crown. New York first recognized him as champion and as he beat man after man, popular opinion considered him to be the best heavyweight around. Finally, in 1970, he knocked out Jimmy Ellis to become THE world champion.

Joe Frazier

Gilbert Odd, the eminent historian, described Frazier (1989 p 50) "... shortish for a heavyweight but he was solidly built and hustled an opponent for the full three minutes of every round, never taking a backward step and hooking viciously with his left."

Only two men defeated him in the professional ring - Muhammad Ali and George Foreman. Frazier fought three bouts with Ali, winning one without question and losing two, both of which were extremely close. He and Ali went 41 rounds against each other and Joe never left his feet. Only two men ever knocked him down - George Foreman and Oscar "Ringo" Bonavena (both men were well over 200 pounds).

On the other hand, he was one of only four men to knock Ali down. He stopped George Chuvalo, who had never been knocked out. He flattened huge Buster Mathis. He leveled the lighter, faster Bob Foster. All of this goes to show Joe's power and quickness.

Stockton (1977 p 92) wrote that Frazier "... was an excellent body puncher and relied primarily on his powerful left hook. He exerted constant pressure and was fairly hard to hit with his bobbing and weaving style. He had no trouble with cuts and took a good punch."

Houston (1975 p 126) said, "Frazier is murder at close and medium-range, ripping vicious hooks and uppercuts to the body and switching to the head, often snorting and grunting as he punches." Litsky (1975 p 111) described Frazier as an "aggressive, relentless fighter who withstood punishment so that he could get close enough to his opponent to deal out punishment."

Cosell (1973 p 218) called him "… a very good, very tough fighter." Carpenter (1975 p 136) said Frazier was "pure aggression." Muhammad Ali said, "Frazier is not a great boxer. He is just a great street fighter" (see McCallum 1975 p 75).

Henry Cooper, British heavyweight, paired Frazier with "Sonny" Liston saying, "They were slugger-killers from the hard American school." He added, "You could hit Frazier with your Sunday punch and you could break your hand" (see Atyeo and Dennis 1975 p 82).

Yank Durham, Frazier's manager, said the things that separated Joe from other good fighters were his determination and strength (see Durant 1976 p 165).

Durant (1976 pp 166 226) wrote, "Joe's great strength comes from his massive shoulders and huge arm and thigh muscles." He described the third Ali-Frazier bout as "… one of the roughest, most dramatic championship bouts ever staged."

Frazier is often compared with Rocky Marciano since their fighting styles were extremely similar. Joe was bigger than Rocky in physical dimensions but whether he was bigger on punch or chin is debatable. Odd (1974 p 68) wrote that he was correctly called "The Black Marciano" due to his physical make-up, fighting style, strength, durability and punching power.

Atyeo and Dennis (1975 p 82) wrote, "Joe Frazier was - perhaps still is - a master slugger, a throwback to the days when men fought each other with bare fists face to face across a chalk mark on the floor. His nickname 'Black Marciano' was an apt description, for like 'The Rock', any finesse Frazier had in his squat chunky body was entirely eclipsed by his unshakable determination to knock out his opponent."

McCallum (1974 p 343) likened Joe unto Marciano saying they were built alike and fought alike, using a "jungle technique." He went on to say that Joe was not vulnerable to cuts like Rocky was.

McCallum (1975 p 74) wrote, "Like Marciano, Frazier came to fight." He added, "Joe was dedicated in his training just as Rocky was. Both of them trained as they fought and their gym fights were wars. They were willing to take a punch to land one of their own. Both men smashed away at the body to soften up an opponent and to open up the head defenses."

Grombach (1977 p 89) wrote that Frazier was often compared to Rocky Marciano because of high dedication to training and explosive punching. Teddy Brenner, former matchmaker for Madison Square Garden, said, "Frazier throws more punches and throws them faster than Marciano" (see McCallum 1974 p 343).

Cooper (1978 p 151) wrote, "Joe was a better fighter than a lot of people believed. There wasn't a lot of finesse with him, but he was something akin to Marciano." He added, "Remember this … He fought Ali when Muhammad was at his best, and he even beat Ali with the title at stake."

Gutteridge (1975 p 35) argued "… Frazier, I am convinced, was strong enough to have walked through many of the idolized heavies of yesterday."

Frazier was durable and had power, determination and heart. All the components that great fighters possess, Joe brought with him into the ring. For sure, he was strong enough to have walked through many of the idolized heavies of yesterday - and today.

Herb Goldman, former Editor of **The Ring Record Book** and the **International Boxing Digest (IBD)** monthly boxing magazine, ranked Frazier as the #10 all-time heavyweight (**The Ring 1987 p 1071**). **The Ring (1999 p 128)** ranked Joe as the #8 all-time heavyweight. Bert Sugar, former Editor of **The Ring Record Book**, in 1991, ranked Frazier as the #7 all-time heavyweight and a poll of historians (International Boxing Research Organization, IBRO) in 2005 ranked Joe as #10. In the opinion of this writer, Frazier was the #13 all-time heavyweight.

Frazier was inducted into the International Boxing Hall of Fame in 1990 and the World Boxing Hall of Fame in 1990.

Joe Frazier-Bob Foster
November 18 1970

Joe Frazier-Muhammad Ali
March 8 1971

12 Mike Tyson ... Iron Mike

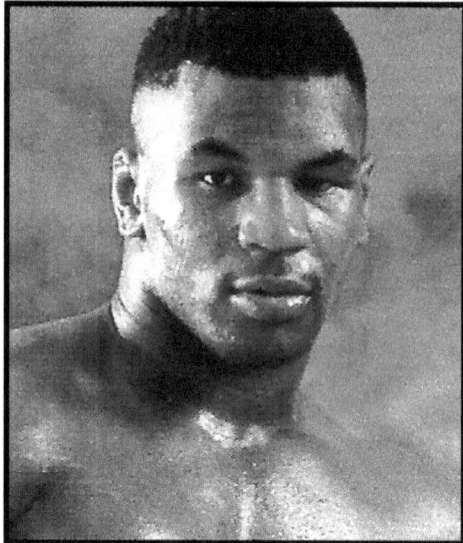

Mike Tyson

Mike Tyson was one of the most brutal inside-punchers ever to enter the ring. He was a human version of a Pit Bull - his goal being the complete destruction of his opponent. He came to fight and went straight after his foe, mindful in style of the great swarming punchers of the past - John L. Sullivan, Tom Sharkey, Rocky Marciano and Joe Frazier. There is a good chance that he was the most powerful puncher ever.

Tyson studied films of the all-time greats and did his best to match their efforts. Jack Dempsey, Joe Louis, Rocky Marciano - all the greats - were watched carefully by Tyson and when he got into the roped square, he resembled them with his awesome hitting. Waiting to attack his foe, he reminded observers of a kid in a candy shop - eagerly awaiting the go-ahead.

Fleischer and Andre (1993 p 183) proclaimed, "Mike Tyson's rise to undisputed heavyweight champion was quicker and more impressive than that of any heavyweight before or since." Arnold (1989 p 72) said he began fighting professionally in 1985 and in 18 months time, won 27 bouts - 25 by knockout. He was all the talk in boxing circles.

Myler wrote (1998 p 354), "With his tight haircut, no robe, plain black shorts and boots without socks, he looked like a throwback to the champions of old. That's exactly what he was. Old-timers imagined they were seeing a black reincarnation of Jack Dempsey." He added, "At his peak, there was no more destructive force in heavyweight history."

Brooke-Ball (1992 p 107) stated, "There was little artistry in Tyson's ring technique, but his brute power and sheer savagery were enough to see off all-comers. Of past greats, the most obvious comparison is with Marciano, and a fight between the two would have been spectacular indeed." Even the eminent historian, Gilbert Odd, was impressed with Mike's punching. Said Odd (1989 p 130), "Few could stay long under his powerful punching, either at short range or long. His speed of punch was devastating, and one on target was usually enough to have his opponent in trouble."

A look at Tyson's record shows he had 58 bouts and won 50 (a winning percentage of 86.21). He scored 44 knockouts (a knockout percentage of 75.86). Thirty-three of his knockouts were scored during the first three rounds. *The Ring (2004 p 137)*, in an article entitled "The 100 Greatest Punchers Of All-Time," ranked Tyson as #16. (Author's comment: He should rank higher.)

His list of wins included the names of Larry Holmes, Frank Bruno, Michael Spinks, Carl "The Truth" Williams, Trevor Berbick, Tony Tubbs, James "Bonecrusher" Smith, Tony Tucker, Donovan "Razor" Ruddock, Bruce Seldon, Pinklon Thomas, "Frans" Botha, Brian Nielsen, James "Quick" Tillis and Tyrell Biggs.

Mike viewed fighters with disdain and once a fight started, he battered his huge adversaries around the ring in an aggressive, mean fashion. Corey Sanders, who fought Andrew Golota and sparred "Frans" Botha and Michael Grant, also sparred with Tyson. Said Sanders *(The Ring 2001 p 100)*, "Mike was one of the calmest, coolest guys I ever worked with sparring, but once he got in that ring, he turned vicious."

Myler (1998 p 354) reported some of Mike's comments about his foes - Tyrell Biggs, "I wanted to make him pay with his health" and Jesse Ferguson, "I wanted to catch him right on the tip of his nose and push the bone into his brain."

As a youngster, life was tough for Mike and trouble was always close by. Coming from a broken home, he was known to the police at an early age. According to Suster (1992 p 298), "Mike Tyson grew up as a bad boy in a bad neighbourhood. Initially he was nothing other than a brutish thug and juvenile delinquent …" Brooke-Ball (1992 p 106) wrote "… as a young teenager he discovered that the easiest way to get money was to mug people."

When Cus D'Amato, fight manager and trainer, gained control of Mike, his life changed for the better. Cus actually became his legal guardian. He shielded Mike from bad influences, taught him boxing skills, showed him ring films and made him a better individual.

When Cus died, Mike's handling was taken over by Jimmy Jacobs, who died about three years afterwards. Next, Bill Cayton, a business partner of Jacobs, directed Tyson's ring affairs. Following squabbles with Cayton over his endless run-ins with citizens on the street, police and a bad marriage, Mike let go of Cayton and acquired Don King to handle his career.

Then, life became topsy-turvy once again for him and he lost focus on his ring career. So dominate was he in his early career that when he lost his title to James "Buster" Douglas, people could hardly believe it. Suster (1992 p 302) called it "… one of the greatest upsets in ring history."

Mullan (1990 pp 156 157) remarked, "He had, undeniably, the stamp of greatness, but there was also about him a sense of vulnerability, and the potential for self-destruction." He called Tyson's loss to Douglas the "biggest upset in boxing history."

Weston and Farhood (1993 p 258) wrote, "In 1985 Mike Tyson exploded on the boxing scene like a tornado. Not since Joe Louis had generated similar excitement almost 50 years before had the world seen any prize fighter as ferocious as this wild dynamo from the streets of Brooklyn. Twenty months after his professional debut, Iron Mike became the youngest heavyweight champion in history."

Suster (1992 p 298) contended, "The supremacy of Mike Tyson over all other heavyweight boxers during his whirlwind reign cannot be disputed. Some thought that he had the potential to become the greatest of all-time and few denied his right to be at least one of their company." He later added (1992 p 303) aside from Muhammad Ali, Joe Louis and Jack Johnson, "one has to call him a great match for any man who ever lived."

Brooke-Ball (1992 p 107) asserted, "Leaving aside events away from the ring, Tyson must be viewed as a truly exceptional champion - a colossus who dominated his age, albeit during a truncated reign. If his power and aggression could have been properly harnessed and controlled, he might well have been the greatest ever." Odd (1989 p 131) contended, "As a champion, he was as impregnable as any had been before him."

Herb Goldman, former Editor of **The Ring Record Book** and the **International Boxing Digest (IBD)** monthly boxing magazine, early in Tyson's career ranked him as the #11 all-time heavyweight (**The Ring 1987 p 1071**). Later, in 1997, he evaluated him as the #4 all-time heavyweight. Bert Sugar, former Editor of **The Ring Record Book**, in 1991, ranked Mike as the #10 all-time heavyweight. Steve Farhood, columnist and one-time editor-in-chief of **The Ring** magazine, in 1999, ranked "Iron Mike" as the #9 all-time heavyweight.

Bill Cayton, former Tyson manager, in 1991 was quoted in Thomas Hauser's book, **Muhammad Ali: His Life and Times**, as ranking Tyson #2 all-time. **The Ring (1999)** ranked Mike as #14 all-time and a poll of historians (International Boxing Research Organization, IBRO) in 2005 ranked Mike as #13. In the opinion of this writer, Tyson was the #12 all-time heavyweight.

Tyson was inducted into the World Boxing Hall of Fame in 2010 and the International Boxing Hall of Fame in 2011.

Mike Tyson-Alfonso Ratliff
September 6 1986

11 George Foreman ... Fairly Hard Hitter

George Foreman

George Foreman was one of the strongest, most powerful men to step into the ring. In all likelihood, he was the most powerful puncher ever. The way to fight "Big George" successfully was to box him - stay away, move quickly, hit him and then run.

Foreman ranks with Jim Jeffries, "Sonny" Liston and Jess Willard as the strongest and most powerful of the all-time heavyweights. It is highly doubtful that anyone besides Jeffries and Liston (and they would have to be at their peaks) could have traded punches and weathered the storm in a toe-to-toe confrontation with George.

For a big man, Foreman was rather fast on his feet and very fast with his fists. He threw punches three or four at a time and was, without question, able to take out most men with a single, crushing blow. An outstanding, thudding jab and vicious uppercuts, hooks and crosses made up his arsenal.

McCallum (1975 p 78) wrote, "Foreman, with arms like wagon tongues and shoulders like a blacksmith, quickly earned the nickname of 'Lightning Destroyer' because of his explosive punching power."

Mee wrote (1997 p 118), "George Foreman didn't worry about subtle techniques. Once he had mastered the basics - a thudding, bone-shuddering jab, how to throw a hook, an uppercut, and a cross - he just went out and hit people. Mostly, they stayed hit." Dick Sadler said, "It's hard to imagine anyone surviving many of those punches, much less remaining on his feet" and added, "George's left jab can stop a man in his tracks" (see McCallum 1975 p 78).

His greatest enemy was not the other man in the ring with him - but his own stamina that seemed to diminish greatly after seven or eight rounds. *The Ring (1999 p 126)* wrote that Foreman "Possessed frightening power in both fists" but "lacked stamina in [his] first career; poise and power would dissolve as bouts wore on."

Foreman actually had two careers. The first one (1969-1977) was fought by an aggressive, angry young man who was confident of his brutal power and anxious to mix it up and hurt people. This big youngster moved fast and possessed awesome strength and hitting power. In addition, he threw heavy, bashing punches rather quickly. The only problems this fighter had were his (1) stamina and (2) lack of experience, which showed against clever boxers who could extend him.

Myler (1998 p 108) wrote, "Once upon a time, there was a fierce giant called George. He devoured his victims as quickly as they were served up to him." Ken Norton said, "He's like a Mack truck." Henry Clark, the California heavyweight and sparring partner of Foreman, called him the strongest man he ever worked with (see McCallum 1975 p 78).

Reflecting upon his first career, the older Foreman once said, "The other Foreman was more interested in hurting people, the fame and the money. Not in that order - I think I liked the hurting more" (see Bunce and Mee 1998 p 225). His rush to finish off his man and his lack of experience caused him to punch himself out in some bouts. His lack of stamina then surfaced. The fact that George relied on his powerful blows magnified this weakness because when his stamina left him, so did his effectiveness as a fighter.

This chink in his armor was revealed on several occasions. An early indication was against Gregorio "Goyo" Peralta, an excellent 175-pound man who extended George in a ten-round bout on February 16, 1970. A little over a year later, on May 10, 1971, Peralta again extended Foreman to ten rounds but George finally hammered him down.

The most famous occurrence was his loss to Muhammad Ali on October 30, 1974 when George pounded the great fighter until he [George] ran out of gas and folded. Later, on March 17, 1977 in a contest against slick-boxing Jimmy Young, Foreman was knocked down and defeated - once again by a tapping, moving "cute" opponent. Following this loss, George retired from the ring.

In 1987, Foreman began a comeback that was laughed at by many. But this time (1987-1997), he was a different fighter - one who still possessed awesome power but was not overly anxious. He was more patient, paced himself well and leaned more on his wonderful jab. He seemed to be as strong as in his first career (or stronger) and he could still take a punch.

However, his punching was not as fast or as crisp as before and his cruel aggression was missing. Nevertheless, the combination of his able hitting along with his newly acquired skills of patience and jabbing seemed to increase his stamina or at least extend it. According to the older Foreman, "There is no killer inside anymore" (see Bunce and Mee 1998 p 224).

It is a well-known fact that he went on to capture the heavyweight championship once again when he knocked out Michael Moorer in ten rounds on November 5, 1994 in Las Vegas. At the age of 45, big George became the oldest man to ever hold the heavyweight championship.

When looking at the two careers, this writer believes George #1 was better. George #2 could not have won the title fighting in the 1970s. The heavyweight talent was better during that period and could have beaten the older, more ponderous George. In assessing Foreman (George #1) versus the other all-time greats, there is no question he is one of the strongest, most powerful fighters and one of the hardest punchers ever. Without doubt, he could bowl over any smaller man who could not "box" him and run. Further, there are few big men who could withstand his awesome hitting.

McCallum (1975 p 78) described Foreman's hitting, "Just watching George train with a heavy punching bag held stationary can be a near-terrifying experience. The rafters shake, the floor rumbles." However, due to his size and tremendous hitting, his stamina usually faded by round seven or eight. Most of the men he fought could not avoid him long enough for this weakness to show up. Anyone who could keep away, would have a chance of defeating him in a long contest.

The older George paced himself better, but in doing so would have difficulty in catching an excellent boxer. Against the best heavyweights of all-time, the excellent "boxer-types" would be extremely difficult for George to catch and batter down. Jack Johnson, Gene Tunney, Muhammad Ali, Jim Corbett and Larry Holmes would be formidable opponents.

George could and would take out the smaller men who did not move quickly - such as Rocky Marciano, Joe Frazier, Mike Tyson, John L. Sullivan and Tom Sharkey. They could not escape him. However, boxer-punchers like Sam Langford, Jack Dempsey and Joe Louis, who moved well and hit hard, would prove difficult for George to defeat.

Against the massive, strongest and most powerful men such as Jim Jeffries, "Sonny" Liston and the prime Jess Willard, outcomes would likely be "first-come, first-serve." All three of these men had tremendous strength, hitting power and tough chins. All moved well and had better stamina than George. Against these men, Foreman would be getting hammered too. On a probable basis, Foreman would beat Willard but lose to Jeffries and Liston. "Sonny" and Jim were as strong as George and both hit about as hard as he did. Liston was a little bouncier in his movement. Jeffries had better, faster footwork, a little better chin and much greater stamina. He also crouched. The memory of George fighting Ron Lyle always comes to mind when comparing Foreman to men like these.

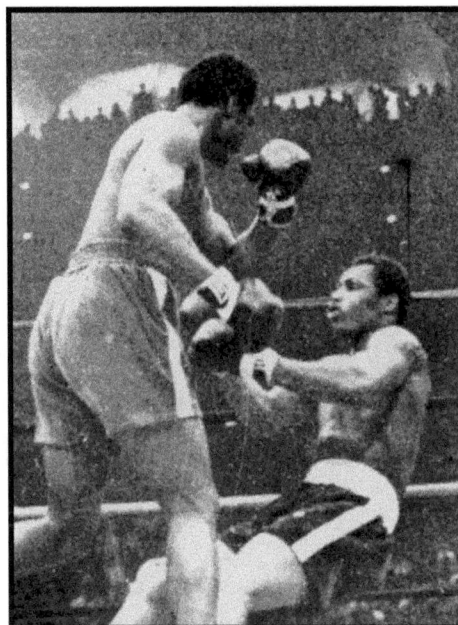

**George Foreman-Ken Norton
March 26 1974**

Surprisingly, some men that George would demolish might do better overall against other opponents. For example, Marciano, Frazier and Tyson might stand a better chance of catching their man than George since they did not have the stamina problem. They could possibly catch up to and beat boxer types such as Johnson, Ali, Tunney, Corbett or Holmes.

Referee Jimmy Rondeau said, "I rate Foreman an even better puncher than Louis. He can hit, he can jab, he wants to get you out of there in a hurry. He's so anxious to finish you off that he'll hit you from any direction he can. It doesn't make any difference what position you're in" (see McCallum 1975 p 80).

A look at Foreman's record confirms Rondeau's observation. He had 81 bouts and won 76, a winning mark of 93.83 percent. He scored 68 knockouts, a knockout percentage of 83.95. Of his knockouts, 15 were scored in round one, 19 in round two and 12 in round three. Sixty-one occurred during the first five rounds. Dick Sadler once said, "I've molded a monster. I've taken the best of Joe Louis, Jack Johnson, and Rocky Marciano and rolled it into one" (Myler 1998 p 110).

Herb Goldman, former Editor of *The Ring Record Book* and the *International Boxing Digest (IBD)* monthly boxing magazine, ranked Foreman as the #9 all-time heavyweight (*The Ring 1987 p 1071*). *The Ring (1999 p 126)* ranked George as the #4 all-time heavyweight. In the opinion of this writer, Foreman was the #11 all-time heavyweight.

Foreman was inducted into the World Boxing Hall of Fame in 2002 and the International Boxing Hall of Fame in 2003.

10 Larry Holmes ... Best Jab In History
(Revised article - from The Cyber Boxing Zone, WAIL! - May 2000)

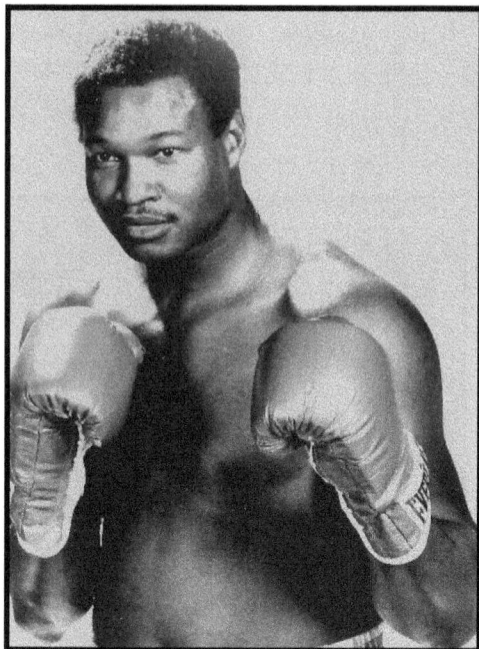

Larry Holmes

Larry Holmes was tall, fast, powerful and tough. He owned an awesome jab. That "thing" was lethal - a hard, thudding blow struck with accuracy and power. It was the "best jab in heavyweight history" (see **The Ring 1999 p 126**). It was usually his "weapon of choice."

And that's not all. He possessed a quick and stunning overhand right that he could deliver "on time," along with a walloping uppercut.

These talents along with his steady movement, outstanding reach and superior reflexes made him a great fighter. Odd (1989 p 60) wrote that he had a "killer punch in each hand." Jay Bright, former trainer of Mike Tyson, said, "Holmes was the consummate boxer, very slick, very cagey, with a terrific jab and a nice right hand. He used every ounce of the ability he had" (see **The Ring November 1996 p 29**).

His greatest weakness was a vulnerability to an inside attack, against which he was always on guard. According to Larry (Holmes 1998 p 99), "I always fought better moving away than coming forward" - beating his man to the punch and then getting away. His anticipation of his opponent's moves on offense and defense was uncanny - "when I was on top of my game, I swear I had a sixth sense that enabled me to see things before they happened" (Holmes 1998 p 112).

A member of a large family and brought up in poverty by his mother, he helped it survive by working as a youth. A possible "hell-raiser" as a teenager (according to Larry, himself), he definitely "raised hell" in the ring.

Holmes was an outspoken man who always said what was on his mind. Never as fancy with his words as was his idol Muhammad Ali, he was sometimes misunderstood - but always honest. Larry once said, "I'm a businessman first and a boxer second" (Myler 1998 p 156). In the ring, he was all business and his record speaks for itself. Incidentally, he was an excellent businessman outside the ring too.

Larry, along with Joe Louis and Muhammad Ali, dominated the heavyweight division as never before. He was called the "most dominant heavyweight king since Joe Louis" and it was written that his "chief weapon was his sterling jab" (see **The Ring November 1996 pp 28 29**).

He was an outstanding amateur fighter and began his professional career in 1973, winning 48 straight fights before losing his first contest in 1985. Mee (1997 p 158) called the loss a "controversial points decision." He defended the title 21 times and gave credibility to the IBF heavyweight title when he accepted it.

During his career, Larry defeated such able men as Ken Norton, Earnie Shavers, Mike Weaver, Trevor Berbick, Leon Spinks, Tim Witherspoon, James "Bonecrusher" Smith, Ray Mercer, Muhammad Ali, Gerry Cooney, Randall "Tex" Cobb and Renaldo Snipes. Larry wrote, "I never felt more alive than when I was fighting my best against a truly good fighter" (Holmes 1998 p 112).

Perhaps his greatest effort came in 1978 when he defeated Ken Norton to capture the WBC heavyweight championship. In a nip-and-tuck bout and one of the greatest fights ever, Larry edged Ken in a disputed split decision.

In this bout, he showed the true grit of which he is made - a great fighter of the mold "when the going gets tough, the tough get going." According to the man himself, "This was the best fight I was ever in" (Holmes 1998 p 112).

In an article in **The Ring (November 1996 pp 28 29)**, Dave Anderson, sports columnist for **The New York Times**, described Holmes, "He could outbox you … he could also outlast you." Teddy Brenner, former matchmaker, said, "Holmes had a good left hand, a great chin, and lots of heart."

Holmes, along with George Foreman, "Jersey" Joe Walcott and Bob Fitzsimmons, proved that "old men" could fight successfully as heavyweights. All four of these talented fighters fought well into their forties and "whomped" many young studs that other top boxers did not want to fight.

Dangerous well past his prime, Holmes tangled with the very best men available - including Ray Mercer, Evander Holyfield and Oliver McCall - and held his own. At the age of forty-seven, he fought Brian Nielsen for the IBO heavyweight championship and pounded the huge Dane before losing a split decision. He actively campaigned for a match with old George Foreman but it never came to pass.

For most of his career, Larry lived in the shadow of Muhammad Ali. As a sparring partner for the champ, the young Holmes knew he could give Ali a "hell of a fight" and began to think he could beat him (Holmes 1998 p 62).

In 1980, he met and defeated the great one in the ring and hated every minute of it. He battered his former mentor and had him at his mercy before the contest was stopped. According to Holmes, "Ali was my idol, a tremendous fighter, but he stepped out of his time into my time" (Bunce and Mee 1998 p 168).

Bert Sugar (1980 p 21) wrote, "A younger, tougher, and better Larry Holmes 'whupped' him in every which way … Ali knew it was all over after the first round." Many fans believe that Larry - with his height, reach and power - may well have been a match for the "real" Ali in his prime.

Mee (1997 p 158) wrote, "Larry Holmes was one of the most highly skilled heavyweights in history ..." Dave Anderson described Holmes as a "terrific boxer with one of the best jabs I've ever seen. He was underrated, more or less ignored, because he succeeded Ali" (see *The Ring November 1996 p 28*). Mullan (1990 p 152) wrote, "he suffered by following one of the sports legends, and he was never accorded the respect that his ability and record merited."

Myler (1998 p 156) recorded, "Despite living in the shadow of Ali throughout most of his championship reign, Holmes earned grudging admiration from many fans as a fine champion."

Bunce and Mee (1998 p 190) wrote, "As the years pass Holmes' status as a modern great increases. He fought on a regular basis and met all of the contenders and pretenders from a period when most of the heavyweights wasted their talents. Holmes is the best heavyweight from the tarnished years between the last of Ali's sweet jabs and the vicious hooks of Tyson. If time had been kinder to Holmes it is possible that he would be held in even higher esteem."

Once at a press conference, Larry made a "Marciano slur" in which he demeaned the skills of the unbeaten slugger. He has since called Marciano a "great champion" and said he didn't mean to impugn "The Blockbuster" as a man but only wanted to emphasize that he felt he could have beaten Rocky (Holmes 1998 pp 236 237).

Owning a 48-0-0 record at the time, he lost his next two fights and fell short of matching the 49-0-0 mark of "The Rock." The two losses were to Michael Spinks. This writer felt that Larry was better than Michael and has always seen these losses as questionable verdicts. Holmes has said, "Don't feel sorry for me, I gave it my all." He has also said, "I owe everything to boxing" (Myler 1998 p 158). But Larry gave back to boxing too.

Sugar (1980 p 23) wrote of Holmes, "A man who invests boxing with a dignity it sometimes doesn't deserve, he deserves better than he has received. This man can do it all." Larry has stated, "Against all odds, I succeeded" (Holmes 1998 p 279).

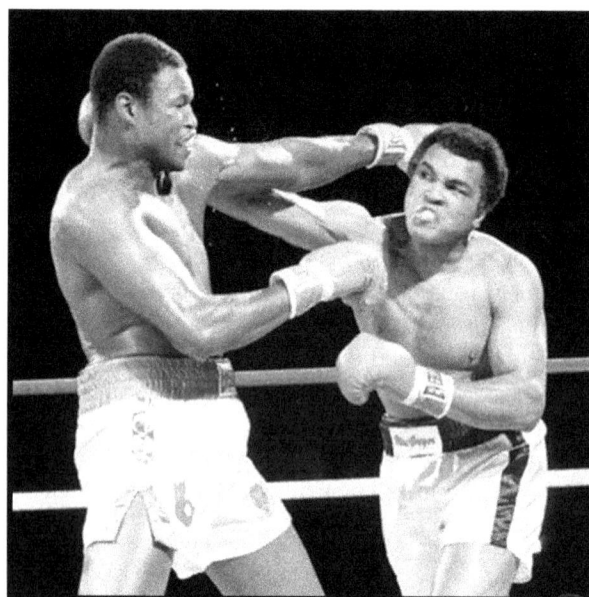

Larry Holmes-Muhammad Ali
October 2 1980

Herb Goldman, former Editor of *The Ring Record Book* and the *International Boxing Digest (IBD)* monthly boxing magazine, ranked Holmes as the #3 all-time heavyweight (*The Ring 1987 p 1071*). *The Ring (1999 p 126)* ranked Larry as the #5 all-time heavyweight. In the opinion of this writer, Holmes was the #10 all-time heavyweight. Holmes was inducted into the World Boxing Hall of Fame in 2007 and the International Boxing Hall of Fame in 2008.

9 Rocky Marciano ... Hardest One Punch
(Revised article - from The Cyber Boxing Zone, WAIL! - October 2000)

Rocky Marciano referred to "Suzy-Q" (his big right-hand punch) when he first came on the scene and the experts laughed. After they saw "The Rock" flatten his opponents for a few years, they referred to "Suzy-Q" and Marciano laughed.

Rocky came out swinging at the opening bell and maintained his attack until he gunned his man down. He gave it his all on each punch. Everything seemed to ride on the one big smash. He was relentless in his pursuit and like the Northwest Mounties, he usually got his man.

No one ever trained harder or took better care of himself than Marciano. He is often compared to Jim Jeffries in terms of brute strength and described as being crude, clumsy, strong and able to hit. He could take a punch - a punch of knockout caliber - and not blink.

Rocky Marciano

Probably a more likely comparison would be that of Marciano to the near-champion Tom Sharkey of the 1890s or Joe Frazier and Mike Tyson of more recent years. Rocky and Sharkey were similar in size except that Sharkey was much larger through the chest. Both had awesome hitting power and endurance, both sought victory any way they could get it and both were aggressive and rough. Marciano possibly had the tougher chin.

A stocky man with short arms, Rocky fought from a semi-crouch and bulled his opponents around with fierce determination using non-stop, swarming tactics. His short reach forced him to get inside and work close. Fists, wrists, forearms, elbows, head butts and low blows comprised his arsenal.

Carpenter (1975 p 114) called him a ruthless attacker and a very dirty fighter who always elbowed and butted. Houston (1975 p 75) said, "He was crude and clumsy, but he was also strong and could hit. He trained arduously, knowing that because of his style he would have to take punches along the way. Marciano developed into a human battering ram of a fighter, seemingly able to take the hardest punches and come right back as if nothing had happened."

Houston asserted that Marciano came to fight and not play. Rocky took no time to be nice. If punches went low or if he butted - too bad! Hmmm, sounds like Tom Sharkey of the 1890s. He added that Rocky's blows were heavy and because he was not a big heavyweight, he got close to his opponents and bulled them to the ropes for body-pounding.

Cooper (1978 p 12) wrote, "… he was a throwback to the old bareknuckle days. He must have been one of the hardest, most physically durable heavyweights of all time." Cannon (1978 p 158) asserted, "The endurance of Rocky Marciano was inhuman, and he was a mercilessly strong man. So hard was his body that [Joe] Louis said he hurt you badly if he bumped into you."

Odd (1974 p 49) described Rocky, "Marciano's brand of belligerent destructiveness had to be seen to be believed. There was no art or finesse about his work, he just bulldozed in and took his opponents apart with his hooks, swings, and uppercuts." Myler (1998 p 247) called him "one of the roughest fighters of them all" and wrote, "He was in the ring to do a job and he did it whichever way he could. If that meant hitting with his elbows, butting, punching low, or after the bell had rung to end a round, then so be it."

Rocky's manager, Al Weill, said, "Rocky has something you don't see unless you're around him all the time. After a while, you know it's there, and so do the guys who get in there with him." He added that nature gave him everything he needed as a champion - unusual strength, stamina, a terrific punch and plenty of guts (see McCallum 1975 p 58).

McCallum (1974 p 244) said, "Rocky Marciano might have been the crudest heavyweight ever to get a crack at the world title, let alone win it, but no one ever beat him." He also asserted (1974 p 254), "With the possible exception of Gene Tunney, no heavyweight could come close to matching the dedication and self-discipline of Marciano."

Grombach (1977 p 83) said that Marciano was "a dedicated, never-say-die, superbly self-disciplined athlete with many physical handicaps. Only Gene Tunney equaled the quite unannounced confidence, discipline, and insurmountable will-to-win of Marciano, although Marciano's physical equipment was far inferior to Tunney's." He added, "Marciano may well have been the hardest hitter in the game."

Gutteridge (1975 pp 101 102 107) described Rocky as a "strong, undisciplined punch swinger" whose impact was that of "brute strength, of almost animal crudity" and that it "mocked the very concept of craft and skill." He wrote, "Marciano's forearm hitting was estimated to be greater than some heavyweights can deliver with their full body force going into a punch."

Fleischer and Andre (1975 p 145) called him "a fighter with iron fists." Dempsey's old manager Jack "Doc" Kearns said, "When it comes to one-punch hitting, this kid is better than Dempsey and Louis" (see Durant 1976 p 119). Red Smith said Rocky "is known as the best one-punch hitter of them all" (see Litsky 1975 p 220).

McCallum (1975 p 57) wrote, "Marciano reminded oldtimers of Dempsey. He had a knockout punch in either hand. He took a punch beautifully. He had guts, a fighting heart. He feared no man, and would not have feared Dempsey."

Gene Tunney thought a Dempsey-Marciano fight would have been a "cheek-to-jowl brawl" and felt that Marciano had at least one asset that matched Dempsey. Tunney stated, "Dempsey could take it. He could take it to a full degree - and so could Rocky" (see McCallum 1974 p 257; McCallum 1975 pp 56 58; and Rice 1954 p 131).

Charley Goldman said Marciano had a "steel-chin" (see McCallum 1974 p 248) and Carpenter (1975 p 114) testified that he never saw Marciano take a backward step. Mee (1997 p 209) insisted, "Rocky Marciano was impossible to discourage, and seemed impervious to pain."

Durant (1976 pp 114 115) described Marciano as follows, "He had determination, he had an exceptionally powerful build and he had a blockbuster of a punch ... he had enormous arms and shoulders and a pair of hands like boulders."

He further wrote (1976 p 123), "Ring critics do not rank Rocky with the great ones, like Jeffries, Johnson, Dempsey, Tunney, and Louis. He never had to face the top-notch fighters that they did. It was not Rocky's fault, of course, that there was not much talent in the heavyweight field when he was fighting. He fought them all, and that is what a champion is supposed to do."

Myler (1998 p 246) wrote, "Forty-nine fights. Forty-nine wins. Rocky Marciano's place in history as the only world champion with a perfect record remains unchallenged."

Herb Goldman, former Editor of **The Ring Record Book** and the **International Boxing Digest (IBD)** monthly boxing magazine, ranked Marciano as the #7 all-time heavyweight (**The Ring 1987 p 1071**). Charley Rose ranked him as the #8 all-time heavyweight and Nat Fleischer ranked him as #10. **The Ring (1999 p 127)** ranked him as the #6 all-time heavyweight and **The Ring (2000 p 132)** ranked him as the #9 all-time greatest fighter of the twentieth century (among all weight classes). In the opinion of this writer, Marciano was the #9 all-time heavyweight.

Rocky Marciano-Rex Layne
July 12 1951

Marciano was inducted into The Ring Boxing Hall of Fame in 1959, the World Boxing Hall of Fame in 1980 and the International Boxing Hall of Fame in 1990.

Rocky Marciano-Archie Moore
September 21 1955

8

Charles "Sonny" Liston ... Menacing Black Bear
(Revised article - from The Cyber Boxing Zone, WAIL! - February 2000)

Charles "Sonny" Liston

Charles "Sonny" Liston was one of the most awesome, massive and powerful heavyweights of all-time. At his peak, he was the closest thing to Jim Jeffries in the last 100 years in terms of raw strength, hard-hitting and ability to take a punch - with the possible exception of George Foreman. If Joe Frazier qualifies as "The Black Marciano," then "Sonny" Liston at his best could be called "The Black Jeffries."

Liston possessed a stiff left jab and vicious hooks from both sides. He moved quickly for a big man and fought from a rather straight-up stance, crouching when attacked. Never off his feet until the second bout with Muhammad Ali, his chin was pure granite. Only his endurance was a question mark since most opponents were unable to extend him.

Liston was avoided by champion Floyd Patterson and labeled as undeserving of a title shot because of his bad character and background. When he was finally given a chance at the crown in 1962, he cleaned up Patterson without breaking a sweat. His reign as champion was short-lived but had his title match with Patterson taken place when it should have, in the mid-fifties, he would easily have been champion from 1958 to 1964 and possibly longer since some mystery surrounds his title fights with Ali.

Many knowledgeable boxing people rate Liston in his prime among the best heavyweights ever. Some even rate him above Muhammad Ali. It is difficult to think of him as better since Muhammad defeated him twice in the ring. But "Sonny" was "over the hill" during these fights. Also, the question of fixed bouts has been raised in connection with these matches.

A few rate him as the greatest ever. They think he could knock out any man he could hit including Dempsey, Louis, Marciano, Foreman and Jeffries. They say the only type of fighter who would have a chance of beating him would be a runner like Muhammad Ali, Gene Tunney or Jim Corbett. And at his best, they feel he would catch up with these guys over the long haul.

Liston flattened Floyd Patterson on two occasions, each fight lasting only one round. He took Patterson's best punches without blinking. He twice stopped the thunderous puncher Cleveland Williams and took his best shots with ease. He required a total of fifteen rounds to finish off the following top eight contenders - Billy Hunter, Julio Mederos, Wayne Bethea, Frankie Daniels, Nino Valdes, Roy Harris, Zora Folley and Albert Westphal.

Gary Cartwright wrote, "No one in his right mind wants to fight Sonny Liston" (see Litsky 1975 p 205). Atyeo and Dennis (1975 p 35) stated, "One by one the top ranking heavyweights crashed beneath Liston's bulldozing tactics and massive fists." Litsky (1975 p 205) called Liston "a big, mean, intimidating brute."

Odd (1974 p 59) said if any man was ever equipped advantageously to be heavyweight champion it was "Sonny" Liston. Muhammad Ali said of Liston, "He was everything they said he was, a mass of muscles, power, force …" (see Durant 1976 p 106). Houston (1975 p 100) called him "one of the most formidable heavyweights in history … powerfully-muscled former convict who oozed menace." He goes on to say (1975 p 101) that Liston's fighting was so impressive that it was difficult to find a weakness. "Sonny" had a "pole-like" left jab, hit heavily with both hands and seemed impossible to knock out due to his tremendous neck muscles.

Carpenter (1975 pp 125 126) said he was massively broad with impressive measurements. He added that Liston's left jab compared favorably with Joe Louis' jab, that he appeared to be impervious to punishment and that he looked like the best champion since Rocky Marciano. According to Reg Gutteridge (1975 p 19), Marciano once told him that he would not relish being in the same ring with Liston.

McCallum (1974 p 300) said about Liston, "There was just too much dynamite in both hands for most fighters to handle him." Joe Louis predicted that Liston would be champion as long as he wanted to be (Durant, 1976 p 150).

In spite of his punch, chin and menacing attitude, there are many who ignore him in the all-time rankings. His personal life was a disgrace as he was constantly in trouble with society and its laws. One of his father's 25 children, Liston could barely read or write. Grombach (1977 p 86) called Liston, "probably one of the most illiterate top performers in modern boxing. He was a mental deficient, hardly able to read and write."

According to Fleischer and Andre (1975 p 159), Liston himself said that when he was thirteen, he joined a bad crowd that was always looking for trouble. McCallum (1975 p 67) said, "His biggest fault lay in the fact that he grew up thinking that criminals were great people." Durant (1976 p 142) wrote, "Liston was a hoodlum, a labor goon, and head-breaker." Jim Bishop said, "Liston had all the character of a mongrel, but he could hit" (see McCallum 1975 p 68).

Cooper (1978 pp 149 150) stated, "People didn't like him, and he didn't like people" and called him "a man with a grudge against everything and just about everybody." He later described Liston's fighting by saying, "looking after himself without needing to use science was nothing but second nature." Cosell (1973 p 169) wrote about an interview he did with Liston saying, "Suddenly, I realized that at heart he was just a big bully."

In the same book, Cosell discussed the possibility of his involvement with gangsters and a fixed fight in Liston's loss of the title to Muhammad Ali. Of the knockout punch in the second fight, Cosell quoted Jimmy Cannon, boxing writer, as saying, "I was sittin' right there. I saw the punch, and it couldn't have crushed a grape" (see Cosell 1973 p 181). Cosell went on to say, "There was a look of absolute relief on Liston's face. I don't think I ever saw 'Sonny' appear so content in his life, and I wondered about that."

Robert Lipsyte, the "accidental sportswriter," wrote, "It must never be forgotten that he was a very good fighter" (see Litsky 1975 p 205).

Herb Goldman, former Editor of **The Ring Record Book** and the **International Boxing Digest (IBD)** monthly boxing magazine, ranked Liston as the #2 all-time heavyweight (**The Ring 1987 p 1071**). In the opinion of this writer, Liston was the #8 heavyweight of all-time - this only after giving in to pressures of colleagues and consideration of a possible lack of stamina in "Sonny." At times, there is a strong feeling he ranks among the four best heavyweights ever.

Liston was inducted into the World Boxing Hall of Fame in 1990 and the International Boxing Hall of Fame in 1991.

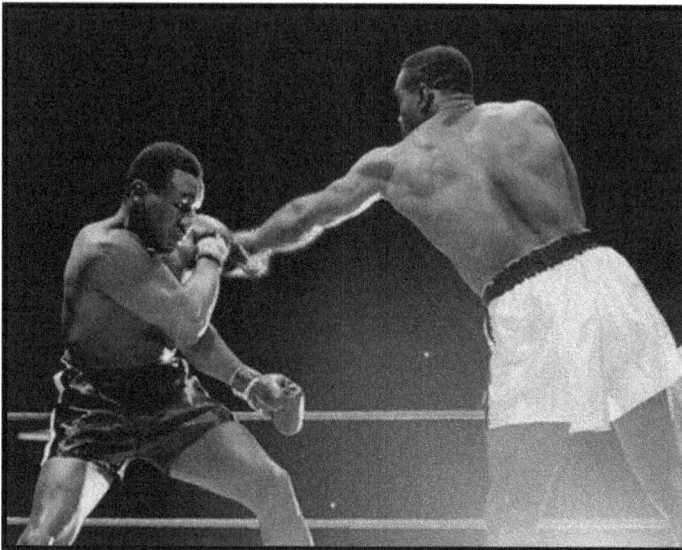

"Sonny" Liston-Julio Mederos
May 14 1958

"Sonny" Liston-Albert Westphal
December 4 1961

7 Jim Corbett ... Always Won "First Blood" Money
(Revised article - from The Cyber Boxing Zone, WAIL! - May 1999)

Jim Corbett

Jim Corbett was a boxer-deluxe. He was fast, clever and elusive with excellent speed of hand and foot. He used a repertoire of jabs, hooks and crosses while keeping his distance during the early part of a fight. But if he chose, Jim could stand within an arm's reach of an opponent and hit him at will without being struck himself. Now and then, when an enemy was flat-footed or off-guard, "The Gent" would move in and slam home a hard one. His punch was stiffer than most people give him credit for.

Many historians said Corbett was the first champion under the Marquis of Queensberry Rules. Some historians wrote that during his entire career (18 years) he never got a black eye or bloody nose. He was "heady" and an exceptional innovator. If a fight did not go according to plan (most did), he could adjust and change tactics in a flash.

Jim was so quick and smooth that his opponent's physical size or boxing skills was never a handicap to him. He knocked out John L. Sullivan, the powerful bully. He went 61 rounds with the two-hundred pound Peter Jackson. He made a mess of Bob Fitzsimmons in the early rounds of their championship fight and had the count been carried out fairly (many sources say it was slow), he would have scored a sixth-round knockout.

But he did err and get too close to Jim Jeffries - more out of disregard than error. Corbett boxed 23 rounds with Jeffries in their first bout and cut the big man's face to shreds. Corbett later joked that he was ahead 22-0 going into the fatal 23rd round.

William Brady, manager of both Corbett and Jeffries, when asked to compare the two, said, "I have a leaning, a slight leaning, toward Corbett. He combined the most desired qualities of brain and brawn to a degree I have never seen in any other fighter, past or present" (see Edgren 1926).

Houston (1975 p 9) said, "He believed in hitting without being hit and moved gracefully about the ring, relying on the speed and accuracy of his hits to wear down opponents ..."

Durant and Bettman (1952 p 82) said Corbett "... could feint, slip punches, side-step, and counter with a left jab so fast that it was a blur to the eye."

Litsky (1975 p 76) said, "James J. Corbett was one of the great heavyweight boxing champions and one of the great innovators ... He originated the counter punch, the feint, and fast footwork." Durant and Rice (1946) called Corbett a skilled boxer who was lightning fast and one of the most scientific fighters of all time. They added, "In the ring he was ice cold. No man before him had ever applied himself to his trade as did Corbett to the study of boxing."

Burrill (1974 pp 50 51) said, "Corbett marked [the] turning point in ring history, replacing mauling sluggers with [the] new school of faster, scientific boxers." Jem Mace, England's great bare-knuckle champion, called Corbett, "... the most scientific boxer ..." he had ever seen (see Durant 1976 pp 38 39).

Grombach (1977 p 48) wrote that Corbett was the first man to introduce defensive tactics into championship competition and the principle that a man cannot be beaten if he cannot be hit. Willoughby (1970 p 358) wrote of Corbett, "... without doubt the greatest of all defensive boxers among the heavyweights ..."

Fleischer and Andre (1975 p 71) stated that at the peak of his career no one could compare with him in quick thinking and cleverness. McCallum (1974 p 22) said, "James John Corbett is down in history as the most intelligent prize fighter the ring has ever known - the supreme master of defensive boxing." Keith (1969 p 114) wrote, "Jim Corbett ... probably had the fastest and cleverest footwork of any man ever to fight for the world's heavyweight championship."

Durant (1976 p 33) said he "... developed the beautifully proportioned body of a Greek athlete" and that he was an accomplished counter-puncher. Odd (1976 p 141) wrote that Corbett appeared to be the perfect athlete with his beautiful muscularity. He earlier wrote (1974 p 16) he [Corbett] placed the science of boxing before brawn and added, "Corbett specialized in a straight left lead and a right cross and he cultivated footwork to a fine degree."

Jim Jeffries said Corbett was "... the cleverest man I ever fought. There isn't a fighter of any weight, living or dead, who could measure up to him as a boxer" (see Litsky 1975 p 76). According to Pollack (2007 p 410) "... at his best, Corbett could hit, elude and neutralize opponents almost at will, and keep it up indefinitely." He added, "In today's world of 12-round bouts, Corbett may well have gone undefeated."

Grantland Rice (1954 pp 142 143) called Corbett "the world's greatest boxer" and wrote that in 1925 Corbett, at the age of 59, sparred three rounds with Gene Tunney. Rice stated that, "Tunney was on the defensive. Corbett was brilliant. He still had bewildering speed! He mixed up his punches better than practically any fighter I've ever seen ..." Tunney commented, "It was the greatest thing I've ever seen in the ring. I learned plenty" (also see McCallum, 1974 p 6).

Lardner (1972 p 69) asserted, "James J. Corbett was the greatest boxer of all time among the heavyweights and one of the greatest ring generals of any weight. No heavyweight ever approached him in the ability to ride with a punch (and so remove part of its sting); slip a punch; make his opponent lead before he was ready and then counter with a series of piston-like jabs; feint an opponent into committing a defensive maneuver and then attack the newly vulnerable area; or drift just out of reach of a punch a split second before it reached its intended target."

Nat Fleischer ranked Corbett as the #5 all-time heavyweight. Charley Rose ranked him as the #9 all-time heavyweight. In the opinion of this writer, Corbett was the fastest heavyweight boxer ever over the entire course of a fight, not just the early rounds, and the #7 all-time heavyweight in boxing history.

"Gentleman Jim" Corbett was inducted into The Ring Boxing Hall of Fame in 1954, the World Boxing Hall of Fame in 1980 and the International Boxing Hall of Fame in 1990.

Jim Corbett in a fighting pose

Jim Corbett-Jake Kilrain
February 18 1890

Jim Corbett-Bob Fitzsimmons
March 17 1897

6 Gene Tunney... The Fighting Marine
(Revised article - from The Cyber Boxing Zone, WAIL! - April 2000)

Gene Tunney was the type of man that comes along once in a hundred years - the looks of a movie star, the intellect of a college professor, a devoted student of Shakespeare and heavyweight boxing champion of the world.

He was the epitome of self-will, discipline, dedication and commitment to purpose. He evaluated his abilities, mapped out a plan, followed it to the letter, achieved his objectives, retired and pursued other goals which he also accomplished.

Blessed with a beautiful, quick left jab and a knack for counter-fighting, Tunney was one of the great defensive fighters of all-time. Gene fought at a fast, steady pace throughout an entire bout and did not seem to tire as the fight progressed.

He was a superb tactician who boxed his man dizzy until the time was right to move in with the heavy blows. His hands did not allow a sustained attack based upon heavy-hitting but when the time came that increased power was needed, it was there.

Gene Tunney

Grantland Rice (1954 p 155) described Tunney as a "man who dedicated himself to a task as no other athlete." From 1919 to 1926, Gene conducted the "Dempsey Analysis" whereby he studied every move of the great champion. He knew the strengths and weaknesses of Dempsey, inside out, upside down and backwards. When he confronted Jack in the ring, he read his moves perfectly except for once - in the seventh round of their second fight when he was knocked down by "The Mauler." Some experts say he won 19 of the 20 rounds he fought with Dempsey.

Gene lost one fight during his professional career and bested that man (Harry Greb) three times afterwards. He was knocked down only once in his career (by Dempsey). Durant and Rice (1946) wrote, "The ex-Marine was a cool, intelligent boxer with a taste for literature. He was not a crowd pleaser but he always won." Litsky (1975 p 325) wrote, "He was a brilliant scientific boxer with agility, speed, quickness, and power."

Durant (1976 p 75) commented, "Like Corbett, Tunney was an intense student of ring craftsmanship. He planned each battle to combat his opponent's style with the thoroughness of a general mapping out a campaign."

He described Tunney as follows (1976 p 77), "Gene was a determined, cool, counter-puncher, a boxer. He was fast and dead game, and a punishing hitter, but he was no knockout artist. He scored his shares of K.O.'s, however, but mostly by wearing down his opponents rather than blasting them out of the ring Dempsey fashion. He was methodical, reserved, and cautious in the ring and out of it. He did not like the fight crowd, nor they him - especially when it became known that he could and did read good books."

Durant and Bettman (1952 p 173) wrote, "A cool, intelligent boxer with unlimited determination, Tunney was not an exciting performer, but he always won." They added, "In many ways he was like Corbett ... essentially a ring scientist."

Odd (1974 pp 29 30) said Tunney had brains in addition to a fine physique. He added that Gene studied every move in boxing, from the feet upwards, and placed the avoidance of a punch above the delivery of one.

Harry Grayson, writer, once said Tunney "... could be mean and cunning in the ring. He liked to break your nose and cut you up. He never cared how much he cut you, he would always take his time. He showed you the difference between great and near-great fighters" (see McCallum 1975 p 30).

Lardner (1972 p 251) wrote, "Tunney was a synthetic fighter. He studied, analyzed, rehearsed, pondered. He saw his opponent as a case history, a specimen, an anatomical object. He analyzed his foe's strengths and weaknesses and constantly analyzed his own - noting improvements - to determine how best to attack and defend. There has never been a fighter who strove as assiduously to correct flaws, physical, mental, or spiritual."

He went on to say that Tunney had weak hands but made the best of the situation by learning how to box, hit accurately and not waste punches. Later, when his hands had toughened to where he could smash hard blows, he profited by combining the boxing skills with the acquired hard-hitting.

McCallum (1975 pp 29 31) wrote, "Tunney's ring career was a literal example of the triumph of mind over matter" and said, "Few athletes in history ever have been better conditioned than Tunney. He developed stamina enough to step around at top speed every second of every round." He added that Gene had "nerves of ice." Gutteridge (1975 p 85) said Tunney was "... an underrated heavy with a fine style and the ability to absorb a hard punch."

Fleischer (1969 pp 277 279) analyzed the great heavyweights and said Tunney was the cleverest of the big boys since Corbett. He wrote that Gene was extremely fast, a master boxer and an intelligent jabber. Further, he labeled Tunney as underrated and described him as being a cool, mechanical technician who was not colorful.

Grombach (1977 p 62) wrote, "The story of Tunney presents a remarkable display of force of character and will to succeed." He was the man who would "rather beat Dempsey than have all the money in the world" (see McCallum 1974 p 111). He beat Dempsey twice and offered to fight him a third time. Dempsey refused.

McCallum (1974 p 123; 1975 pp 29 30) asserted, "Tunney never entered the prize ring with the natural, instinctive fighting equipment of a Jeffries, a Johnson - or a Dempsey. He wasn't a natural born puncher, his physique was not adapted to fighting, and although he did possess superb reflexes, they had to be adjusted to boxing. Through sheer willpower and mental exertion, Gene converted ordinary equipment into one of the finest fighting machines the ring has ever known."

Nat Fleischer ranked Tunney as the #8 all-time heavyweight. Charley Rose ranked him as the #6 all-time heavyweight. In the opinion of this writer, Tunney was the #1 all-time light-heavyweight and the #6 all-time heavyweight.

Tunney was inducted into The Ring Boxing Hall of Fame in 1955, the World Boxing Hall of Fame in 1980 and the International Boxing Hall of Fame in 1990.

**Gene Tunney-Georges Carpentier
July 24 1924**

**Gene Tunney-Jack Dempsey
September 22 1927**

5 Muhammad Ali … Float Like A Butterfly
(Revised article - from The Cyber Boxing Zone, WAIL! - February 2001)

Muhammad Ali

Muhammad Ali claimed he was "The Greatest" from the early days of his boxing career. His assertion that he was the "All-Time Best" gained support of boxing fans and experts with each passing year. His admirers said that he was not bragging when he sounded off - merely stating the facts.

There is no doubt that he was the best fighter in the heavyweight division for thirteen years, from 1964-1977. He is living proof that there is nothing like nerve if you have the ability to back it up.

Ali had the fastest hands in heavyweight history with the possible exception of Joe Louis and Floyd Patterson. Ali, however, lacked the benumbing power that Louis possessed. But Ali's body motion, leg movement, head and neck control, and overall ability were second to none in the annals of the big boys.

In the early part of a fight, he was sometimes untouchable. As the fight progressed, Ali, being a large man, tended to slow somewhat from the blistering pace of the first five rounds to a moderate pace for the remainder of the bout. However, due to exceptional anticipation, he was still hard to hit squarely.

A master strategist, Muhammad would "psych-out" his opponents by pre-fight talk, predictions and frequently by writing a poem about how he was going to knock them out or handle them during the match. Many times the outcome was exactly as he predicted. Gilbert Odd (1975) called him "The Fighting Prophet."

Usually Muhammad would outrun his adversary, pepper him heavily with jabs and combinations, and when his man tired, move in for the kill. Against stronger and more aggressive opposition, he would back-peddle, tantalize them with jabs and when they charged forward excitedly, he would brace himself and greet them with a straight right that shook them apart from head to toe. On many occasions, it was obvious that he was "carrying" his man to prolong the fight - even against topflight competition.

A government enforced suspension from the ring during the years 1967-1970 because of his stand against the Vietnam War prevented him from fighting in what were possibly his best years. Many claim that had he fought during that period, he would have been "The Greatest" beyond any shadow of a doubt. They may be right!

Durant (1976 p 151) described him as having "lightning-fast hands and a pair of legs that took him around the ring like a ballet dancer. He would float just out of range with his hands dangling at his sides as if to taunt his opponent." He added (1976 p 172) "he was black pride out loud."

Houston (1975 p 112) said, "He moved gracefully and punched fluently. He was not a particularly damaging hitter with one punch, but his combinations of blows made their mark." He added that speed and remarkable reflexes enabled him to box with hands dangling at his sides and simply not be there when an opponent went to hit him - "He swayed back from the waist to make punches miss by inches."

Cooper (1978 p 13) asserted, "What Ali was, at his best, was the fastest moving heavyweight of all time." He added (1978 p 15), "the second of Ali's great assets, and one which no other boxer can surely have possessed to the same degree, was the ability to judge distances … he knew to an inch when he was safely out of range."

Odd (1974 p 60) wrote, "Speed, perfect timing, sharp perception and correct punching have been the secret of Ali's success." Rocky Marciano was quoted as saying, "I never saw a fighter with hands that fast" (see Ali and Durham 1975 p 299).

Litsky (1975 p 16) wrote about Ali, "He is the fastest heavyweight boxing champion ever and, in the opinion of some, one of the best. He is by far the greatest box-office attraction in boxing history … his athletic talent is only half of his renown. He is colorful and charismatic, charming and abrasive, fascinating and mischievous, loud, antagonistic, magnetic."

Grombach (1977 p 88) called him "probably the most controversial, strange, and most unbelievable character in the history of prize-fighting from … around 1700 to our present era and probably beyond."

McCallum (1975 p 69) wrote, "There is no telling what heights Ali might have reached had his battle with the federal government over his military draft status not lopped three and a half years off his career. At his peak, he stood 6 ft. 3 in. and weighed 210 lbs. and he moved with the grace of a ballet dancer and punched with a speed hard to follow with the naked eye."

He also stated, "At his peak, 1964-1968, Muhammad Ali deserved to be ranked with the best heavyweights in history."

Carpenter (1975 p 156) expressed his thoughts following Ali's 1974 knockout of George Foreman to regain the title, "How many years had I been hearing Ali say 'I am the Greatest?' Always I had listened, laughed, enjoyed, and yet kept a doubt aflame in my mind.

The Greatest? With Johnson, Dempsey, Louis, Marciano there before him?" He went on to say, "I reflected on what I had just seen and admitted to myself - yes, very likely he is The Greatest."

Gutteridge (1975 p 13) said, "Until Ali regained the richest prize in sport in 1974, I was not totally convinced that he is the greatest heavyweight of all. Joe Louis held sway. Jack Johnson was also a master. Others would argue the case for deadly hitters Jack Dempsey and Rocky Marciano.

He continued, "But, Ali has brought a new conception to the art of boxing … he is not the hardest of heavyweight hitters and his in-fighting is practically non-existent. Ali's greatness, apart from the grace, the speed and the beautiful art of swaying out of harm's way, is more basic. He takes a blow better than anyone else. Behind the show off is a brave heart and a body that has recuperative powers beyond all other big men."

Howard Cosell (1973 p 188) wrote, "I am of the opinion that the finest fighter of my lifetime was Muhammad Ali."

Herb Goldman, former Editor of **The Ring Record Book** and the **International Boxing Digest (IBD)** monthly boxing magazine, ranked Ali as the #1 all-time heavyweight (**The Ring 1987 p 1071**). **The Ring (1999 p 124)** ranked him as the #1 all-time heavyweight and **The Ring (2000 p 124)** ranked him as the #1 all-time greatest fighter of the twentieth century among all weight classes.

However, a close analysis of his boxing career reveals that, in addition to his five official losses, he had a number of extremely close bouts that he could have or should have lost (i.e. Jimmy Young, Ken Norton #2 and #3, possibly Joe Frazier #2 and possibly Henry Cooper #1). Granted, these contests were against fine competition, but surely he would have had even more difficult bouts against the very best heavyweights in history. This writer believes he would have lost those bouts to the best men ever and accordingly ranks Ali as the #5 all-time heavyweight.

Ali was inducted into the World Boxing Hall of Fame in 1986 and the International Boxing Hall of Fame in 1990.

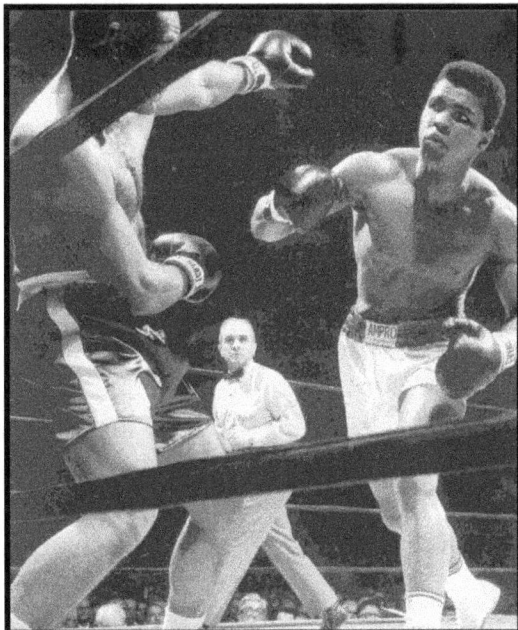

Muhammad Ali-Zora Folley
March 22 1967

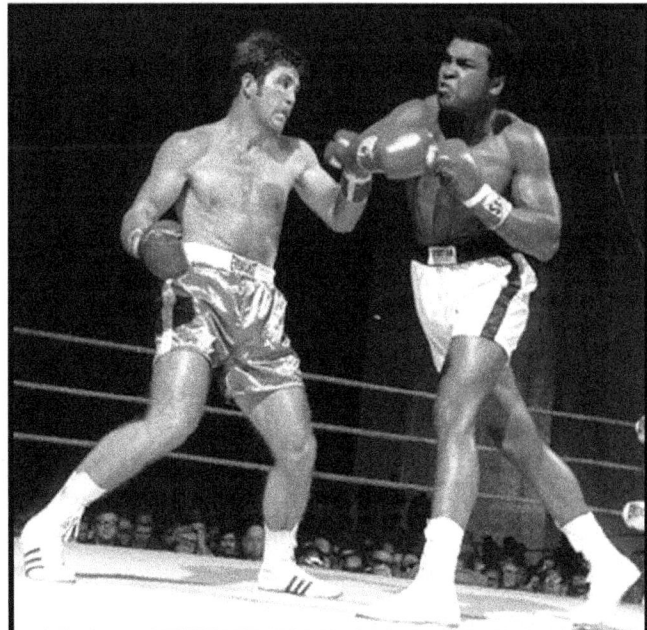

Muhammad Ali-Jerry Quarry
October 26 1970

4 Joe Louis … His Fists Did The Talking
(Revised article - from The Cyber Boxing Zone, WAIL! - July 2000)

Joe Louis

Joe Louis was sad-eyed, solemn, patient and deadly. His methodical, almost mechanical attack was backed up by strong shoulders and lightning-fast hands. In those hands was "TNT." Joe stalked his man, expressionless, striding forward with "that" jab which was equal to many a man's "Sunday Punch."

Many experts consider him to be the greatest counter-puncher among the heavyweights. When the slightest opportunity presented itself, the right-left exploded. Sportswriters of his day described him as "a combined boxer-puncher with the fastest pair of hands and the hardest punch ever seen" (see Durant 1976 p 99).

His offensive capability was most likely unequaled in the ring. He performed at optimum efficiency with little wasted motion. His style was that of a standup boxer with quick reflexes. He carried his guard moderately low. His defense consisted of a superb offense.

Gutteridge (1975 p 41) said that Louis "was unquestionably the most complete heavyweight of them all." He wrote, "The power he packed looked capable of lopping a man's head from his shoulders. He was the most correct hitter I have seen and he turned the destruction of his opponents into an art form." Further he stated, "Using his left jab he could set up his victim for either a lethal left-hook, delivered with unerring accuracy, or for the text book right-cross." He concluded, "Louis did his job with a cold detachment, fighting with a deadpan expression that never changed in victory or defeat."

In many ways, he was the ideal champion. His conduct in and out of the ring was that of a gentleman. His sportsmanship was first class. He was at the same time both modest and confident. He dodged no man. He gave a title shot to all deserving contenders … and beat them.

Louis did not run his mouth like some fighters. He let his fists do the talking and when they spoke, everyone listened. In fact, they spoke so loudly that the echoes can still be heard. He was champion for eleven years and eight months. He defended the title 25 times. He knocked out six other heavyweight champions - Primo Carnera, Max Baer, Jack Sharkey, Max Schmeling, Jim Braddock and "Jersey" Joe Walcott.

Henry Cooper (1978 p 10) contended, "He was a beautiful mover, compact, and with a great left jab which more often than not opened the door for a right cross that might just as well have had the word curtains tattooed on the glove."

He added (1978 p 11), "Joe always let his fists do his talking." Max Schmeling said the same, "He [Louis] says nothing with his mouth ... He says it with his fists" (see Astor 1974 p 171). Jim Braddock said, "Nobody hits like Louis ... A punch is a punch. But that Louis. Take the first jab he nails you. You know what it's like? It's like someone jammed an electric bulb in your face and busted it" (see McCallum 1975 p 45).

Durant (1976 p 101) wrote, "The Brown Bomber ... did not have the whirlwind aggressiveness of Dempsey or the beautiful ring science of Corbett or Tunney but he combined a good portion of these qualities, and, in addition, had the fastest pair of hands in ring history. He was one of the very few who could knock a man out with a left jab, and his straight right spelled destruction. Joe could end a fight suddenly and completely with either hand with a punch that did not have to travel more than a few inches."

Bromberg (1958 p 59) said, "In the cold recording of successes, one is apt to lose sight of the fact that Louis was much more than an effective automation. Anyone who breathed the boxing air through Joe's generation would be quick to confirm that he had a capacity to respond electrically to a tense situation."

Fleischer and Andre (1975 p 127) wrote that Joe Louis was colorful and one of the greatest fighters in modern boxing. Joe was described as having the "grace of a gazelle" and the "cold fury of an enraged mountain lion."

Grombach (1977 p 64) recorded, "Louis showed an easy, relaxed style, delivering lightning left hooks, and two-handed attacks to the body. He displayed in addition nice pacing and unusual ability to handle a much bigger and heavier man in clinches." He evaluated Louis by writing, "Joe Louis, even seen through contemporary eyes too often prone to look to the past for great fighters, was definitely one of the finest fighters in the history of boxing."

Durant and Bettman (1952 p 229) called Louis, "a superb fighting machine, a combined boxer-puncher who punched so fast and accurately that they (fans) could scarcely follow the course of his blows." They also asserted he was "one of the greatest fighters of them all" (1952 p 269).

McCallum (1974 p 198) called Louis "a great champion" and a "clean and fair sportsman" and rated his ring record the best among the heavyweight champions. Carpenter (1975 pp 76 88) wrote that Louis was sleek and quick, punched with short blows and became the greatest of all champions.

Houston (1975 p 57) wrote, "If any heavyweight champion could be called a perfect fighting machine, it was Joe Louis. Louis was considered unbeatable at his peak." He added (1975 p 58), "He was one of the most destructive heavyweight punchers and a great combination hitter. When he had an opponent in trouble he was merciless."

Further, Houston wrote, "Louis had a jarring left jab, which he used to set up an opponent for the heavier artillery - the hooks, uppercuts, and the smashed straight right-handers. He punched in jarring sequences, not just one blow but a whole series, all deliberately aimed and driven in fast and hard. He shuffled forward and sought to cut off the ring and pin down his opponents."

Jimmy Cannon (1978 p 113) quoted Billy Conn as saying, "Louis was just the greatest." Cannon, himself, said (1978 p 157), "The greatest heavyweight I've ever covered was Joe Louis. The hands were quick, and a left hook or a right hand would stun the other guy and then he would put the combinations together with a rapid accuracy."

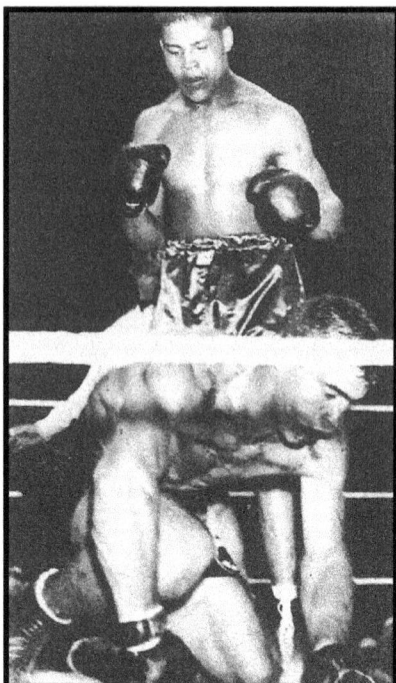

Joe Louis-Primo Carnera
June 25 1935

Odd (1974 p 40) asserted that Louis was "Undoubtedly the finest fighting machine ever to step into a ring" and described him as "a poker-faced, deliberate attacking fighter, who came forward in a shuffle behind an almost mechanical left jab, that traveled the shortest distance between any two points, was straight, true, and deadly. It would snap a man's head back with sickening monotony until he wavered under the steady punishment."

Odd went on to say Louis would then finish off his opponent quickly with swift and accurate hooks from both hands. He stated that Joe was ice-cold, rarely wasting a punch and able to anticipate and avoid a blow by the mere movement of his head.

Nat Fleischer rated Louis as the #6 all-time heavyweight. Charley Rose rated Joe as the #4 all-time heavyweight. *The Ring (1999 p 125)* ranked him as the #2 all-time heavyweight and *The Ring (2000 p 125)* ranked him as the #2 all-time greatest fighter of the twentieth century (among all weight classes). In the opinion of this writer, Louis was the #4 heavyweight of all-time.

Joe Louis-Jim Braddock
June 22 1937

Louis was inducted into The Ring Boxing Hall of Fame in 1954, the World Boxing Hall of Fame in 1980 and the International Boxing Hall of Fame in 1990.

3 Jack Dempsey ... Lean and Mean, Skill and Will
(Revised article - from The Cyber Boxing Zone, WAIL! - December 1999)

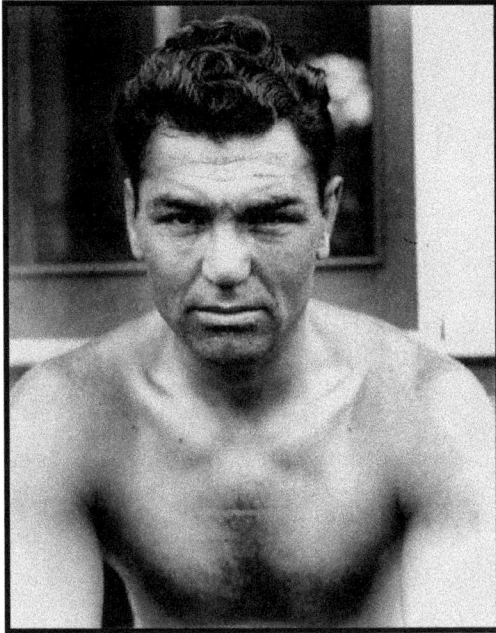

Jack Dempsey

Jack Dempsey has been called "The Eternal Champion," the ultimate yardstick by which all heavyweight fighters are judged. He was the most thrilling, brutal and savage fighter who ever ruled the ring. His vicious intent was the complete and total destruction of his opponent and he didn't care how he did it. This usually meant disaster for his foe.

He had the equipment to carry out his intentions. As Litsky (1975 p 86) put it, he had "fast hands, fast feet, and frightening power." He was durable, with high cheekbones that protected his eyes. He could take a punch. Dark-bearded, mahogany-skinned, busted nose, hair cropped close and high above his ears, Dempsey "came to fight" (see McCallum 1975 p 23).

Durant (1976 p 68) described him as follows, "He had a perfect build and appearance of a fighter - high cheekbones, deep-set eyes, a bull neck, and a beautifully proportioned body. He was hard all over, in muscles and in mind. He was always in condition." He went on to say, "He was an exciting fighter, an aggressive two-fisted cyclone in action, all flame and power. He seemed to burn with a white rage at the sound of the bell."

Crouching, bobbing and weaving, chin-on-chest, teeth bared, scowling at his victim, smashing with piston-like, bone-crushing hooks and uppercuts, Dempsey attacked. He was rough and dirty, the prime example of anything goes. He hit low, after the bell, and on breaks. He butted and used rabbit punches, thumbs and laces. The killer instinct was always visible. If a man wanted a fight, he had it. If he didn't, he'd better not get in the ring with Dempsey.

Grantland Rice (1954 pp 116 117) called Jack the "greatest attacking" star in sports that he'd ever seen and stated that he was keen, lithe and fast. He writes, "It was his speed, speed of hand as well as foot, that made him such a dangerous opponent ... In the ring, he was a killer - a superhuman wildman ... He was a fighter - one who used every trick to wreck the other fighter" (also see McCallum, 1974 p 89).

Durant and Bettman (1952 p 170) wrote, "He was all fighter - a tough, 190-pounder with whipcord muscles and a scowling face." Jack was a two-handed hitter who could knock out a man with one punch from either hand. He threw heavy, blockbuster punches that pulverized and flattened bigger, stronger men. Keith (1969 p 127) asserted that Jack's hook was a "close second" to that of Jim Jeffries.

Often he threw controlled punches so that he could follow one stiff blow quickly with another. He had great balance and quick hands that could get to vulnerable spots and therefore beat or knock out light, fast men - although he had his toughest times against this type of fighter.

He was accused of using plaster of paris in his gloves but Carpenter (1975 pp 64 67) asserted that his hands alone were enough to tear out a man's heart and guts.

Joe Benjamin, old-time fighter, once said, "Jack's hands were hard as rocks. He was the perfect fighting machine - hands, legs, fighting brain, and disposition. He was simply a super-human wild man" (see McCallum 1975 p 23).

Cooper (1978 p 7) called Dempsey "mean and merciless" and said (1978 p 9), "He let his fists hammer out their own message, and if he had to trade punches, take two to land one, well, the one that landed was going to be a good one." John J. Romano (1931 p 94) said, "Dempsey was known for his terrific punching. A tiger man in the ring he did not know the meaning of the word 'quit'."

Gutteridge (1975 p 71) wrote, "He was once the most powerful, ruthless, and dangerous unarmed man in the world" and added (1975 p 76), "Dempsey's greatness, apart from the power of his punches, was his ability to crush much heavier opposition with the sheer viciousness of his attacks."

He was scintillating and explosive and lost little time in getting his man. His 25 one-round knockouts, the highest total among the heavyweight champions, attest to this fact. Houston (1975 p 31) called him "a true hungry fighter" and contended, "It is doubtful if any heavyweight fighter before or since could have surpassed Jack Dempsey's sheer savagery in the ring. His style was one of unbridled aggression."

Bromberg (1958 p 39) wrote, "his ring savagery was the outgrowth of a wandering adolescence in the hobo jungles of the far west." Grombach (1977 p 54) commented that he bowled over opposition with "startling speed and dynamic knockouts" and observed that a nonstop "two-handed attack and killer instinct" was his order of the day. He later added (1977 p 100) that Dempsey, in his prime, was probably the greatest boxing champion of modern times.

Odd (1974 p 25) wrote, "To name Jack Dempsey as the most exciting of all the heavyweight champions is no exaggeration, for he packed more thrills and drama into his ring battles than any other and carried a knockout punch in each fist." He further said Dempsey was game, durable, and dedicated to physical fitness, and these qualities made him a terrifying opponent for anyone.

Jack had the upper body strength of the old school fighters but could move on his feet like the new. Tipping the scales at 190 pounds, his upper torso was equivalent to that of a 210-pound man. He was lean and mean with the skill and will, 190 pounds of hate!

Lardner (1972 p 217) remarked, "He may not have been the greatest fighter who ever lived - though denying it will get you a stiff argument in any bar in the land - but he was certainly the most exciting, the most colorful, the most dynamic, and the most savage. There was an immense fury coiled inside him waiting to be released."

He asserted that Dempsey's appeal lay in the fact that "he was willing to take six blows to land one," had a "panther-like concentration on demolishing his enemy" and carried "explosive charges in both hands." He called Dempsey a swift and accurate hitter who was able to flatten a foe with a blow traveling no more than eight inches, and said the punch could come at any moment.

Gene Tunney felt that Dempsey was the greatest of all heavyweights (1952 pp 36 38) and pointed out Dempsey's ability to take it, saying "Jack could recover faster than any man I ever fought. He was dangerous with a five-second interval" (also see McCallum 1975 p 27 and Rice 1954 p 131).

Nat Fleischer ranked Dempsey as the #4 all-time heavyweight. Charley Rose ranked him as the #3 all-time heavyweight. In the opinion of this writer, Dempsey was the #3 heavyweight of all-time.

Dempsey was inducted into The Ring Boxing Hall of Fame in 1954, the World Boxing Hall of Fame in 1980 and the International Boxing Hall of Fame in 1990.

Jack Dempsey-Billy Miske
September 6 1920

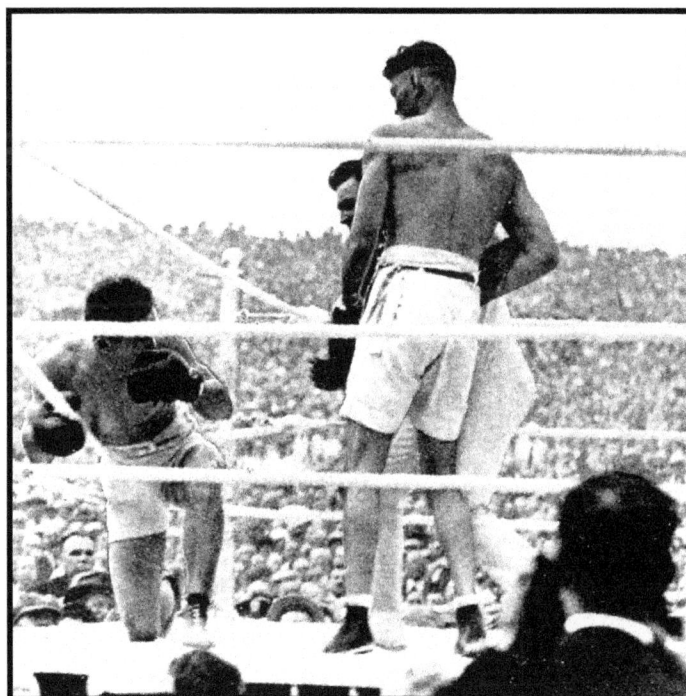

Jack Dempsey-Georges Carpentier
July 2 1921

2 Jack Johnson ... Bad Nigger
(Revised article - from The Cyber Boxing Zone, WAIL! - November 2000)

Jack Johnson

Jack Johnson was the first black heavyweight champion and as such, was the hero of his race. His ability in the ring is unquestioned, possibly unequalled. He could do it all, do it well and do it with ease.

His personal conduct outside the ring and many times within it was a different matter. Modesty and humility were no part of this man. He was extremely arrogant and fun-loving and lived life at a reckless, carefree, helter-skelter, "get out of my way," breakneck speed and manner. His behavior has been described as a public scandal and an irritant to white America. As a result, he was easily the most hated champion.

The effort to dethrone him brought about the search for the "Great White Hope" during his 1908-1915 reign and according to Nat Fleischer, produced an array of talent that has rarely been matched in any other period. But even they could not touch Johnson in his prime.

Johnson began a fight extremely cautious, quiet and on the defensive. As he slowly and surely turned the tide of battle his way, he became more aggressive and destructive in his style of fighting and abusive with his tongue. He preferred to punish his man rather than knock him out.

Jack gave the impression of holding back during a fight, never going all out and never pushing to the limit. "Dumb" Dan Morgan said, "I had the feeling he could demolish an opponent any time he chose."

Yes, he could get rough if he wanted. He cracked "Fireman" Jim Flynn's jaw, broke Stanley Ketchel's teeth off at the gum, flattened Bob Fitzsimmons and left him glassy eyed and mumbling to himself. He beat up Sam Langford, breaking his nose in the process, and left an old Jim Jeffries in a battered heap.

He knocked Marvin Hart out of the ring and put Tommy Burns down twice in the first two rounds, broke his nose and then taunted him for the next twelve rounds before he got bored and finished him off.

Jack Dempsey described him as a combination of Jim Corbett and Joe Louis. Others said he was as vicious as Dempsey but faster; smarter and more powerful than Louis (see McCallum 1975 p 17).

224

Durant and Bettman (1952 p 123) stated, "There was no denying Johnson's ability. He was a superb boxer with a punishing blow in either hand and was amazingly fast for a big man."

Fleischer and Andre (1975 pp 85 86) described him as cautious, tantalizing and having great ring science. A fighter with the perfect stance, he was a master of feinting a punch and carried punishing power in his stiff jabs.

Cooper (1978 p 9) wrote, "Many a time, Johnson could have knocked the guy out. But, if his opponent was white he'd have to suffer." He added (1978 p 17), "his main object in life was to put the white man in his place." (Author's Comment: Johnson probably could have scored knockouts 75 percent of the time had he not chosen to carry or punish his man.)

Lardner (1972 p 172) called him the grinning negro whose delight was in whipping caucasian fighters with taunts pouring from his mouth and described Johnson (1972 p 170), "He fought in a stand-up style, careful never to be caught off-balance … developed an effective snakelike left … and he fashioned the greatest right uppercut in prizefight history."

Keith (1969 p 134) asserted that Johnson rarely shot lead punches but fought mostly with counter-blows. However, Odd (1974 p 22) said, "Jack's skill at leading, picking his punches and whipping in precision blows was unequalled, so too was his uncanny ability to deflect punches aimed at him."

He went on to say that Johnson could make a foe miss by a fraction of an inch by side-stepping or drawing his head back and called Johnson's left jab straight and true, his right cross sheer artistry and his uppercuts devastating.

Gutteridge (1975 p 94) stated, "Johnson was a master of defense. While his style gave the impression that he was toying with an opponent, he had an explosive leopard-like reflex which was often overwhelming." Houston (1975 p 20) wrote, "He was a master defensive boxer who tricked opponents into making errors. Johnson fought with his hands held low, but had such fast reflexes he could pick off a rival's punches in mid-air."

He commented that Johnson's cautious style made him unexciting to watch as he often grabbed his opponent and tied up his arms. Nevertheless, Jack was nearly unbeatable because it was so difficult to hit him cleanly. Because of his tormenting style, opponents lunged recklessly to hit him while he placed his counter blows.

Durant (1976 p 58) wrote, "… he was a genius in the ring. He was a flawless boxer with an almost perfect defense, and he could hit hard with either hand. A superb counter puncher, he was never off balance, always in a position to hit, and he was a master of the art of feinting. Many competent ring critics believe that he was the greatest fighter who ever lived."

Carpenter (1975 p 45) said Johnson was the Muhammad Ali of his time and described him as having a super-ego with the boxing wizardry to back it up. Bromberg (1958 p 32) reported, "In overall ring assay, some have called him the finest of the heavyweight champions. He had grace, know-how, and hitting power."

McCallum (1974 pp 65 73) described Johnson as having a bullet head, wide face, gold-toothed grin, with a magnificent physique and the arms and torso of a gorilla. His strength is considered to be similar to that of James J. Jeffries. McCallum also wrote (1975 p 17) that catfooted Johnson came about as close to being an unbeatable fighter as ever lived.

Durant (1976 p 58) quoted Nat Fleischer as saying, "In all-around ability he was tops. After years devoted to the study of heavyweight fighters, I have no hesitation in naming Jack Johnson as the greatest of them all. He possessed every asset" (also see Fleischer 1949 p 153).

Charley Rose ranked Jack as the #2 all-time heavyweight. **The Ring (1999 p 129)** ranked him as the #9 all-time heavyweight and **The Ring (2000 p 128)** ranked him as the #5 all-time greatest fighter of the twentieth-century among all weight classes. In the opinion of this writer, Johnson was the #2 heavyweight of all-time.

Johnson was inducted into The Ring Boxing Hall of Fame in 1954, the World Boxing Hall of Fame in 1980 and the International Boxing Hall of Fame in 1990.

Jack Johnson-Jim Jeffries
July 4 1910

Jack Johnson-"Fireman" Jim Flynn
July 4 1912

1 Jim Jeffries ... Warhorse of Yesteryear
(Revised article - from The Cyber Boxing Zone, WAIL! - April 2001)

Jim Jeffries

Jim Jeffries was the "Champion of the Old Guard," the strong man from the school of brute strength. He was a self-punishing fighter in training, thriving on hard work. In combat, he stepped up the pace as a fight wore on and seemed to get stronger with each passing round.

Jeffries preferred to bide his time and hammer out a deliberate win but fought harder when challenged to mix it up. The rougher it got, the rougher he got.

He fought from a crouch, leading with his left. In this position, he was somewhat difficult to hit and impossible to hurt. He resembled a bear as he ambled towards his opponent. An awesome left-hand hitter, he was able to deliver knockout punches or telltale blows from a short distance rather quickly.

He was massive in size with large arms, shoulders, neck, head and legs. But at the same time, he was sinewy, shapely and muscular. In spite of his huge size, he moved on springy, bouncy legs. He could run 100 yards in a little over ten seconds and high jump over six feet. John L. Sullivan called him "the fastest big man I ever saw in the ring" (see Willoughby 1970 p 362).

Old-time referee Billy Roche described Jeffries as having the "acrobatic springiness of a circus tumbler in his legs. He was no lumbering ox, anchored to one spot, but a natural athlete" (see McCallum 1975 p 11).

Surly in nature and stubborn, he did not care much for foolishness or jokes. He was sometimes referred to as "The Beast" because of his rough battle tactics. Fighting from his crouch, he would suddenly spring forward, sometimes clanging heads with his foe - this never hurt Jeffries but often stunned his man.

Butting heads, ramming shoulders into opponents, hitting with elbows, shoving his foe around and leaning on his man in clinches were all part of his style.

William Brady, who managed both Jeffries and Jim Corbett, remarked, "There never was a man better fitted anatomically, physically, and temperamentally for the role of World's Heavyweight Champion" (see Edgren 1926).

Testimonies to Jeffries' strength are numerous. Houston (1975 p 15) said, "There was nothing fancy about James J. Jeffries. He was a die-hard fighter of the old school, relying on his considerable strength and durability to bring him victory."

He added that Jeffries had a bear-like appearance in his slightly crouched stance, was almost impossible to hurt or discourage and delivered clubbing blows that took their toll. He also said, "If Jeffries could not outbox an opponent, he could certainly outlast the best of them."

Odd (1974 p 18) said that Jeffries was the strongest of the heavyweight champions in both hitting power and build. Carpenter (1975 p 34) called Jeffries a bull of a man out of the California iron foundries who traded on strength. It has been written that no man was the same after being pounded by Jeffries' fists. With "TNT" in each hand, he delivered heavy, relentless blows that imparted their damage to the foe.

He cracked two of Bob Fitzsimmons' ribs in one of their bouts. He battered Tom Sharkey, breaking his nose and two ribs. Diamond (1954 p 62) said Sharkey was hospitalized for three days and suffered three broken ribs. He bashed in Jim Corbett's right side in their second match. He sent Joe Goddard to bed with a severe beating and dealt "Mexican" Pete Everett head and back injuries that kept him bed-ridden for days. Yet, Jeffries himself said he never hit a man with all his strength for fear of killing him.

Grombach (1977 p 50) said Jeffries was a natural puncher who was so big and powerful that he could deliver damaging blows from an almost extended left-hand that did not have to travel more than a few inches. Keith (1969 p 127) asserted, "Jeffries probably owned the deadliest left hook the prize ring has ever known."

"Tex" Rickard, famed fight promoter, said, "There's no style to him, but he's the hardest hitter I ever saw. And that includes Dempsey" (see McCallum 1975 p 15; Durant 1976 p 47). Diamond (1954 p 60) described Jeffries, "he was something more than a mere slugger. He was a rough, tough battler, with a mighty punch."

Sports columnist Ned Brown said, "He was one of the most powerfully built, could take a solid punch, and had acquired a fair amount of boxing skill by the time he tangled with Jim Corbett in their second match. Jeff had as deadly wallop as any I've ever seen" (see McCallum 1975 p 12).

Odd (1976 p 163) quoted Fitzsimmons describing Jeffries in battle, "The first time he really hit me in the body, I thought his fist had gone right through me. His crouching stance and the way he tossed that long left. Every time I hit him, he punched back even harder." Cooper (1978 p 107) remarked, "James J. Jeffries was one of the ring's indestructibles" and asserted, "Apart from having a punch that might have knocked a horse out, Jeffries' greatest asset was sheer patience."

It has been said that Jeffries could endure more punishment than any other prizefighter. He had a cast-iron chin attached to a large, bowling ball head. Fight fans in New York called him a "primitive," a "caveman." He was never knocked down during his prime.

According to Farr (1964 p 34), "Jim Jeffries was tough. Let us examine the word. Since Jeffries' time, it has suffered such abuse as a vogue-word as to be almost without meaning ... But, at the time the word was applied to Jeffries, it had a meaning that was both broad and exact.

A tough man's bone structure was heavier than that of an ordinary person; his muscular integument was thicker, so that it protected his nervous system from shock, and also was more supple, thus giving him superior ease and freedom of movement. He had a higher threshold of pain than the average man, and so could take a punch, as the handlers of prizefighters put it. The completing element of toughness, however, was emotional, and it lay in willingness to hit or kick another man, or maim him, before he could go into action."

Suster (1994 p 31) reported, "Certainly he was tough. Possibly no heavyweight champion has ever demonstrated a greater capacity for enduring pain." Lardner (1972 p 135) said, "Jeffries, far from a natural boxer, picked up the rawest fundamentals. But, given Jeffries' extraordinary physical skills, fundamentals were enough." He added, "nature had furnished him with nearly impenetrable armour."

Bob Fitzsimmons, one of the ring's deadliest hitters, broke his fists on Jeffries' head. Reportedly, Fitz even used plaster of paris in his wraps and still couldn't knock Jeffries down. Jim Corbett said, "Nobody can ever hurt him, not even with an ax" (see Litsky 1975 p 166). Gene Tunney (1941 p 139) wrote, "Jeffries' decisive quality was his tremendous physical toughness and endurance. The brawny giant could hardly be hurt" (also see McCallum 1974 p 49).

Jim Carney Jr. (2009 p 246) wrote, "His left jab rivals those of Sonny Liston and Joe Louis in potency, and perhaps no one else had as deadly a short, straight left. Jeff's left hook was also lethal, and he packed power in his right too. His combination left hook/uppercut to the body was legendary. As for durability, he is probably in a class by himself."

W.W. Naughton (1902 p 122) recorded, "To sum up his qualities of ringmanship, it may be said that he is fairly talented in every branch of self-defense. He boxes cleverly, defends himself well and strikes a hard blow. But, back of all these are the qualities which have made him a champion, to wit, magnificent strength and wonderful endurance."

Willoughby (1970 p 358) wrote, "Certainly, among all the heavyweights up to the year 1905, when he retired from the ring, Jim Jeffries was the greatest all-around performer. While he could not hit with the lightning-speed of Fitzsimmons, he had a powerful punch in each hand, and a good defense in the form of his famous 'crouch.' Most of all, however, he was impervious to blows, either to his head, face, or body."

John L. Sullivan said "... I never saw the man that I thought could stand a chance to lick Jeffries" (see Pollack 2009 p 666).

Kelly Nicholson (2002 p 165) commented "... I would rate Jeffries ... over most of his successors to this day. And under the older rules of the London prize ring, there is not a heavyweight in history whom I would choose over him."

Durant and Bettman (1952 p 122) stated that Jeffries was a fighting champion, putting his title on the line to anyone who deserved a crack at it. All the good men he fought prior to becoming champion received a title shot. Edgren (1926 p 56) said he even offered to fight Fitzsimmons, Corbett and Sharkey - all on the same night - but they refused.

Jess Willard said, "Jim Jeffries was a great, big, rugged fella, hard t'beat." He added, "Very tough man … Jeffries in his prime would lick anybody - he did!" (see Suster 1994 p 31). Tom Sharkey asserted, "Jeffries would have licked Jack Dempsey and Joe Louis on the same night. He was strong as a bull and quick on his feet like a cat" (see Diamond 1954 p 62).

McCallum (1974 p 47) described Jeffries as "big, strong and hard as granite" and said if he "wasn't the greatest heavyweight who ever fought certainly he stands out as one of the more formidable." Hugh Fullerton (1929 Foreword) wrote, "James J. Jeffries was the greatest heavyweight fighter in the history of the ring. A huge, hairy mountain of a man, fast with the deceptive speed of a grizzly, seemingly stolid, almost sullen, he was the least known of the great champions - and the most misunderstood."

John J. Romano (1931 p 93) wrote, "Jeff is sometimes referred to as the greatest of them all, and his record certainly justifies the title." Fighter and manager for over forty years, "Dumb" Dan Morgan, called Jeffries his "Champion of Champions" and firmly believed Jeff would whip all the others (see McCallum 1975 pp 11 12).

In a survey of a number of old-timers, conducted by John McCallum, Jeffries was ranked as the #1 all-time heavyweight (see McCallum 1975 p 322). Nat Fleischer ranked Jim as the #2 all-time heavyweight. Charley Rose ranked him as #5. In the opinion of this writer, Jeffries was the #1 heavyweight of all-time.

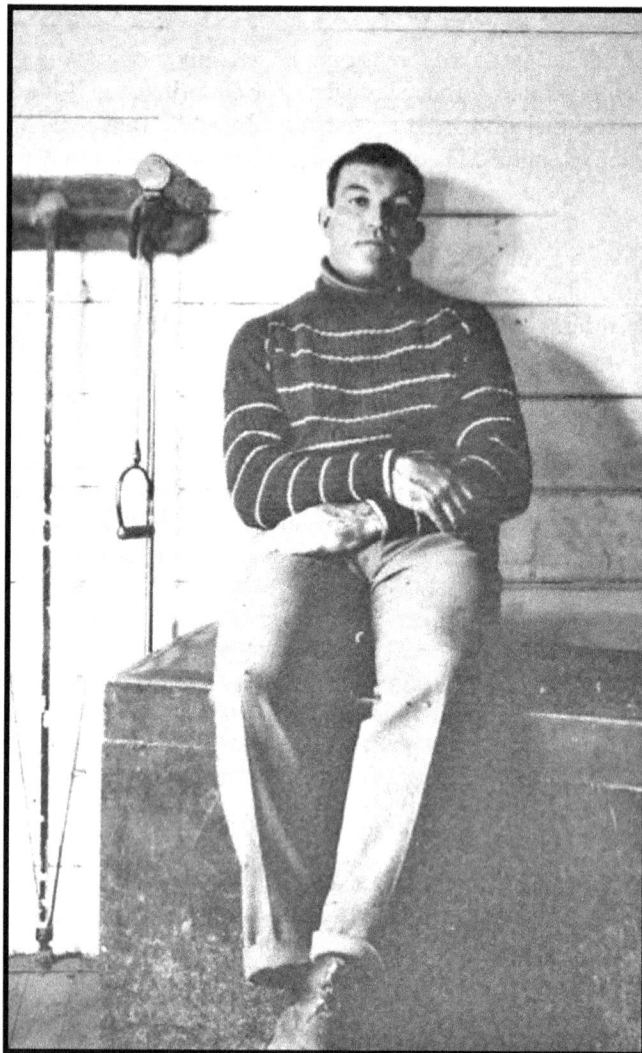

Jim Jeffries in the gym

Jeffries was inducted into The Ring Boxing Hall of Fame in 1954, the World Boxing Hall of Fame in 1980 and the International Boxing Hall of Fame in 1990.

JIM JEFFRIES AND OTHER GREAT HEAVYWEIGHTS
(Revised article - from The Cyber Boxing Zone, WAIL! - April 2003)

JIM JEFFRIES

Jim Jeffries

Jim Jeffries won the heavyweight championship of the world the same way he accomplished most things in his life - he made up his mind he wanted it and battered down anyone who got in his way. Jeffries, along with Rocky Marciano, are two of the most highly criticized heavyweight champions, due to their crude styles of fighting, but they were also the only two men to retire unbeaten during their active careers.

Unfortunately, Jeffries was talked into a comeback after being out of the ring for six years and experienced the only loss of his career. For this fight, he shed 70 pounds, had no warm-up fights prior to the contest - only sparring sessions and a few exhibitions - and fought in 100 degree weather against a very, very good fighter, Jack Johnson. Johnson was at his peak and had fought thirty bouts since Jeffries had retired. Jeffries was rusty and "over the hill." Yet today, many analysts rate him on the basis of this fight.

As a fighter, Jeffries traded on strength, power hitting, a tough chin, wonderful stamina and an indomitable will. He was a heavy hitter with both fists and caved in the ribs of many opponents with his sledge-hammer left hook - Bob Fitzsimmons, Jim Corbett, Tom Sharkey, Gus Ruhlin and "Mexican" Pete Everett - to name five. He also sent Joe Goddard to bed after a heavy battering.

Keith (in his book, *Sports and Games, 1969 p 127*) said, "Jeffries probably owned the deadliest left hook the prize ring has ever known" and "Tex" Rickard said, "he's the hardest hitter I ever saw and that includes Dempsey." Jeffries himself once said he never hit a man as hard as he could for fear of killing him.

Some critics portray Jeffries as slow-moving and ponderous. This is not true. He was able to move very fast. He tracked down and knocked out clever Peter Jackson, the all-time great boxer-puncher. He cornered and hammered Bob Armstrong, the 6'3" fast-moving, sharp-jabbing black. He outran the speedy Jim Corbett, Bob Fitzsimmons and Joe Choynski in footraces and all of these men were fast runners. In addition, Jeffries could jump over six feet vertically.

Other critics call Jeffries a "one-armed" fighter. This is false. He threw short, straight, jolting blows with each fist when fighting in close. He also used a thundering right uppercut. From a distance, he utilized a punishing left jab and a bashing left hook.

During his bouts, he used a crouch which made it difficult to hit him cleanly. When an opponent moved in to hit him, he ran the risk of getting hammered with that left hook or having Jeffries spring forward and pound away with those short, bludgeoning left-right blasts. Sometimes heads collided but that never fazed Jeffries.

If a skirmish became distasteful, Jeffries would take hold of his man and shove him backward 5-6 feet with his enormous strength and resume the battle from there - stalking his man, resembling a bear as he moved forward. Interestingly enough, Jeffries also reminds one of a bulldog when seen in his crouch.

The Jeffries chin was a phenomenal structure and it would certainly hold up against most of the "best ever" hitters. The dynamite puncher Tom Sharkey punched at it in two contests and could not hurt it. Bob Fitzsimmons and a number of others broke their hands and injured their wrists hitting it.

The Jeffries stamina was awesome too - if he could not outbox an opponent, he could certainly outlast him. He fought two grueling fights with Tom Sharkey, endured two punishing battles with Bob Fitzsimmons and chased down shifty Jim Corbett in two long contests.

THE STRONGEST BIG FELLOWS

Jeffries, George Foreman, "Sonny" Liston and possibly Jess Willard were probably the strongest and most powerful big men among the heavyweights of boxing history. Comparing these four men, Foreman was possibly (slightly) the hardest hitter, Liston was the bounciest and quickest heavy hitter and Willard was an awesome hitter when he landed his big punch on a man. Recall that he snapped "Bull" Young's neck. Jeffries was, without a doubt, the strongest. He also possessed the greatest stamina and the toughest chin. He could hit hard too. I suspect he had the best legs as well. Rating these four men against each other, I would rank them (1) Jeffries (2) Liston (3) Foreman (4) Willard.

GREAT FIGHTERS AND HYPOTHETICAL MATCHES

Today, many analysts "put down" the skills of Jim Corbett, Bob Fitzsimmons and Tom Sharkey - three of Jeffries' top rivals. But the people who actually saw them fight rated these men highly and continued to do so even after Jack Dempsey, Gene Tunney and Joe Louis appeared on the scene.

JIM CORBETT

Corbett was "jack-rabbit" quick with very fast hands and feet. He could maintain his speed for the duration of a fight (15-20 rounds) and not slow significantly. Gene Tunney sparred with him in the 1920s and was impressed. The quick-hitter Bob Fitzsimmons said he couldn't hit Corbett in the head. Most men who faced him couldn't strike him effectively. Jim was probably the fastest of all heavyweights over the entire course of a fight. Muhammad Ali was equally fast in the early part of a fight but as the fight wore on, Ali's weight had its say and he slowed as he tired. In spite of Corbett's speed, Jeffries defeated him twice in larger rings than the ones used today.

BOB FITZSIMMONS

Bob Fitzsimmons was a quick-hitting, devastating puncher with his whipcord muscles molded by his work at the blacksmith's anvil. Many who saw Fitz in action considered him to be the best hitter ever. He was compared favorably with Dempsey even when the latter was champion. Nat Fleischer ranked him higher than Jack on his all-time heavyweight list. Yet Jeffries defeated him twice, the first time in only Jeffries' 13th fight with the heavyweight championship at stake.

TOM SHARKEY

Many critics question Jeffries' close wins over Tom Sharkey and point to the easy Fitzsimmons victory over "Sailor" Tom. But Sharkey was a great fighter and just about the equal of Rocky Marciano in size, strength, style, ruggedness and power. He was a tough warrior. Had he fought at any other time in history, he might have been champion.

So, when Jeffries fought Sharkey, in essence he fought Marciano - no easy task. Tom had engaged in 34 fights, scoring 24 knockouts. He had been in the ring against John L. Sullivan, Jim Corbett, Bob Fitzsimmons, Peter Maher, Joe Choynski and Joe Goddard. It was just Jeffries' 11th fight. In spite of this disadvantage in experience, Jeffries won a close decision.

When they fought the second time in what many historians call the "greatest heavyweight fight in ring history," it was for the heavyweight championship and only Jeffries' 14th fight. During training, Jeffries injured his left shoulder and the fight was delayed. After a short time, a physical checkup revealed the injury was not fully healed and the contest was postponed again. Following a third physical examination, the medical doctor recommended putting off the bout once more. But Jeffries went ahead with the fight and got in against Sharkey with his greatest weapon - the left hook - weakened and ailing. In a furious, brutal battle, Jeffries floored Sharkey, broke two of his ribs and battered him to a pulp. One of Sharkey's ears was swollen to the size of a softball.

After a time, Jeffries offered to fight Corbett, Fitzsimmons and Sharkey all on the same night - they refused.

JACK DEMPSEY

Some contend that Jack Dempsey was just a little too small to defeat the very best heavyweights of all-time. This writer has never bought into that argument. Dempsey was an exceptional fighter who moved well and hit with tremendous power. He used a crouch and bobbed and weaved. His greatest weakness was his long-term stamina. In the case of Dempsey versus Jim Jeffries, size and stamina would be the deciding factors in favor of Jeffries - after a "war."

JOE LOUIS

Joe Louis was a magnificent fighter who was patient and powerful - and possessed two very fast hands. But Joe had considerable trouble with men who fought from a crouch - Tony Galento, Tommy Farr and Arturo Godoy, for example - and they were nowhere near a Jim Jeffries. Further, Joe did not have the toughest chin. After a patient but tense battle with flurries of hard punching from time to time, Jeffries would finish Louis.

ROCKY MARCIANO

Rocky Marciano was a determined, bulldog of a fighter who hit with power much like the Tom Sharkey of the 1890s who gave Jeffries two great, desperate battles. A Jeffries-Marciano fight would be a replay of the Sharkey fights. After rounds of hard slugging, Jeffries would batter Rocky enough to win.

CHARLES "SONNY" LISTON

Charles "Sonny" Liston was "The Black Jeffries." He was big and strong and could take a solid punch. In his movements, he was quicker than Jeffries but his strength and stamina were not as great as Jim's. Their hitting power was about the same. In a Jeffries-Liston bout, these two men would go toe-to-toe, each man pounding away and then covering up until one finally gave out. Jeffries' stamina and chin would prevail in a close, close fight.

JOE FRAZIER - GEORGE FOREMAN - MUHAMMAD ALI

The chin and stamina figure in greatly when contemplating Jeffries-Frazier, Jeffries-Foreman and Jeffries-Ali fights. Recall that Foreman, Frazier and Ali pounded George Chuvalo unmercifully but could not put him down. Chuvalo's chin was not what Jeffries' was and these men would not put Jeffries down either. In addition, Jeffries was a much greater overall fighter than Chuvalo and a much better hitter as well. These three wonderful fighters would be getting hit against Jeffries whereas they were not against Chuvalo.

JOE FRAZIER

Joe Frazier was a very good fighter who was tough, fought from a crouch, bobbed as he moved and carried a dangerous left hook. He came to fight - not run. Versus Jeffries, he would be in against a man with the size and power of George Foreman. Jeffries would be too big and strong for Joe who could not run from him.

GEORGE FOREMAN

When considering a Jeffries-Foreman fight, one cannot help but think of the Foreman-Ron Lyle fight. Allowing Lyle credit as being a near-equal of Jeffries as a hitter (questionable and doubtful), he nearly finished Foreman. But Lyle had nowhere near Jeffries' stamina - his wind and chin gave out. Jeffries would not have wilted and it would have been Foreman who ended up on the canvas.

"CUTE" FIGHTERS

Jeffries would have his most trouble against the "cute" type of fighter - Corbett, Johnson, Tunney, Ali and Holmes. These men would have to "hit and run" because any man Jeffries could hit, he would beat. None of these men would put Jeffries on the floor. But they could cut him up. Each would have to keep his distance, move, jab and pick his moments to move in and hit hard. After hitting, they would have to move away quickly.

They would have to be careful in anticipating Jeffries' moves - the bashing left hook, the springing from his crouch so he could catch them (also the possibility of cracking heads as he sprang forward) and the left-right slams in close. If they carried out their plan, kept up their pace of movement and did not slow as they tired, they would have a chance. But they would have to do it for the entire fight.

MIKE TYSON - EVANDER HOLYFIELD - RIDDICK BOWE
LENNOX LEWIS - WLADIMIR KLITSCHKO - VITALI KLITSCHKO

Of the heavyweights since the 1961-1980 years, Mike Tyson, Evander Holyfield and Riddick Bowe stand out but all fall short of being a serious threat to defeat Jeffries. Tyson fell into the category of Tom Sharkey, Rocky Marciano and Joe Frazier - hard-hitting and tough but not tough enough. Jeffries would beat him. Holyfield was an all-around fighter who found a way to win. But, like Jack Dempsey and Joe Louis, he would not be strong enough to hold off Jeffries. Riddick Bowe was big and strong but he was battered by Andrew Golota, a man whose fighting style and strength was similar to Jeffries' but who was not nearly Jeff's equal as a fighter. Jeffries would beat Bowe. Lennox Lewis was a talented fighter with a good jab, stiff punches and pretty good boxing techniques. However, he appeared up-and-down in his performances and had a tendency to sometimes let some good in-fighters get close to him - just like Larry Holmes did from time to time. It would prove fatal against Jeffries. At other times, he tended to get into a rock 'em, sock 'em style and that would spell disaster against Jeff.

In recent years, Wladimir Klitschko and Vitali Klitschko have gained significant stature as heavyweight fighters. Both were quite tall, both possessed good jabs and both struck very hard blows. Punches by these men - right on the button - could put anyone to the floor and might have put Jeffries down too. But keeping him down would be a problem. Wladimir had a definite stamina problem and if he could not put Jeffries out early on in a bout, he would fall prey to Jeff's big blows. Vitali, with his tough chin and strength, would pose a stern problem for Jeffries but this writer sees him falling victim after seven or eight rounds.

MUHAMMAD ALI

Now, a few comments about Muhammad Ali, the self-proclaimed "Greatest" and a man whose claim is supported by many fans today. Ali was a remarkable boxer. He was fluid, quick and able to anticipate his opponents' moves. As a fighter, he made a number of mistakes, as all fighters do, but was able to outrun them due to his outstanding speed and the caliber of many of his foes.

He possessed wonderful quickness, especially during the early part of a fight. But due to his weight, he tired and slowed as the fight wore on. During his era, Ali was able to defeat his competition when he slowed during a fight due to his superior skills, but it is doubtful if he could have done this against the very best heavyweights of all-time.

Ali was bothered by the crouch as are most fighters. He also got tagged with some tremendous shots during his "second career." When he got hit he usually was able to take the punch or roll with it to reduce its effect. But, by his own admission, he was "out on his feet" three times from punches by George Foreman. When Foreman's stamina gave out, Ali won. Would Ali be able to withstand the punches of Jeffries for an entire fight? Jeffries possessed power similar to Foreman's but his stamina did not give out.

A close analysis of his performance in the ring reveals that fate smiled upon Ali in the first Henry Cooper fight following his visit to the canvas. He could have been knocked out. Ken Norton beat him once officially and in the opinion of this writer, deserved wins in all three of their bouts. Jimmy Young outboxed him and deserved the win. Joe Frazier beat him in their first battle and possibly the second fight. George Foreman was duped in Africa but the big slugger probably would have won in a return match. Leon Spinks beat him too.

Against Jeffries, Ali would have faced a man who crouched - always troublesome - like Joe Frazier and at the same time had the size and power of George Foreman. In addition, Jeffries had much greater stamina than George and faster footwork than either Frazier or Foreman. Jeffries would edge Ali, overcoming him at the end.

ERAS

Different periods of history, due to existing conditions and philosophies, impart certain characteristics to its people. The early years of last century bestowed better capabilities onto its fighters to perform and survive in the ring. A period of manual labor, hard work and hunger cultivated in its people the determination, mental discipline, strong willpower, physical conditioning, perseverance and the willingness to struggle and endure in order to survive. Its fighters, from all races and nationalities, showed more persistence, spunk and energy than in more recent, affluent years. Since all groups of people were significantly deprived in those days, they all produced great fighters.

Some analysts assert that technique improves over the years and makes the fighters better. Generally speaking, this is true. But in the case of men who have size and strength - Jeffries, Liston, Foreman, Willard, etc. - they need technique less than other men do. It is the opposition that needs improved techniques in order to avoid these powerful men.

THE J'S HAVE IT

In rating the greatest heavyweights of all-time, the J's have it. The four all-time best heavyweights were Jim Jeffries, Jack Johnson, Jack Dempsey and Joe Louis. The younger Ali was very fast but not strong enough to hold off these all-time greats. The older Ali was very strong but not fast enough to hold off these same all-time greats.

Many people hypothesize that during the "lost years," Ali would have put it all together - speed and strength - and would have been the greatest heavyweight ever. Possibly - but this is speculation. It just might have been that during this transition period, he had not yet acquired the strength necessary to carry him through his toughest battles after he had lost his super quickness.

Acknowledging that Ali dominated his era and was the greatest heavyweight fighter since Joe Louis, he belongs in the top echelon of all-time heavyweight greats as the #5 man.

THE GREATEST

In the view of this writer, the greatest athletes of history could compete with each other on a "near-equal" basis, some a little better than others, some not as well. Further, the "Jim Browns" of history are the greatest athletes. Howard Cosell once said Muhammad Ali was the best heavyweight he had seen - that is, until Jim Brown decided to enter the ring. Well, Jim Jeffries was the "Jim Brown" of his time and Jeffries did enter the ring.

In 1899, Jim Jeffries was heavyweight champion of the world and the greatest heavyweight fighter ever to enter the ring. Today, in 2013, more than one hundred years later, he is still the greatest heavyweight fighter ever to enter the ring.

ATHLETES - BIGGER, FASTER, STRONGER

(Revised article - from The Cyber Boxing Zone, WAIL! - June 1998)

INTRODUCTION

Are athletes of today better than those of the past? Was Muhammad Ali the greatest heavyweight boxer ever? Was Michael Jordan the greatest basketball player ever? Was Barry Bonds the greatest baseball homerun hitter ever?

The argument that athletes are bigger, faster and stronger is heard frequently today and there is little doubt that this is true. It is also heard that because they are bigger, faster and stronger, many of the top performers in today's sports are rated better than their predecessors. But are they really?

One must be careful in making a judgment. Various sports require different skills, comply with different rules and are played using different methods. In some sports, man competes against nature on a time or distance basis. In other sports, man competes against man on an action/reaction basis and style of play becomes more important than time or distance.

BIGGER, FASTER AND STRONGER

A magnificent book, ***The Super Athletes,*** written by David Willoughby and published in 1970, analyzes athletic performances in many sports and is referenced in this article.

Willoughby wrote "... the records of modern athletes, sport, industry, and medical science combine to show that the civilized portion of the human race is bigger, stronger, and healthier in general today than ever before in history" (***Introduction, The Super Athletes***).

All one has to do is check the height and weight statistics to see that the athletes are larger. Perhaps the strongest argument that modern athletes are better is the continuous setting of new records in track, field and swimming events where precise measurements of performances can be made.

Willoughby stated, "The reason why date of performance is important is because with the passage of time there is an increase in population, and the larger the population the greater the probability of an extraordinary record. In short, athletic records, like those of height and weight, or any other expressions of human diversity that can be measured, range in magnitude in ratio to the size of the population from which the record is drawn. Accordingly, in a large population of competitors (no matter what the events), the best performance should be expected to be of high caliber, and vice-versa" (***page 585, The Super Athletes***).

Further, Willoughby contended, "A second factor that should be taken into account in the 'weight' events is the size of the performer. This means not only his bodyweight, but also his height. Since greater height and weight assist a performer in such events as weightlifting, the shot put, the hammer throw, the 56-pound weight throw, and even the lightweight javelin throw ..." (***pages 585 586, The Super Athletes***).

MAN-AGAINST-NATURE

In "man-against-nature" events, such as track, field and swimming, the best technique, coupled with specific athletic abilities, bring about better performance. Judgment is clear on time and distance. Putting the shot sixty-five feet is better than putting it sixty. Running one hundred meters in 10.5 seconds is better than running it in 10.7 seconds.

As time passes and people get bigger, faster and stronger and utilize better techniques, athletic performances improve. Times get faster and distances farther. So, do the athletes get better over the years in these sports? It appears that they do.

Yet, even in these man-against-nature sports, there are rules changes and innovations which assist the human in his battle against the physical world - starting blocks, fiberglass poles, corked tracks and springy boards for launching broad jumps, etc. Factors other than pure athletic ability creep into the picture and complicate the task of comparing athletes.

GENERALIZATION

A dangerous mistake in judgment may occur. A generalization might take place - since athletes perform better than they used to in man-against-nature sports (i.e. a recent 65 foot shot put is better than the old 60 foot shot put), they perform better in all sports.

MAN-AGAINST-MAN

In "man-against-man" sports or "team-against-team" sports (which ultimately boil down to man-against-man), performance is based upon a reaction by one competitor to an action by the other competitor (and not simply a case of running fast or throwing an object a great distance). Speed, power and quickness offer advantages but often are not as important as savvy, anticipation and the correct action/reaction.

In baseball, a team-against-team sport (really man-against-man when batters face pitchers), certainly seventy-three homeruns in a season is a better number than seventy-one. But did the performer do better? The number was not attained by strictly competing against nature so much as it was by a man competing against other men on an action/reaction basis. In boxing, a 75 percent knockout ratio is better than 70 percent but it is accomplished by a man competing against other men on an action/reaction basis too.

NUMBERS

It can be argued that in man-against-man competition, big numbers do not truly indicate a superior athlete or better performance - but just the opposite. It is easier to beat a weaker or lesser-skilled man than it is to beat a stronger or better-skilled man. It is easier to rack up numbers against lesser-skilled men than against highly-skilled ones. An athlete is more likely to break records against weaker opposition than against better opposition.

STYLE

In man-against-nature sports, a change in technique can be an improvement in that it enables a man to do better in his quest for a faster time or greater distance. In man-against-man sports, technique also can improve performance and is very closely related to the style of play. Depending upon the sport, style can be a dominant factor. It often offsets "bigger, faster and stronger."

As difficult as it is to compare athletic performances over the years in man-against-man or team-against-team sports such as boxing, baseball, basketball and football, any comparison is confounded further by the styles used by the men.

Willoughby addressed this as it relates to boxing "... the matter of differing styles ... makes fighters (boxers vs. sluggers) so difficult to rate. Instead of more or less uniform techniques - such as apply in running, jumping, swimming and other athletic events - that can be measured, in boxing (and for that matter wrestling, judo, etc.) no such exact measurement is possible. In these man-to-man encounters, unless a decisive victory - such as a knockout or a fall - is scored, the decision as to the winner rests with the referee and the judges. And, needless to say, the official decision is frequently rejected by the majority - sometimes the great majority - of spectators and followers" (*page 355, The Super Athletes*).

SUMMARY (ATHLETES)

Today, athletes are bigger, faster and stronger but it all depends upon the sport as to whether they are truly better than those of the past. Different sports have different rules and different objectives (jump, run, throw, etc.). One example was Michael Jordan in baseball. He was bigger. Was he better? Another example was Deion Sanders in baseball. He was faster. Was he better? What about Nikolai Valuev in boxing? He is bigger. Is he better?

The skills needed to succeed in a given sport must be such that they enable a man to compete successfully against others. A man who has an abundance of a particular skill may be better than others who possess better all-around skills. A standout athlete in one sport may be simply average in another. And, as strange as it seems, the daily activities of a particular period in past history may have equipped individuals better for a certain type of competition than today's activities.

It is the opinion of this writer that the best athletes of all-time could compete with each other on a near-equal basis with slight advantages here and there going to certain men who possessed this or that skill or attribute (depending upon the sport and how the various traits match up). The modern athlete is not necessarily better than his predecessors.

Rules of the game, mental discipline and style as well as improved equipment affect outcomes of competition possibly as often as size, speed, quickness, agility, strength and stamina do.

HOW DOES THIS RELATE TO BOXERS?

Boxing is a man-against-man sport in which being bigger, faster and stronger offers an advantage. But style offsets this physical edge. So, in this sport, those who combine physical advantages with good technique have the upper hand.

Is the modern fighter the only man to possess the physical advantages or the skills? No. There have been men with size, speed and strength advantages throughout history and yet, other fighters have been better, even within the same era. Various styles and tactics have been developed over the years to counter physical advantages and these have produced many exceptional fighters.

Could Muhammad Ali of the 1960s fight the athletes of today? Yes - and be better. Go back thirty or forty years before Ali. Could Joe Louis of the 1930s or Jack Dempsey of the 1920s fight with the men of the 1960s, the 1990s or today? Again, a resounding yes - and be better! Go back yet further. Could Jim Jeffries of the early 1900s or Jack Johnson of the teens fight with men of the 1930s, the 1960s, the 1990s or today? Once more, yes - and be better.

Two recent examples of older fighters proving their merit against the modern men are George Foreman and Larry Holmes (of the 1970s and 1980s). They held their own against the fighters of recent years and pounded most of them. For style to offset the physical advantages, one must possess enough technique, mental discipline and physical conditioning to be better.

TECHNIQUE

A specific procedure or technique is designed to be a better (or best) way of doing this or that. It came about as a way to use an individual's particular combination of height, weight, speed, quicknes, agility and strength in an effort to beat the physical advantage or skills of an opponent. Foot movement, head movement, bobbing-and-weaving, crouching, hand feints, doubling up on jabs, straight punches, etc., are examples of technique.

Most techniques used by today's fighters were well-known by the 1920s and used regularly by fighters since then. Little, if any, advantage is seen here for the modern fighters over the early fighters.

WEIGHTS

Weights are utilized by boxers today in training much more than ever. A strength advantage is seen for the modern fighter due to his more frequent use of weights. But, care must be exercised to prevent the fighter from becoming too heavily muscled or stiff because limber arm and shoulder movement is a valuable asset which a fighter does not want to lose.

Weights were used in the old days too, as evidenced by many old films, but not to the extent that they are used today. However, years ago much manual labor was carried out by everyone, including boxers who worked at other jobs. So, hard work, chopping, digging, moving, lifting, carrying, positioning for leverage - on a daily basis - provided advantages which those boxers utilized in the ring. This fact might serve to counter the strength advantage of the modern fighters.

SOCIO-ECONOMIC "HUNGER"

The "hungry" athlete is a worthy adversary and is usually a product of the "have-not" environment. A study conducted by Weinberg and Arond and reported in *The American Journal of Sociology (1952)* revealed that most fighters and, consequently, most good fighters, are likely to come from poor families that are at the bottom of the socio-economic scale. Of course, there are some exceptions.

The fighter who comes from this type of background possesses this edge. But, as one looks back through history, it is seen that more and more families - black, white and otherwise - all - came from poorer socio-economic levels. So it seems that the earlier years of our history produced more "hungry" fighters and provided this advantage to its fighters.

MENTAL DISCIPLINE

The society of earlier years in this nation (and most other nations) insisted upon stricter adherence to its rules. This attitude prevailed in athletics as well. An athlete who was trained in a certain manner, to fight a certain way, generally followed the rules while in training and fought his fight according to plan.

Absolute or strict insistence to follow the rules by those in charge developed a resolution to do so on the part of the fighter. This, in turn, cultivated an absolute will - an indomitable will - in many cases. So, it seems that an earlier time in our history produced men of a greater will and has the advantage here.

Furthermore, many of today's boxers do not fight smart. They follow their opponent around almost in a straight-line, they do not cut off the ring, they fight in a straight-up stance, they hardly ever crouch, they position themselves at a range which is perfect for the opponent to strike and they do not train to avoid head-butts. No wonder Ali was able to jab his foes so easily (and this is not a putdown to him).

PHYSICAL CONDITION

The rather lax mental attitude of today's society has affected its trainers and boxers. Many boxers today fail to train adequately and abandon their fight plan during the course of a fight. Many times the poor physical condition is obvious. Many trainers do not insist upon rigid adherence to his rules of training. Many give in to the whims of the lazy or rich or ranked pugilist.

Consequently, the fighters are not as well conditioned physically as they could be/should be. Those who are in good shape usually win. If an athlete is bigger and heavier and not in condition, he will be a sitting duck when he becomes tired. Many boxers have layers of fat hanging over their trunks and consequently, tire after three or four rounds.

Wrestling is one training activity the old-time boxers went through. It enhanced their strength, dynamic tension, stamina, maneuverability, agility and would be a good drill for modern fighters to utilize as well. It would definitely enhance their physical condition.

SUMMARY (BOXERS)

Boxing is a sport in which "bigger, faster and stronger" provides a definite advantage but does not necessarily equate to being better. As useful as height, weight, speed, quickness, agility and strength are, they are no more important than correct action/reaction which is generally associated with style and technique.

A fighter needs savvy, mental discipline, physical conditioning and stamina. The modern fighters seem to have an edge in strength and a slight edge in technique. The fighters of the past appear to have the advantage in mental discipline, physical conditioning, stamina and hunger. It is the opinion of this writer that fighters of the past were better.

Gene Tunney and Jim Corbett sparring
1925

Jack Dempsey and Peter Maher
1936

TALKIN' 'BOUT THE HEAVIES

The heavyweights have always captured the bulk of attention when it comes to boxing. The big fellows are seen as bigger, stronger, better and able to beat men of the lighter weight classes.

Like all human endeavors, sooner or later questions arise as to who was better, which was better, what was better, etc. This is true of the heavyweight boxers too. In the case of these men, observers question which era of fighting was the best, how good were the skills of the various time periods, what years had the best or most talented fighters, etc.?

One approach to analyzing some of these questions was to break the years into periods like this: 1881-1900, 1901-1920, 1921-1940, 1941-1960, 1961-1980, 1981-2000 and 2001-2010. Of course, there are other breakdowns for time such as "London Prize Ring Rules" years or "Bare-Knuckle" years, "Early Glove" years or "Early Marquis of Queensberry Rules" years, "The Teens" years, "Modern Heavyweights" years, "Super Heavyweights" years, etc. But the first named set seemed to be as good as any for studying the big men.

To look at the question of which time period had the best heavyweights, certainly one of them was the 1961-1980 group loaded with men like Muhammad Ali, the older Charles "Sonny" Liston, Larry Holmes, George Foreman, Joe Frazier, Ken Norton, Jerry Quarry, Earnie Shavers, Ron Lyle, George Chuvalo, the older Floyd Patterson, Henry Cooper, Ernie Terrell and Zora Folley.

But if one goes way back to the pre-1900 years, there was an abundance of quality fighters such as Jim Jeffries, Jim Corbett, John L. Sullivan, Peter Jackson, Bob Fitzsimmons, Tom Sharkey, Peter Maher, Frank "Paddy" Slavin, Joe Goddard, Bob Armstrong and Joe Choynski.

There was top talent in other time periods too. The 1901-1920 years had many of the pre-1900 men still fighting and many other outstanding men such as Jack Johnson, Jack Dempsey, Sam Langford, Joe Jeannette, Sam McVea, Harry Wills, Luther "Luck" McCarty, Jess Willard, Fred Fulton, Carl Morris, Ed "Gunboat" Smith, Tommy Burns, Bill Lang and Al Kaufman.

The 1921-1940 time period had, in addition to some of those previously named, Joe Louis, Gene Tunney (now, a full-fledged heavyweight), the Baer brothers - Max and "Buddy," Max Schmeling, Jack Sharkey, George Godfrey, W.L. "Young" Stribling, Primo Carnera, Jim Braddock and Jim Maloney.

Moving to the 1941-1960 years, among the top men who appeared on the scene were Joe Louis, Charles "Sonny" Liston, Rocky Marciano, Ezzard Charles, "Jersey" Joe Walcott, Floyd Patterson, Cleveland Williams, Ingemar Johansson and Eddie Machen.

Not to be ignored is the 1981-2000 time interval with Larry Holmes still going strong, Mike Tyson, Evander Holyfield, Gerry Cooney, Frank Bruno, Tony Tubbs, Tony Tucker, Tim Witherspoon, John Tate, Mike Weaver, Gerrie Coetzee, Riddick Bowe and a young Lennox Lewis.

A matured Lennox Lewis, along with the outstanding European fighters, dominated the recent 2001-2010 years. Wladimir Klitschko, Vitali Klitschko, Hasim Rahman, Ruslan Chagaev, Oleg Maskaev and John Ruiz were names often seen.

A question that always surfaces when discussing the heavyweight boxers is - who had the best boxing skills? Certainly Jim Corbett, Jack Johnson, Jack Dempsey, Gene Tunney, Joe Louis, Muhammad Ali, Larry Holmes and Evander Holyfield are names that pop up in any such talk.

Who was the hardest hitter? Well, there is no question that John L. Sullivan, Pat Killen, Bob Fitzsimmons, Peter Maher, Jim Jeffries, Tom Sharkey, Jack Dempsey, Luis Angel Firpo, George Godfrey, Joe Louis, Rocky Marciano, Bob Satterfield, Charles "Sonny" Liston, Ingemar Johansson, Joe Frazier, George Foreman, Earnie Shavers, Mike Tyson, David Tua, Wladimir Klitschko and Vitali Klitschko will be mentioned here.

Who was the quickest or who moved better? Surely, Jim Corbett, Jack Johnson, Jack Dempsey, Gene Tunney, Muhammad Ali and Larry Holmes rank highly on movement.

What about the strongest or toughest? Jim Jeffries has long been talked of in these terms but Jess Willard, Max Baer, Rocky Marciano, Charles "Sonny" Liston, George Chuvalo, Joe Frazier, George Foreman, Ron Lyle, Riddick Bowe and the modern Klitschkos rank highly too.

Regarding chin, who could take punishment and hard blows and keep on fighting? Again, Jim Jeffries must be ranked highly along with Jess Willard, Tony Galento, Rocky Marciano, Charles "Sonny" Liston, George Chuvalo, George Foreman, Randall "Tex" Cobb, Ray Mercer, Oliver McCall and Vitali Klitschko.

As to which fighter was the best poet, there is absolutely no doubt. Muhammad Ali reigns supreme here - he was the "greatest" poet, without question, and a tremendous showman! However, witty Jim Corbett earns consideration for his confidence, smart-alec comments and antics too.

Many of today's fans ask if Jim Corbett could fight with the big heavyweights of today. My question to them is, "How big is the ring?" If it's bigger than 16 by 16, the big boys wouldn't touch him.

Even Herb Goldman, a most knowledgeable man of boxing history, said it's hard to imagine Corbett holding off Charles "Sonny" Liston. My response - it's hard to imagine "Sonny" touching Jim in a large ring.

At his peak, "Gentleman Jim" had those special gifts from Mother Nature - exceptional boxing savvy and quickness. It is difficult to see any man defeating him in a short distance fight of four or six rounds. In a longer fight, maybe he could be beaten by quick men such as Jack Johnson, Muhammad Ali, Gene Tunney, Larry Holmes and Peter Jackson but even they would have difficulty in eight rounds or less.

Jim Corbett

When speaking of John L. Sullivan and Peter Jackson, one must acknowledge that they were outstanding fighters during the bare-knuckle years and early-glove years. They were talented pugilists and legends in their day - a time period of very tough men. Their records prove they were exceptional. For boxing historians, Sullivan and Jackson continue to be fistic icons to this day.

There exists little film footage for all the pre-1900 fighters but what film there is seems to match up well with the newspaper descriptions of the early day fighters and validate their skills (in this writer's opinion). Therefore, I believe that John L. and Peter can be viewed much as they are described in their ring encounters.

Bob Fitzsimmons

It is the opinion of this writer that Sullivan and Jackson must be included in any all-time ranking of heavyweight fighters. Accordingly, they are included in my list along with an apology for their not being ranked higher than they are. There is every reason to believe that they merit much higher rankings. Both were inducted into The Ring Boxing Hall of Fame, the World Boxing Hall of Fame and the International Boxing Hall of Fame.

Now, a few words about Bob Fitzsimmons, the man I consider the greatest pound-for-pound fighter who ever stepped into the ring. Fitz fought mostly at middleweight and light-heavyweight poundage and possessed rare, phenomenal firepower. In addition, he moved quickly and got in explosive, paralyzing punches. Many observers feel the great "Sugar" Ray Robinson was the best pound-for-pound fighter ever. However, in a match-up between the two, I believe that Bob could handle Ray's punches but Ray could not handle his.

Fitzsimmons reminds this observer of the talented light-heavyweight Bob Foster. Both were lanky with monster hitting capability. Foster could clean up men of his own weight and many good heavyweights too. However, he had trouble with the very best big men. I tend to see Fitz much the same way - but a much harder, sharper hitter than Foster and a lot more durable too.

With his cleverness and punching power, he just might come out on top in an exchange with Jack Dempsey and Joe Louis - although he would have a tough time with Dempsey's movement and ruggedness. Joe's quick hands and punches would be a challenge too.

Top heavyweights like Jim Jeffries, Charles "Sonny" Liston, Rocky Marciano, Joe Frazier, Mike Tyson and John L. Sullivan would pose very tough problems for Fitz. These particular men were rugged and durable and possessed awesome power similar to that of "Ruby Robert." He would have difficulty holding them off.

The big hitter George Foreman would likewise pose a severe test for Bob. But if he could avoid George's punches for a few rounds, then Foreman's stamina problem just might kick in and put him in jeopardy against the hard-hitting Fitzsimmons.

Larry Holmes with his excellent boxing skills would trouble Bob but Holmes got careless every so often. If he did, then Fitz might slip inside and down Larry. The case of Peter Jackson is similar to that of Holmes. If Peter allowed Bob to get inside, it could spell curtains for Peter.

Fitzsimmons simply would not catch up to the quickness of Jack Johnson, Muhammad Ali, Gene Tunney and Jim Corbett at their peaks. But they would have to be at their best.

Therefore, I place Bob as a near-miss in the all-time top fifteen heavyweights. Yet, based upon what was said by those who saw him in action as well as those who tangled with him, he likely should be in the group. His punching power far exceeded his size and weight - it was off the charts. In addition, he was a very clever fighter. Quite possibly he should be included and just maybe he belongs in the all-time top five or top ten. I apologize to Mr. Fitzsimmons if I have assessed him incorrectly. However, I do rate him as the greatest middleweight of all-time and the #2 light-heavyweight of all-time as well as the best pound-for-pound man ever (as stated earlier).

Fitzsimmons was inducted into The Ring Boxing Hall of Fame in 1954, the World Boxing Hall of Fame in 1980 and the International Boxing Hall of Fame in 1990.

Ifs and buts, candy and nuts, what if - Jim Jeffries had not come out of retirement, Jack Dempsey had immediately gone to a neutral corner against Gene Tunney in 1927, Billy Conn had boxed Joe Louis the last few rounds instead of trying to knock him out in 1941, Al Berl had stopped the second Rocky Marciano-Ezzard Charles bout in round seven, Floyd Patterson had fought "Sonny" Liston in 1958, Henry Cooper's knockdown of Cassius Clay in 1963 had occurred earlier in the round, Muhammad Ali had fought "Sonny" Liston in Liston's prime, and the judges had scored the Muhammad Ali-Ken Norton bouts like the sportswriters did?

Regarding athletes and the heavyweight boxers, my conclusion is as follows -

There exists, in the sporting world, a widely held view that athletes get bigger, faster and stronger with the passage of time. Among reasons advanced for this view are improvement in nutrition and improvement in the techniques employed in the sporting activity itself. While this notion of improvement with time has some truth, I would qualify it in the following way. Some sports, essentially "man-against-nature," involve singular techniques to be practiced, in rote fashion, time and again. Examples of this kind include swimming events and events of running, jumping and distance throwing. Other sports, "man-against-man," have to do additionally with head to head ability - with elements of nerve, heart and savvy, each quite real, even if hard to measure. In these sports, which include disciplines like boxing and wrestling, such elements are crucial and may offset advantages elsewhere.

In this latter regard, old-timers concede nothing to athletes of the present day. **In Jim Jeffries, furthermore, is the extraordinary:** *an athlete built on the dimensions of the present day, but one also with the grit of his time and the deep elements of which I speak. Thus, after years of study, and bearing in mind that athletes, on the whole, do get measurably bigger, faster and stronger, and that they are heir always to the day's advancement in training science,* **I am of the view that Jeffries' combination of assets makes him yet the greatest heavyweight boxer of all-time.**

Tracy Callis, Boxing Historian

SELECTED ALL-TIME TOP TEN LISTS

Nat Fleischer 1954 and 1971

1. Jack Johnson
2. Jim Jeffries
3. Bob Fitzsimmons
4. Jack Dempsey
5. Jim Corbett
6. Joe Louis
7. Sam Langford
8. Gene Tunney
9. Max Schmeling
10. Rocky Marciano

Charley Rose 1968

1. Sam Langford
2. Jack Johnson
3. Jack Dempsey
4. Joe Louis
5. Jim Jeffries
6. Gene Tunney
7. Sam McVey
8. Rocky Marciano
9. Jim Corbett
10. Max Baer

Nat Loubet 1975

1. Joe Louis
2. Jack Dempsey
3. Jim Jeffries
4. Jack Johnson
5. Rocky Marciano
6. Gene Tunney
7. Bob Fitzsimmons
8. Jim Corbett
9. Muhammad Ali
10. Joe Frazier

SELECTED ALL-TIME TOP TEN LISTS (Cont'd.)

John Durant 1976

1. Joe Louis
2. Jack Johnson
3. Jack Dempsey
4. Muhammad Ali
5. Gene Tunney
6. Joe Frazier
7. Jim Jeffries
8. Jim Corbett
9. Rocky Marciano
10. Max Schmeling

Herb Goldman 1987

1. Muhammad Ali
2. Charles "Sonny" Liston
3. Larry Holmes
4. Jack Johnson
5. Jack Dempsey
6. Joe Louis
7. Rocky Marciano
8. Harry Wills
9. George Foreman
10. Joe Frazier

IBRO 2005

1. Joe Louis
2. Muhammad Ali
3. Jack Johnson
4. Jack Dempsey
5. Rocky Marciano
6. Larry Holmes
7. Jim Jeffries
8. George Foreman
9. Charles "Sonny" Liston
10. Joe Frazier

Heavyweight Championship of the World 1892-1989

Date	Winner	Verdict	Rounds	Loser	Location	Referee
1892-09-07	Jim Corbett	KO	21	John L. Sullivan	New Orleans, Louisiana, United States	John Duffy
1894-01-25	Jim Corbett	KO	3	Charlie Mitchell	Jacksonville, Florida, United States	John Kelly
1897-03-17	Bob Fitzsimmons	KO	14	Jim Corbett	Carson City, Nevada, United States	George Siler
1899-06-09	Jim Jeffries	KO	11	Bob Fitzsimmons	New York, New York, United States	George Siler
1899-11-03	Jim Jeffries	W	25	Tom Sharkey	New York, New York, United States	George Siler
1900-04-06	Jim Jeffries	RTD	1	John Finnegan	Detroit, Michigan, United States	George Siler
1900-05-11	Jim Jeffries	KO	23	Jim Corbett	New York, New York, United States	Charlie White
1901-11-15	Jim Jeffries	RTD	5	Gus Ruhlin	San Francisco, California, United States	Harry Corbett
1902-07-25	Jim Jeffries	KO	8	Bob Fitzsimmons	San Francisco, California, United States	Eddie Graney
1903-08-14	Jim Jeffries	RTD	10	Jim Corbett	San Francisco, California, United States	Eddie Graney
1904-08-26	Jim Jeffries	TKO	2	Jack Monroe	San Francisco, California, United States	Eddie Graney
1907-12-02	Tommy Burns	KO	10	James "Gunner" Moir	London, England, United Kingdom	Eugene Corri
1908-02-10	Tommy Burns	KO	4	Jack Palmer	London, England, United Kingdom	Robert Watson
1908-03-17	Tommy Burns	KO	1	Jem Roche	Dublin, Leinster, Ireland	Robert Watson
1908-04-18	Tommy Burns	KO	5	Joseph "Jewey" Smith	Paris, Paris, France	Phelin Roux
1908-06-13	Tommy Burns	KO	8	Bill Squires	Paris, Paris, France	Phelin Roux
1908-08-24	Tommy Burns	KO	13	Bill Squires	Sydney, New South Wales, Australia	Harry Nathan
1908-09-02	Tommy Burns	KO	6	Bill Lang	Melbourne, Victoria, Australia	Harry Nathan
1908-12-26	Jack Johnson	W	14	Tommy Burns	Sydney, New South Wales, Australia	Hugh McIntosh
1909-09-09	Jack Johnson	ND	10	Al Kaufman	Colma, California, United States	Eddie Smith
1909-10-16	Jack Johnson	KO	12	Stanley Ketchel	Colma, California, United States	Jack Welch
1910-07-04	Jack Johnson	RTD	15	Jim Jeffries	Reno, Nevada, United States	George "Tex" Rickard
1912-07-04	Jack Johnson	W	9	"Fireman" Jim Flynn	Las Vegas, New Mexico, United States	Eddie Smith
1915-04-05	Jess Willard	KO	26	Jack Johnson	Havana, Havana Province, Cuba	Jack Welch
1916-03-25	Jess Willard	ND	10	Frank Moran	New York, New York, United States	Charlie White
1919-07-04	Jack Dempsey	RTD	3	Jess Willard	Toledo, Ohio, United States	Ollie Pecord
1920-09-06	Jack Dempsey	KO	3	Billy Miske	Benton Harbor, Michigan, United States	Jim Dougherty
1920-12-14	Jack Dempsey	KO	12	"K.O." Bill Brennan	New York, New York, United States	Johnny Haukop
1921-07-02	Jack Dempsey	KO	4	Georges Carpentier	Jersey City, New Jersey, United States	Harry Ertle
1923-07-04	Jack Dempsey	W	15	Tommy Gibbons	Shelby, Montana, United States	Jim Dougherty
1923-09-14	Jack Dempsey	KO	2	Luis Angel Firpo	New York, New York, United States	Johnny Gallagher
1926-09-23	Gene Tunney	W	10	Jack Dempsey	Philadelphia, Pennsylvania, United States	Tommy "Pop" Reilly
1927-09-22	Gene Tunney	W	10	Jack Dempsey	Chicago, Illinois, United States	Dave Barry
1928-07-26	Gene Tunney	TKO	11	Tom Heeney	New York, New York, United States	Eddie Forbes
1930-06-12	Max Schmeling	DSQ	4	Jack Sharkey	New York, New York, United States	Jim Crowley
1932-06-21	Jack Sharkey	W	15	Max Schmeling	New York, New York, United States	Ed "Gunboat" Smith
1933-06-29	Primo Carnera	KO	6	Jack Sharkey	New York, New York, United States	Arthur Donovan
1933-10-22 &	Primo Carnera	W	15	Paulino Uzcudun	Rome, Lazio, Italy	Maurice Nicod
1934-03-01	Primo Carnera	W	15	Tommy Loughran	Miami, Florida, United States	Leo Shea
1934-06-14	Max Baer	TKO	11	Primo Carnera	New York, New York, United States	Arthur Donovan
1938-06-22	Joe Louis	RTD	1	Max Schmeling	New York, New York, United States	Arthur Donovan
1939-01-25	Joe Louis	TKO	1	John Henry Lewis	New York, New York, United States	Arthur Donovan
1939-04-17	Joe Louis	KO	1	Jack Roper	Los Angeles, California, United States	George Blake
1939-06-28	Joe Louis	TKO	4	Tony Galento	New York, New York, United States	Arthur Donovan
1939-09-20	Joe Louis	KO	11	Bob Pastor	Detroit, Michigan, United States	Sam Hennessey
1940-02-09	Joe Louis	W	15	Arturo Godoy	New York, New York, United States	Arthur Donovan
1940-03-29	Joe Louis	TKO	2	Johnny Paychek	New York, New York, United States	Arthur Donovan
1940-06-20	Joe Louis	TKO	8	Arturo Godoy	New York, New York, United States	Billy Cavanaugh
1940-12-16	Joe Louis	RTD	6	Al McCoy	Boston, Massachusetts, United States	Johnny Martin
1941-01-31	Joe Louis	KO	5	"Red" Burman	New York, New York, United States	Frank Fullam
1941-02-17	Joe Louis	KO	2	Gus Dorazio	Philadelphia, Pennsylvania, United States	Irving Kutcher
1941-03-21	Joe Louis	TKO	13	Abe Simon	Detroit, Michigan, United States	Sam Hennessey
1941-04-08	Joe Louis	TKO	9	Tony Musto	St. Louis, Missouri, United States	Arthur Donovan

The above bouts were recognized by the major organizations of the time; This list is primarily, but not entirely, based upon www.boxrec.com/hugman
& Also recognized by the International Boxing Union (IBU)

Heavyweight Championship of the World 1892-1989 (Cont'd.)

Date	Winner	Verdict	Rounds	Loser	Location	Referee
1941-05-23	Joe Louis	DSQ	7	Jacob "Buddy" Baer	Washington, District of Columbia, United States	Arthur Donovan
1941-06-18	Joe Louis	KO	13	Billy Conn	New York, New York, United States	Eddie Joseph
1941-09-29	Joe Louis	TKO	6	Lou Nova	New York, New York, United States	Arthur Donovan
1942-01-09	Joe Louis	KO	1	Jacob "Buddy" Baer	New York, New York, United States	Frank Fullam
1942-03-27	Joe Louis	KO	6	Abe Simon	New York, New York, United States	Eddie Joseph
1946-06-19	Joe Louis	KO	8	Billy Conn	New York, New York, United States	Eddie Joseph
1946-09-18	Joe Louis	KO	1	Tami Mauriello	New York, New York, United States	Arthur Donovan
1947-12-05	Joe Louis	W	15	"Jersey" Joe Walcott	New York, New York, United States	Ruby Goldstein
1948-06-25	Joe Louis	KO	11	"Jersey" Joe Walcott	New York, New York, United States	Frank Fullam
1952-06-05	"Jersey" Joe Walcott	W	15	Ezzard Charles	Philadelphia, Pennsylvania, United States	Zach Clayton
1952-09-23	Rocky Marciano	KO	13	"Jersey" Joe Walcott	Philadelphia, Pennsylvania, United States	Charlie Daggert
1953-05-15	Rocky Marciano	KO	1	"Jersey" Joe Walcott	Chicago, Illinois, United States	Frank Sikora
1953-09-24	Rocky Marciano	TKO	11	Roland LaStarza	New York, New York, United States	Ruby Goldstein
1954-06-17	Rocky Marciano	W	15	Ezzard Charles	New York, New York, United States	Ruby Goldstein
1954-09-17	Rocky Marciano	KO	8	Ezzard Charles	New York, New York, United States	Al Berl
1955-05-16	Rocky Marciano	TKO	9	Don Cockell	San Francisco, California, United States	Frankie Brown
1955-09-21	Rocky Marciano	KO	9	Archie Moore	New York, New York, United States	Harry Kessler
1956-11-30	Floyd Patterson	KO	5	Archie Moore	Chicago, Illinois, United States	Frank Sikora
1957-07-29	Floyd Patterson	TKO	10	Tommy "Hurricane" Jackson	New York, New York, United States	Ruby Goldstein
1957-08-22	Floyd Patterson	KO	6	Pete Rademacher	Seattle, Washington, United States	Tommy Loughran
1958-08-18	Floyd Patterson	RTD	12	Roy Harris	Los Angeles, California, United States	Mushy Callahan
1959-05-01	Floyd Patterson	KO	11	Brian London	Indianapolis, Indiana, United States	Frank Sikora
1959-06-26	Ingemar Johansson	TKO	3	Floyd Patterson	New York, New York, United States	Ruby Goldstein
1960-06-20	Floyd Patterson	KO	5	Ingemar Johansson	New York, New York, United States	Arthur Mercante
1961-03-13	Floyd Patterson	KO	6	Ingemar Johansson	Miami Beach, Florida, United States	Billy Regan
1961-12-04	Floyd Patterson	TKO	4	Tom McNeeley	Toronto, Ontario, Canada	"Jersey" Joe Walcott
1962-09-25	Charles "Sonny" Liston	KO	1	Floyd Patterson	Chicago, Illinois, United States	Frank Sikora
1963-07-22	Charles "Sonny" Liston	KO	1	Floyd Patterson	Las Vegas, Nevada, United States	Harry Krause
1964-02-25	Cassius Clay	RTD	6	Charles "Sonny" Liston	Miami Beach, Florida, United States	Barney Felix
1967-02-06	Muhammad Ali	W	15	Ernie Terrell	Houston, Texas, United States	Harry Kessler
1967-03-22	Muhammad Ali	KO	7	Zora Folley	New York, New York, United States	Johnny LoBiano
1970-02-16	Joe Frazier	RTD	5	Jimmy Ellis	New York, New York, United States	Tony Perez
1970-11-18	Joe Frazier	KO	2	Bob Foster	Detroit, Michigan, United States	Tom Briscoe
1971-03-08	Joe Frazier	W	15	Muhammad Ali	New York, New York, United States	Arthur Mercante
1972-01-15	Joe Frazier	TKO	4	Terry Daniels	New Orleans, Louisiana, United States	Herman Dutreix
1972-05-25	Joe Frazier	TKO	4	Ron Stander	Omaha, Nebraska, United States	Zach Clayton
1973-01-22	George Foreman	TKO	2	Joe Frazier	Kingston, Surrey, Jamaica	Arthur Mercante
1973-09-01	George Foreman	KO	1	Jose "King" Roman	Tokyo, Kanto Region, Japan	Jay Edson
1974-03-26	George Foreman	TKO	2	Ken Norton	Caracas, Metropolitan District of Caracas, Venezuela	Jimmy Rondeau
1974-10-30	Muhammad Ali	KO	8	George Foreman	Kinshasa, Zaire, Democratic Republic Of The Congo	Zach Clayton
1975-03-24	Muhammad Ali	TKO	15	Chuck Wepner	Richfield, Ohio, United States	Tony Perez
1975-05-16	Muhammad Ali	TKO	11	Ron Lyle	Las Vegas, Nevada, United States	Ferd Hernandez
1975-07-01	Muhammad Ali	W	15	Joe Bugner	Kuala Lumpur, Federal Territory of Kuala Lumpur, Malaysia	Takeo Ugo
1975-10-01	Muhammad Ali	RTD	14	Joe Frazier	Quezon City, Metro Manila, Philippines	Carlos Padilla
1976-02-20	Muhammad Ali	KO	5	Jean-Pierre Coopman	San Juan, San Juan District, Puerto Rico	Ismael Quinones Falu
1976-04-30	Muhammad Ali	W	15	Jimmy Young	Landover, Maryland, United States	Tom Kelly
1976-05-25	Muhammad Ali	TKO	5	Richard Dunn	Munich, Bayern, Germany	Herbert Tomser
1976-09-28	Muhammad Ali	W	15	Ken Norton	New York, New York, United States	Arthur Mercante
1977-05-16	Muhammad Ali	W	15	Alfredo Evangelista	Landover, Maryland, United States	Harry Cecchini
1977-09-29	Muhammad Ali	W	15	Earnie Shavers	New York, New York, United States	Johnny LoBianco
1978-02-15	Leon Spinks	W	15	Muhammad Ali	Las Vegas, Nevada, United States	Davey Pearl
1987-08-01	Mike Tyson	W	12	Tony Tucker	Las Vegas, Nevada, United States	Mills Lane
1987-10-16	Mike Tyson	TKO	7	Tyrell Biggs	Atlantic City, New Jersey, United States	Tony Orlando

The above bouts were recognized by the major organizations of the time; This list is primarily, but not entirely, based upon www.boxrec.com/hugman

& Also recognized by the International Boxing Union (IBU)

Heavyweight Championship of the World 1892-1989 (Cont'd.)

Date	Winner	Verdict	Rounds	Loser	Location	Referee
1988-01-22	Mike Tyson	TKO	4	Larry Holmes	Atlantic City, New Jersey, United States	Joe Cortez
1988-03-21	Mike Tyson	TKO	2	Tony Tubbs	Tokyo, Kanto Region, Japan	Arthur Mercante
1988-06-27	Mike Tyson	KO	1	Michael Spinks	Atlantic City, New Jersey, United States	Frank Cappuccino
1989-02-25	Mike Tyson	TKO	5	Frank Bruno	Las Vegas, Nevada, United States	Richard Steele

The above bouts were recognized by the major organizations of the time; This list is primarily, but not entirely, based upon www.boxrec.com/hugman

& Also recognized by the International Boxing Union (IBU)

WBA Heavyweight Championship 1962-2010

Date	Winner	Verdict	Rounds	Loser	Location	Referee
1962-09-25	Charles "Sonny" Liston	KO	1	Floyd Patterson	Chicago, Illinois, United States	Frank Sikora
1963-07-22	Charles "Sonny" Liston	KO	1	Floyd Patterson	Las Vegas, Nevada, United States	Harry Krause
1964-02-25	Cassius Clay	RTD	6	Charles "Sonny" Liston	Miami Beach, Florida, United States	Barney Felix
1965-03-05	Ernie Terrell	W	15	Eddie Machen	Chicago, Illinois, United States	Bernie Weismann
1965-11-01	Ernie Terrell	W	15	George Chuvalo	Toronto, Ontario, Canada	Sammy Luftspring
1966-06-28	Ernie Terrell	W	15	Doug Jones	Houston, Texas, United States	Ernie Taylor
1967-02-06	Muhammad Ali	W	15	Ernie Terrell	Houston, Texas, United States	Harry Kessler
1967-03-22	Muhammad Ali	KO	7	Zora Folley	New York, New York, United States	Johnny LoBianco
1968-04-27	Jimmy Ellis	W	15	Jerry Quarry	Oakland, California, United States	Elmer Costa
1968-09-14	Jimmy Ellis	W	15	Floyd Patterson	Stockholm, Södermanland and Uppland, Sweden	Harold Valan
1970-02-16	Joe Frazier	RTD	5	Jimmy Ellis	New York, New York, United States	Tony Perez
1970-11-18	Joe Frazier	KO	2	Bob Foster	Detroit, Michigan, United States	Tom Briscoe
1971-03-08	Joe Frazier	W	15	Muhammad Ali	New York, New York, United States	Arthur Mercante
1972-01-15	Joe Frazier	TKO	4	Terry Daniels	New Orleans, Louisiana, United States	Herman Dutreix
1972-05-25	Joe Frazier	TKO	4	Ron Stander	Omaha, Nebraska, United States	Zach Clayton
1973-01-22	George Foreman	TKO	2	Joe Frazier	Kingston, Surrey, Jamaica	Arthur Mercante
1973-09-01	George Foreman	KO	1	Jose "King" Roman	Tokyo, Kanto Region, Japan	Jay Edson
1974-03-26	George Foreman	TKO	2	Ken Norton	Caracas, Metropolitan District of Caracas, Venezuela	Jimmy Rondeau
1974-10-30	Muhammad Ali	KO	8	George Foreman	Kinshasa, Zaire, Democratic Republic Of The Congo	Zach Clayton
1975-03-24	Muhammad Ali	TKO	15	Chuck Wepner	Richfield, Ohio, United States	Tony Perez
1975-05-16	Muhammad Ali	TKO	11	Ron Lyle	Las Vegas, Nevada, United States	Ferd Hernandez
1975-07-01	Muhammad Ali	W	15	Joe Bugner	Kuala Lumpur, Federal Territory of Kuala Lumpur, Malaysia	Takeo Ugo
1975-10-01	Muhammad Ali	RTD	14	Joe Frazier	Quezon City, Metro Manila, Philippines	Carlos Padilla
1976-02-20	Muhammad Ali	KO	5	Jean-Pierre Coopman	San Juan, San Juan District, Puerto Rico	Ismael Quinones Falu
1976-04-30	Muhammad Ali	W	15	Jimmy Young	Landover, Maryland, United States	Tom Kelly
1976-05-25	Muhammad Ali	TKO	5	Richard Dunn	Munich, Bayern, Germany	Herbert Tomser
1976-09-28	Muhammad Ali	W	15	Ken Norton	New York, New York, United States	Arthur Mercante
1977-05-16	Muhammad Ali	W	15	Alfredo Evangelista	Landover, Maryland, United States	Harry Cecchini
1977-09-29	Muhammad Ali	W	15	Earnie Shavers	New York, New York, United States	Johnny LoBianco
1978-02-15	Leon Spinks	W	15	Muhammad Ali	Las Vegas, Nevada, United States	Davey Pearl
1978-09-15	Muhammad Ali	W	15	Leon Spinks	New Orleans, Louisiana, United States	Lucien Joubert
1979-10-20	John Tate	W	15	Gerrie Coetzee	Pretoria, Transvaal [Gauteng], South Africa	Carlos Barrocal
1980-03-31	Mike Weaver	KO	15	John Tate	Knoxville, Tennessee, United States	Ernesto Magana
1980-10-25	Mike Weaver	KO	13	Gerrie Coetzee	Sun City, Bophuthatswana [North West], South Africa	Jesus Celis
1981-10-03	Mike Weaver	W	15	James "Quick" Tillis	Rosemont, Illinois, United States	Stanley Christodoulou
1982-12-10	Michael Dokes	TKO	1	Mike Weaver	Las Vegas, Nevada, United States	Joey Curtis
1983-05-20	Michael Dokes	D	15	Mike Weaver	Las Vegas, Nevada, United States	Richard Steele
1983-09-23	Gerrie Coetzee	KO	10	Michael Dokes	Richfield, Ohio, United States	Tony Perez
1984-12-01	Greg Page	KO	8	Gerrie Coetzee	Sun City, Bophuthatswana [North West], South Africa	Isidro Rodriguez
1985-04-29	Tony Tubbs	W	15	Greg Page	Buffalo, New York, United States	Vincent Rainone
1986-01-17	Tim Witherspoon	W	15	Tony Tubbs	Atlanta, Georgia, United States	Nate Morgan
1986-07-19	Tim Witherspoon	TKO	11	Frank Bruno	London, England, United Kingdom	Isidro Rodriguez
1986-12-12	James "Bonecrusher" Smith	TKO	1	Tim Witherspoon	New York, New York, United States	Luis Rivera
1987-03-07	Mike Tyson	W	12	James "Bonecrusher" Smith	Las Vegas, Nevada, United States	Mills Lane
1987-05-30	Mike Tyson	TKO	6	Pinklon Thomas	Las Vegas, Nevada, United States	Carlos Padilla
1987-08-01	Mike Tyson	W	12	Tony Tucker	Las Vegas, Nevada, United States	Mills Lane
1987-10-16	Mike Tyson	TKO	7	Tyrell Biggs	Atlantic City, New Jersey, United States	Tony Orlando
1988-01-22	Mike Tyson	TKO	4	Larry Holmes	Atlantic City, New Jersey, United States	Joe Cortez
1988-03-21	Mike Tyson	TKO	2	Tony Tubbs	Tokyo, Kanto Region, Japan	Arthur Mercante
1988-06-27	Mike Tyson	KO	1	Michael Spinks	Atlantic City, New Jersey, United States	Frank Cappuccino
1989-02-25	Mike Tyson	TKO	5	Frank Bruno	Las Vegas, Nevada, United States	Richard Steele

The above bouts are primarily, but not entirely, based upon www.boxrec.com/hugman

* Interim WBA title bout

& Some sources report this as an IBA title bout also; Toney won the contest but tested positive for illegal substances and the bout was declared "No Decision"

! Chagaev was the WBA "champion in recess"

Date	Winner	Verdict	Rounds	Loser	Location	Referee
1989-07-21	Mike Tyson	TKO	1	Carl Williams	Atlantic City, New Jersey, United States	Randy Neumann
1990-02-11	James "Buster" Douglas	KO	10	Mike Tyson	Tokyo, Kanto Region, Japan	Octavio Meyran
1990-10-25	Evander Holyfield	KO	3	James "Buster" Douglas	Las Vegas, Nevada, United States	Mills Lane
1991-04-19	Evander Holyfield	W	12	George Foreman	Atlantic City, New Jersey, United States	Rudy Battle
1991-11-23	Evander Holyfield	TKO	7	Bert Cooper	Atlanta, Georgia, United States	Mills Lane
1992-06-19	Evander Holyfield	W	12	Larry Holmes	Las Vegas, Nevada, United States	Mills Lane
1992-11-13	Riddick Bowe	W	12	Evander Holyfield	Las Vegas, Nevada, United States	Joe Cortez
1993-02-06	Riddick Bowe	TKO	1	Michael Dokes	New York, New York, United States	Joe Santarpia
1993-05-22	Riddick Bowe	TKO	2	Jesse Ferguson	Washington, District of Columbia, United States	Larry Hazzard
1993-11-06	Evander Holyfield	W	12	Riddick Bowe	Las Vegas, Nevada, United States	Mills Lane
1994-04-22	Michael Moorer	W	12	Evander Holyfield	Las Vegas, Nevada, United States	Mills Lane
1994-11-05	George Foreman	KO	10	Michael Moorer	Las Vegas, Nevada, United States	Joe Cortez
1995-04-08	Bruce Seldon	RTD	7	Tony Tucker	Las Vegas, Nevada, United States	Mills Lane
1995-08-19	Bruce Seldon	TKO	10	Joe Hipp	Las Vegas, Nevada, United States	Richard Steele
1996-09-07	Mike Tyson	TKO	1	Bruce Seldon	Las Vegas, Nevada, United States	Richard Steele
1996-11-09	Evander Holyfield	TKO	11	Mike Tyson	Las Vegas, Nevada, United States	Mitch Halpern
1997-06-28	Evander Holyfield	DSQ	3	Mike Tyson	Las Vegas, Nevada, United States	Mills Lane
1997-11-08	Evander Holyfield	RTD	8	Michael Moorer	Las Vegas, Nevada, United States	Mitch Halpern
1998-09-19	Evander Holyfield	W	12	Vaughn Bean	Atlanta, Georgia, United States	Brian Garry
1999-03-13	Evander Holyfield	D	12	Lennox Lewis	New York, New York, United States	Arthur Mercante Jr.
1999-11-13	Lennox Lewis	W	12	Evander Holyfield	Las Vegas, Nevada, United States	Mitch Halpern
2000-08-12	Evander Holyfield	W	12	John Ruiz	Las Vegas, Nevada, United States	Richard Steele
2001-03-03	John Ruiz	W	12	Evander Holyfield	Las Vegas, Nevada, United States	Joe Cortez
2001-12-15	John Ruiz	D	12	Evander Holyfield	Mashantucket, Connecticut, United States	Steve Smoger
2002-07-27	John Ruiz	DSQ	10	Kirk Johnson	Las Vegas, Nevada, United States	Joe Cortez
2003-03-01	Roy Jones Jr.	W	12	John Ruiz	Las Vegas, Nevada, United States	Jay Nady
2003-12-13 *	John Ruiz	W	12	Hasim Rahman	Atlantic City, New Jersey, United States	Randy Neumann
2004-04-17	John Ruiz	TKO	11	Fres Oquendo	New York, New York, United States	Wayne Kelly
2004-11-13	John Ruiz	W	12	Andrew Golota	New York, New York, United States	Randy Neumann
2005-04-30 &	John Ruiz	ND	12	James Toney	New York, New York, United States	Steve Smoger
2005-12-17	Nikolai Valuev	W	12	John Ruiz	Prenzlauer Berg, Berlin, Germany	Stanley Christodoulou
2006-06-03	Nikolai Valuev	TKO	3	Owen Beck	Hannover, Niedersachsen, Germany	Luis Pabon
2006-10-07	Nikolai Valuev	TKO	11	Monte Barrett	Rosemont, Illinois, United States	John O'Brien
2007-01-20	Nikolai Valuev	RTD	3	Jameel McCline	Basel, Canton of Basel-Stadt, Switzerland	John Coyle
2007-04-14	Ruslan Chagaev	W	12	Nikolai Valuev	Stuttgart, Baden-Württemberg, Germany	Luis Pabon
2008-01-19	Ruslan Chagaev	W	12	Matt Skelton	Düsseldorf, Nordrhein-Westfalen, Germany	Guillermo Perez Pineda
2008-08-30	Nikolai Valuev	W	12	John Ruiz	Prenzlauer Berg, Berlin, Germany	Derek Milham
2008-12-20	Nikolai Valuev	W	12	Evander Holyfield	Zurich, Canton of Zurich, Switzerland	Luis Pabon
2009-02-07 !	Ruslan Chagaev	TW	6	Carl Davis Drumond	Rostock, Mecklenburg-Vorpommern, Germany	Gustavo Padilla
2009-11-07	David Haye	W	12	Nikolai Valuev	Nuremberg (Nürnberg), Bayern, Germany	Luis Pabon
2010-04-03	David Haye	TKO	9	John Ruiz	Manchester, England, United Kingdom	Guillermo Perez Pineda
2010-11-13	David Haye	TKO	3	Audley Harrison	Manchester, England, United Kingdom	Luis Pabon

The above bouts are primarily, but not entirely, based upon www.boxrec.com/hugman

* Interim WBA title bout

& Some sources report this as an IBA title bout also; Toney won the contest but tested positive for illegal substances and the bout was declared "No Decision"

! Chagaev was the WBA "champion in recess"

WBC Heavyweight Championship 1963-2010

Date	Winner	Verdict	Rounds	Loser	Location	Referee
1963-07-22	Charles "Sonny" Liston	KO	1	Floyd Patterson	Las Vegas, Nevada, United States	Harry Krause
1964-02-25	Cassius Clay	RTD	6	Charles "Sonny" Liston	Miami Beach, Florida, United States	Barney Felix
1965-05-25	Muhammad Ali	TKO	1	Charles "Sonny" Liston	Lewiston, Maine, United States	"Jersey" Joe Walcott
1965-11-22	Muhammad Ali	TKO	12	Floyd Patterson	Las Vegas, Nevada, United States	Harry Krause
1966-03-29	Muhammad Ali	W	15	George Chuvalo	Toronto, Ontario, Canada	Jackie Silvers
1966-05-21	Muhammad Ali	TKO	6	Henry Cooper	London, England, United Kingdom	George Smith
1966-08-06	Muhammad Ali	KO	3	Brian London	London, England, United Kingdom	Harry Gibbs
1966-09-10	Muhammad Ali	TKO	12	Karl Mildenberger	Frankfurt, Hessen, Germany	Teddy Waltham
1966-11-14	Muhammad Ali	TKO	3	Cleveland Williams	Houston, Texas, United States	Harry Kessler
1967-02-06	Muhammad Ali	W	15	Ernie Terrell	Houston, Texas, United States	Harry Kessler
1967-03-22	Muhammad Ali	KO	7	Zora Folley	New York, New York, United States	Johnny LoBianco
1970-02-16	Joe Frazier	RTD	5	Jimmy Ellis	New York, New York, United States	Tony Perez
1970-11-18	Joe Frazier	KO	2	Bob Foster	Detroit, Michigan, United States	Tom Briscoe
1971-03-08	Joe Frazier	W	15	Muhammad Ali	New York, New York, United States	Arthur Mercante
1972-01-15	Joe Frazier	TKO	4	Terry Daniels	New Orleans, Louisiana, United States	Herman Dutreix
1972-05-25	Joe Frazier	TKO	4	Ron Stander	Omaha, Nebraska, United States	Zach Clayton
1973-01-22	George Foreman	TKO	2	Joe Frazier	Kingston, Surrey, Jamaica	Arthur Mercante
1973-09-01	George Foreman	KO	1	Jose "King" Roman	Tokyo, Kanto Region, Japan	Jay Edson
1974-03-26	George Foreman	TKO	2	Ken Norton	Caracas, Metropolitan District of Caracas, Venezuela	Jimmy Rondeau
1974-10-30	Muhammad Ali	KO	8	George Foreman	Kinshasa, Zaire, Democratic Republic Of The Congo	Zach Clayton
1975-03-24	Muhammad Ali	TKO	15	Chuck Wepner	Richfield, Ohio, United States	Tony Perez
1975-05-16	Muhammad Ali	TKO	11	Ron Lyle	Las Vegas, Nevada, United States	Ferd Hernandez
1975-07-01	Muhammad Ali	W	15	Joe Bugner	Kuala Lumpur, Federal Territory of Kuala Lumpur, Malaysia	Takeo Ugo
1975-10-01	Muhammad Ali	RTD	14	Joe Frazier	Quezon City, Metro Manila, Philippines	Carlos Padilla
1976-02-20	Muhammad Ali	KO	5	Jean-Pierre Coopman	San Juan, San Juan District, Puerto Rico	Ismael Quinones Falu
1976-04-30	Muhammad Ali	W	15	Jimmy Young	Landover, Maryland, United States	Tom Kelly
1976-05-25	Muhammad Ali	TKO	5	Richard Dunn	Munich, Bayern, Germany	Herbert Tomser
1976-09-28	Muhammad Ali	W	15	Ken Norton	New York, New York, United States	Arthur Mercante
1977-05-16	Muhammad Ali	W	15	Alfredo Evangelista	Landover, Maryland, United States	Harry Cecchini
1977-09-29	Muhammad Ali	W	15	Earnie Shavers	New York, New York, United States	Johnny LoBianco
1978-02-15	Leon Spinks	W	15	Muhammad Ali	Las Vegas, Nevada, United States	Davey Pearl
1978-06-09	Larry Holmes	W	15	Ken Norton	Las Vegas, Nevada, United States	Mills Lane
1978-11-10	Larry Holmes	KO	7	Alfredo Evangelista	Las Vegas, Nevada, United States	Richard Greene
1979-03-23	Larry Holmes	TKO	7	Osvaldo "Ossie" Ocasio	Las Vegas, Nevada, United States	Carlos Padilla
1979-06-22	Larry Holmes	TKO	12	Mike Weaver	New York, New York, United States	Harold Valan
1979-09-28	Larry Holmes	TKO	11	Earnie Shavers	Las Vegas, Nevada, United States	Davey Pearl
1980-02-03	Larry Holmes	KO	6	Lorenzo Zanon	Las Vegas, Nevada, United States	Ray Solis
1980-03-31	Larry Holmes	TKO	8	Leroy Jones	Las Vegas, Nevada, United States	Richard Greene
1980-07-07	Larry Holmes	TKO	7	Scott LeDoux	Bloomington, Minnesota, United States	Davey Pearl
1980-10-02	Larry Holmes	RTD	10	Muhammad Ali	Las Vegas, Nevada, United States	Richard Greene
1981-04-11	Larry Holmes	W	15	Trevor Berbick	Las Vegas, Nevada, United States	Mills Lane
1981-06-12	Larry Holmes	TKO	3	Leon Spinks	Detroit, Michigan, United States	Richard Steele
1981-11-06	Larry Holmes	TKO	11	Renaldo Snipes	Pittsburgh, Pennsylvania, United States	Rudy Ortega
1982-06-11	Larry Holmes	TKO	13	Gerry Cooney	Las Vegas, Nevada, United States	Mills Lane
1982-11-26	Larry Holmes	W	15	Randall "Tex" Cobb	Houston, Texas, United States	Steve Crosson
1983-03-27	Larry Holmes	W	12	Lucien Rodriguez	Scranton, Pennsylvania, United States	Carlos Padilla
1983-05-20	Larry Holmes	W	12	Tim Witherspoon	Las Vegas, Nevada, United States	Mills Lane
1983-09-10	Larry Holmes	TKO	5	Scott Frank	Atlantic City, New Jersey, United States	Tony Perez
1984-03-09	Tim Witherspoon	W	12	Greg Page	Las Vegas, Nevada, United States	Mills Lane
1984-08-31	Pinklon Thomas	W	12	Tim Witherspoon	Las Vegas, Nevada, United States	Richard Steele
1985-06-15	Pinklon Thomas	KO	8	Mike Weaver	Las Vegas, Nevada, United States	Carlos Padilla
1986-03-22	Trevor Berbick	W	12	Pinklon Thomas	Las Vegas, Nevada, United States	Richard Steele
1986-11-22	Mike Tyson	TKO	2	Trevor Berbick	Las Vegas, Nevada, United States	Mills Lane

The above bouts are primarily, but not entirely, based upon www.boxrec.com/hugman

* Interim WBC title bout

254

WBC Heavyweight Championship 1963-2010 (Cont'd.)

Date	Winner	Verdict	Rounds	Loser	Location	Referee
1987-03-07	Mike Tyson	W	12	James "Bonecrusher" Smith	Las Vegas, Nevada, United States	Mills Lane
1987-05-30	Mike Tyson	TKO	6	Pinklon Thomas	Las Vegas, Nevada, United States	Carlos Padilla
1987-08-01	Mike Tyson	W	12	Tony Tucker	Las Vegas, Nevada, United States	Mills Lane
1987-10-16	Mike Tyson	TKO	7	Tyrell Biggs	Atlantic City, New Jersey, United States	Tony Orlando
1988-01-22	Mike Tyson	TKO	4	Larry Holmes	Atlantic City, New Jersey, United States	Joe Cortez
1988-03-21	Mike Tyson	TKO	2	Tony Tubbs	Tokyo, Kanto Region, Japan	Arthur Mercante
1988-06-27	Mike Tyson	KO	1	Michael Spinks	Atlantic City, New Jersey, United States	Frank Cappuccino
1989-02-25	Mike Tyson	TKO	5	Frank Bruno	Las Vegas, Nevada, United States	Richard Steele
1989-07-21	Mike Tyson	TKO	1	Carl Williams	Atlantic City, New Jersey, United States	Randy Neumann
1990-02-11	James "Buster" Douglas	KO	10	Mike Tyson	Tokyo, Kanto Region, Japan	Octavio Meyran
1990-10-25	Evander Holyfield	KO	3	James "Buster" Douglas	Las Vegas, Nevada, United States	Mills Lane
1991-04-19	Evander Holyfield	W	12	George Foreman	Atlantic City, New Jersey, United States	Rudy Battle
1992-06-19	Evander Holyfield	W	12	Larry Holmes	Las Vegas, Nevada, United States	Mills Lane
1992-11-13	Riddick Bowe	W	12	Evander Holyfield	Las Vegas, Nevada, United States	Joe Cortez
1993-05-08	Lennox Lewis	W	12	Tony Tucker	Las Vegas, Nevada, United States	Joe Cortez
1993-10-01	Lennox Lewis	TKO	7	Frank Bruno	Cardiff, Wales, United Kingdom	Mickey Vann
1994-05-06	Lennox Lewis	TKO	8	Phil Jackson	Atlantic City, New Jersey, United States	Arthur Mercante
1994-09-24	Oliver McCall	TKO	2	Lennox Lewis	London, England, United Kingdom	Jose Guadalupe Garcia
1995-04-08	Oliver McCall	W	12	Larry Holmes	Las Vegas, Nevada, United States	Richard Steele
1995-09-02	Frank Bruno	W	12	Oliver McCall	London, England, United Kingdom	Tony Perez
1996-03-16	Mike Tyson	TKO	3	Frank Bruno	Las Vegas, Nevada, United States	Mills Lane
1997-02-07	Lennox Lewis	TKO	5	Oliver McCall	Las Vegas, Nevada, United States	Mills Lane
1997-07-12	Lennox Lewis	DSQ	5	Henry Akinwande	Stateline, Nevada, United States	Mills Lane
1997-10-04	Lennox Lewis	TKO	1	Andrew Golota	Atlantic City, New Jersey, United States	Joe Cortez
1998-03-28	Lennox Lewis	TKO	5	Shannon Briggs	Atlantic City, New Jersey, United States	Frank Cappuccino
1998-09-26	Lennox Lewis	W	12	Zeljko Mavrovic	Uncasville, Connecticut, United States	Frank Cappuccino
1999-03-13	Lennox Lewis	D	12	Evander Holyfield	New York, New York, United States	Arthur Mercante Jr.
1999-11-13	Lennox Lewis	W	12	Evander Holyfield	Las Vegas, Nevada, United States	Mitch Halpern
2000-04-29	Lennox Lewis	KO	2	Michael Grant	New York, New York, United States	Arthur Mercante Jr.
2000-07-15	Lennox Lewis	TKO	2	Francois "Frans" Botha	London, England, United Kingdom	Larry O'Connell
2000-11-11	Lennox Lewis	W	12	David Tua	Las Vegas, Nevada, United States	Joe Cortez
2001-04-22	Hasim Rahman	KO	5	Lennox Lewis	Brakpan, Gauteng, South Africa	Daniel Van de Wiele
2001-11-17	Lennox Lewis	KO	4	Hasim Rahman	Las Vegas, Nevada, United States	Joe Cortez
2002-06-08	Lennox Lewis	KO	8	Mike Tyson	Memphis, Tennessee, United States	Eddie Cotton
2003-06-21	Lennox Lewis	TKO	6	Vitali Klitschko	Los Angeles, California, United States	Lou Moret
2004-04-24	Vitali Klitschko	TKO	8	Corrie Sanders	Los Angeles, California, United States	Jon Schorle
2004-12-11	Vitali Klitschko	TKO	8	Danny Williams	Las Vegas, Nevada, United States	Jay Nady
2005-08-13 *	Hasim Rahman	W	12	Monte Barrett	Chicago, Illinois, United States	Jay Nady
2006-03-18	Hasim Rahman	D	12	James Toney	Atlantic City, New Jersey, United States	Eddie Cotton
2006-08-12	Oleg Maskaev	TKO	12	Hasim Rahman	Las Vegas, Nevada, United States	Jay Nady
2006-12-10	Oleg Maskaev	W	12	Peter Okhello	Moscow, Central Federal District, Russia	Jose Guadalupe Garcia
2007-10-06 *	Samuel Peter	W	12	Jameel McCline	New York, New York, United States	Mike Ortega
2008-03-08	Samuel Peter	TKO	6	Oleg Maskaev	Cancun, Quintana Roo, Mexico	Jose Guadalupe Garcia
2008-10-11	Vitali Klitschko	RTD	8	Samuel Peter	Kreuzberg, Berlin, Germany	Massimo Barrovecchio
2009-03-21	Vitali Klitschko	TKO	9	Juan Carlos Gomez	Stuttgart, Baden-Württemberg, Germany	Daniel Van de Wiele
2009-09-26	Vitali Klitschko	RTD	10	Chris Arreola	Los Angeles, California, United States	Jon Schoele
2009-12-12	Vitali Klitschko	W	12	Kevin Johnson	Bern, Canton of Bern, Switzerland	Kenny Bayless
2010-05-29	Vitali Klitschko	KO	10	Albert Sosnowski	Gelsenkirchen, Nordrhein-Westfalen, Germany	Jay Nady
2010-10-16	Vitali Klitschko	W	12	Shannon Briggs	Altona, Hamburg, Germany	Ian John-Lewis

The above bouts are primarily, but not entirely, based upon www.boxrec.com/hugman

* Interim WBC title bout

IBF Heavyweight Championship 1984-2010

Date	Winner	Verdict	Rounds	Loser	Location	Referee
1984-11-09	Larry Holmes	TKO	12	James "Bonecrusher" Smith	Las Vegas, Nevada, United States	Davey Pearl
1985-03-15	Larry Holmes	TKO	10	David Bey	Las Vegas, Nevada, United States	Carlos Padilla
1985-05-20	Larry Holmes	W	15	Carl Williams	Reno, Nevada, United States	Mills Lane
1985-09-21	Michael Spinks	W	15	Larry Holmes	Las Vegas, Nevada, United States	Carlos Padilla
1986-04-19	Michael Spinks	W	15	Larry Holmes	Las Vegas, Nevada, United States	Mills Lane
1986-09-06	Michael Spinks	TKO	4	Steffen Tangstad	Las Vegas, Nevada, United States	Richard Steele
1987-05-30	Tony Tucker	TKO	10	James "Buster" Douglas	Las Vegas, Nevada, United States	Mills Lane
1987-08-01	Mike Tyson	W	12	Tony Tucker	Las Vegas, Nevada, United States	Mills Lane
1987-10-16	Mike Tyson	TKO	7	Tyrell Biggs	Atlantic City, New Jersey, United States	Tony Orlando
1988-01-22	Mike Tyson	TKO	4	Larry Holmes	Atlantic City, New Jersey, United States	Joe Cortez
1988-03-21 *	Mike Tyson	TKO	2	Tony Tubbs	Tokyo, Kanto Region, Japan	Arthur Mercante
1988-06-27	Mike Tyson	KO	1	Michael Spinks	Atlantic City, New Jersey, United States	Frank Cappuccino
1989-02-25	Mike Tyson	TKO	5	Frank Bruno	Las Vegas, Nevada, United States	Richard Steele
1989-07-21	Mike Tyson	TKO	1	Carl Williams	Atlantic City, New Jersey, United States	Randy Neumann
1990-02-11	James "Buster" Douglas	KO	10	Mike Tyson	Tokyo, Kanto Region, Japan	Octavio Meyran
1990-10-25	Evander Holyfield	KO	3	James "Buster" Douglas	Las Vegas, Nevada, United States	Mills Lane
1991-04-19	Evander Holyfield	W	12	George Foreman	Atlantic City, New Jersey, United States	Rudy Battle
1991-11-23	Evander Holyfield	TKO	7	Bert Cooper	Atlanta, Georgia, United States	Mills Lane
1992-06-19	Evander Holyfield	W	12	Larry Holmes	Las Vegas, Nevada, United States	Mills Lane
1992-11-13	Riddick Bowe	W	12	Evander Holyfield	Las Vegas, Nevada, United States	Joe Cortez
1993-02-06	Riddick Bowe	TKO	1	Michael Dokes	New York, New York, United States	Joe Santarpia
1993-05-22	Riddick Bowe	TKO	2	Jesse Ferguson	Washington, District of Columbia, United States	Larry Hazzard
1993-11-06	Evander Holyfield	W	12	Riddick Bowe	Las Vegas, Nevada, United States	Mills Lane
1994-04-22	Michael Moorer	W	12	Evander Holyfield	Las Vegas, Nevada, United States	Mills Lane
1994-11-05	George Foreman	KO	10	Michael Moorer	Las Vegas, Nevada, United States	Joe Cortez
1995-04-22	George Foreman	W	12	Axel Schulz	Las Vegas, Nevada, United States	Joe Cortez
1995-12-09 #	Francois "Frans" Botha	NC	12	Axel Schulz	Stuttgart, Baden-Württemberg, Germany	Rudy Battle
1996-06-22	Michael Moorer	W	12	Axel Schulz	Dortmund, Nordrhein-Westfalen, Germany	William Conners
1996-11-09	Michael Moorer	TKO	12	Francois "Frans" Botha	Las Vegas, Nevada, United States	Mills Lane
1997-03-29	Michael Moorer	W	12	Vaughn Bean	Las Vegas, Nevada, United States	Mitch Halpern
1997-11-08	Evander Holyfield	RTD	8	Michael Moorer	Las Vegas, Nevada, United States	Mitch Halpern
1998-09-19	Evander Holyfield	W	12	Vaughn Bean	Atlanta, Georgia, United States	Brian Garry
1999-03-13	Evander Holyfield	D	12	Lennox Lewis	New York, New York, United States	Arthur Mercante Jr.
1999-11-13	Lennox Lewis	W	12	Evander Holyfield	Las Vegas, Nevada, United States	Mitch Halpern
2000-04-29	Lennox Lewis	KO	2	Michael Grant	New York, New York, United States	Arthur Mercante Jr.
2000-07-15	Lennox Lewis	TKO	2	Francois "Frans" Botha	London, England, United Kingdom	Larry O'Connell
2000-11-11	Lennox Lewis	W	12	David Tua	Las Vegas, Nevada, United States	Joe Cortez
2001-04-22	Hasim Rahman	KO	5	Lennox Lewis	Brakpan, Gauteng, South Africa	Daniel Van de Wiele
2001-11-17	Lennox Lewis	KO	4	Hasim Rahman	Las Vegas, Nevada, United States	Joe Cortez
2002-06-08	Lennox Lewis	KO	8	Mike Tyson	Memphis, Tennessee, United States	Eddie Cotton
2002-12-14	Chris Byrd	W	12	Evander Holyfield	Atlantic City, New Jersey, United States	Randy Neumann
2003-09-20	Chris Byrd	W	12	Fres Oquendo	Uncasville, Connecticut, United States	Eddie Cotton
2004-04-17	Chris Byrd	D	12	Andrew Golota	New York, New York, United States	Randy Neumann
2004-11-13	Chris Byrd	W	12	Jameel McCline	New York, New York, United States	Wayne Kelly
2005-10-01	Chris Byrd	W	12	DaVarryl Williamson	Reno, Nevada, United States	Vic Drakulich
2006-04-22	Wladimir Klitschko	TKO	7	Chris Byrd	Mannheim, Baden-Württemberg, Germany	Wayne Kelly
2006-11-11	Wladimir Klitschko	TKO	7	Calvin Brock	New York, New York, United States	Wayne Kelly
2007-03-10	Wladimir Klitschko	TKO	2	Ray Austin	Mannheim, Baden-Württemberg, Germany	Eddie Cotton
2007-07-07	Wladimir Klitschko	RTD	6	Lamon Brewster	Cologne, Nordrhein-Westfalen, Germany	Sam Williams
2008-02-23	Wladimir Klitschko	W	12	Sultan Ibragimov	New York, New York, United States	Wayne Kelly
2008-07-12	Wladimir Klitschko	KO	11	Tony Thompson	Altona, Hamburg, Germany	Joe Cortez
2008-12-13	Wladimir Klitschko	TKO	7	Hasim Rahman	Mannheim, Baden-Württemberg, Germany	Tony Weeks

The above bouts are primarily, but not entirely, based upon www.boxrec.com/hugman

* Japan did not recognize this as an IBF title bout

Botha won the contest but tested positive for illegal substances and the bout was declared "No Contest"

Date	Winner	Verdict	Rounds	Loser	Location	Referee
2009-06-20	Wladimir Klitschko	RTD	9	Ruslan Chagaev	Gelsenkirchen, Nordrhein-Westfalen, Germany	Eddie Cotton
2010-03-20	Wladimir Klitschko	KO	12	Eddie Chambers	Düsseldorf, Nordrhein-Westfalen, Germany	Genaro Rodriguez
2010-09-11	Wladimir Klitschko	TKO	10	Samuel Peter	Frankfurt, Hessen, Germany	Robert Byrd

The above bouts are primarily, but not entirely, based upon www.boxrec.com/hugman

* Japan did not recognize this as an IBF title bout

\# Botha won the contest but tested positive for illegal substances and the bout was declared "No Contest"

WBO Heavyweight Championship 1989-2010

Date	Winner	Verdict	Rounds	Loser	Location	Referee
1989-05-06	Francesco Damiani	KO	3	Johnny du Plooy	Syracuse, Sicily, Italy	Tony Perez
1989-12-16	Francesco Damiani	RTD	2	Daniel Eduardo Neto	Cesena, Emilia-Romagna, Italy	Bernie Soto
1991-01-11	Ray Mercer	KO	9	Francesco Damiani	Atlantic City, New Jersey, United States	Rudy Battle
1991-10-18	Ray Mercer	TKO	5	Tommy Morrison	Atlantic City, New Jersey, United States	Tony Perez
1992-05-15	Michael Moorer	TKO	5	Bert Cooper	Atlantic City, New Jersey, United States	Joe O'Neil
1993-06-07	Tommy Morrison	W	12	George Foreman	Las Vegas, Nevada, United States	Mills Lane
1993-08-30	Tommy Morrison	RTD	4	Tim Tomashek	Kansas City, Missouri, United States	Danny Campbell
1993-10-29	Michael Bentt	TKO	1	Tommy Morrison	Tulsa, Oklahoma, United States	Danny Campbell
1994-03-19	Herbie Hide	KO	7	Michael Bentt	London, England, United Kingdom	Paul Thomas
1995-03-11	Riddick Bowe	KO	6	Herbie Hide	Las Vegas, Nevada, United States	Richard Steele
1995-06-17	Riddick Bowe	KO	6	Jorge Luis Gonzalez	Las Vegas, Nevada, United States	Mills Lane
1996-06-29	Henry Akinwande	KO	3	Jeremy Williams	Indio, California, United States	Raul Caiz Sr.
1996-11-09	Henry Akinwande	TKO	10	Alexander Zolkin	Las Vegas, Nevada, United States	Richard Steele
1997-01-11	Henry Akinwande	W	12	Scott Welch	Nashville, Tennessee, United States	William Conners
1997-06-28	Herbie Hide	TKO	2	Tony Tucker	Norwich, England, United Kingdom	Raul Caiz Sr.
1998-04-18	Herbie Hide	TKO	1	Damon Reed	Manchester, England, United Kingdom	Rudy Battle
1998-09-26	Herbie Hide	TKO	2	Willi Fischer	Norwich, England, United Kingdom	Joe Cortez
1999-06-26	Vitali Klitschko	KO	2	Herbie Hide	London, England, United Kingdom	Genaro Rodriguez
1999-10-09	Vitali Klitschko	TKO	3	Ed Mahone	Oberhausen, Nordrhein-Westfalen, Germany	Rudy Battle
1999-12-11	Vitali Klitschko	RTD	9	Obed Sullivan	Alsterdorf, Hamburg, Germany	Joe Cortez
2000-04-01	Chris Byrd	RTD	9	Vitali Klitschko	Neukölln, Berlin, Germany	Genaro Rodriguez
2000-10-14	Wladimir Klitschko	W	12	Chris Byrd	Cologne, Nordrhein-Westfalen, Germany	Lou Moret
2001-03-24	Wladimir Klitschko	TKO	2	Derrick Jefferson	Munich, Bayern, Germany	Genaro Rodriguez
2001-08-04	Wladimir Klitschko	TKO	6	Charles Shufford	Las Vegas, Nevada, United States	Kenny Bayless
2002-03-16	Wladimir Klitschko	TKO	8	Francois "Frans" Botha	Stuttgart, Baden-Württemberg, Germany	Genaro Rodriguez
2002-06-29	Wladimir Klitschko	TKO	6	Ray Mercer	Atlantic City, New Jersey, United States	Randy Neumann
2002-12-07	Wladimir Klitschko	RTD	10	Jameel McCline	Las Vegas, Nevada, United States	Jay Nady
2003-03-08	Corrie Sanders	TKO	2	Wladimir Klitschko	Hannover, Niedersachsen, Germany	Genaro Rodriguez
2004-04-10	Lamon Brewster	TKO	5	Wladimir Klitschko	Las Vegas, Nevada, United States	Robert Byrd
2004-09-04	Lamon Brewster	W	12	Kali Meehan	Las Vegas, Nevada, United States	Jay Nady
2005-05-21	Lamon Brewster	TKO	1	Andrew Golota	Chicago, Illinois, United States	Genaro Rodriguez
2005-09-28	Lamon Brewster	RTD	9	Luan Krasniqi	Altona, Hamburg, Germany	Jose Hiram Rivera
2006-04-01	Sergei [Serguey] Liakhovich	W	12	Lamon Brewster	Cleveland, Ohio, United States	Ernie Sharif
2006-11-04	Shannon Briggs	TKO	12	Sergei [Serguey] Liakhovich	Phoenix, Arizona, United States	Robert Ferrara
2007-06-02	Sultan Ibragimov	W	12	Shannon Briggs	Atlantic City, New Jersey, United States	Eddie Cotton
2007-10-13	Sultan Ibragimov	W	12	Evander Holyfield	Moscow, Central Federal District, Russia	Raul Caiz Sr.
2008-02-23	Wladimir Klitschko	W	12	Sultan Ibragimov	New York, New York, United States	Wayne Kelly
2008-07-12	Wladimir Klitschko	KO	11	Tony Thompson	Altona, Hamburg, Germany	Joe Cortez
2008-12-13	Wladimir Klitschko	TKO	7	Hasim Rahman	Mannheim, Baden-Württemberg, Germany	Tony Weeks
2009-06-20	Wladimir Klitschko	RTD	9	Ruslan Chagaev	Gelsenkirchen, Nordrhein-Westfalen, Germany	Eddie Cotton
2010-03-20	Wladimir Klitschko	KO	12	Eddie Chambers	Düsseldorf, Nordrhein-Westfalen, Germany	Genaro Rodriguez
2010-09-11	Wladimir Klitschko	TKO	10	Samuel Peter	Frankfurt, Hessen, Germany	Robert Byrd

The above bouts are primarily, but not entirely, based upon www.boxrec.com/hugman

IBC Heavyweight Championship 1990-2010

Date	Winner	Verdict	Rounds	Loser	Location	Referee
1990-12-14	Phil Jackson	KO	1	Olian Alexander	Kansas City, Missouri, United States	
1992-06-26	Donovan Ruddock	KO	4	Phil Jackson	Cleveland, Ohio, United States	Tony Perez
1994-12-03	Tim Puller	TKO	8	Sherman Griffin	Harlingen, Texas, United States	
1995-06-10	Tommy Morrison	TKO	6	Donovan Ruddock	Kansas City, Missouri, United States	Ron Lipton
1995-10-07	Lennox Lewis	TKO	6	Tommy Morrison	Atlantic City, New Jersey, United States	Mills Lane
1996-06-28	Jerry Ballard	TKO	6	Corey Sanders	Upper Marlboro, Maryland, United States	
1996-11-22	John Kiser	W	12	George Stephens	Denver, Colorado, United States	
1997-06-20	Michael Grant	RTD	10	Alfred "Ice" Cole	Atlantic City, New Jersey, United States	Eddie Cotton
1997-11-07	Michael Grant	TKO	1	Jorge Luis Gonzalez	Las Vegas, Nevada, United States	Joe Cortez
1998-01-17	Michael Grant	TKO	5	David Izon	Atlantic City, New Jersey, United States	Frank Cappuccino
1998-05-30	Michael Grant	TKO	9	Obed Sullivan	Atlantic City, New Jersey, United States	Tony Orlando
2000-01-14	Brian Nielsen	KO	8	Troy Weida	Kolding, Region Syddanmark, Denmark	Pete Podgorski
2000-04-28	Brian Nielsen	TKO	5	Jeremy Williams	Copenhagen, Region Hovedstaden, Denmark	Pete Podgorski
2001-06-16	Brian Nielsen	W	12	Orlin Norris	Brondby, Region Hovedstaden, Denmark	Marty Denkin
2005-11-26	Tomasz Bonin	W	12	Fernely Feliz	Chicago, Illinois, United States	Pete Podgorski
2006-05-20	Tomasz Bonin	KO	3	Adenilson Rodrigues	Ketrzyn, Warmian-Masurian Voivodeship, Poland	Bela Florian
2009-04-18	Hector Ferreyro	W	12	Cisse Salif	Laredo, Texas, United States	Wilfredo Esperon
2009-08-21	Hector Ferreyro	KO	2	Matt Hicks	Laredo, Texas, United States	Wilfredo Esperon
2010-03-26	Hector Ferreyro	W	12	Arron Lyons	Laredo, Texas, United States	Wilfredo Esperon
2010-08-06	Hector Ferreyro	W	12	Homero Fonseca	Laredo, Texas, United States	Tony Garcia

The above bouts are primarily, but not entirely, based upon www.boxrec.com

IBO Heavyweight Championship 1992-2010

Date	Winner	Verdict	Rounds	Loser	Location	Referee
1992-11-14	Pinklon Thomas	W	12	Craig Payne	Greenville, South Carolina, United States	
1993-02-23	Lionel Butler	TKO	5	Tony Willis	Reseda, California, United States	Chuck Hassett
1994-08-04	Danell Nicholson	W	12	John Ruiz	Mashantucket, Connecticut, United States	Matt Mullaney
1994-10-29	Jimmy Thunder	W	12	Richard Mason	Atlantic City, New Jersey, United States	Eddie Cotton
1994-12-06	Jimmy Thunder	W	12	Tony Tubbs	Auburn Hills, Michigan, United States	Sam Williams
1995-08-08	Jimmy Thunder	TKO	7	Ray Anis	Coachella, California, United States	Robert Ferrara
1996-01-12	Brian Nielsen	TKO	2	Tony LaRosa	Copenhagen, Region Hovedstaden, Denmark	
1996-03-29	Brian Nielsen	TKO	6	Phil Jackson	Copenhagen, Region Hovedstaden, Denmark	Marty Denkin
1996-05-31	Brian Nielsen	TKO	5	Mike Hunter	Copenhagen, Region Hovedstaden, Denmark	Pete Podgorski
1997-01-24	Brian Nielsen	W	12	Larry Holmes	Brondby, Region Hovedstaden, Denmark	Marty Denkin
1997-11-14	Brian Nielsen	KO	2	Don Steele	Copenhagen, Region Hovedstaden, Denmark	Steve Smoger
1998-11-06	Brian Nielsen	KO	1	Lionel Butler	Copenhagen, Region Hovedstaden, Denmark	James Santa
1999-11-13	Lennox Lewis	W	12	Evander Holyfield	Las Vegas, Nevada, United States	Mitch Halpern
2000-04-29	Lennox Lewis	KO	2	Michael Grant	New York, New York, United States	Arthur Mercante Jr.
2000-07-15	Lennox Lewis	TKO	2	Francois "Frans" Botha	London, England, United Kingdom	Larry O'Connell
2000-11-11	Lennox Lewis	W	12	David Tua	Las Vegas, Nevada, United States	Joe Cortez
2001-04-22	Hasim Rahman	KO	5	Lennox Lewis	Brakpan, Gauteng, South Africa	Daniel Van de Wiele
2001-11-17	Lennox Lewis	KO	4	Hasim Rahman	Las Vegas, Nevada, United States	Joe Cortez
2002-06-08	Lennox Lewis	KO	8	Mike Tyson	Memphis, Tennessee, United States	Eddie Cotton
2003-06-21	Lennox Lewis	TKO	6	Vitali Klitschko	Los Angeles, California, United States	Lou Moret
2006-04-22	Wladimir Klitschko	TKO	7	Chris Byrd	Mannheim, Baden-Württemberg, Germany	Wayne Kelly
2006-11-11	Wladimir Klitschko	TKO	7	Calvin Brock	New York, New York, United States	Wayne Kelly
2007-03-10	Wladimir Klitschko	TKO	2	Ray Austin	Mannheim, Baden-Württemberg, Germany	Eddie Cotton
2007-07-07	Wladimir Klitschko	RTD	6	Lamon Brewster	Cologne, Nordrhein-Westfalen, Germany	Sam Williams
2008-02-23	Wladimir Klitschko	W	12	Sultan Ibragimov	New York, New York, United States	Wayne Kelly
2008-07-12	Wladimir Klitschko	KO	11	Tony Thompson	Altona, Hamburg, Germany	Joe Cortez
2008-12-13	Wladimir Klitschko	TKO	7	Hasim Rahman	Mannheim, Baden-Württemberg, Germany	Tony Weeks
2009-06-20	Wladimir Klitschko	RTD	9	Ruslan Chagaev	Gelsenkirchen, Nordrhein-Westfalen, Germany	Eddie Cotton
2010-03-20	Wladimir Klitschko	KO	12	Eddie Chambers	Düsseldorf, Nordrhein-Westfalen, Germany	Genaro Rodriguez
2010-09-11	Wladimir Klitschko	TKO	10	Samuel Peter	Frankfurt, Hessen, Germany	Robert Byrd

The above bouts are primarily, but not entirely, based upon www.boxrec.com

260

WBF Heavyweight Championship 1993-2010

Date	Winner	Verdict	Rounds	Loser	Location	Referee
1993-01-29	Lawrence Carter	TKO	7	Pinklon Thomas	Columbia, South Carolina, United States	
1993-07-23	Jimmy Thunder	TKO	5	Melton Bowen	Townsville, Queensland, Australia	Denzil Creed
1993-11-19	Johnny Nelson	W	12	Jimmy Thunder	Auckland, North Island, New Zealand	
1994-11-05	Johnny Nelson	W	12	Nikolay Kulpin	Chiang Mai, Chiang Mai Province, Thailand	
1995-08-22	Adilson Rodrigues	W	12	Johnny Nelson	Sao Paulo, Sao Paulo, Brazil	
1995-12-03	Adilson Rodrigues	W	12	Johnny Nelson	Sao Paulo, Sao Paulo, Brazil	
1996-05-18	Adilson Rodrigues	KO	3	Dave Fiddler	Araraquara, Sao Paulo, Brazil	
1997-01-23	Lionel Butler	KO	1	Marcos Gonzalez	Reseda, California, United States	Jon Schorle
1997-07-29	Bert Cooper	KO	1	Richie Melito	New York, New York, United States	Wayne Kelly
1998-07-04	Joe Bugner	RTD	1	James "Bonecrusher" Smith	Gold Coast, Queensland, Australia	Bruce McTavish
1999-06-25	Joe Hipp	W	12	Everett Martin	St. Charles, Missouri, United States	Myrl Taylor
2000-05-12	Mike Bernardo	TKO	6	Daniel Jerling	Szekszard, Tolna, Hungary	
2001-06-08	Mike Bernardo	TKO	1	Peter McNeeley	Cape Town, Western Cape, South Africa	Isaac Tshabalala
2002-05-11	Furkat Tursunov	W	12	Ralf Packheiser	Munich, Bayern, Germany	
2003-05-16	Richel Hersisia	KO	9	Sandro Abel Vazquez	The Hague, South Holland, Netherlands	Harry Hemelrijk
2003-08-09	Richel Hersisia	W	12	Sami Elovaara	Salzburg, Salzburg Land Province, Austria	
2009-10-24	Francois "Frans" Botha	D	12	Pedro Carrion	Dessau, Sachsen-Anhalt, Germany	Ian John-Lewis
2010-04-10	Evander Holyfield	TKO	8	Francois "Frans" Botha	Las Vegas, Nevada, United States	Russell Mora

The above bouts are primarily, but not entirely, based upon www.boxrec.com

WBU Heavyweight Championship 1995-2005

Date	Winner	Verdict	Rounds	Loser	Location	Referee
1995-04-22	George Foreman	W	12	Axel Schulz	Las Vegas, Nevada, United States	Joe Cortez
1996-11-03	George Foreman	W	12	Crawford Grimsley	Urayasu, Chiba, Japan	Max Parker Jr.
1997-04-26	George Foreman	W	12	Lou Savarese	Atlantic City, New Jersey, United States	Eddie Cotton
1997-11-15	Corrie Sanders	W	12	Ross Puritty	Temba, North West, South Africa	Dave Parris
1998-06-12	Corrie Sanders	TKO	2	Bobby Czyz	Uncasville, Connecticut, United States	Mickey Vann
1999-07-02	Corrie Sanders	TKO	1	Jorge Valdes	Bristol, England, United Kingdom	Dave Parris
2000-02-19	Corrie Sanders	TKO	1	Alfred "Ice" Cole	Brakpan, Gauteng, South Africa	Dave Parris
2000-05-20	Hasim Rahman	TKO	7	Corrie Sanders	Atlantic City, New Jersey, United States	Eddie Cotton
2001-11-24	Johnny Nelson	W	12	Alexander Vasiliev	London, England, United Kingdom	Mickey Vann
2002-12-21	George Kandelaki	TKO	12	Alexander Vasiliev	St. Petersburg, Northwestern Federal District, Russia	Jean-Louis Legland
2005-02-25	Matt Skelton	TKO	6	Fabio Eduardo Moli	London, England, United Kingdom	Dave Parris

The above bouts are primarily, but not entirely, based upon www.boxrec.com

IBA Heavyweight Championship 1996-2008

Date	Winner	Verdict	Rounds	Loser	Location	Referee
1996-11-03	George Foreman	W	12	Crawford Grimsley	Urayasu, Chiba, Japan	Max Parker Jr.
1998-06-25	Lou Savarese	KO	1	James "Buster" Douglas	Mashantucket, Connecticut, United States	Steve Smoger
2004-09-23	James Toney	W	12	Rydell Booker	Temecula, California, United States	Raul Caiz Sr.
2005-04-30 *	James Toney	ND	12	John Ruiz	New York, New York, United States	Steve Smoger
2005-10-01	James Toney	W	12	Dominick Guinn	Reno, Nevada, United States	Jay Nady
2006-09-02	Samuel Peter	W	12	James Toney	Los Angeles, California, United States	Raul Caiz Sr.
2008-12-13	James Toney	W	12	Fres Oquendo	Cabazon, California, United States	Lou Moret

The above bouts are primarily, but not entirely, based upon www.boxrec.com

* Some sources report this as a WBA title bout also; Toney won the contest but tested positive for illegal substances and the bout was declared "No Decision"

IBU Heavyweight Championship 1933-1935, 2001-2006

Date	Winner	Verdict	Rounds	Loser	Location	Referee
1933-10-22 *	Primo Carnera	W	15	Paulino Uzcudun	Rome, Lazio, Italy	Maurice Nicod
1935-10-02 *	George Godfrey	W	15	Pierre Charles	Brussels, Bruxelles-Capitale, Belgium	Rene Scheman
2001-10-01	Dirk Wallyn	TKO	9	Jukka Jarvinen	Helsinki, Southern Finland, Finland	Esa Lehtosaari
2002-02-04	Adnan Serin	TKO	3	Jukka Jarvinen	Helsinki, Southern Finland, Finland	Erkki Meronen
2003-07-19	Shannon Briggs	TKO	1	John Sargent	Fort Lauderdale, Florida, United States	Jorge Alonso
2005-03-24	Robert Hawkins	TKO	5	John Poore	Philadelphia, Pennysylvania, United States	Blair Talmadge
2005-09-09	Eddie Chambers	W	12	Robert Hawkins	Philadelphia, Pennysylvania, United States	Robert Grasso
2006-05-20	Gene Pukall	TKO	3	Ingo Jaede	Bautzen, Sachsen, Germany	

The above bouts are primarily, but not entirely, based upon www.boxrec.com

* An earlier and different IBU organization

Heavyweight Championship of England 1860-1900

Date	Winner	Verdict	Rounds	Loser	Location	Referee
1860-01-01	Tom Sayers was the reigning champion					
1860-04-17 *	Tom Sayers	D	42	John Heenan	Farnborough, England, United Kingdom	Frank Dowling
1860-11-06 * $	Sam Hurst	W	5	Tom Paddock	near Hungerford, England, United Kingdom	
1861-06-18 *	Jem Mace	W	8	Sam Hurst	Medway Island, England, United Kingdom	
1862-01-28 * #	Jem Mace	W	42	Tom King	Godstone, England, United Kingdom	
1862-11-26 *	Tom King	W	21	Jem Mace	Thames Haven, England, United Kingdom	
1863-12-10 *	Tom King	W	24	John Heenan	Wadhurst, England, United Kingdom	
1865-01-04 *	Joe Wormald	W	18	Andrew Marsden	Horley, England, United Kingdom	
1866-05-24 *	Jem Mace	D	1	Joe Goss	Meopham, England, United Kingdom	
1866-08-06 *	Jem Mace	W	21	Joe Goss	Purfleet, England, United Kingdom	
1877-10-29	Tom Allen	RTD	7	Tompkin [Thompkin] Gilbert	London, England, United Kingdom	Robert Watson
1878-04-04	Tom Allen	DSQ	5	Charles Davis	London, England, United Kingdom	Charles Conquest
1879-04-22	Tom Allen	D	24	Jem Stewart	London, England, United Kingdom	Charles Conquest
1879-09-06	Jem Stewart	DSQ	13	Tompkin [Thompkin] Gilbert	Glasgow, Scotland, United Kingdom	John Riddell
1880-02-26	Alfred "Alf" Greenfield	DSQ	20	Jem Stewart	London, England, United Kingdom	Charles Bedford
1884-10-14	John Knifton	RTD	10	Wolf Bendoff	London, England, United Kingdom	
1884-12-17	Jem Smith	RTD	12	Wolf Bendoff	London, England, United Kingdom	
1885-12-16 *	Jem Smith	KO	6	Jack Davis [Davies]	near Lingfield, England, United Kingdom	
1886-02-16 *	Jem Smith	D	13	Alfred "Alf" Greenfield	near Paris, Paris, France	Jem Mace
1889-09-30	Jem Smith	W	10	Jack Wannop	London, England, United Kingdom	W.J. King
1889-11-11	Peter Jackson	DSQ	2	Jem Smith	London, England, United Kingdom	George Vize
1889-12-23 *	Frank "Paddy" Slavin	D	14	Jem Smith	near Bruges, West Flanders, Belgium	J. Vesey
1891-07-27	Ted Pritchard	RTD	3	Jem Smith	London, England, United Kingdom	
1892-05-30 &	Peter Jackson	TKO	10	Frank "Paddy" Slavin	London, England, United Kingdom	Bernard J. Angle
1895-05-10	Jem Smith	KO	2	Ted Pritchard	London, England, United Kingdom	Joe Steers
1895-11-26	Jem Smith	DSQ	9	Dick Burge	London, England, United Kingdom	Bernard J. Angle
1896-01-27 !	Dan Creedon	KO	2	Jem Smith	London, England, United Kingdom	Bernard J. Angle
1900-12-17	George Chrisp	KO	14	Harry Smith	Newcastle, England, United Kingdom	Thomas W. Gale

* Prize Ring rules and bare-knuckles were used

$ Some sources report the date as 1860-11-05

\# Some sources report the result as "W 43"

& Also for Australian, Fox, Police Gazette and Imperial British Empire Heavyweight Championship

! Imperial British Empire Heavyweight Championship

Heavyweight Championship of America 1860-1889

Date	Winner	Verdict	Rounds	Loser	Location	Referee
1860-05-28	John Hennan was awarded a championship belt					
1863-05-05	Joe Coburn	W	67	Mike McCoole	Charlestown, Cecil County, Maryland, United States	Ned Price
1865-05-16	Jim Dunn	W	43	Bill Davis	Pike County, Pennsylvania, United States	Joe Coburn/Tim Hurley
1866-09-19	Mike McCoole	RTD	34	Bill Davis	Chouteau Island, Madison County, Illinois, United States	Pat Coyle
1867-08-31	Mike McCoole	W	34	Aaron Jones	Busenbark's Station, Ohio, United States	Rufus Hunt
1869-01-12	Tom Allen	W	43	Bill Davis	Chouteau Island, Madison County, Illinois, United States	Bill Collins
1869-02-23	Charley Gallagher	W	2	Tom Allen	Carroll Island, near St. Louis, Missouri, United States	James Donald
1869-06-15	Mike McCoole	WF	9	Tom Allen	Foster's Island, near St. Louis, Missouri, United States	Val McKinney
1869-08-17 $	Tom Allen	W	9	Charley Gallagher	Foster's Island, near St. Louis, Missouri, United States	Larry Wessell
1870-05-10 !	Jem Mace	W	10	Tom Allen	Kennerville, Louisiana, United States	Rufus Hunt
1871-05-11 !	Jem Mace	D	1	Joe Coburn	Port Ryerse [Port Dover], Ontario, Canada	Dick Hollywood
1871-11-30 ! $	Jem Mace	D	12	Joe Coburn	Bay St. Louis, Mississippi, United States	Rufus Hunt
1873-09-23	Tom Allen	W	7	Mike McCoole	Chouteau Island, Madison County, Illinois, United States	Jack Looney
1873-11-18	Tom Allen	D	3	Ben Hogan	Pacific City, Iowa, United States	Tom Riley
1876-09-07 #	Tom Allen	D	7	Joe Goss	near Walton, Kenton County, Kentucky, United States	E.H. Holland
1876-09-07 #	Joe Goss	WF	14	Tom Allen	near Walton, Boone County, Kentucky, United States	E.H. Holland
1880-05-30	Paddy Ryan	RTD	87	Joe Goss	Collier's Station, West Virginia, United States	Goss Schell
1882-02-07	John L. Sullivan	W	9	Paddy Ryan	Mississippi City, Mississippi, United States	Alex Brewster/Jack Hardy
1885-08-29 *	John L. Sullivan	DSQ	7	Dominick McCaffrey	Cincinnati, Ohio, United States	Billy Tait
1887-06	Richard K. Fox declared Jake Kilrain the Fox (Police Gazette) Heavyweight Champion of America and Champion of the World					
1889-07-08 &	John L. Sullivan	RTD	75	Jake Kilrain	Richburg, Mississippi, United States	John Fitzpatrick

All contests utilized Prize Ring rules and bare-knuckles except the Sullivan-McCaffrey bout

$ Some sources report the verdict as "D 11"

! Also for the Championship of the World

Same fight continued in different locations

* Queensberry Rules and gloves were used; Some sources report this as a world title bout

& Some sources report this as a Fox (Police Gazette) world title bout

Heavyweight Championship of Australia 1879-1900

Date	Winner	Verdict	Rounds	Loser	Location	Referee
1879-03-20 b	Laurence "Larry" Foley	RTD	16	Abe Hicken	near Echuca, New South Wales, Australia	Sam Baldock
1881	Bill Farnan	KO	6	Charlie "Darkie" Richardson	Melbourne, Victoria, Australia	
1883-05-28	William Miller	D	40	Laurence "Larry" Foley	Sydney, New South Wales, Australia	William Forrester
1884-07-26	Bill Farnan	RTD	3	Peter Jackson	Melbourne, Victoria, Australia	
1884-09-23	Bill Farnan	D	6	Peter Jackson	Sydney, New South Wales, Australia	
1885-05-20	Tom Lees	KO	12	Bill Farnan	Melbourne, Victoria, Australia	
1886-04-19 !	Tom Lees	D	18	Bill Farnan	Melbourne, Victoria, Australia	
1886-04-20 !	Tom Lees	RTD	4	Bill Farnan	Essendon, Victoria, Australia	
1886-09-25	Peter Jackson	RTD	30	Tom Lees	Sydney, New South Wales, Australia	George Searle
1888-12-08	Frank "Paddy" Slavin	KO	1	Nicholas "Mick" Dooley	Sydney, New South Wales, Australia	Sid Bloomfield
1890-06-24	Joe Goddard	RTD	21	Nicholas "Mick" Dooley	Sydney, New South Wales, Australia	Sid Bloomfield
1890-08-25	Owen Sullivan	KO	11	Jim Hall	Broken Hill, New South Wales, Australia	R.B. Pell
1890-10-20	Joe Goddard	D	8	Peter Jackson	Melbourne, Victoria, Australia	William Miller
1890-11-01	Joe Goddard	RTD	7	Nicholas "Mick" Dooley	Melbourne, Victoria, Australia	William Miller
1891-02-10	Joe Goddard	RTD	4	Joe Choynski	Sydney, New South Wales, Australia	Sid Bloomfield
1891-05-23	Joe Goddard	DSQ	9	Tom Lees	Charters Towers, Queensland, Australia	
1891-07-20	Joe Goddard	KO	4	Joe Choynski	Melbourne, Victoria, Australia	W.R. Virgoe
1891-09-21 *	Joe Goddard	D	8	Tom Lees	Melbourne, Victoria, Australia	Bill Curran
1891-10-02 *	Joe Goddard	W	8	Jack Ashton	Melbourne, Victoria, Australia	W.R. Virgoe
1891-12-31 *	Joe Goddard	RTD	4	Ned Ryan	Melbourne, Victoria, Australia	
1892-05-30 &	Peter Jackson	TKO	10	Frank "Paddy" Slavin	London, England, United Kingdom	Bernard J. Angle
1893-02-14	Steve O'Donnell	D	10	Ned Ryan	Sydney, New South Wales, Australia	Harry Cansdell
1894-01-01	Harry Laing	RTD	12	Joe Goddard	Melbourne, Victoria, Australia	Harry Nathan
1894-06-23	Nicholas "Mick" Dooley	W	20	James "Tut" Ryan	Melbourne, Victoria, Australia	
1896-04-04	Nicholas "Mick" Dooley	KO	2	Peter Felix	Melbourne, Victoria, Australia	
1897-07-03	Nicholas "Mick" Dooley	D	10	Peter Felix	Brisbane, Queensland, Australia	Horace Brinsmead
1898-09-07	Nicholas "Mick" Dooley	RTD	6	Bill Doherty	Freemantle, Western Australia, Australia	William Miller
1898-10-08	Peter Felix	D	20	James "Tut" Ryan	Melbourne, Victoria, Australia	
1898-12-26	Nicholas "Mick" Dooley	RTD	2	Will Bell	Coolgardie, Western Australia, Australia	
1899-01-21	Nicholas "Mick" Dooley	KO	2	Jim Fogarty	Coolgardie, Western Australia, Australia	
1899-02-25	Bill Doherty	KO	6	Nicholas "Mick" Dooley	Kalgoorlie, Western Australia, Australia	R.B. Pell
1899-04-03	Bill Doherty	KO	4	Nicholas "Mick" Dooley	Kalgoorlie, Western Australia, Australia	R.B. Pell
1899-06-17	Bill Doherty	DSQ	12	James "Tut" Ryan	Kalgoorlie, Western Australia, Australia	R.B. Pell
1899-08-14	Bill Doherty	RTD	16	James "Tut" Ryan	Kalgoorlie, Western Australia, Australia	R.B. Pell
1899-12-02	Peter Felix	RTD	7	Bill Doherty	Kalgoorlie, Western Australia, Australia	
1900-07-16	Bill Doherty	W	20	Peter Felix	Sydney, New South Wales, Australia	
1900-08-11	Bill Doherty	KO	3	Nicholas "Mick" Dooley	Sydney, New South Wales, Australia	Wally Weekes
1900-12-03 $	Bill Doherty	D	20	Peter Felix	Kalgoorlie, Western Australia, Australia	R.B. Pell

The above bouts are primarily, but not entirely, based upon www.boxrec.com/hugman

b Bare-knuckles were used; Some sources report the date as 1879-03-13

! Same fight continued on consecutive days

* Scheduled for less than ten rounds

& Also for English, Fox, Police Gazette and Imperial British Empire Heavyweight Championships

$ Held on two nights; Lights went out on 1900-12-01 after eight rounds; Remaining twelve rounds held on 1900-12-03

Heavyweight Championship of New Zealand 1885-1889

Date	Winner	Verdict	Rounds	Loser	Location	Referee
1885-03-16	Dick Matthews	KO	2	Jim Pettengell	Dunedin, South Island, New Zealand	R. Wilson
1885-07-25	Dick Matthews	KO	7	Jack "John" O'Neill	Hokitika, South Island, New Zealand	T. McFarlane
1885-08-19	Dick Matthews	KO	5	Bill Wilkinson	Auckland, North Island, New Zealand	George Belcher
1886-08 *	Harry Laing	KO		Mick Dillon	Wanganui, North Island, New Zealand	
1887-05-09	Harry Laing	KO	5	Jim Pettengell	Wanganui, North Island, New Zealand	George Stevenson
1887-06-04	Dick Matthews	KO	3	Charlie "Darkie" Richardson	Auckland, North Island, New Zealand	Jack Kirby
1887-06-28	Harry Laing	TKO	17	John "Jack" Cunningham	Wellington, North Island, New Zealand	E. Brooks
1887-07-20	Dick Matthews	DSQ	10	Charlie "Darkie" Richardson	Wellington, North Island, New Zealand	H.F. Woods
1887-10-17	Harry Laing	TKO	11	Charlie "Darkie" Richardson	Wellington, North Island, New Zealand	George Cloake
1887-11-21	Harry Laing	KO	6	Charlie "Darkie" Richardson	Wanganui, North Island, New Zealand	George Stevenson
1888-01-06	Harry Laing	KO	4	Dick Matthews	Wanganui, North Island, New Zealand	Chavanne
1888-03-29	Harry Laing	TKO	2	Dick Matthews	Otahuhu, North Island, New Zealand	J. Wakefield
1888-04-25	Frank "Paddy" Slavin	KO	6	Harry Laing	Wanganui, North Island, New Zealand	John Chaafe
1889-04-24	Harry Laing	D	13	"Australian" Billy Smith	Wanganui, North Island, New Zealand	Tommy Williams

The above bouts are primarily, but not entirely, based upon www.boxrec.com

* Bare-knuckles were used

Other Selected Heavyweight Championships 1867-1991

Title	Date	Winner	Verdict	Rounds	Loser	Location	Referee
AM *	1867-05-10	Jimmy Elliott	DSQ	9	Bill Davis	Point Peelee Island, Ontario, Canada	
WORLD-AM *	1870-05-10	Jem Mace	W	10	Tom Allen	Kennerville, Louisiana, United States	Al Smith
WORLD-AM *	1871-05-11	Jem Mace	D	1	Joe Coburn	Port Ryerse [Port Dover], Ontario, Canada	Dick Hollywood
WORLD-AM *	1871-11-30	Jem Mace	D	12	Joe Coburn	Bay St. Louis, Mississippi, United States	Rufus Hunt
AM *	1879-05-09	John J. Dwyer	W	12	Jimmy Elliott	Long Point, Ontario, Canada	Al Smith
WORLD-AM	1885-08-29	John L. Sullivan	DSQ	7	Dominick McCaffrey	Cincinnati, Ohio, United States	Billy Tait
FOX-PG *	1887-12-19	Jake Kilrain	D	106	Jem Smith	Isle des Souverains, Seine Maritime, France	George Atkinson
WORLD *	1888-03-10	John L. Sullivan	D	39	Charlie Mitchell	Chantilly, Oise, France	Bernard J. Angle
FOX-PG-AM *	1889-07-08	John L. Sullivan	RTD	75	Jake Kilrain	Richburg, Mississippi, United States	John Fitzpatrick
FOX-PG	1890-09-27	Frank "Paddy" Slavin	RTD	2	Joe McAuliffe	London, England, United Kingdom	Bernard J. Angle/ George Vize
FOX-PG	1891-06-16	Frank "Paddy" Slavin	W	9	Jake Kilrain	Hoboken, New Jersey, United States	Jere Dunn
AUS-BRIT-ENG-FOX-PG	1892-05-30	Peter Jackson	TKO	10	Frank "Paddy" Slavin	London, England, United Kingdom	Bernard J. Angle
WORLD	1895-11-11	Peter Maher	KO	1	Steve O'Donnell	New York, New York, United States	Tim Hurst
WORLD	1896-02-21	Bob Fitzsimmons	KO	1	Peter Maher	In Coahuila, Mexico, near Langtry, Texas, United States	George Siler
SA-WORLD	1896-11-07	Joe Goddard	KO	4	"Denver" Ed Smith	Johannesburg, Transvaal [Gauteng], South Africa	Clem Webb
WORLD	1896-12-02	Tom Sharkey	DSQ	8	Bob Fitzsimmons	San Francisco, California, United States	Wyatt Earp
WORLD	1897-06-09	Tom Sharkey	D	7	Peter Maher	New York, New York, United States	Jimmy Colville
WORLD	1897-11-18	Tom Sharkey	TKO	6	Joe Goddard	San Francisco, California, United States	Bob McArthur
WORLD	1898-03-11	Tom Sharkey	D	7	Joe Choynski	San Francisco, California, United States	George Green
WORLD	1898-05-06	Jim Jeffries	W	20	Tom Sarkey	San Francisco, California, United States	Alec Greggains
WORLD	1898-05-20	Charles "Kid" McCoy	W	20	Gus Ruhlin	Syracuse, New York, United States	George Siler
WORLD	1898-11-22	Tom Sharkey	DSQ	9	Jim Corbett	New York, New York, United States	John Kelly
WORLD	1899-01-10	Tom Sharkey	KO	10	Charles "Kid" McCoy	New York, New York, United States	Tim Hurst
WORLD-USA	1905-07-03	Marvin Hart	KO	12	Jack Root	Reno, Nevada, United States	Jim Jeffries
WORLD	1905-10-27	"Philadelphia" Jack O'Brien	KO	17	Al Kaufman	San Francisco, California, United States	Jack Welch
WORLD	1905-12-20	"Philadelphia" Jack O'Brien	RTD	13	Bob Fitzsimmons	San Francisco, California, United States	Ed Graney
WORLD-USA	1906-02-23	Tommy Burns	W	20	Marvin Hart	Los Angeles, California, United States	Charles Eyton
WORLD-USA	1906-10-02	Tommy Burns	KO	15	"Fireman" Jim Flynn	Los Angeles, California, United States	Eddie Robinson
WORLD-USA	1906-11-28	Tommy Burns	D	20	"Philadelphia" Jack O'Brien	Los Angeles, California, United States	Jim Jeffries
WORLD	1907-04-15	Mike Schreck	KO	9	John Wille	Tonopah, Nevada, United States	Otto Floto
WORLD	1907-05-03	Mike Schreck	KO	13	Tony Ross	Dayton, Ohio, United States	
WORLD-USA	1907-05-08	Tommy Burns	W	20	"Philadelphia" Jack O'Brien	Los Angeles, California, United States	Charles Eyton
WORLD	1907-05-30	Mike Schreck	RTD	21	Marvin Hart	Tonopah, Nevada, United States	George Siler
WORLD-USA	1907-07-04	Tommy Burns	KO	1	Bill Squires	Colma, California, United States	Jim Jeffries
WORLD-USA	1909-05-19	Jack Johnson	ND	6	"Philadelphia" Jack O'Brien	Philadelphia, Pennsylvania, United States	Jack McGuigan

Queensberry Rules and gloves were used unless otherwise noted

* Bare-knuckles were used

AM - Heavyweight Championship of America

AUS - Claimed Heavyweight Championship of Australia

BBBC - Recognized by the British Boxing Board of Control

BRIT - Imperial British Empire Heavyweight Championship

C - Colored Heavyweight Championship

EBU - Recognized by the European Boxing Union

ENG - Claimed Heavyweight Championship of England

FBF - Recognized by the French Boxing Federation

FOX - Richard K. Fox Heavyweight Championship

GB - Recognized in Great Britain; Based upon www.boxrec.com/hugman

NBA - Recognized by the National Boxing Association; Based upon www.boxrec.com/hugman

NYSAC - Recognized by the New York State Athletic Commission; Based upon www.boxrec.com/hugman

PG - Police Gazette Heavyweight Championship

SA - Heavyweight Championship of South Africa

USA - Recognized in the United States

WBC - Some sources report this as a WBC title bout

WHITE - White Heavyweight Championship

WORLD - Claimed Heavyweight Championship of the World

Title	Date	Winner	Verdict	Rounds	Loser	Location	Referee
WORLD-USA	1909-06-30	Jack Johnson	ND	6	Tony Ross	Pittsburgh, Pennsylvania, United States	Jimmy Dime
WHITE	1913-01-01	Luther "Luck" McCarty	KO	18	Al Palzer	Vernon, California, United States	Charles Eyton
WHITE	1913-04-30	Luther "Luck" McCarty	ND	10	Frank Moran	New York, New York, United States	
WHITE	1913-05-24	Arthur Pelkey	KO	1	Luther "Luck" McCarty	Calgary, Alberta, Canada	Eddie Smith
NYSAC	1913-12-19	Jack Johnson	D	10	"Battling" Jim Johnson	Paris, Paris, France	Emile Maitrot
C-FBF	1913-12-20	Sam Langford	W	20	Joe Jeannette	Paris, Paris, France	Franz Reichel
WHITE	1914-01-01	Ed "Gunboat"Smith	KO	15	Arthur Pelkey	San Francisco, California, United States	Jim Griffin
FBF	1914-06-27	Jack Johnson	W	20	Frank Moran	Paris, Paris, France	Georges Carpentier
WHITE	1914-07-16	Georges Carpentier	DSQ	6	Ed "Gunboat"Smith	London, England, United Kingdom	Eugene Corri
NYSAC	1922-07-24	Jack Dempsey	W	4	Jimmy Darcy	Buffalo, New York, United States	
NBA	1931-07-03	Max Schmeling	TKO	15	W.L. "Young" Stribling	Cleveland, Ohio, United States	George Blake
GB-NBA-NYSAC	1935-06-13	Jim Braddock	W	15	Max Baer	New York, New York, United States	Johnny McAvoy
GB-NBA-NYSAC	1937-06-22	Joe Louis	KO	8	Jim Braddock	Chicago, Illinois, United States	Tommy Thomas
GB-NBA-NYSAC	1937-08-30	Joe Louis	W	15	Tommy Farr	New York, New York, United States	Arthur Donovan
GB-NBA-NYSAC	1938-02-23	Joe Louis	KO	3	Nathan Mann	New York, New York, United States	Arthur Donovan
GB-NBA-NYSAC	1938-04-01	Joe Louis	KO	5	Harry Thomas	Chicago, Illinois, United States	Davey Miller
NYSAC	1944-11-14	Joe Louis	KO	1	Johnny Davis	Buffalo, New York, United States	Billy Cavanaugh
NBA	1949-06-22	Ezzard Charles	W	15	"Jersey" Joe Walcott	Chicago, Illinois, United States	Davey Miller
NBA	1949-08-10	Ezzard Charles	RTD	7	Gus Lesnevich	New York, New York, United States	Ruby Goldstein
NBA	1949-10-14	Ezzard Charles	KO	8	Pat Valentino	San Francisco, California, United States	Jack Downey
GB-EBU	1950-06-06	Lee Savold	TKO	4	Bruce Woodcock	London, England, United Kingdom	Andrew Smythe
NBA	1950-08-15	Ezzard Charles	TKO	14	Freddie Beshore	Buffalo, New York, United States	Barney Felix
NBA-NYSAC	1950-09-27	Ezzard Charles	W	15	Joe Louis	New York, New York, United States	Mark Conn
NBA-NYSAC	1950-12-05	Ezzard Charles	KO	11	Nick Barone	Cincinnati, Ohio, United States	Tony Warndorf
NBA-NYSAC	1951-01-12	Ezzard Charles	TKO	10	Lee Oma	New York, New York, United States	Ruby Goldstein
NBA-NYSAC	1951-03-07	Ezzard Charles	W	15	"Jersey" Joe Walcott	Detroit, Michigan, United States	Clarence Rosen
NBA-NYSAC	1951-05-30	Ezzard Charles	W	15	Joey Maxim	Chicago, Illinois, United States	Frank Gilmer
BBBC	1951-06-15	Joe Louis	KO	6	Lee Savold	New York, New York, United States	Ruby Goldstein
NBA-NYSAC	1951-07-18	"Jersey" Joe Walcott	KO	7	Ezzard Charles	Pittsburgh, Pennsylvania, United States	Buck McTiernan
NYSAC	1968-03-04	Joe Frazier	TKO	11	Buster Mathis	New York, New York, United States	Arthur Mercante
NYSAC	1968-06-24	Joe Frazier	TKO	2	Manuel Ramos	New York, New York, United States	Arthur Mercante
NYSAC	1968-12-10	Joe Frazier	W	15	Oscar "Ringo" Bonavena	Philadelphia, Pennsylvania, United States	Joe Sweeney
NYSAC	1969-04-22	Joe Frazier	KO	1	Dave Zyglewicz	Houston, Texas, United States	Jimmy Webb
NYSAC	1969-06-23	Joe Frazier	TKO	7	Jerry Quarry	New York, New York, United States	Arthur Mercante
WBC	1983-11-25	Larry Holmes	TKO	1	Marvis Frazier	Las Vegas, Nevada, United States	Mills Lane
WBC	1991-11-23	Evander Holyfield	TKO	7	Bert Cooper	Atlanta, Georgia, United States	Mills Lane

Queensberry Rules and gloves were used unless otherwise noted

* Bare-knuckles were used

AM - Heavyweight Championship of America

AUS - Claimed Heavyweight Championship of Australia

BBBC - Recognized by the British Boxing Board of Control

BRIT - Imperial British Empire Heavyweight Championship

C - Colored Heavyweight Championship

EBU - Recognized by the European Boxing Union

ENG - Claimed Heavyweight Championship of England

FBF - Recognized by the French Boxing Federation

FOX - Richard K. Fox Heavyweight Championship

GB - Recognized in Great Britain; Based upon www.boxrec.com/hugman

NBA - Recognized by the National Boxing Association; Based upon www.boxrec.com/hugman

NYSAC - Recognized by the New York State Athletic Commission; Based upon www.boxrec.com/hugman

PG - Police Gazette Heavyweight Championship

SA - Heavyweight Championship of South Africa

USA - Recognized in the United States

WBC - Some sources report this as a WBC title bout

WHITE - White Heavyweight Championship

WORLD - Claimed Heavyweight Championship of the World

Colored Heavyweight Championship 1876-1935

Date	Winner	Verdict	Rounds	Loser	Location	Referee
1876-1878	Charles Smith was the recognized colored champion					
1878-1881	Morris Grant claimed the colored championship					
1881-01-14	Reportedly, Charles Hadley defeated Morris Grant to claim the colored championship					
1882-04-06	Charles Hadley	KO	2	Morris Grant	New York, New York, United States	
1882-12-07	Charles Hadley	RTD	3	Morris Grant	New York, New York, United States	Harry Hill
1883-01-25	Charles Hadley	TKO	3	Harry Woodson (Black Diamond)	New York, New York, United States	
1883-02-23 *	George Godfrey	TKO	6	Charles Hadley	Boston, Massachusetts, United States	John L. Sullivan
1884-05-10 *	George Godfrey	D	6	McHenry Johnson	Boston, Massachusetts, United States	
1884-06-28 *	McHenry Johnson	D	2	Billy Wilson	New York, New York, United States	
1886-12-02	McHenry Johnson	D	10	Billy Wilson	St. Paul, Minnesota, United States	Michael Roche
1888-01-25	McHenry Johnson	DSQ	4	George Godfrey	Boulder County, Colorado, United States	Dick Williams
1888-08-24	Peter Jackson	RTD	19	George Godfrey	San Francisco, California, United States	Hiram Cook
1889-07-25 *	Peter Jackson	TKO	3	George Peters	Detroit, Michigan, United States	
1896-12-21	Bob Armstrong	KO	19	Charley Strong	New York, New York, United States	
1897-03-06	Bob Armstrong	TKO	6	Joe Butler	New York, New York, United States	Dick Roche
1897-04-23	Bob Armstrong	RTD	1	Sam Pruitt	San Francisco, California, United States	Hiram Cook
1897-09-13 *	Bob Armstrong	RTD	2	Jack Douglass	Chicago, Illinois, United States	
1898-01-29	Frank Childs	RTD	2	Bob Armstrong	Chicago, Illinois, United States	George Siler
1898-02-07 *	Frank Childs	W	6	George Grant	Chicago, Illinois, United States	
1898-02-26 *	Frank Childs	DSQ	3	John "Klondike" Haines	Chicago, Illinois, United States	
1898-06-03 *	Frank Childs	D	6	Charley Strong	Chicago, Illinois, United States	Malachy Hogan
1898-09-14	George Byers	W	20	Frank Childs	New York, New York, United States	Charlie White
1898-11-08 *	Frank Childs	W	6	Charley Strong	Chicago, Illinois, United States	
1899-01-21 *	Frank Childs	DSQ	2	Joe Butler	Chicago, Illinois, United States	
1899-03-04	Frank Childs	RTD	6	Bob Armstrong	Cincinnati, Ohio, United States	Johnny Murphy
1899-05-06 *	John "Klondike" Haines	KO	5	Jack Johnson	Chicago, Illinois, United States	Malachy Hogan
1899-05-12 *	John "Klondike" Haines	W	6	George Grant	Chicago, Illinois, United States	
1899-05-27 *	John "Klondike" Haines	TKO	2	"Scaldy" Bill Quinn	Chicago, Illinois, United States	
1899-07-24	George Byers	TKO	9	Charley Strong	New York, New York, United States	
1899-08-11 *	Frank Childs	W	6	John "Klondike" Haines	Chicago, Illinois, United States	
1899-10-28 *	Frank Childs	KO	3	John "Klondike" Haines	Chicago, Illinois, United States	Joe Choynski
1900-03-16 *	Frank Childs	D	6	George Byers	Chicago, Illinois, United States	
1900-12-15	Frank Childs	KO	4	Joe Butler	Chicago, Illinois, United States	George Siler
1901-03-16	Frank Childs	KO	17	George Byers	Hot Springs, Arkansas, United States	Bat Masterson
1902-01-18 *	Frank Childs	W	6	Walter Johnson	Chicago, Illinois, United States	
1902-02-24 *	"Denver" Ed Martin	W	6	Frank Childs	Chicago, Illinois, United States	
1902-07-25	"Denver" Ed Martin	W	15	Bob Armstrong	London, England, United Kingdom	Tom Scott
1902-08-16	"Denver" Ed Martin	RTD	3	Frank Craig	Newcastle, England, United Kingdom	Sam Francis
1902-08-30	"Denver" Ed Martin	KO	4	Frank Craig	Newcastle, England, United Kingdom	Sam Francis
1902-10-09	Frank Childs	NC	3	Joe Walcott	Chicago, Illinois, United States	
1902-10-21	Jack Johnson	RTD	12	Frank Childs	Los Angeles, California, United States	John Brink
1902-12-10 *	"Denver" Ed Martin	ND	6	Bob Armstrong	Philadelphia, Pennsylvania, United States	
1903-02-05	Jack Johnson	W	20	"Denver" Ed Martin	Los Angeles, California, United States	Harry Stuart
1903-02-26	Jack Johnson	W	20	Sam McVea	Los Angeles, California, United States	
1903-05-11 *	Jack Johnson	KO	3	Joe Butler	Philadelphia, Pennsylvania, United States	William Rocap
1903-10-27	Jack Johnson	W	20	Sam McVea	Los Angeles, California, United States	Charles Eyton
1904-02-15 *	Jack Johnson	ND	6	Black Bill (Claude Brooks)	Philadelphia, Pennsylvania, United States	
1904-04-22	Jack Johnson	KO	20	Sam McVea	San Francisco, California, United States	Eddie Graney
1904-06-02 *	Jack Johnson	W	6	Frank Childs	Chicago, Illinois, United States	
1904-10-18	Jack Johnson	KO	2	"Denver" Ed Martin	Los Angeles, California, United States	
1905-05-02 *	Jack Johnson	KO	4	Black Bill (Claude Brooks)	Philadelphia, Pennsylvania, United States	

The above bouts are primarily, but not entirely, based upon www.boxrec.com/hugman

* Scheduled for less than ten rounds

! Both bouts held the same date

Both bouts held the same date

& Also recognized as the French Boxing Federation (FBF) Heavyweight Championship

Date	Winner	Verdict	Rounds	Loser	Location	Referee
1905-05-09 * !	Jack Johnson	ND	3	Joe Jeannette	Philadelphia, Pennsylvania, United States	
1905-05-09 * !	Jack Johnson	KO	3	Walter Johnson	Philadelphia, Pennsylvania, United States	
1905-07-13 * #	Jack Johnson	KO	1	Morris Harris	Philadelphia, Pennsylvania, United States	
1905-07-13 * #	Jack Johnson	ND	3	Black Bill (Claude Brooks)	Philadelphia, Pennsylvania, United States	
1905-11-25 *	Joe Jeannette	DSQ	2	Jack Johnson	Philadelphia, Pennsylvania, United States	
1905-12-01	Jack Johnson	D	12	"Young" Peter Jackson	Baltimore, Maryland, United States	
1905-12-02 *	Jack Johnson	ND	6	Joe Jeannette	Philadelphia, Pennsylvania, United States	
1906-01-16 *	Jack Johnson	ND	3	Joe Jeannette	New York, New York, United States	
1906-03-14	Jack Johnson	W	15	Joe Jeannette	Baltimore, Maryland, United States	Fred Sweigert
1906-04-16	Jack Johnson	KO	6	Black Bill (Claude Brooks)	Wilkes-Barre, Pennsylvania, United States	Buck Kelly
1906-04-26	Jack Johnson	W	15	Sam Langford	Chelsea, Massachusetts, United States	Martin Flaherty
1906-09-20 *	Jack Johnson	ND	6	Joe Jeannette	Philadelphia, Pennsylvania, United States	
1906-11-26	Jack Johnson	D	10	Joe Jeannette	Portland, Maine, United States	Martin Sullivan
1907-02-19	Jack Johnson	KO	1	Peter Felix	Sydney, New South Wales, Australia	Beckett
1909-02-20	Sam McVea	W	20	Joe Jeannette	Paris, Paris, France	
1909-04-09	Sam McVea	KO	2	Billy Warren	Paris, Paris, France	
1909-04-17	Joe Jeannette	RTD	49	Sam McVea	Paris, Paris, France	
1909-07-13 *	Sam Langford	ND	6	John "Klondike" Haines	Pittsburgh, Pennsylvania, United States	
1909-09-28	Sam Langford	RTD	5	Dixie Kid (Aaron Brown)	Boston, Massachusetts, United States	
1909-11-02	Sam Langford	KO	2	John "Klondike" Haines	Boston, Massachusetts, United States	Fleming
1909-12-11	Joe Jeannette	D	30	Sam McVea	Paris, Paris, France	
1910-01-10 *	Sam Langford	KO	3	Dixie Kid (Aaron Brown)	Memphis, Tennessee, United States	
1910-05-14 *	Sam Langford	ND	6	"Battling" Jim Johnson	Philadelphia, Pennsylvania, United States	
1910-07-01	Joe Jeannette	ND	10	Morris Harris	New York, New York, United States	
1910-09-06	Sam Langford	W	15	Joe Jeannette	Boston, Massachusetts, United States	Charlie White
1910-11-10	Sam Langford	TKO	2	Jeff Clark	Joplin, Missouri, United States	
1910-12-06	Sam Langford	KO	2	Morris Harris	Boston, Massachusetts, United States	
1911-01-10	Sam Langford	W	12	Joe Jeannette	Boston, Massachusetts, United States	Charlie White
1911-01-16	Sam Langford	TKO	3	Fred Atwater	Utica, New York, United States	
1911-04-01	Sam Langford	D	20	Sam McVea	Paris, Paris, France	Eugene Corri
1911-05-30	Sam Langford	TKO	4	Ralph Calloway	Syracuse, New York, United States	Jack Lewis
1911-09-05	Sam Langford	ND	10	Joe Jeannette	New York, New York, United States	
1911-12-26	Sam McVea	W	20	Sam Langford	Sydney, New South Wales, Australia	Snowy Baker
1912-04-08	Sam Langford	W	20	Sam McVea	Sydney, New South Wales, Australia	Arthur Scott
1912-08-03	Sam Langford	W	20	Sam McVea	Sydney, New South Wales, Australia	
1912-10-09	Sam Langford	TKO	11	Sam McVea	Perth, Western Australia, Australia	
1912-12-26	Sam Langford	KO	13	Sam McVea	Sydney, New South Wales, Australia	Arthur Scott
1913-03-24	Sam Langford	D	20	Sam McVea	Brisbane, Queensland, Australia	Frank Craig
1913-09-09	Sam Langford	KO	1	John Lester Johnson	New York, New York, United States	
1913-10-03	Sam Langford	ND	10	Joe Jeannette	New York, New York, United States	Billy Joh
1913-12-20 &	Sam Langford	W	20	Joe Jeannette	Paris, Paris, France	Franz Reichel
1914-03-23	Sam Langford	TKO	1	Bill Watkins	New York, New York, United States	Patsy Haley
1914-03-27	Sam Langford	ND	10	"Battling" Jim Johnson	New York, New York, United States	
1914-04-15 *	Sam Langford	W	8	George "Kid" Cotton	Chattanooga, Tennessee, United States	
1914-04-20 *	Sam Langford	TKO	5	"Rough House" Ware	Memphis, Tennessee, United States	Billy Haack
1914-05-01	Sam Langford	ND	10	Harry Wills	New Orleans, Louisiana, United States	Buddy Griffin
1914-05-25	Sam Langford	KO	4	Bill Watkins	Rochester, New York, United States	Harry Pollock
1914-06-09	Harry Wills	ND	10	Joe Jeannette	New Orleans, Louisiana, United States	Buddy Griffin
1914-08-12	Sam Langford	ND	10	"Battling" Jim Johnson	New York, New York, United States	
1914-08-25	Sam Langford	KO	4	George "Kid" Cotton	Boston, Massachusetts, United States	Jack Sheehan
1914-09-15	Sam Langford	D	12	"Battling" Jim Johnson	Boston, Massachusetts, United States	George Tuohey

The above bouts are primarily, but not entirely, based upon www.boxrec.com/hugman

* Scheduled for less than ten rounds

! Both bouts held the same date

Both bouts held the same date

& Also recognized as the French Boxing Federation (FBF) Heavyweight Championship

Date	Winner	Verdict	Rounds	Loser	Location	Referee
1914-10-01	Sam Langford	ND	10	Joe Jeannette	New York, New York, United States	
1914-10-26	Sam Langford	ND	10	Jeff Clark	Joplin, Missouri, United States	
1914-10-30 *	Harry Wills	W	4	Jim Cameron	San Francisco, California, United States	
1914-11-16 *	Sam Langford	RTD	6	Jim Cameron	San Diego, California, United States	
1914-11-26	Sam Langford	KO	14	Harry Wills	Vernon, California, United States	George Blake
1915-04-06	Sam Langford	ND	10	"Battling" Jim Johnson	New York, New York, United States	
1915-04-13	Joe Jeannette	W	12	Sam Langford	Boston, Massachusetts, United States	Jack McGuigan
1915-04-19	Joe Jeannette	KO	4	"Battling" Jack Brooks	New York, New York, United States	
1915-04-27	Joe Jeannette	D	12	Sam McVea	Boston, Massachusetts, United States	
1915-05-10	Joe Jeannette	ND	10	"Battling" Jim Johnson	Montreal, Quebec, Canada	
1915-05-19	Sam McVea	ND	10	Harry Wills	New York, New York, United States	
1915-06-09	Sam McVea	ND	10	"Battling" Jim Johnson	Montreal, Quebec, Canada	
1915-06-29	Sam McVea	W	12	Sam Langford	Boston, Massachusetts, United States	
1915-07-02	Joe Jeannette	ND	10	Bill Watkins	New York, New York, United States	
1915-09-07	Harry Wills	W	12	Sam McVea	Boston, Massachusetts, United States	
1915-12-03	Harry Wills	ND	10	Sam Langford	New York, New York, United States	
1916-01-03	Harry Wills	W	20	Sam Langford	New Orleans, Louisiana, United States	Tommy Burns
1916-02-11	Sam Langford	KO	19	Harry Wills	New Orleans, Louisiana, United States	Sammy Goldman
1916-02-17	Sam Langford	ND	10	Sam McVea	New York, New York, United States	
1916-02-25	Joe Jeannette	KO	6	Silas Green	Montreal, Quebec, Canada	
1916-02-28	Sam Langford	ND	10	Cleve Hawkins	New York, New York, United States	
1916-03-07	Sam Langford	ND	10	Harry Wills	New York, New York, United States	
1916-03-23	Sam Langford	TKO	2	Dave Mills	Syracuse, New York, United States	Tom Cawley
1916-03-24	Joe Jeannette	KO	2	George "Kid" Cotton	New York, New York, United States	
1916-03-31	Sam Langford	TKO	5	Jeff Clark	St. Louis, Missouri, United States	
1916-04-07	Sam Langford	ND	10	Sam McVea	Syracuse, New York, United States	
1916-04-25 *	Sam Langford	ND	8	Harry Wills	St. Louis, Missouri, United States	
1916-05-02	Sam Langford	ND	12	Sam McVea	Akron, Ohio, United States	
1916-05-12	Sam Langford	KO	7	Joe Jeannette	Syracuse, New York, United States	Tom Cawley
1916-08-12	Sam Langford	D	20	Sam McVea	Avellaneda, Buenos Aires Province, Argentina	
1916-11-30	Sam Langford	ND	10	"Big" Bill Tate	Syracuse, New York, United States	
1916-12-12	Sam Langford	KO	12	"Battling" Jim Johnson	St. Louis, Missouri, United States	
1917-01-01	Sam Langford	W	12	"Battling" Jim Johnson	Kansas City, Missouri, United States	
1917-01-25	"Big" Bill Tate	W	12	Sam Langford	Kansas City, Missouri, United States	
1917-05-01	Sam Langford	KO	5	"Big" Bill Tate	St. Louis, Missouri, United States	
1917-05-11 *	Sam Langford	ND	6	Harry Wills	Philadelphia, Pennsylvania, United States	
1917-09-14	Sam Langford	ND	12	Joe Jeannette	Toledo, Ohio, United States	
1917-09-17	Sam Langford	KO	2	Andrew Johnson	Ardmore, Maryland, United States	
1917-09-20	Sam Langford	ND	10	Harry Wills	New York, New York, United States	
1917-11-12	Sam Langford	ND	12	Harry Wills	Toledo, Ohio, United States	Ollie Pecord
1917-12-17	Sam Langford	KO	2	Kid Norfolk	Denver, Colorado, United States	
1918-04-14	Harry Wills	KO	6	Sam Langford	Panama City, Panama Province, Panama	
1918-05-19	Harry Wills	TKO	7	Sam Langford	Panama City, Panama Province, Panama	
1918-06-16	Harry Wills	W	20	Sam McVea	Panama City, Panama Province, Panama	
1918-08-19 *	Harry Wills	TKO	5	Jeff Clark	Atlantic City, New Jersey, United States	
1918-09-14 *	Harry Wills	ND	6	Jack Thompson	Philadelphia, Pennsylvania, United States	
1918-11-15 *	Harry Wills	ND	8	Jack Thompson	Atlantic City, New Jersey, United States	
1919-06-10 *	Harry Wills	ND	8	John Lester Johnson	Jersey City, New Jersey, United States	
1919-07-04 *	Harry Wills	ND	8	Sam Langford	St. Louis, Missouri, United States	
1919-08-18	Harry Wills	TKO	4	Jeff Clark	Syracuse, New York, United States	

The above bouts are primarily, but not entirely, based upon www.boxrec.com/hugman

* Scheduled for less than ten rounds

! Both bouts held the same date

Both bouts held the same date

& Also recognized as the French Boxing Federation (FBF) Heavyweight Championship

Date	Winner	Verdict	Rounds	Loser	Location	Referee
1919-09-30	Harry Wills	ND	10	Sam Langford	Syracuse, New York, United States	
1919-10-20 *	Harry Wills	ND	8	Joe Jeannette	Jersey City, New Jersey, United States	
1919-10-21	Sam Langford	D	15	Jack Thompson	Tulsa, Oklahoma, United States	
1919-11-05	Harry Wills	W	15	Sam Langford	Tulsa, Oklahoma, United States	Edward Cochrane
1920-01-01 *	Harry Wills	NC	3	Jack Thompson	San Francisco, California, United States	
1920-01-12	Harry Wills	W	15	Jack Thompson	Tulsa, Oklahoma, United States	
1920-03-17	Harry Wills	KO	1	Andrew Johnson	St. Paul, Minnesota, United States	
1920-04-23	Harry Wills	W	15	Sam Langford	Denver, Colorado, United States	
1920-06-01 *	Harry Wills	TKO	1	Ray Bennett	Bridgeport, Connecticut, United States	
1920-09-08 *	Harry Wills	NC	6	Sam McVea	Philadelphia, Pennsylvania, United States	
1920-09-15	Harry Wills	TKO	4	Jeff Clark	Atlanta, Georgia, United States	
1921-01-17	Harry Wills	KO	2	"Big" Bill Tate	Buffalo, New York, United States	
1921-02-11	Harry Wills	TKO	2	Jeff Clark	Baltimore, Maryland, United States	
1921-04-08 *	Harry Wills	ND	8	Jack Thompson	St. Louis, Missouri, United States	
1921-05-27	Harry Wills	KO	1	Andrew Johnson	New York, New York, United States	
1921-06-03	Harry Wills	KO	7	Jim McCreary	Syracuse, New York, United States	Tommy Connolly
1921-06-04	Harry Wills	KO	1	Ray Bennett	New York, New York, United States	
1921-07-02	Harry Wills	TKO	6	"Big" Bill Tate	New York, New York, United States	
1921-11-18	Harry Wills	KO	1	"Denver" Ed Martin	Milwaukie, Oregon, United States	
1921-11-30	Harry Wills	ND	5	Jack Thompson	Denver, Colorado, United States	
1921-12-08	Harry Wills	W	12	"Big" Bill Tate	Denver, Colorado, United States	
1922-01-02	"Big" Bill Tate	DSQ	1	Harry Wills	Milwaukie, Oregon, United States	Tom Louttit
1922-01-06	Harry Wills	D	10	"Big" Bill Tate	Milwaukie, Oregon, United States	
1922-01-17	Harry Wills	W	10	Sam Langford	Milwaukie, Oregon, United States	
1922-02-06 *	"Big" Bill Tate	KO	2	"Battling" Owens	Memphis, Tennessee, United States	
1922-03-02	Harry Wills	KO	2	Kid Norfolk	New York, New York, United States	Billy McPartland
1922-03-20	"Big" Bill Tate	TKO	2	"Rough House" Ware	Columbus, Ohio, United States	
1922-03-27 *	"Big" Bill Tate	ND	8	Sam Langford	Memphis, Tennessee, United States	
1922-06-17	"Big" Bill Tate	KO	1	Boston Bearcat	Porter, Indiana, United States	
1922-06-21	Jack Thompson	W	15	"Big" Bill Tate	New Orleans, Louisiana, United States	
1922-06-30	Harry Wills	RTD	2	Jeff Clark	Trenton, New Jersey, United States	
1922-07-17	Harry Wills	KO	3	Jeff Clark	Winnipeg, Manitoba, Canada	Mike McNulty
1922-08-21	Harry Wills	KO	2	Buddy Jackson	Newark, New Jersey, United States	Harry McCoy
1922-08-29	Harry Wills	KO	3	James "Tut" Jackson	New York, New York, United States	
1922-09-29	Harry Wills	TKO	12	Clem Johnson	New York, New York, United States	
1923-11-05	Harry Wills	TKO	4	Jack Thompson	Newark, New Jersey, United States	Hank Lewis
1926-11-08	George Godfrey	TKO	6	Larry Gains	Buffalo, New York, United States	
1926-11-23	George Godfrey	NC	10	Ed "Bearcat" Wright	Portland, Oregon, United States	Ralph Gruman
1926-12-03 *	George Godfrey	TKO	8	"Cowboy" Billy Owens	Chicago, Illinois, United States	
1927-04-18	George Godfrey	KO	4	Leon "Bombo" Chevalier	Los Angeles, California, United States	
1927-05-13	George Godfrey	KO	7	"Long" Tom Hawkins	San Diego, California, United States	
1927-06-23	George Godfrey	W	10	Jake Kilrain	Culver City, California, United States	
1927-07-05	George Godfrey	KO	7	Neil Clisby	Los Angeles, California, United States	
1927-11-21 *	George Godfrey	KO	1	Clem Johnson	Atlantic City, New Jersey, United States	
1927-11-22 *	George Godfrey	W	4	Jack Townsend	New York, New York, United States	
1928-08-15	Larry Gains	DSQ	3	George Godfrey	Toronto, Ontario, Canada	Alex Sinclair
1928-12-20	Larry Gains	ND	10	Cecil "Seal" Harris	Indianapolis, Indiana, United States	
1929-04-02	Bob Lawson	W	10	Al Walker	Atlanta, Georgia, United States	Jack Denham
1929-05-07	Cecil "Seal" Harris	W	10	Neil Clisby	Los Angeles, California, United States	Frank Holborow
1929-05-17	Cecil "Seal" Harris	D	10	"Long" Tom Hawkins	San Diego, California, United States	Billy McMahon
1929-06-07	Bob Lawson	DSQ	4	Al Walker	Atlanta, Georgia, United States	Cy "Kid" Young

The above bouts are primarily, but not entirely, based upon www.boxrec.com/hugman

* Scheduled for less than ten rounds

! Both bouts held the same date

Both bouts held the same date

& Also recognized as the French Boxing Federation (FBF) Heavyweight Championship

Date	Winner	Verdict	Rounds	Loser	Location	Referee
1929-06-21	"Long" Tom Hawkins	TKO	7	Cecil "Seal" Harris	San Diego, California, United States	
1929-07-19	"Long" Tom Hawkins	KO	1	Cecil "Seal" Harris	San Francisco, California, United States	
1929-08-13	"Long" Tom Hawkins	DSQ	3	George Godfrey	Los Angeles, California, United States	Larry McGrath
1929-10-01	"Long" Tom Hawkins	W	10	Al Walker	Los Angeles, California, United States	Harry Lee
1929-10-25	Ed "Bearcat" Wright	TKO	9	"Long" Tom Hawkins	San Francisco, California, United States	
1929-11-12	Ed "Bearcat" Wright	KO	2	"Cowboy" Billy Owens	Des Moines, Iowa, United States	
1929-12-23	George Godfrey	KO	3	Leonard Dixon	Roanoke, Virginia, United States	
1930-01-10	Ed "Bearcat" Wright	W	10	"Long" Tom Hawkins	San Diego, California, United States	William Lovejoy
1930-03-24	George Godfrey	KO	7	Roy "Ace" Clark	Philadelphia, Pennsylvania, United States	
1930-05-16	George Godfrey	TKO	1	Jack Rozier	Baltimore, Maryland, United States	
1930-06-17	Al Walker	W	10	Ed "Bearcat" Wright	Atlanta, Georgia, United States	
1930-06-23 *	Al Walker	W	6	Leonard Dixon	Philadelphia, Pennsylvania, United States	
1930-08-20	George Godfrey	TKO	1	Elijah Lee	Indianapolis, Indiana, United States	
1930-09-05	Al Walker	NC	6	Carl Carter	East Hartford, Connecticut, United States	
1930-11-07	George Godfrey	KO	4	Cecil "Seal" Harris	Lansing, Michigan, United States	
1930-12-08	George Godfrey	KO	3	Cecil "Seal" Harris	Milwaukee, Wisconsin, United States	
1930-12-19	George Godfrey	D	10	Ed "Bearcat" Wright	Atlanta, Georgia, United States	
1931-08-24	George Godfrey	KO	2	Cecil "Seal" Harris	Toronto, Ontario, Canada	
1932-09-05	George Godfrey	KO	5	Roy "Ace" Clark	Nuevo Laredo, Tamaulipas, Mexico	Fred Maly
1933-01-31	George Godfrey	W	10	"Tiger" Jack Fox	Indianapolis, Indiana, United States	
1933-02-10	George Godfrey	NC	6	Ed "Bearcat" Wright	Kansas City, Missouri, United States	Walter Bates
1933-10-09	Obie Walker	W	10	George Godfrey	Philadelphia, Pennsylvania, United States	
1935-07-20	Larry Gains	W	15	Obie Walker	Leicester, England, United Kingdom	

The above bouts are primarily, but not entirely, based upon www.boxrec.com/hugman

* Scheduled for less than ten rounds

! Both bouts held the same date

Both bouts held the same date

& Also recognized as the French Boxing Federation (FBF) Heavyweight Championship

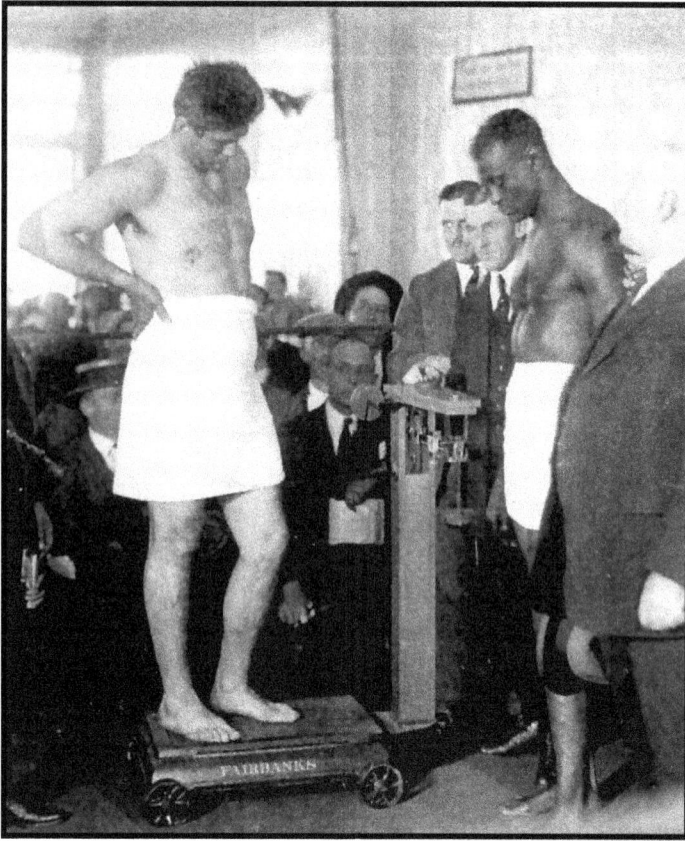

Luis Angel Firpo-Harry Wills weigh in
September 1924

Bud Gorman, Gene Tunney, Bill Vidabeck and Harold Mays
1926

ABOUT THE AUTHOR

Tracy Callis has been researching boxing history and the records of boxers for 47 years and has produced rare, updated records for many boxers. He possesses an outstanding knowledge of boxing history and has a strong interest in boxers of all weight classes from every historical period.

Callis is the **Director of Historical Research** for **The Cyber Boxing Zone (www.cyberboxingzone.com)** internet website, an elector to the **International Boxing Hall of Fame** and a member of the **Advisory Board of the Boxing Hall of Fame - Luxor Hotel Las Vegas.** He is also a member of the **International Boxing Research Organization (IBRO).**

In the past, he was a contributing editor to **The Ring Record Book** for a number of years, a contributor to the **British Boxing Board of Control Yearbook** and a member of the **World Boxing Historians Association (WBHA).** In 2002, Tracy co-authored the book, **Philadelphia's Boxing Heritage 1876-1976**, was a historical consultant on the Jim Jeffries book by Kelly Nicholson, **A Man Among Men**, in 2003 and co-authored the book, **Boxing in the Los Angeles Area 1880-2005** in 2007. In 2008, he was a historical consultant on the Fox Sports presentation **Amazing Sports Stories: Billy Miske: Dead Man Fighting** and in 2009 was a consultant on the Jim Jeffries book by Jim Carney Jr., **Ultimate Tough Guy**. In 2010, Tracy consulted with Adam Pollack on his book, **In the Ring With Marvin Hart**, Kelly Nicholson on his book, **Hitters, Dancers and Ring Magicians** and with Greg Lewis and Moira Sharkey on their book, **I Fought Them All**, about Tom Sharkey. In 2011, Tracy again consulted with Adam Pollack on his book, **In the Ring With Tommy Burns** and also with Clay Moyle on his book, **Billy Miske: The St. Paul Thunderbolt.**

Tracy Callis

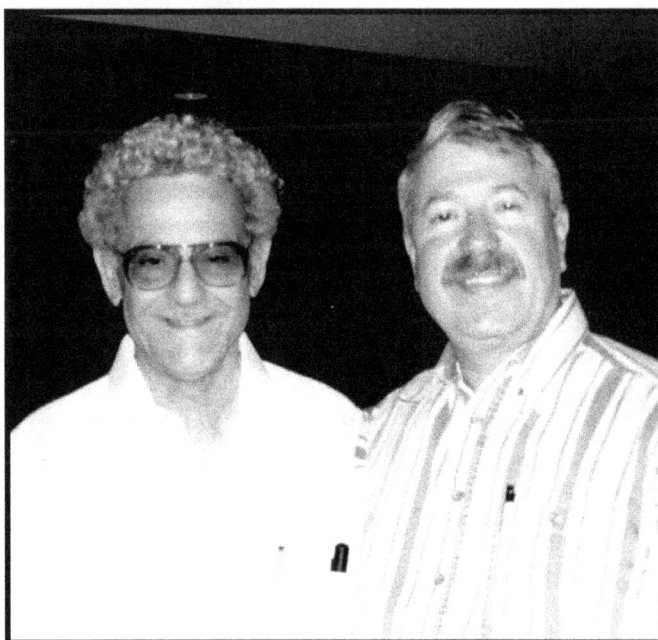

Ralph Citro (left), former Director of IBRO
Dan Cuoco (right), current Director of IBRO

Muhammad Ali and Joe Louis

Ron Lyle, Dan Cuoco (Director of IBRO) and Earnie Shavers

BIBLIOGRAPHY

Ali, M. and Durham, R. 1975. The Greatest - My Own Story (Muhammad Ali). New York: Random House Publishers

Arnold, P. 1989. The Illustrated Encyclopedia pf World Boxing. New York: W.H. Smith, Publishers Inc.

Astor, G. 1974. "… And a Credit to His Race" (Joe Louis). New York: Saturday Review Press/E.P. Dutton and Company, Inc.

Atyeo, D. and Dennis, F. 1975. The Holy Warrior - Muhammad Ali. New York: Simon and Schuster

Bromberg, L. 1958. World's Champs. Retail Distributors, Inc.

Brooke-Ball, P. 1992. The Boxing Album: An Illustrated History. London: Anness Publishing Limited

Bunce, S. and Mee, B. 1998. Boxing Greats. Philadelphia: Courage Books

Burrill, B. 1974. Who's Who in Boxing. New Rochelle, New York: Arlington House

Cannon, J. 1978. Nobody Asked Me, But … (The World of Jimmy Cannon). New York: Holt, Rinehart, and Winston (Edited by Jack Cannon and Tom Cannon)

Carney, J. Jr. 2009. Ultimate Tough Guy: The Life and Times of James J. Jeffries. Westlake, Ohio: Achill Publishing

Carpenter, H. 1975. Boxing: A Pictorial History. Chicago: Henry Regnery Company

Cooper, H. 1978. The Great Heavyweights. Secaucus, New Jersey: Chartwell Books, Inc.

Corbett, J. J. 1926. The Roar of the Crowd (James J. Corbett). New York: Garden City Publishing Company

Cosell, H. 1973. Cosell. Chicago: The Playboy Press

Diamond, W. 1954. Kings of the Ring. London: The World's Work (1913) Ltd.

Durant, J. 1976. The Heavyweight Champions. New York: Hastings House Publishers

Durant, J. 1977. Private Correspondence

Durant, J. and Bettman, O. 1952. Pictorial History of American Sports. Cranbury, New Jersey: A.S. Barnes and Co.

Durant, J. and Rice, E. 1946. Come Out Fighting. Cincinnati: Zebra Picture Books

Edgren, R. 1926. The Big Fellow (Jim Jeffries - contained in Liberty magazine for seven weekly issues from July 31 to September 11, 1926)

English, A. 2008. Ringside at Richburg. Baltimore, Maryland: Gateway Press, Inc.

Farhood, S. 1999. www.hbo.com/boxing/columnsfeatures/farhood/ (no longer exists)

Farnol. J. 1928. Famous Prize Fights. Boston: Little, Brown, and Company

Farr, F. 1964. Black Champion (The Life and Times of Jack Johnson). New York: Charles Scribner's Sons

Fleischer, N. 1938. Black Dynamite (Volume I). New York: C. J. O'Brien, Inc.

Fleischer, N. 1939. Black Dynamite (Volume IV). New York: C. J. O'Brien, Inc.

Fleischer, N. 1942. Gentleman Jim - The Story of James J. Corbett. New York: The Ring, Inc.

Fleischer, N. 1949. The Heavyweight Championship. New York: G. P. Putnam's Sons

Fleischer, N. 1969. 50 Years at Ringside. New York: Greenwood Press, Publishers

Fleischer, N. 1972. Jack Dempsey. New Rochelle, NY: Arlington House

Fleischer, N. and Andre, S. 1959. A Pictorial History of Boxing. New York: Bonanza Books

Fleischer, N. and Andre, S. 1975. A Pictorial History of Boxing. Secaucus, NJ: Castle Books

Fleischer, N. and Andre, S. 1993. A Pictorial History of Boxing. New York: Carol Publishing Group

Fullerton, H. 1929. Two-Fisted Jeff. Chicago: Consolidated Book Publishers, Inc.

Gilmore, A.T. 1975. Bad Nigger! The National Impact of Jack Johnson. Port Washington, NY: Kennikat Press Corp.

Goldman, H. 1997. International Boxing Digest, November-December 1997 p 24

Gordon, G. 2007. Master of the Ring. Wrea Green, England: Milo Books

Grombach, J. 1977. The Saga of Fist. New York: A.S. Barnes and Company, Inc.

Grombach, J. 1977. The Saga of Sock. London : Thomas Yoseloff Ltd.; Cranbury, New Jersey: A.S. Barnes and Company, Inc.

Gutteridge, R. 1975. Boxing: The Great Ones. London: Pelham Books Ltd.

Hauser, T. 1991. Muhammad Ali: His Life and Times. New York: Simon & Schuster Paperbacks

Holmes, L. 1998. Against the Odds. New York: St. Martin's Press

Houston, G. 1975. SuperFists. New York: Bounty Books

Keith, H. 1969. Sports and Games. New York: Thomas Y. Crowell Company

Langley, T. 1973. The Life of John L. Sullivan. Leicester, England: Vance Harvey Publishing

BIBLIOGRAPHY (Cont'd.)

Langley, T. 1974. The Life of Peter Jackson. Leicester, England: Vance Harvey Publishing

Lardner, R. 1972. The Legendary Champions. New York: American Heritage Press

Lerner, P. 2012. Private Correspondence

Litsky, F. 1975. Superstars. Secaucus, New Jersey: Derbibooks, Inc.

McCallum, J. 1974. The World Heavyweight Boxing Championship. Radnor, Pa.: Chilton Book Company

McCallum, J. 1975. The Encyclopedia of World Boxing Champions. Radnor, Pa.: Chilton Book Company

Mee, B. 1997. Boxing: Heroes & Champions. Edison, NJ: Chartwell Books, Inc.

Mullan, H. 1990. The Great Book of Boxing. New York: Crescent Books

Myler, P. 1998. A Century of Boxing Greats. New York: Robson/Parkwest Publications

Naughton, W. 1902. Kings Of The Queensberry Realm. Chicago: The Continental Publishing Company

Nicholson, K. 2002. A Man Among Men. Draper, Utah: Homeward Bound Publishing Company, Inc.

Odd, G. 1974. Boxing: The Great Champions. London: The Hamlyn Publishing Group Limited

Odd, G. 1975. The Fighting Prophet. London: Pelham Books Ltd.

Odd, G. 1976. The Fighting Blacksmith. London: Pelham Books Ltd.

Odd, G. 1989. The Encyclopedia of Boxing. London: The Hamlyn Publishing Group Limited

Odd, G. 1989. The Encyclopedia of Boxing. Secaucus, NJ: Chartwell Books, Inc.

Page, J. 2011. Primo Carnera. Jefferson, NC: McFarland & Company, Inc.

Petersen, R.C. 2011. Peter Jackson. Jefferson, NC: McFarland & Company, Inc.

Pollack, A. 2007. In the Ring With James J. Corbett. Iowa City, Ia: Win By KO Publications

Pollack, A. 2009. In the Ring With James J. Jeffries. Iowa City, Ia: Win By KO Publications

Pollack, A. 2012. Private Correspondence

Rice, G. 1954. The Tumult and the Shouting. New York: A.S. Barnes and Company

Romano, J. 1931. Champions All. In Everlast Boxing Record, pp 92-126

Stockton, R. 1977. Who Was the Greatest. Phoenix: Boxing Enterprises

Sugar, B. 1980. Holmes-Ali:The Last Hurrah (contained in The Ring, December 1980, pp 20-23). New York: The Ring Publishing Corp.

Sugar, B. 1991. Boxing Illustrated, December 1991 pp 69-89

Suster, G. 1992. Champions of the Ring. London: Robson Books, Ltd.

Suster, G. 1994. Champions of the Ring. London: Robson Books Ltd.

The Ring. 1987. The Ring Record Book and Boxing Encyclopedia. New York: The Ring Publishing Corp.

The Ring. 1996. Battle of the Legends (contained in The Ring, November 1996, pp 28-29). Fort Washington, Pa: London Publishing Co.

The Ring. 1999. The 1999 Boxing and Book of Facts. Fort Washington, Pa: London Publishing Co.

The Ring. 2000. The 20 Greatest Fighters of the 20th Century by William Detloff (contained in The 2000 Boxing Almanac and Book of Facts). Fort Washington, Pa: London Publishing Co.

The Ring. 2001. The 2001 Boxing Almanac and Book of Facts. Fort Washington, Pa: London Publishing Co.

The Ring. 2004. The 2004 Boxing Almanac and Book of Facts. Fort Washington, Pa: London Publishing Co.

Tunney, G. 1941. Arms For Living. New York: Wilfred Funk, Inc.

Tunney, G. 1952, September 23. "Dempsey Could Flatten Today's Heavies All in One Night" (contained in Look, pp 36-38)

Weinberg, S.K. and Arond, H. 1952. The Occupational Culture of the Boxer (contained in The American Journal of Sociology, Vol. 57, pp 460-469 March 1952)

Weston, S. and Farhood, S. 1993. The Ring Chronicle of Boxing. London: Hamlyn Publishing Group Limited

Willoughby, D. 1970. The Super Athletes. Cranbury, New Jersey: A.S. Barnes and Co., Inc.

Introduction. The Years 1860-1880

Chapter One. The Years 1881-1900

Chapter Two. The Years 1901-1920

JIM FLYNN DROPS KAUFMAN IN TENTH AFTER TERRIFIC BATTLE, The Colorado Springs (Co) Gazette, May 6 1911

LANGFORD KNOCKS OUT GUNBOAT SMITH, The Naugatuck (Ct) Daily News, October 21 1914

CARL MORRIS ROCKS PELKY TO SLEEP, The Oakland (Ca) Tribune, February 12 1916

FULTON STOPS SAM LANGFORD IN SIXTH, The Racine (Wi) Journal-News, June 20 1917

Chapter Three. The Years 1921-1940

BIG WILLARD A COMEBACK, The Sunday State Journal, May 13 1923. Reprinted with permission of the Lincoln (Ne) Journal Star

FIRPO WINNER OVER WILLARD IN THE EIGHTH, The Traverse City (Mi) Record-Eagle, July 13 1923

Jack Johnson Flop in Simmons Fight; Monte in Victory, The San Antonio (Tx) Light, September 7 1926

Gene Tunney, the Fighting Marine, Slugs Heavyweight Crown Off Dempsey's Head, The Charleston (WV) Gazette, September 24 1926

Gene Tunney Remains World's Champion; Gets Decision in 10th Round, The Palatine (Il) Enterprise, September 23 1927; Reprinted by permission of the Daily Herald, Arlington Heights, Illinois

A Square Sport, The Salt Lake (Ut) Tribune, January 7 1929

WIGGINS ADDDED TO CARNERA VICTIMS, The Monitor-Index and Democrat (Moberly, Mo), March 18 1930

The Baer-Campbell Fight, The Greeley (Co) Daily Tribune, August 27 1930

MAX BATTERS WALKER FOR RIGHT TO MEET SHARKEY AGAIN, The Sun (Lowell, Ma), September 27 1932. All rights reserved. Reproduced with the permission of MediaNews Group Inc.

BAER TRIUMPHS OVER GRIFFITHS, The Monitor-Index (Moberly, Mo), September 27 1932

Thomas Goes Out In Fifth, The Hutchinson (Ks) News, April 2 1938

Louis Looks Forward to Conn Fight After Battering McCoy, The Sun (Lowell, Ma), December 17 1940. All rights reserved. Reproduced with the permission of MediaNews Group Inc.

Chapter Four. The Years 1941-1960

Louis Stops Buddy Baer In Rousing Title Fight, The Salt Lake (Ut) Tribune, May 24 1941

Conn Stops Knox In Eighth Round, The Salt Lake (Ut) Tribune, May 27 1941

Rocky Decisions La Starza In N.Y., The Oakland (Ca) Tribune, March 25 1950

Charles Injured In Title Clash; To Be Sidelined For Two Months, The Kingsport (Tn) Times, March 8 1951

Henry Upsets Baker in Explosive Eighth-Round Kayo, The Sun (Lowell, Ma), November 24 1951. All rights reserved. Reproduced with the permission of MediaNews Group Inc.

Jersey Joe Decisions Charles To Keep Heavyweight Title, The Salt Lake (Ut) Tribune, June 6 1952

Rocky Kayoes Joe in 2:25 of 1st, The Racine (Wi) Journal-Times, May 16 1953

Swede KOs Machen In 2:16 of 1st Round, The Tokyo (Japan) Pacific Stars and Stripes, September 15 1958

Patterson Retains Title By Knocking Out London in 11th, Republished with permission of The Galveston County (Tx) Daily News, May 2 1959

Ingo to Quit Training Five Days Before Bout, The Sun (Lowell, Ma), June 18 1959. All rights reserved. Reproduced with the permission of MediaNews Group Inc.

Chapter Five. The Years 1961-1980

Clay Forced to Rally to Whip Doug Jones, The Racine (Wi) Journal-Times, March 14 1963

Ernie Terrell Awarded Decision over Machen, The Racine (Wi) Journal-Times, March 6 1965

Terrell Retains Title Amid 'Low Blow' Yells, The Logansport (In) Pharos-Tribune, June 29 1966

Jimmy Ellis Retains WBA Heavyweight Title, The Logansport (In) Pharos-Tribune and Press, September 15 1968

Olympic king Foreman making noise as a pro, The Jefferson City (Mo) Daily Capital News, August 20 1969

Joe Frazier Is The Undisputed King Of Heavyweights After Victory Over Jimmy Ellis, But Now Has No One Left To Fight, The Gettysburg (Pa) Times, February 17 1970

Frazier Decisions Britain's Bugner, The Naugatuck (Ct) Daily News, July 3 1973

Foreman dethrones 'King' Roman in two minutes, The Great Bend (Ks) Tribune, September 2 1973

"He shouldn't ever fight again, and I'm sure he won't … His time has come", The Logansport (In) Pharos-Tribune, October 3 1980

Chapter Six. The Years 1981-2000

Holmes survives bout with Witherspoon, The Cedar Rapids (Ia) Gazette, May 21 1983

Witherspoon decisions Page to capture title, The Hutchinson (Ks) News, March 10 1984

NEWSPAPER HEADLINES (Cont'd.)

Page KOs Coetzee for WBA crown, The Intelligencer (Doylestown, Pa), December 2 1984

Witherspoon batters Tubbs, The Daily Herald (Chicago, Il), January 18 1986; Reprinted by permission of the Daily Herald, Arlington Heights, Illinois

Spinks decks Cooney in fifth round, The Intelligencer (Doylestown, Pa), June 16 1987

Foreman eyes title after KO, From an Associated Press article published in The Ukiah (Ca) Daily Journal, January 16 1990

Holyfield tops Foreman in 12, The Daily Herald (Chicago, Il), April 20 1991; Reprinted by permission of the Daily Herald, Arlington Heights, Illinois

Tyson accused of rape, The Cedar Rapids (Ia) Gazette, July 27 1991

BOXING, From an Associated Press article published in The Gettysburg (Pa) Times, October 19 1991

Split Decision, The Santa Fe (NM) New Mexican, December 15 1992

Holyfield regains crown; fight delayed by chutist, The Colorado Springs (Co) Gazette Telegraph, November 7 1993

Former champion Tyson ends 3-year prison term, The Daily Herald (Chicago, Il), March 26 1995; Reprinted by permission of the Daily Herald, Arlington Heights, Illinois

Tyson makes quick return - 1:29, The Daily Herald (Chicago, Il), August 20 1995; Reprinted by permission of the Daily Herald, Arlington Heights, Illinois

Holyfield KOs Tyson in 11th, The Colorado Springs (Co) Gazette Telegraph, November 10 1996

Chapter Seven. The Years 2001-2010

John Ruiz defeats Holyfield in decision, The Logansport (In) Pharos-Tribune, March 4 2001

Klitschko Ponders Future, The Harrisonburg (Va) Daily News-Record, April 12 2004

Ibragimov beats Briggs, The Salina (Ks) Journal, June 3 2007

Klitschko stops Chagaev:, The Daily Herald (Chicago, Il), June 21 2009; Reprinted by permission of the Daily Herald, Arlington Heights, Illinois

Ranking The All-Time Great Bouts

Choynski Knocked Out by Corbett, The Boston (Ma) Daily Globe, June 6 1889

FOUGHT A DRAW, The Boston (Ma) Daily Globe, May 3 1899

Where Are They Now? Coronet, October 1949 p 14. Chicago: Esquire, Inc.

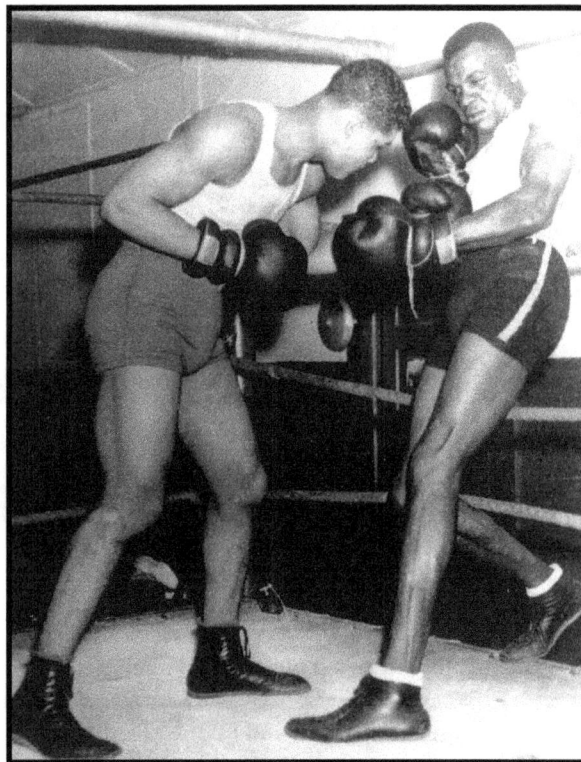

Joe Louis and Leonard Dixon Sparring
1935

"Big" Bill Tate, Jack Dempsey, Terry Kellar and George "One-Round" Davis
1919

Georges Carpentier and "Babe" Ruth
1921

INDEX

INDEX (Cont'd.)

INDEX (Cont'd.)

290

www.ingramcontent.com/pod-product-compliance
Lightning Source LLC
Chambersburg PA
CBHW050409110426
42812CB00006BA/1843